D1431681

RUFFIN

RUFFIN

Family and Reform in the Old South

David F. Allmendinger, Jr.

New York • Oxford
OXFORD UNIVERSITY PRESS
1990

Oxford University Press

Oxford   New York   Toronto
Delhi   Bombay   Calcutta   Madras   Karachi
Petaling Jaya   Singapore   Hong Kong   Tokyo
Nairobi   Dar es Salaam   Cape Town
Melbourne   Auckland

and associated companies in
Berlin   Ibadan

Copyright © 1990 by David F. Allmendinger, Jr.

Published by Oxford University Press, Inc.,
200 Madison Avenue, New York, New York 10016

Oxford is a registered trademark of Oxford University Press

Library of Congress Cataloging-in-Publication Data
Allmendinger, David F.
Ruffin : family and reform in the Old South / David F.
Allmendinger, Jr.
p. cm.   Bibliography: p.   Includes index.
ISBN 0-19-504415-0
1. Ruffin, Edmund, 1794-1865. 2. Statesmen—Virginia—Biography.
3. Slavery—Southern States—History—19th century 4. Agricultural
ecology—Virginia—History—19th century. 5. Agricultural ecology—
United States—History—19th century. 6. Secession. 7. Southern
States—Politics and government—1775-1865. I. Title.
F230.R932A45   1990
973.7'092—dc20   89-16098   CIP

9 8 7 6 5 4 3 2 1

Printed in the United States of America
on acid-free paper

To Marjorie K. Allmendinger
and to the memory of
David F. Allmendinger, Sr.

Contents

Illustrations and Tables

Map

Graphs

Illustrations following page   110

Tables

Preface

Edmund Ruffin first set foot on soil that was his own property two months after his nineteenth birthday, early in 1813. When he claimed the farm he had inherited at Coggin's Point on the James River, he was an orphan with no living older relatives. He began alone. He ended his career in similar circumstances in 1865, when, alone in his room at Redmoor Farm in Amelia County, he committed suicide. He probably was aware of this circular pattern, for despite a separation from his family's past, Ruffin had a sense of personal history.

He constructed that history himself, beginning upon his arrival at Coggin's Point. He started a farm journal in which he entered precise details about slaves, crops, and yields. Eventually he would write three volumes of memoirs, and in 1856 he began one of the great diaries of the Civil War period, linking an individual and family record with events of national historic significance. Through personal history he developed both an interpretation of his career and a sense of his own identity. He was not always conscious of the way this history influenced his thinking, but it was a constant presence. Since he accumulated an archive of his own manuscripts, the documents of his past were always at hand, and he consulted them frequently. When he died they were his most treasured possessions.

Most of the materials available to Ruffin have survived, and they have provided most of the documents for this study. They make it possible to determine which elements of his thinking changed or remained constant. This study uses those materials to analyze Ruffin's assumptions about family and career, slavery and race, rejuvenation and death. In scope and method this is not a comprehensive biography like those by Avery Craven and Betty L. Mitchell, nor is it primarily an attempt to assess Ruffin's influence on farming and rural society in the antebellum South, in the manner of work by Eugene Genovese and W. M. Mathew. The original pattern for the book came from

Alan Macfarlane's *The Family Life of Ralph Josselin* (1970), though the character of Ruffin's writing opened other options. This study became an effort to combine intellectual and social history, focusing on Ruffin's thought as it developed through his experience.

The limits of a study dealing with one individual are evident. Ruffin's case does not prove that science and slavery were compatible (as he thought they were), or that patriarchy was not a feature of slavery or the family in the antebellum South, or that the rejuvenation he sought for Virginia did in fact begin. A study of an individual life does have its virtues, nonetheless, and they remain very much as Christopher Lasch defined them two decades ago.[1] In this instance, it was Ruffin who articulated experiences peculiar to this place and time. His quality of constant self-examination (even when talking about fields, shells, malaria, or migration) makes it possible to examine the responses of a thinker who perceived his society in decline. This quality makes it possible to explain shifts in Ruffin's thinking, and to establish the timing of those shifts. It reveals Ruffin's sense of himself as an agent of change, pressing his contemporaries to alter ideas in definable ways, particularly in assumptions about the earth.

Though much has been written about Ruffin, there was much to discover when this study began. He seemed to appear from nowhere. Almost nothing has been published about his family of origin, as the obscurity of his mother, for example, would indicate. The ideas of this thinker and reformer have received no systematic analysis by intellectual historians. There has been no agreement even on the date of his suicide. Most previous work has focused primarily on his public life, using the family as a setting for other events. Ruffin's papers and published works indicated that discoveries might be made about the connection between his family life, his thought, and his career in reform.

In addressing the family I have not focused, therefore, on its vital or structural history. Nor have I treated the Ruffins in terms of the resurgent, social history of inanimate objects and thoughtless activities. The evidence has permitted another approach. The family history of Edmund Ruffin shaped his thinking, writing, and his career in reform, even though he lived in an age when people commonly separated domestic and public spheres. And if the great events of political and social history ever became entwined with one man's personal affairs, they certainly did so in the family life and in the death of Edmund Ruffin.

Acknowledgments

I first want to thank two great teachers, Merle Curti and William R. Taylor. Their influence has remained with students who worked with them during a wonderful time twenty-five years ago at the University of Wisconsin. Merle Curti also offered me the practical advice that pointed me toward Ruffin. And William R. Taylor provided his own, classic interpretation of Ruffin. For their advice, their example, and their friendship, I thank them.

Colleagues in Australia and the United States offered generous attention and criticism. I thank in particular Greg Bowen, Greg Tobin, and Donald DeBats of the Flinders University of South Australia, together with the social history group at Flinders and Adelaide universities. Paul Bourke, now of the Australian National University, helped me interpret Ruffin's suicide and his role as a symbolic figure. In Adelaide, Rosanne DeBats pressed me to write as much as possible in narrative form. In Melbourne my early chapters received a critical hearing from historians at Melbourne, Monash, and LaTrobe universities; I thank in particular Donna Merwick, Greg Dening, Rhys Isaac, and Kenneth Lockridge.

Closer to home, I thank my colleagues John Hurt, Edward Lurie, and Svend Holsoe, who read drafts of early chapters. Susan A. Allmendinger also read those early chapters. William K. Scarborough of the University of Southern Mississippi shared both his knowledge of Ruffin and his magnificent edition of Ruffin's diary. The Chester Avenue Seminar in Philadelphia was a collegial, critical audience: Marion Roydhouse, Eric Schneider, Janet Golden, Patricia Cooper, Brian Greenberg, Emma Lapsansky, Randall Miller, Cynthia Little, Len Braitman, and George Dowdall. Dorothy J. Wurman, who shared with me her interest in ecological history, drew the map of lower Virginia for this book. Descendants of Ruffin in Virginia and Georgia provided important family records and generous hospitality. I owe many debts to James S. Gilliam and Corinna R. Gilliam, to whom I was first introduced by the late Mary Denmead Ruffin. James Gilliam has saved me from many errors of fact; if errors remain, they are all mine. Marion Ruffin Jones, Jane R. Grubb, and Tilghman Broaddus also provided ideas and crucial materials. Through these people I was able to visit the places Ruffin lived, including Coggin's Point, Marlbourne, and Redmoor. I also learned much from the research and writings of David Ruffin about his family history.

At the Virginia Historical Society, Nelson Lankford, Sara Bearss, and Frances Pollard assisted in innumerable ways. Lyndon Hart of the Virginia State Library provided the clue that helped identify Ruffin's mother; and staff members at the Southern Historical Collection gave their thoughtful assistance. I also thank John Ingram of the Colonial Williamsburg Foundation Library, Ellen R. Strong and Margaret Cook of the Swem Library at the College of William and Mary, Frank V. Emmerson and Jane Emmerson of Surry County, and Steven Colvin of Mechanicsville, all of whom offered suggestions for my research.

The National Endowment for the Humanities provided a Travel to Collections Program Grant. Research trips were made possible by a fellowship from the Delaware Humanities Forum and by a supplemental funds grant from the College of Arts and Science, University of Delaware. For permission to quote from manuscripts in their collections, I want to thank the Southern Historical Collection, University of North Carolina Library, Chapel Hill; the Manuscripts Department, University of Virginia Library; Manuscripts and Rare Books Department, Swem Library, College of William and Mary; and the Virginia Historical Society. I also thank the *Virginia Magazine of History and Biography* for permission to publish revised portions of Chapter 2, which appeared in that journal in slightly different form.

RUFFIN

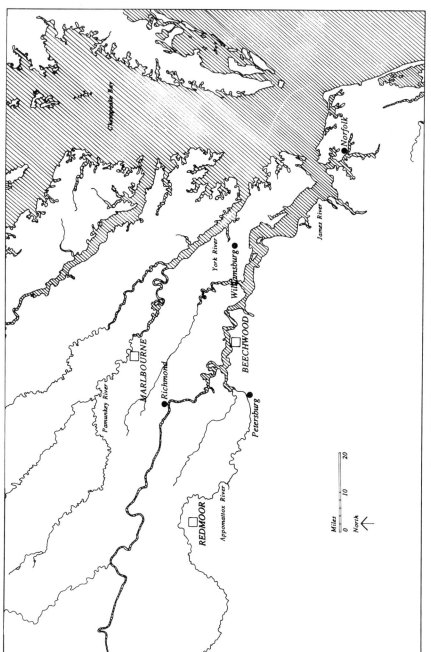

Lower Virginia and the Ruffin family farms, 1865

Prologue:
The Death of Thomas Cocke

I feel strongly impelled to write down the strange & horrible circumstances which have just occurred, & thus to record & preserve, even if but for my own eye, the many minute details which would otherwise soon fade away from a frail memory.

EDMUND RUFFIN, 1840

Facts Edmund Ruffin gathered late in February 1840 demonstrated that Thomas Cocke, Ruffin's oldest and best friend, had planned for months to commit suicide. No signs of impulsiveness appeared in the evidence; Cocke had acted in a rational, calculating manner. He had established routines that gave him hours of solitude, and he had feigned a new appetite for wild duck, making necessary a gun and ammunition. Cocke aroused no one's suspicion, therefore, when he left his house at Tarbay after 10:00 a.m. on 22 February 1840, and walked concealed through the grounds east of the house and into the field and woods. He kept the dwelling house as a screen between himself and his servants in the detached Tarbay kitchen. When he reached a favorite secluded oak he had chosen in advance, he sat down, placed the muzzle of the gun in his mouth, and shot off his head. Ruffin's son later retraced Cocke's route, "following his foot prints on the soft earth."[1]

Ruffin, who had visited Thomas Cocke just two days earlier, heard the news that night at his home in Petersburg, Virginia, where he was editor of the *Farmers' Register*. He ordered a coffin and early next morning drove the fifteen miles back to Prince George County, to his son's home at Beechwood, a farm immediately east of Tarbay. Both farms lay on the south shore of the James River, twenty-five

3

miles southeast of Richmond. After the burial on 25 February, "returning what was now earth to earth," Ruffin remained at his son's house. That night he wrote eleven pages about the "closing scenes" of Cocke's life. In that manuscript Ruffin revealed that while he did not view Cocke's body, he did walk to the oak; and what he observed left an impression more lasting than anyone knew. "Pieces of the scull, some of them black from the burnt powder, and the brains, were scattered all around," he wrote. "I aided in the gathering up as many of these widely scattered fragments as could be found."[2]

He then began to gather details for a narrative that would help him understand Cocke's decision and help him deal with his own shock. Part of the horror lay in the deliberateness of the act. When connected into narrative form, the evidence made it clear that Cocke had planned his exit with precision. "I have no doubt but that he had long before fixed the place, the day, the very hour, for the deed," Ruffin wrote. First, there was the gun, which Cocke had ordered to be kept "always at hand," and which he ordered "the young negro man who waited on table" to use in hunting ducks. "Such an order, & directed to so inexpert a gunner, was thought strange, but only as a whim, that attracted no consideration." A week before the suicide, Cocke had sent a request to Beechwood for percussion caps, "as if for his servant's use." Three of these caps were found later in his pocket. "This was another precaution against not finding the gun ready, & against its missing fire, even if ready." Cocke carried his razor, "obviously to finish the deed, if the gun should by possibility fail." To manipulate the gun, he had held the muzzle with his hands and used his toe to push the trigger. Apparently even this maneuver had been planned, for Cocke had cut away the end of his stocking beforehand.[3]

On the morning of his final day, a Saturday, Cocke varied only once from his contrived routine. He rose for breakfast and then shaved himself, "which was so unusual on that day, that it attracted his servants' notice." His son, Nathaniel, had gone to oversee work at another farm five miles away, leaving Cocke alone with the servants. Apparently Cocke spent part of that morning reading one of the newspapers Ruffin had brought him three days earlier: Edmund Ruffin, Jr., found them "thrown carelessly" on the sofa beside his spectacles, "as if he had but just left his seat, & in usual manner." He also wrote a note, which he left on a parlor table, "as if for observation." In a steady hand he recorded his intention and disclosed that his body could be found by "the large oak below the multicaulis planting."

Even the place had been planned. "I consider the summons of a jury unnecessary," he wrote, "as this paper announces the fact of my exit by my own operation." Finally he had signed his name, noted the hour (ten o'clock) and the date, and left the house.[4]

Horror lay also in the fact that Cocke had expressed his intention openly beforehand. Though Ruffin had suspected Cocke's intention, he had lulled himself into disbelief. On his trip to Prince George the previous week, he had visited Cocke on Wednesday, 19 February, from noon until sunset; on Thursday evening he returned to Tarbay for two more hours.[5] Cocke complained of pain and "intolerable sufferings," though he seemed cheerful. "Indeed I saw no change, save an increase of the disposition which I had witnessed for years, to express his anxiety to die."[6]

Cocke's motives were clear. He was a widower whose daughter had married and moved to New York and whose son had recently returned from school to begin farming, and his family no longer depended on him. The note on the parlor table contained a sentence depicting Cocke himself as the dependent individual: "I find myself not only a burthen on myself, but entertain no hope that my permanence in this world can essentially aid my dear children."[7] At sixty-five he felt like an old man. Some years before 1840, according to Ruffin, Cocke had suffered an apoplectic attack that nearly killed him, "leaving bodily feebleness, lethargy, torpor, difficulty of breathing, & a state of general suffering, too heavy to bear, & which made the coming of death to him the most desirable of all earthly events." He had withdrawn to a "hermit-like life," confined by infirmity to his room, unable to take pleasure in reading, due to "prostration of all vigor of mind & reasoning power." Life had become "a regular succession of one wretched day added to another," but death would not come naturally. Several times that previous week, Ruffin recalled, Cocke had declared "I cannot bear it—& I *will not* bear it." Ruffin guessed that his friend was touching upon suicide and tried to change the subject. "I affected to be ignorant of the import of his expressions, & merely observed that suicide must always be the effect of temporary insanity." "In that," Cocke responded, "you are *altogether* mistaken."[8] Cocke had concluded that in some instances suicide was a rational act.

There were many clues. Even as their talk drifted, it remained on the subject of death: the expense of Western burial customs compared to the Chinese, and Cocke's desire for a plain burial of his own body.

"And what folly the attempt to prevent the designed operation of the universal law of nature," Cocke declared, "by burying our dead 6 feet deep." The Chinese were wise to forbid graves deeper than eighteen inches. "But," Ruffin replied, "whether at our depth or theirs' the final result is the same; & the flesh passes into grass." "True," Cocke said, "but that proper & natural result is much longer delayed."

> It is not frustrated however. Grass grows & receives its bulk & substance from the man's buried body; the ox or the hog eats the grass, & what was first man's flesh, & next grass, becomes part of the brute, which when killed & eaten, again becomes part of man again. Thus, there is a perpetual round of changes; of greater or of less extent & duration.[9]

He forbade any "parade or formalities" over his body. Ruffin recalled that when he prepared to leave, Cocke urged him strongly to stay longer in the country, further proof that a plan was in progress, "& that he wished me to be at hand when it was consummated." He now reproached himself for not combatting Cocke's opinions, but decided that, "with a man of such strong mind, who had reasoned with himself in solitude for years, & had considered & measured the subject in every aspect," he would have failed.[10]

As he constructed his melancholy narrative of Cocke's closing scene, Ruffin realized that this event had caused trauma in his own mind. The passage of two days had not lessened his pain, but rather had added "weight to the first shock." A desire to preserve details of "the strange & horrible circumstances" impelled him to write the narrative, "even if but for my own eye," so he would not forget. Never in real life or in fiction had anyone imagined a suicide like Thomas Cocke's. Ruffin thanked God he had not witnessed the discovery of the bloody corpse. "For even from the description, it is continually coming before my mental vision." He did not believe in supernatural visitations, but as he wrote, "alone & in the depth of night," he felt "almost afraid to look around, lest the object which so dwells on my mind's eye should be more palpably present, & thus demand of me more strongly & sternly than does my own heart, 'Why did you make no effort to prevent this deed?' " Grief became remorse.[11]

The most painful consequences of Thomas Cocke's suicide did not lie in the moral or religious questions such a death might have raised. Despite his shock over this "dreadful catastrophe," Ruffin refused to condemn Cocke's decision. "When death calls me from this world," he concluded simply, "may my dread account of sins over-balancing

virtues, be not greater than that of my self-slaughtered friend!"[12] He
withheld all other judgment. The truly painful aspect of this "last
act" lay in family history. In the death of Thomas Cocke, Ruffin lost
not only his closest friend but his only link to the distant past. Cocke
had been the friend of Ruffin's father and must have known even his
mother and his grandparents. When Ruffin's father died in 1810,
Thomas Cocke became his legal guardian. From that year onward,
when Ruffin was sixteen, Cocke had taken a father's place. It was
Cocke who handed Ruffin his inheritance in 1813, the farm on which
Beechwood now stood, where Ruffin now wrote. For thirty years
Cocke had collaborated in the effort to rejuvenate that farm and the
soils of farms all over the county. Ruffin was now forty-six, a husband,
and the father of nine children. Cocke's death completed a sense of
isolation in Ruffin that stemmed from his early family history. And
so he wrote the narrative of Cocke's closing scenes as near to the
events as possible, to keep the connection in "frail memory."

1

Among the Survivors: Mortality and Isolation

One son only has been left to continue the stock in two successive generations of my branch of the family, and in two other branches, one male only has been left alive in each, out of a large number of brothers. But we have broken the charm, if there was one, and I am heartily glad of it.

EDMUND RUFFIN, 1834

Survival itself distinguished Edmund Ruffin from nearly all members of his family who had lived and perished along the James River in the eighteenth century. Long after the general population of Tidewater Virginia was supposed to have seasoned itself against malaria and other killer diseases of the Chesapeake, families in that stretch of the James between Williamsburg and Richmond still found survival from generation to generation a matter of chance. For them, mortality remained as powerful a force as it had been for settlers in the seventeenth century, cutting ties to grandparents and parents, aunts, uncles, and cousins, and their own family histories.[1]

Ruffin always recalled his boyhood in terms indicating that reaching adulthood had been problematic for him, too. He was born 5 January 1794 at the farm his father inherited near Jordan's Point, on the south side of the James in Prince George County, ten miles northeast of Petersburg. At sixty-five, in 1859, he remembered himself as a delicate youth with a "weak constitution."[2] Even as an adult he was thin. He stood five feet, eight inches tall. At forty, in 1834, he weighed 130 pounds.[3]

From the time of his youth Ruffin knew that on both sides of his family the passage of generations had been a precarious matter. One reminder of this fact was the very place he was born. Ruffin's great-grandfather, Edmund Ruffin I (1713–1790), had established the farm near Jordan's Point between 1750 and 1772. A carpenter, it was probably he who built the family's first house there. Down to the year 1800, this farm had been the home of no more than nine Ruffins in four generations.[4]

The Origins of Isolation

After 1800 the Ruffin family experienced a dramatic change in its vital history, a transformation symbolized by the large, new house in which Ruffin spent some of his childhood. This was Evergreen. Ruffin's father, George Ruffin (1765–1810), built the house after 1795, apparently on the site of the original dwelling.[5] It stood away from the river, barely within sight of the water; it was in new condition when George Ruffin insured the property in 1808. In that year Evergreen was among the three largest houses on the south bank between City Point and Surry County, a distance of more than twelve miles.[6] It was a brick, five-bay, Georgian house, two stories high, with central hall, four large rooms on each floor, a full basement, and a detached kitchen.[7] This was a mansion built for a large family, based on expectations about infant survival that differed dramatically from assumptions in the past.

Before the nineteenth century the Ruffin family had known only one period—between 1700 and 1720—when a large number of children had lived into adulthood. Edmund Ruffin I (known as Captain Edmund) was a member of that first Ruffin generation to count a large number of live siblings, including four brothers and three sisters.[8] As a young man, Edmund I found himself among a cohort of brothers too numerous to divide their family's land. Their survival necessitated an exodus from old Surry County and sent them to new lands in Sussex, Southampton, Dinwiddie, and King William counties, and eventually to North Carolina. Captain Edmund joined the migration to Sussex and Southampton around 1735; finally he became the first of Ruffin's ancestors to settle in Prince George County.[9] As his generation scattered away from the lower Tidewater, their migration had the effect of cutting generational ties with family members down the river. Captain Edmund, at about the age of twenty-five, detached himself and became in effect an only, isolated offspring.

After these Ruffins moved on to new lands, the vital history of the family reassumed its pattern of seventeenth-century mortality, suggesting that the common nemeses of these people were either typhoid, dysentery, or malaria and its opportunistic allies.[10] They cannot have bequeathed to newborn children acquired immunities against malaria; after moving from Surry County they certainly confronted malaria-bearing mosquitoes anew as they cleared new lands. Even among seasoned people, malaria was known to strike especially hard among pregnant women and new mothers. Whether the problem lay in malaria, water-borne organisms, or diseases of childbirth and childhood, between 1740 and 1800 the Ruffin line in Prince George nearly disappeared.

In each of the following two generations, only one son survived. Captain Edmund and Anne Simmons Edmunds (who died after childbirth in 1749) had only two children who lived through infancy. One of these was a daughter who died at twenty-eight.[11] The other was Edmund II (1745–1807), who became Edmund Ruffin's grandfather. In the early years of the Revolution, this man, known as Edmund, Jr., bought a farm at Coggin's Point, also on the James River in Prince George County.[12] Edmund II and his wife, Jane Skipwith (who died about 1783), had a son, George (1765–1810), who was for his entire life his parents' only son and child.[13] This meant that Edmund Ruffin's father and his paternal grandfather both had been only sons, establishing the demographic preconditions for isolation before Ruffin was born. As late as 1794, the "charm" had not been broken.

Of his mother's family Ruffin knew almost nothing. He may never have discovered the date she died, since it occurred so early in his life that its details disappeared among those of the other deaths he observed in his first sixteen years. Jane Lucas, who married George Ruffin in probably 1792, survived Ruffin's birth in 1794 but was dead by 1797. The last trace of her being alive was recorded in Surry Court House on 19 May 1794, when she joined her husband in a suit against her brother Samuel II (who died within a year) for settlement of debts. In the record of that suit she was identified as the former Jane Lucas, now the wife of George Ruffin. Apart from one other instance a decade after she died, that court case was the only precise record of her identity after marriage.[14] In 1856, when Ruffin constructed his genealogical chart of the Ruffin family, the only fact he knew about her was her name.[15]

The death of Jane Lucas ended a calamitous life history that was to remain obscure throughout Ruffin's lifetime. Surry County court records would have permitted him to establish her identity only with difficulty.[16] She was the second daughter and youngest child of Samuel and Elizabeth Lucas, who lived in Southwark Parish, near Surry Court House, across the James River from Williamsburg. She was born in 1770, a few months after her father died. Samuel Lucas I died before he was thirty, leaving a young widow with orphaned children: Thomas, Samuel II, Sarah, and the unborn Jane; the terms of his will made it clear that he knew he was dying, and that he insisted on leaving an equal portion for the "Child or Children that my loving Wife Elizabeth is now Pregnant with." Jane Lucas' mother, Elizabeth, disappeared from the official records of Surry County, almost certainly through death; Edmund Ruffin did not know her as his grandmother, just as he did not know the long-dead Samuel Lucas as his grandfather.[17]

Nor did he know either of his maternal uncles, Samuel II (dead by 1795) and Thomas (dead by 1805).[18] In 1805 his father joined Jane Lucas Ruffin's sister, Sarah Lucas Burgess, in a suit to recover the value of three slaves, remainders of the estate Samuel I had left in 1770: at the time the suit began, Sarah Lucas Burgess (Ruffin's aunt) was the only survivor of the Lucas family, apart from three or more of Ruffin's young cousins in Surry County whom he apparently never met. By the time the suit came to court, the first executor of Samuel Lucas' estate had died, and so had the second. It was a bizarre suit in which all but one of the original heirs (the principal complainants) were dead, and the defendant (Travis Harris) was executor for a dead man (Samuel Lucas I) whose estate had passed through the hands of two previous executors (John Cocke and Walter Cocke), both of whom were now dead.[19]

This joining in court was the only time Ruffin appears to have been linked to his mother's family. George Ruffin must have maintained some contact with his former sister-in-law, for in 1805 he joined her in the suit concerning her father's estate; but Edmund Ruffin, the infant named as a complainant in that suit, probably heard little of this matter. The fact that his mother was an orphan born after her father's death, and that she herself died before Ruffin could know her, removed him from social connections with the Lucases. The fact that the Lucases proceeded to die at prodigious rates prevented Ruffin from knowing them or their history. Concerning these people, half of his family of origin, he knew nothing.

The death of Jane Lucas gave the young Edmund Ruffin one thing in common with his father, a characteristic that illuminated the equally disastrous vital history of the Ruffin family. When Jane Lucas died, she left the infant Edmund Ruffin as his father's only son and only child, his position until 1800. George Ruffin remarried in 1799 and became the father of a daughter in 1800; but as late as 1810 Edmund Ruffin still was his father's only surviving son.[20] In this he was like his father and his grandfather; he was in fact the only son of an only son of an only son. The Ruffin male line was thin.

The peculiar circumstances under which Edmund Ruffin passed his childhood and youth have lain buried for two centuries in the vital biological history of the Ruffins and the families into which they married. In his lifetime Ruffin knew very few people over the age of sixty, man or woman, black or white, family or distant kin.[21] For his first thirteen years, it is true, he did know his paternal grandfather, from 1794 to 1807; it is also true that Ruffin's father, George Ruffin, had known his own paternal grandfather, Edmund I, from 1765 to 1790—the longest period the family ever experienced with three generations alive and near one another.[22] Edmund Ruffin knew about Captain Edmund only in legend as a man of herculean frame who lived seventy-seven years, longer than any ancestor.[23] Neither Ruffin nor his father ever knew a grandmother, and neither man knew a maternal grandfather. Ruffin never discovered even the names of his mother's parents, who lived and died twenty miles downstream in Surry County before he was born.[24]

This history of family mortality and migration culminated in the isolation of young Edmund Ruffin between 1794 and 1799, during his first five years of life. He lived in a social setting in which the family had barely enough members to constitute a domestic circle. The Ruffins and their neighbors did not live in three-generation households or kin groups that gathered together grandparents, parents, and the new generation of children. Their experience was closer to that of people who had settled in Virginia in the seventeenth century. Between 1795 and 1799 four years passed when Ruffin's father found it impossible to gather even two full generations into his household: George lived alone with just young Edmund and the slaves. At some point, probably in 1807 and 1808, young Edmund went away for secondary schooling, perhaps in North Carolina.[25] Between 1809 and 1813 he lived for long periods apart from his family, first at the college, then in the militia, then at Coggin's Point, the farm he inherited from his grandfather. By the time he

reached the age of nineteen, he had spent as many as ten full years—
more than half his life—outside a complete family.

The Broken Charm: A Malthusian Revolution

Ruffin's father was remarried on 19 September 1799, to Rebecca
Cocke (1771–1837), another woman from Surry County with a family
history like that of Jane Lucas.[26] Rebecca Cocke had lost both of her
parents: her father, George Ruffin's friend John Cocke, was a widower
who had died in 1798 at about fifty-five, leaving Rebecca one "good
feather Bed and furniture," one "good Horse," and an equal—but
unspecified—share of "all my negroes not already given away." His
survivors in January 1798 included Rebecca, her brother Walter (who
was soon to die in 1802 at thirty-four), and her three adult sisters.[27]

Edmund Ruffin at the age of five thus acquired a parentless woman
as his stepmother, just as soon as George Ruffin possibly could have
won the hand (and slaves) of Rebecca Cocke. George and Rebecca
Ruffin settled in 1799 on the property soon to be known as Evergreen
Farm, which George had inherited from his grandfather.[28] The marriage pattern George Ruffin followed in selecting orphans as spouses—
a pattern followed later by his son Edmund and daughter Jane—
revealed how Tidewater families struck by death took care of their
orphaned sons and daughters: immediate and early marriage became
the means of securing places in other families for young survivors.
Unless guardians themselves were willing to assume the expense of
supporting wards, these young solitaries had no choice but to marry
as soon as possible; this was particularly true for females over sixteen
(when orphans could choose their own guardians) and males over
twenty-one. Young people who found themselves alone in the world
at these ages quickly formed their own families whenever an orphan-
bride's inherited dowry matched an orphan-groom's inherited property. Everyone's interest dictated that these marriages proceed
quickly, for no one had to support, sustain, or supervise orphans once
they had formed their own legitimate matches.[29]

In the decade after his father's second marriage, vital events of
family history changed Ruffin's life abruptly. First, his father and
stepmother produced six children. Only two of these six died in
infancy (George R., born 1801; and Rebecca S., born 1803). Four
survived, including Jane (1800), Juliana (1806?), Elizabeth (1807),

Graph 1   Ancestors of Ruffin in Prince George County: Life Spans,
1700–1820

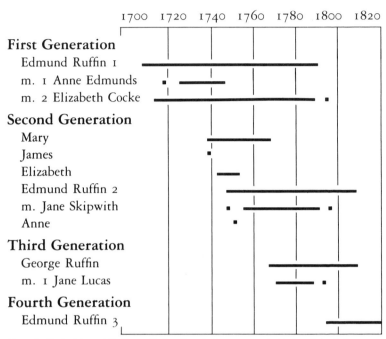

Note: Ruffin is Edmund Ruffin 3. Broken lines indicate uncertain birth and death dates.

and George Henry (1810).[30] George Henry broke the three-generation
spell under which the Ruffins produced only one living son. His
survival and that of his three sisters constituted a revolution in family
size. For the first time since the early eighteenth century, this line
of Ruffin children would form a significant cohort of brothers and
sisters. While their life spans fell slightly short of those for surviving
Ruffins in the eighteenth century, many more members of the family
would be alive at the same time. (See Graphs 1 and 2.)

In the midst of this vital revolution, two other events changed
Ruffin's life. First came the death of his grandfather, Edmund II, in
May 1807, at sixty-two.[31] Then, in May 1810, when Ruffin was
sixteen years old and a student at William and Mary, his father died.[32]
Ruffin himself now legally became an orphan. With these two deaths
came a total separation from older kin. His parents and all of his

Graph 2   Relatives of Ruffin in Prince George County: Life Spans, 1780–1880

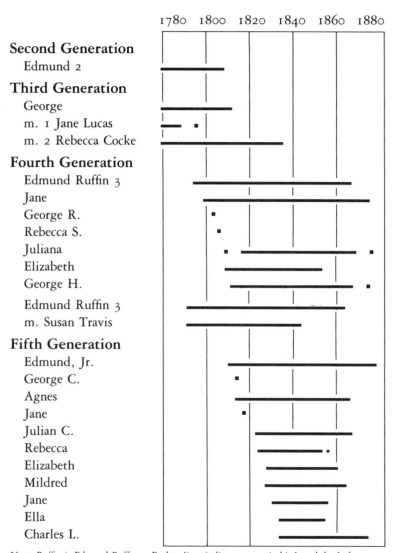

Note: Ruffin is Edmund Ruffin 3. Broken lines indicate uncertain birth and death dates.

grandparents were dead. Since his father had been an only child, he had no Ruffin aunts or uncles. His Lucas uncles both were dead, and his mother's one surviving sister either had died by 1810 or had migrated from Surry County. There was no comforting, sustaining circle of relatives from older generations to surround him.[33]

He did have his stepmother, it is true, a woman described in 1851 as "kind" and who permitted him to return to Evergreen from col-lege.[34] It was also true that Rebecca Cocke Ruffin had a material interest in securing the welfare of herself and her own children, an interest that did not always coincide with that of Edmund Ruffin. In 1812 she filed suit in Prince George County Court to overturn specific provisions in her husband's will favoring Edmund Ruffin at the expense of herself and her own children. She refused to accept the guardians her husband named for her own children (letting Ed-mund remain in alien hands); for herself she demanded guardianship of her children, possession of all slaves she had brought to her mar-riage, "and also such negroes accustomed to waiting and attending in the house," together with assurances that Evergreen and two other plantations owned by George Ruffin would descend to her daughters and to George Henry Ruffin. Edmund Ruffin kept his right to the farm his grandfather had willed him at Coggin's Point, and to four court-awarded slaves, Lydia, Molly, Giles, and Moses.[35] (Some of these slaves once may have been Jane Lucas' property and thus provided links to Ruffin's maternal ancestors.) Rebecca Ruffin would care for her own.

It was true, too, that Ruffin now had three half-sisters (one of whom he came to love dearly the rest of his life) and a half-brother, but all were much younger than he; his half-brother, an infant, was sixteen years younger. In terms of kin and family of origin, Ruffin was utterly alone. For the rest of his youth and young adulthood, Ruffin had but one adult ally, the man his father named to be his guardian, who was in the legal terminology of the day his "next friend" and who granted the wish expressed in George Ruffin's will, assuming between 1810 and 1840 the role of a father. This friend was Thomas Cocke.[36]

From the experience of losing parents and relatives Ruffin emerged with that quality of solitariness he always remembered about himself. His later memories of childhood at Evergreen, even as that house became populated with younger Ruffins, seldom involved family members or other people in the household.[37] In his diary entries after

1857 he recalled days alone in the library at Evergreen, reading what he came to regard as a meager collection—newspapers, children's books, Adam Smith, Walter Scott, Joseph Addison, Jonathan Swift, Henry Fielding, Edmund Burke, the Bible, Shakespeare.[38] He did not go to the fields with his father or grandfather.[39]

His behavior followed the same pattern of bookishness and solitariness at the College of William and Mary, where he studied in 1810.[40] Ruffin did not board or room in the college but did so in town, with perhaps half the student population of Williamsburg. He therefore knew only the small circle of students who shared quarters in the same house; one of these students, William C. Rives from Prince George, he later claimed to despise.[41] He read what he wanted, picking up books as if he were still in the library at Evergreen. He attended especially to geometry, which he could apply to surveying fields; he learned no chemistry. In later memories of his youth he recalled his lackadaisicalness, fondness for drink, and the need he felt even at that time to exercise self-control.[42] Even at the college, Ruffin lived on his own in social conditions that led him to feel that he was alone in the world.

In the tradition of most William and Mary students, Ruffin took no degree. His grandfather, a classmate of Thomas Jefferson, had studied at Williamsburg for two of the three years required for a bachelor's degree.[43] The bursar did not record Ruffin's departure from the college; probably it was after his father's death in May 1810 that he returned to Evergreen. There, at loose ends, he lived two years on the hospitality of Rebecca Cocke Ruffin. In 1812, after his eighteenth birthday, he joined the militia in Prince George; between August 1812 and February 1813 he served six months as a private during the War of 1812. Early in 1813, when he was just nineteen, he persuaded Thomas Cocke to give him his inheritance, the farm at Coggin's Point.[44] Ruffin now was the orphaned owner of a poor, depleted farm four miles downstream from Evergreen, five miles northwest of Cocke's farm at Aberdeen. In the center of his 1,582 acres stood his grandfather's old complex of farm buildings, isolated completely on a point jutting into the James River, and two miles by carriage road from the nearest house at Tarbay.

Ruffin's grandfather, who had grown up at the farm that became Evergreen, had purchased this property about 1778; by 1781 the Coggin's Point farm had at least one small house, and Edmund II had established his household there.[45] With the these properties the

Ruffins had acquired two farms of sufficient size to provide permanent homes for three generations in the same county, diminishing chances that children would have to migrate to find land. Evidence in Ruffin family inheritance patterns suggests that they ingeniously planned to pass the Evergreen property from Captain Edmund, the carpenter, to George (from grandfather to grandson). Edmund II, son of the carpenter, in turn would pass Coggin's Point to his own grandson, Edmund Ruffin. A son would grow up on his father's farm and then take possession of his grandfather's. Always, three generations could be together—fate willing. This plan was based on the assumption that just one son in each generation would survive, an assumption that held true from 1740 to 1810. The Ruffins had no experience in planning for the survival of daughters.

When Edmund Ruffin moved alone to Coggin's Point early in 1813, he was entering a material environment created by his deceased grandfather. Vastly less impressive than the home of his youth at Evergreen, it was a reminder that one could decline in the world. The mansion at Evergreen had a replacement value in 1808 of $9,150. At Coggin's Point Ruffin found two small frame dwellings standing close together, with perhaps two rooms in each. One house measured thirty-six by eighteen feet (648 square feet), the other thirty-two by eighteen (576 square feet); their combined replacement value in 1808 was $1,350. They sat in the middle of a field, with few trees for shade.[46] In one of these houses Ruffin discovered his grandfather's manuscripts, documenting that ancestor's role in repelling the British when their fleet anchored off City Point during the Revolution and drove the Ruffins from their farms. Ruffin kept these manuscripts for forty-five years.[47] These were his first documents in local history, his first evidence that dramatic events had occurred where he lived, his most prized intellectual connection with the past. Through these papers he acquired an identification with his grandfather.

At Coggin's Point he also encountered his grandfather's slaves, about fifty in number. In 1782 there had been thirty slaves at Coggin's Point. His great-grandfather, by comparison, had fifty-one slaves in Prince George that year, and forty-one more on property in Charlotte County.[48] In 1820, seven years after Ruffin arrived, the total number at Coggin's Point stood at fifty-two.[49] In 1813, when he entered this community of fifty black slaves, Ruffin experienced an extreme form of the racial distribution he would know all his life: he was that year the only representative of a slaveholding family living in the midst of a black slave majority.[50]

This racial setting would reinforce his isolation and shape his thinking about black people, about race, about intelligence, about success, and about himself. He was a stranger to most of these people, though most of them had known his grandfather. Later in his life he became conscious of the fact that some of his father's slaves and at least one of Thomas Cocke's slaves knew much about the history of his family and their farms. But this was always a wonder to him, that a black man could remember years when crops were poor, or that a black woman might remember things his great-grandfather had done.[51] Their slavery, contrasted with Ruffin's literacy, education, comparative leisure, responsibility, and power, confirmed his separation from these people. His ambition, when it yielded success, prosperity, and fame—all through his own efforts, he thought—would make him contemptuous of them.

Ruffin remained alone with his slaves at Coggin's Point almost a full year, until some time near the end of 1813. Then he married Susan Hutchings Travis (1793–1846), a woman one year older than he, but barely twenty years old herself. The daughter of Champion Travis and Elizabeth Boush Travis, she came from one of Williamsburg's most prominent colonial and Revolutionary families. She and Ruffin must have met while he was a student at William and Mary. The Travis family had wealth, though they did not stand absolutely at the top of the pyramid in James City County. In 1810 Champion Travis owned 802.75 acres in that county, ranking eleventh among its landholders; in personal property he stood forty-fourth out of 332, below the top ten percent.[52]

Reasons other than a match between wealthy families lay behind this marriage. Champion Travis, who had inherited his family's property on Jamestown Island, died on 22 August 1810, just three months after George Ruffin expired at Evergreen.[53] Aged sixty-five at his death, Travis left behind his wife and seven children, at least three of whom were still his dependents. Susan Travis, his sixth child and second daughter, thus was orphaned at the age of eighteen, during the same year Edmund Ruffin lost his father. Here was a match made in heaven.

Travis' third son, Samuel, became his father's executor and took possession of most of the Williamsburg property. Other lands in

Tennessee and Kentucky went to other sons.[54] For young Susan, Edmund Ruffin (soon to inherit fifteen hundred acres) offered more than romance. He offered a way to restore her to the security of a family without moving her across the mountains. Thus orphan married orphan. In this match Edmund Ruffin acquired no father-in-law to represent the older generation or to instruct him or challenge his authority. Never did Ruffin have to allow for the give-and-take of argument with his wife's kin. At Coggin's Point, the new couple settled in isolation from kin and the past. At nineteen he was his own master.

Probably they married in October or November 1813, for their first son, Edmund Ruffin, Jr., was born 31 August 1814.[55] After this child came ten more. Their rate of survival was as unprecedented as that of Ruffin's half-siblings in the previous decade: George Champion, born in 1815 (died as an infant); Agnes, 1817; Jane, 1819 (died as an infant); Julian Calx, 1821; Rebecca, 1823; Elizabeth, 1824; Mildred Campbell, 1827; Jane, 1829; Ella and Charles (twins), 1832. Eleven births, nine surviving children.[56]

These nine survivors at Ruffin's house, added to the five earlier survivors at Evergreen, completed a revolution in Ruffin family reproductive history between 1800 and 1832. No Ruffin ever had confronted such numbers or had had to find places for so many surviving children. "But we have broken the *charm*," Ruffin wrote to his distant cousin in 1834, "and I am heartily glad of it."[57] He wanted them to live. He decided, therefore, to move away from the disease-ridden environment of the river and marshes for the summer of 1828, a decision whose wisdom reinforced his sense that their welfare lay in his hands.[58]

All of these children arrived just as the soil in Prince George County was judged at last to be wasted and barren. Edmund Ruffin then confronted twin problems that would determine his future: a Malthusian crisis in the family he had fathered, and a depletion of the soil on which he lived. Success in conquering these problems, he came to believe, was the result of his own intelligence and effort. In this he shared the thinking of other antebellum Americans north and south. These were the terms in which he thought about his early life at Evergreen and Coggin's Point: independence, self-reliance, achievement, and success through hard work. Family history led him to think in these terms whenever he judged the worth of human beings and, ultimately, when he measured the value of his own life.

The Consequences of Isolation

Early isolation had consequences that influenced Ruffin's career and thinking in ways he made manifest. Isolation made possible the way he formed his own marriage and family. It fixed in his mind an image of himself as a father. Though he thought of family history in terms of the male line, and though he assumed that paternal authority was necessary for family survival, this conservative Southern slaveholder did not adhere to a concept of strict patriarchy.[59] Experience would teach him that his authority was not absolute, but limited and finite. As he would discover when he became guardian briefly for his two youngest sisters and brother, his legal power ended the instant those wards married, became adults, or chose another guardian. He would rediscover the limits of paternal authority in dealing with his children, who made nearly all the crucial decisions regarding their marriages and vocations. In fact, Ruffin did not try to keep paternal authority for life. Rather, he waited impatiently for his children to take it away. Before he was sixty he divided his estate and gave equal portions to each child, male and female. And with this property he intended to transfer power.

This nineteenth-century father did insist that his children follow his instruction, but only as a preparation before they cast themselves into a world of mobility, mortality, and competition. Here his youthful isolation led him to draw on assumptions originating not in the Middle Ages, but in the eighteenth century. He did not assume that a good family name would assure his children a place in society. The family did not have that power. This family—his own creation, whose survival was his triumph—might prepare sons and daughters for lives on their own, but it could not convey to them ascribed status. It could only help them achieve a competency, and their father's instruction was merely a means to that end. This appears to have been a way of thinking about the family that Ruffin developed for himself, though he certainly understood the implications of his ancestors' experience. Neither his father nor his grandfather left clues in writing about their assumptions, but they behaved as if they thought in similar terms.[60]

Isolation also permitted Ruffin to think of himself as the sole agent of his success, to view himself as a totally independent, competent man. This concept appeared at the latest by 1821 (when he was twenty-seven), by which time he had established his wife and children securely in one household, had begun the successful rejuvenation of his farm, and had begun to write about his triumphs.[61] He began to judge himself and other men not simply in terms of Virginia or Carolina family lineage, but according to their intelligence and achievements. In time this would make him a harsh judge of failure and weakness. His way of assessing human beings eventually confirmed his notions about race, drawing him toward contempt for blacks, in whom he could detect no apparent ambition or independence. The origin of these ideas and judgments lay in his early isolation: the self-history he began to construct in those years permitted him to interpret his past as a record of independent triumphs over adversity.

In the end, too, isolation would influence the way he thought about death. By the time he was twenty-seven and the father of three living children, Ruffin began to reveal that he had carried from his youth an assumption that even survival was a matter within the power of human beings to control. He came to believe he could control the effects of malaria by draining ponds and swamps and by moving to high ground.[62] Like nineteenth-century reformers in the North, Ruffin developed a passion for controlling processes of material life that his ancestors had accepted as inevitable. He may have begun this way of thinking when he was a student at the College of William and Mary, controlling himself in matters of diet, drink, health, and work.[63] Near the end of his life, in 1865, he reached the conclusion that he could control the very hour of his death. This sense of competence and control over life fixed itself in Ruffin at Coggin's Point Farm after 1818, the year he taught himself how to increase the fertility of the earth.

2

The Early Career
of Edmund Ruffin

Especially he valued my theoretical views of the causes of & means for producing fertility.

EDMUND RUFFIN, 1851

Discoveries Edmund Ruffin made between 1813 and 1821, during the first decade of his career as a farmer, changed assumptions about the agricultural crisis facing eastern Virginia in the early nineteenth century. When he published his first findings in the *American Farmer* in 1821, Ruffin was only twenty-seven years old, but he knew already he had introduced a new idea about soil exhaustion. He argued for a notion of expanded human control over soil fertility and raised the possibility of rejuvenating farmlands of the East. At the same time, he altered suppositions that prevailed all along the Atlantic seaboard about ecology and population. Ruffin's theory offered a way for Virginia farmers to free themselves from the bleak belief that their lands were caught in a downward spiral of depletion and depopulation, feeding only an exodus to the West.

Five years later, in 1826, while still a farmer, Ruffin finished a draft of his first book, *An Essay on Calcareous Manures* (1832). In this, his most famous book, he realized he was also changing an old idea of farming. Ruffin conceptualized a reconstruction of rural Virginia led by individuals possessing the calculating mentality of scientific farmers. Because the kind of scientific agriculture Ruffin knew in 1826 required much labor, his reconstruction also demanded the work of slaves. He saw no contradiction between science and slavery: his concept required both.[1]

Events much later in Ruffin's life would entangle him in a chain of argument and agony that eventually made him seem to be an

alienated man possessed by a sense of failure. After 1832 he experienced a series of occupational changes, most of which he viewed with
regret. For only a dozen of his first fifty years did he dedicate himself
totally to farming—from 1813 to about 1825.[2] In this pursuit he
had great success, and his rejuvenation of Coggin's Point Farm made
it a model for others to study. Nonetheless, he sought constantly to
leave farming. From 1833 he edited a distinguished journal, the
Farmers' Register; then he testily abandoned it in 1842. After a second
brief period of farming in the 1840s, he embarked on another career
in reform, during which he became involved in the movement for
secession. In his mid-fifties he began to play a role that made him
the archetype of the proslavery Southerner. The despair he finally
came to feel in the spring of 1865 made it appear that Ruffin had
linked the collapse of the Old South with a failure of his reforms,
particularly those in agriculture.[3] Events after 1840 had obscured,
even to Edmund Ruffin, his role as an agent of intellectual change.

The Experimental Farmer

Ruffin's most influential experiments on soil fertility took place between 1813 and 1821, the first nine years he owned Coggin's Point
Farm, in Prince George County, Virginia. He made his discoveries
in a specific social setting that influenced the direction of those experiments. More was involved than his well-known reading of John
Taylor's essays on agricultural reform and Sir Humphry Davy's treatise
on agricultural chemistry; Ruffin encountered a need to experiment
even before he found those books. Conditions peculiar to his life and
social situation in Prince George County between 1813 and 1820
shaped his thinking. Relationships with neighbors, his own family
history, and the history of local farms defined the problems that
worried him.

When Ruffin took possession of Coggin's Point Farm in 1813, he
moved into a community of neighbors who believed their lands in
Prince George County were dead. They saw themselves confronting
an ecological crisis of insurmountable proportions, as an inevitable
decline in soil fertility created a crisis of population surplus. All of
Ruffin's early farming experiments addressed the assumption that he
and his neighbors now lived in "barren country."[4] Ruffin confronted

a mentality more deterministic in its view of soil and population than anything conceived of in the works of T. R. Malthus.

One neighbor who voiced this fatalism most clearly was Thomas Cocke himself. Cocke played a significant role in Ruffin's first career as a farmer. Their relationship, though forgotten by the world after 1840, constituted one long scientific debate, with Cocke playing the role of skeptic of Ruffin's ideas.[5] Cocke gave articulate expression to a stubborn skepticism that apparently was common among farmers in the county, challenging Ruffin to provide evidence that agricultural reform could succeed. Thomas Cocke's friendly opposition made it possible for Ruffin's theories to emerge from debates about very practical farming experiences in Prince George County. These two men lived at a time when research into the chemistry of soils in Virginia took place outside formal institutions such as agricultural societies and colleges. Research depended on institutions of family and friendship. Ruffin and Cocke conducted field experiments on their own farms, analyzing soil samples apparently in their own houses, where chemical apparatus could be assembled. Neither Ruffin nor Cocke felt limited by this situation, for at the start of their experimenting this was the only institutional setting they knew or could imagine. The conditions of discovery were dictated by a situation they took for granted.[6] Even after Ruffin founded the Agricultural Society of Prince George in 1818, it was Thomas Cocke who provided the crucial audience for him. It was Cocke who had to be convinced.

Though awareness of the legal ties between these two men disappeared after 1840 (at least outside their families), the relationship between Ruffin and Cocke became crucial. At the time of Ruffin's birth Cocke lived at Aberdeen Farm, five miles from Coggin's Point and about seven miles from Evergreen. When Ruffin's father remarried in 1799 to Rebecca Cocke, a distant cousin of Thomas Cocke, the two families became linked through marriage as well as friendship. This connection probably led George Ruffin to designate Cocke as his choice for Edmund's guardian.[7] When Cocke conveyed Coggin's Point to his young ward early in 1813, he created a situation in Edmund Ruffin's life that made innovation necessary. Ruffin knew that the circumstances under which he received his portion of George Ruffin's estate seemed odd. He was too young, "barely nineteen years of age." Odder yet, Ruffin had never worked at farming. Cocke knew his ward "was totally ignorant of practical agriculture." From Ruffin's point of view, Cocke handed him the farm "out of easy indulgence."

Indifference, too, may have played a part, since Cocke was a careless farmer, and the land at Coggin's Point had declined to near worthlessness by 1813.[8] As soon as Ruffin got his land, however, he persuaded Thomas Cocke to help him save their farms. In 1816 Cocke moved from Aberdeen Farm to Tarbay, immediately next to Ruffin. At this point a research society of two had formed through friendship and family connections.[9]

Ruffin and Cocke began to argue at once about theories of soil fertility. Between 1813 and 1818 Ruffin tried to undermine one assumption Cocke had gathered "from some old and ignorant, but experienced practical cultivators of his neighborhood," a notion that their lands could not "hold manure" and could not be rejuvenated. "For years I heard this opinion frequently expressed by him," Ruffin remarked in 1839, "and the evident inference therefrom, that the far greater part of our lands, and of the whole country, was doomed to hopeless sterility."[10]

Coggin's Point Farm in 1812 did stand in barren condition, its recovery debatable. Ruffin described the property in clichés common among men who assumed control of run-down farms in the early nineteenth century. Its 1,582 acres on the south bank of the James River lay directly across from the Westover and Berkeley plantations. In 1813 it had 472 arable acres. Only one hundred acres along the river had good, neutral soil, and even that part had been "reduced below its great original fertility, by severe and careless tillage."[11] Records Ruffin kept between 1813 and 1826 proved that he was not exaggerating the miserableness of Coggin's Point merely to inflate his achievements; in 1813 the farm yielded eighteen bushels of corn per acre, and in 1814 it yielded only eight, when lands in the West were yielding thirty-five and more.[12]

Ruffin confronted his decaying fields without skill or knowledge handed down from his family. Here the isolation created by deaths in the Ruffin and Lucas families had still more consequences. With the demise of his grandfather in 1807 and his father in 1810, he had no older male Ruffins alive to instruct him in farming. He had no older brothers, no uncles, and no father-in-law. By the time he married Susan Travis in 1813 (after obtaining his farm), she was herself an orphan, and the couple lived remote from her older brothers, who survived in Williamsburg.[13] The impulse to reform his farm and Virginia came necessarily, from himself.

He found himself unable to follow farming traditions of the Tidewater simply because he never learned them. He had not gone to the fields with his father and grandfather, so he knew nothing from them. He would have been ignorant, "even if my farming labors had been postponed to a mature age," he admitted, given the "usual want of training of farmers of Virginia." (Ruffin himself never trained his own sons to farm.) At first, in 1813, he tried to emulate his neighbors, but stopped that course within a few months. "The agriculture of my neighborhood, like all that I ever witnessed, was wretched in execution, and as erroneous as well could be in system."[14] There were no models in Prince George County. At Coggin's Point, where a run-down farm had been inherited by an innocent orphan with a guardian indifferent to details of farming, there inevitably would occur some innovation.

Books alone gave guidance and provided Ruffin with a link to farming practices of the eighteenth century. In the winter of 1813–14 he began his oft-told encounter with John Taylor's *Arator* essays, immediately after their publication in book form.[15] He began at once to follow Taylor's instructions, enclosing his largest field on the Point (to prevent animals from damaging soil), spreading animal and vegetable manures, and plowing deeply. Apparently he persuaded Thomas Cocke to follow the same instructions at Aberdeen. For four years (and perhaps as many as six years in some experiments) Ruffin and Cocke tried Taylor's methods, paying special attention to using animal manure and cornstalks as fertilizer. By 1817, after four years of debate, Thomas Cocke convinced Ruffin that Taylor was wrong. Mere fertilizers had not revived their soil. Cocke persuaded Ruffin that their land "was and always had been sterile."[16]

In the crisis of 1817 Ruffin momentarily became convinced that Thomas Cocke had won the debate and that Virginia soil could not be revived. He claimed in later years that he tried to sell his farm in early 1817, falling back on "the universal approved resort, in all such cases, of emigrating to the rich western wilderness." But he found no buyer. Coggin's Point could not produce enough food and profit to support a "small but fast growing family," along with the slaves.[17] At that point Ruffin had only one or two young children, but Edmund and Susan Travis Ruffin knew they would conceive more offspring, given their youthfulness (he was twenty-three and she, twenty-four). Given recent family history, Ruffin knew the chances were good that some of those children would survive. He also had to consider the survival of his slaves, who numbered about fifty in 1817.[18] He faced a miniature Malthusian crisis on his own farm. In his case, the crisis assumed the harshest possible form—population increasing while an ecological disaster drove down the fertility of the land.

The Death of the Earth

Not even T. R. Malthus anticipated a crisis of subsistence like the one farmers in Prince George County thought they faced between 1800 and 1820. Malthus, whose *Essay on the Principle of Population* had been read in various editions by Virginians at this time, believed the crisis would occur when population surpassed the power of the earth to increase the food supply. While Malthus did not have a completely static concept of the earth, he did not imagine—except in a few, brief passages—significant increases or decreases in soil fertility. He saw the power of the earth as limited, but not "defined." He thought food production might increase through the introduction of "fertile uncultivated land," animal manures, and by the invention of new machinery and division of labor. He did consider the possibility of an "exhaustion of cultivable land," but he mentioned it only peripherally. Soil depletion did not become one of Malthus' central concerns, and he did not list it among his theoretical checks to the growth of population. He did not envision an ecological disaster stemming from soil depletion as a cause of population crisis.[19]

Edmund Ruffin detected in his neighbors a decidedly harsher, more deterministic view of the subsistence crisis. In their view, land itself acted as the agent of change; its declining fertility was the agency creating an ecological crisis, supporting fewer people and creating by its decline a population surplus. In their view, population did not have to increase for the crisis to occur. The soil simply wasted away. These farmers of Prince George could imagine the death of the earth and the decline of the East.[20]

Failure pushed Ruffin in 1817 toward his neighbors' point of view, as expressed by Thomas Cocke. By 1821, however, he had reached conclusions that took him far from the thinking of his neighbors, and from Malthus, too. Between 1826 and 1832, in discussing the laws of population as they applied to slaves, he did adopt terms almost identical to those of Malthus. He spoke of "prudential, moral, or physical" checks to reproduction.[21] Yet Ruffin moved beyond Malthus to an idea of perpetual renewal of the earth, a new idea for which he relied on no previous authority. This change in thinking came after Ruffin had decided to surrender at Coggin's Point, while he was waiting for a buyer in 1817. It came when he discovered a new book, Sir Humphry Davy's *Elements of Agricultural Chemistry*, which appeared first in London in 1812 and then in 1815 in four American cities, including Fredericksburg, Virginia. In Chapter 4 Ruffin found an engraving of Davy's pneumatic apparatus for testing the chemical composition of soils. He also found descriptions of sterile soils in England that Davy had analyzed.[22] Early in 1817 Ruffin reproduced Davy's pneumatic apparatus and began testing soil samples from Coggin's Point and neighboring farms. Henceforth, Ruffin's life course was determined not so much by material conditions of rural life in Virginia, or by forces of class, race, and economics, as by the ideas in a book.

In the manner of other country naturalists of the early nineteenth century, Ruffin gathered soil samples and presented his findings in papers that made his scientific research famous. He analyzed four samples from Coggin's Point, one from James City County, another from a farm near Norfolk. Other samples followed from all over Virginia, from Pennsylvania, and from the Mississippi Valley.[23] His discovery that soils in Virginia's Tidewater differed from those Davy described in England not only challenged all European authorities on agricultural chemistry, but changed local ways of thinking as well. Essentially, Ruffin had discovered the principle of pH acting in Virginia soils that varied in their acidity and alkalinity. Soils he found in Virginia contained no "calcareous earth," no carbonate of lime, an ingredient necessary to maintain a neutral soil capable of retaining its fertility. His discovery of high concentrations of acid in fields abandoned or covered with second-growth pines changed completely the way Virginians defined the problem of soil depletion. Moreover, Ruffin discovered in the galls and ravines on his own farm the cure for acid soil: layer upon layer of fossil shells ("marl," as it was called in Virginia) that had the *"power of neutralizing acids."* Once the marl had been applied, putrescent manures of animal and vegetable waste could work effectively as fertilizer. Shells neutralized soil; manures then fertilized it. This discovery, Ruffin thought, was his.[24]

Elated, he told the news to Thomas Cocke. That skeptic responded by declaring marl "not worth the trouble." Cocke himself had made "several small applications, in 1803, on soils of different kinds," with no visible benefit. He had neglected to mention this early trial, Ruffin

said, "until induced by my remark." Ruffin must have insisted that
Cocke take him immediately to the field that had been marled in
1803. There, in 1817, Ruffin could still see the results in the mere
appearance of three places Cocke had treated. One had been ruined
by too heavy an application; but the other two remained rejuvenated,
superior to surrounding plots. The results had lasted fourteen years;
but Ruffin wanted to prove they would last forever, so he cast about
for traces of other old experiments.[25] What he discovered then was
the unknown history of much earlier attempts to revive Virginia using
precisely the methods he himself had devised. Ruffin reconstructed
a local history of farm reform dating from the Revolution, a reform
abandoned because no one understood theories of soil rejuvenation.
Through local history, Ruffin supplemented his experiments in soil
chemistry and, incidentally, made it possible to date the first local
efforts at agricultural reform.

His distant kinsman, Francis Ruffin, showed him a field in Surry
County in early 1819 that had been marled in 1775 or 1776, about
the time Thomas Cocke was born. Even in January 1819, when Francis
Ruffin's field was under grass, Edmund Ruffin reported he could
"easily discover the commencement of the marling by the difference
in growth." Francis Ruffin did not remember the actual marling,
since he was too young to recall events before 1801.[26]

Later in 1819 Ruffin appears to have persuaded Thomas Cocke to
experiment once more with marl. It was then that Ruffin discovered
the earliest such experiment he ever recorded. When Thomas Cocke
ordered his elderly gardener at Aberdeen to apply marl to the garden,
the slave objected; he knew "the stuff was good for nothing" because
his old master had once tried marl, "and it had never done the least
good." This experiment had taken place about 1771 at Bonaccord,
the farm once owned by James Cocke, father of Thomas Cocke. The
gardener had been a witness. "Being asked whether he could show
the spot where this trial had been made," Ruffin wrote, "he answered
that he could easily, as he drove the cart which carried out the marl."
Ruffin went to this field, too, and could see where the deposit had
been laid, covering almost an acre of ground. It was still so much
better than all the surrounding field that it was never dressed with
barnyard manure, "though the cause was not then suspected."[27]

This field had been marled in 1771, before the lifetime of Thomas
Cocke. The present generation of whites knew nothing about it until
an elderly slave remembered it. For Ruffin, Bonaccord proved that

the original fertility of soil, if restored by marling, was perpetual. The worst assumptions of the farmers of Prince George County were wrong.[28] Through science and family history, Ruffin had devised a new idea of the earth.

In February 1818 there began at Coggin's Point the field experiments with marl that convinced Edmund Ruffin that the ecological crisis in Virginia could be overcome, at least to the extent of disproving local notions that soil inevitably declined and died. Most of his experiments took place in a single field of twenty-six acres, on a ridge near the James River. Near this field slaves dug a pit three or four feet deep, but this first pit filled with water and had to be abandoned. Ruffin then moved excavations to a second site, where his laborers removed the fossil shells and carted them to the plots. For the next ten years Ruffin continued to clear and marl, until by 1827 he had treated 555 acres at Coggin's Point.[29] Two neighbors joined the experiments between 1818 and 1823. One of them, Ruffin said, was "my old friend Thomas Cocke—who though he had led me to find the disease, could not be speedily convinced of its true nature, or of the value of the remedy." Cocke still played the skeptic, and Ruffin knew other neighbors were watching skeptically:

> As late as 1822, when he [Cocke] walked with me to an enormous excavation which I was then making in carrying out marl, he said to me, that, "In future time, if marling shall then have been abandoned as unprofitable, this place will probably be known by the name of 'Ruffin's Folly.' "[30]

Within five years the extent of marl deposits under neighboring farms had been discovered; the shells underlay the entire county and Tidewater Virginia. Within ten years, Ruffin boasted, most of his neighbors had begun to follow his theory, if not his precise instructions for application. "There were no exceptions, as might have been expected—because of the poverty of some, or the old age or infirmities of others."[31] For a time Ruffin thought marling was a reform that farmers of all classes could join.

Ruffin published enthusiastic accounts of his success, relying on measurements he recorded carefully until 1828. In one of his first experiments he used a scaled method to test the effect of marl on corn, comparing two identically sized plots of 588 stalks of corn. Marling increased yields: in the end, he estimated it doubled corn production. Moreover, as early as 1823, Ruffin discovered that his applications of fossil shells and manure had added topsoil, from an original thinness of one to three inches, to a new thickness of seven inches and more.[32] Soil that was perpetually fertile could now be created.

Enthusiasm produced by this triumph over nature nearly obscured two other significant changes implicit in Ruffin's work. Marling demanded new farming methods and a larger scale in farming, both of which had begun to worry Ruffin by 1826, at the latest. He had anticipated that marling might create its own disruptions in rural Virginia, and that it might not merely revive a once-productive farming society in its old social form. He took pains, however, to deny the consequences of new methods and scale. Eventually he became frustrated by these changes: frustration appeared as early as 1832, when he published *An Essay on Calcareous Manures*. By that time, the complexities of applying calcareous manures had driven him from farming.

The Difficulties of Reform

Descriptions in the *Essay* of experiments between 1818 and 1831 revealed Ruffin's frustrations and his fears about the social consequences of agricultural reform. By 1832 he had become aware that marling demanded not only a new way of thinking about soil, but also a new way of farming. His autobiographical accounts of applying calcareous manures were documents in precision, planning, and calculation—in maddening detail. Marling required precision at every turn. Ruffin had to know the strength and quantity of marl he applied; he had to know the extent of land to be fertilized; he had to apply marl in straight lines, in order to determine the bounds of experiments and to avoid disastrous double-marling; he had to plant at specific distances and measure yields precisely. He had to analyze soil, survey fields, oversee loading and harvesting, and keep records. Finally, as early as 1821, Ruffin discovered marling had to be incorporated into the regular routine of his work force. It could not be a leisure-time activity. Horses and mules had to be assigned the same tasks constantly or they did not become accustomed to carting; the slave force had to be devoted to specific tasks routinely or they made mistakes through inexperience and forgetfulness. Marling had to proceed with the order and scale of a bureaucracy.[33]

This troubled Ruffin, for he knew that not every farmer could proceed so precisely or quickly as he. No "cultivator," he knew, could "bestow enough care and patient observation" to obtain the kind of measured results produced at Coggin's Point, a pattern farm. His great fear in the *Essay* was that he might undercut reform by leading his readers to despair that marling cost too much. He feared that reform might be class-specific, that it might be an option open only to wealthy planters. In the *Essay* and other writings through 1842, Ruffin assumed an attitude hostile to the formation of an elite class holding large acreages; such a class of farmers might become absentee landlords, not farming the lands they owned. The *Essay* followed a tradition of rural writing in the Atlantic states that favored land-holdings farmed by people who owned their own land. Ruffin wanted his readers to believe that even light marling, advancing slowly on a small scale, could work. His central task in writing *An Essay on Calcareous Manures*, therefore, was to convince his readers that they could apply marl without enormous expense or scale. He offered prescriptions for standard quantities of marl for acid and exhausted soils (250 to 300 bushels per acre), and for newly cleared land (twice as much). This standard prescription would be easier to follow, particularly for smaller farms and poorer farmers.[34]

One concession to science and change he did insist that even small farmers must make: all farmers had to measure the strength of the marl they applied. He urged everyone to use Davy's apparatus, consisting of three glass bottles, a glass tube, a stop-cock, a bladder, and muriatic acid. If this proved too complicated, Ruffin permitted a simpler (and less accurate) apparatus consisting of a large drinking glass and water. "The most experienced eye may be much deceived in the strength of marl, and still more gross and dangerous errors would be made by an inexperienced marler." No longer would the eye suffice to estimate quantities or composition. "Whoever uses marl, ought to know how to analyze it."[35] In the non-institutional setting of the early nineteenth century, this meant that each farmer had to become his own chemist, with his own apparatus. This, in turn, demanded a change in mentality and skill.

The sheer amount of labor also worried Ruffin. He feared marling would demand too much "force," a problem particularly for those without large numbers of slaves. He began to worry about this as early as 1821, when he confessed, "The labour required for using shell marl, is now the greatest obstacle to the practice."[36] This worry never subsided, for in fact marling did demand a large expenditure in labor.

In 1820 Ruffin owned fifty-two slaves; in 1830, sixty-six. He kept detailed records of costs per acre and of slave tasks in marling, hoping to dispel fears that this reform was a remedy only for planters with large slave holdings. He devised tasks that permitted the division and specialization of labor for different categories of slaves, and he found new uses for small boys and old men. "Strong labourers are required in the pit for digging and loading: but boys who are too small for any other regular farm labour, are sufficient to drive the carts." Yet the labor was great. In 1818 Ruffin did not have enough "spare labor" to marl more than twelve acres. On one job in April 1824, he employed nineteen slaves for four days to remove earth—just clearing the area for a pit required nine young men, six young women, two boys, one girl, and one old man. Removing the marl from the pit then required two men for digging and two boys for carting, for six weeks.[37] In 1839 he confessed that once his land had been marled it demanded more labor for harvest and maintenance than he could muster, and the farm got "wretchedly out of order." This problem of labor was not resolved until 1836, when Edmund Ruffin, Jr., married a wealthy woman who brought more slaves to Coggin's Point.[38]

Edmund Ruffin had wanted to find in marling a method of rejuvenation that would be inexpensive, in order to save the lands of everyone in Virginia and along the Atlantic seaboard. He did not find marling inexpensive. His own accounts revealed that this rejuvenation of the soil demanded much labor and that it entailed at least one serious social consequence. Marling, it appeared, would fasten slavery upon Virginia in large-scale holdings. Indeed, in 1832 the case could be made that scientific agriculture now required the preservation of slavery. Ruffin discovered the need on his own land for more slaves. This need, in turn, made it necessary to farm on an ever-larger scale, leading to the consolidation of smaller farms, and feeding the emigration to the West. Ruffin himself bought at least four farms in addition to Coggin's Point. He wanted none of this change in scale, but discovered that even he had become implicated in creating it.

All of his experiments had proceeded on a scale he could supervise in person. He simply assumed the cultivator ought to direct every operation. On farms of larger scale this would not be possible; the overseers (whom he detested) would have to direct the rejuvenation. Even on the moderate scale of his own operations, Ruffin found his efforts confounded by error. His work force frustrated him. "Careless labourers" loaded carts too lightly—time after time—and then they would injure the unsuspecting horse by suddenly "putting in a load much too heavy." He devised a smaller cart to foil this sabotage (which he always saw as ineptitude). If he did not watch carefully, his loaders still found ways to vary the amounts they put into the carts, so he sometimes had to guess at the amounts being applied. He removed the tailgate on each cart to stop this imprecision; excess shells would spill immediately back into the pit. He complained of carts breaking down, "which was very often, owing to careless driving, and worse carpentry." In 1831 he found that "another accidental circumstance" prevented measurement of a crucial corn crop. Contrary to his explicit, standing instructions, his laborers shucked the corn before he had a chance to measure it. His fields suffered an accidental fire in the spring of 1830, preventing comparisons.[39] Amid the science, the precision, the history and record-keeping, the exhortation, and the boasting in his *Essay*, Ruffin wrote of his frustrations.

Between 1826 and 1832 Ruffin's first career in farming drew to an end: by the time he was thirty-two years old, he had shifted his attention to reading, writing, teaching himself French, and discussing calcareous manures with Thomas Cocke. "He was privy to my every thought on this, as on most other subjects; & of course, knew, from our frequent & full conversations, every view that I entertained, before all were laid before him, arranged in writing, for his opinion & friendly censure." In 1826 Ruffin read aloud to his friend the entire manuscript of *An Essay on Calcareous Manures*. After 1826 Ruffin quit keeping records on Coggin's Point. In 1831, after doubling his patrimony (not merely through marling, but also through the lucky stroke of having a large surplus of corn on hand when a disastrous drought struck farms to the south), he left that farm permanently for another three miles away, which he called Shellbanks, and which he also proceeded to revive.[40] One motive in moving to Shellbanks was to preserve the health of the children by escaping the river and marshes, with their malaria and bilious fevers.[41] This strategy worked: all of the Ruffin children born after 1821 survived, bringing their number in 1832 to nine. Yet the move to Shellbanks really indicated that Ruffin was losing interest in farming. He continued to keep some perfunctory records on Shellbanks, but in 1835 he abandoned that farm, too, and moved into Petersburg. Thwarted in his early desire to abandon Coggin's Point in 1817, Ruffin finally left the country altogether in November 1835 and became an absentee landholder.[42]

He had come to hate farming for reasons he listed in his private memoirs in 1851. He was "deficient in order & method," and had serious deficiencies as a farmer. He had no "genius for, and little knowledge of machinery & its proper working—even of ploughs & of gearing." He was no judge of horses or livestock. He took no pleasure in "their care & management." He was a bad slave master, he thought. "I cannot exercise that uniform & inflexible demeanor which is necessary for the proper & easy government & discipline of subordinates, & especially of slaves." Ruffin was criticizing himself according to standards of a new regime. He hated supervising slaves, particularly under a system that demanded bureaucratic, almost industrial methods. "At last," he wrote about this period in his life, "my farming business became actually distasteful to me." He hated the new kind of farming he had created for himself, with all of its fussing over details, its keeping of records, its administration over minions bent on his defeat. Between 1835 and 1839, when Ruffin's son assumed direction of Coggin's Point, Ruffin rid himself of farming completely and moved away. "I did not spend in all my visits as much as 20 hours on the premises," he wrote in his memoirs. "At each visit I gave but a few hours to my farm, & the remainder of the time to my old friend Thomas Cocke, who lived at Tarbay, close adjoining."[43]

Ruffin's attitude toward his early career may have revealed a sense of failure. He himself became the source of conflicting interpretations of his work and of agricultural reform in the antebellum South. He developed an uncertainty about his achievements, alternately expressing feelings of success and failure. He would boast about changes in Southern agriculture, then despair that his instruction was being ignored by Virginia farmers. Ruffin neither believed he had transformed the reality of farming practice throughout the South, nor thought his methods could be applied to every kind of soil. The obvious depression he felt much later, at the end of his life, seemed to put a final emphasis upon his doubts. There the matter remained, in terms he defined, as he tried to determine what, if anything, he had changed.[44]

The Editor

Editing the *Farmers' Register* from 1833 through 1842 gave Ruffin the chance to discover whether his theory of soil rejuvenation had influenced other farmers. The impulse to found the new journal was stimulated by the success of *An Essay on Calcareous Manures*, but also by the desire to extend that influence.[45] He issued a prospectus in the winter of 1832–33 and began publishing the journal in June 1833; after suffering delays at the shop of his Richmond printer, he installed a press in one of the farm buildings in the Shellbanks yard. For a year and a half in 1834 and 1835 he published the *Register* as a family enterprise in the country. Then, acknowledging the difficulty of operating a print shop on a farm, he moved into Petersburg.[46] If his records on crops were kept less scrupulously after 1833, the explanation lay in this new work.

In each monthly issue of sixty-four pages Ruffin sought original contributions from his readers; when those did not come forth, he filled the *Register* with his own essays, many of them published anonymously.[47] While he addressed many agricultural subjects in the *Register*, he nearly always circled around to the subject of calcareous manures and the cycle of returning flesh and bone to the earth. In disposing of human waste, Virginia towns should learn from Europeans, who routinely shipped bones ("composed of phosphate of lime") to England where they were sold for manure. European battlefields had been gleaned for this purpose, he noted in 1833, "and the bones of the ten thousand British heroes who fell on the field of Waterloo, are now performing the less glorious but more useful purpose of producing wheat for their brothers at home."[48] In the effort to find new topics, he began to scan the countryside for evidence of innovation and change, for proof about the consequences of his work. He became skeptical of casual observations and enthusiastic reports. Increasingly he sought evidence he could perceive with his eyes and also measure with chemical apparatus. The search for such evidence engrossed his attention. Thus, every year in his decade as an editor he rode into the countryside searching for facts.

Ruffin's Rides

What he found as an "agricultural traveller" changed everything Virginians knew about the ecological history of the Tidewater and about the history of their farms. Equally significant, the experience of traveling through Virginia changed Edmund Ruffin. Places he never had seen, facts he never had suspected, surprised him. He found himself changing his own notion of evidence as he developed needs for a new kind of fact that could not be gathered on leisurely rides through rural Virginia, no matter how well he trained his eye.

Even before he issued the first number of the *Register*, Ruffin began to take excursions through the Tidewater, writing notes and preparing essays for his press. He knew the genre well, having read Arthur Young's accounts of travels in England and France and John Skinner's descriptions of Maryland and Virginia in the *American Farmer*.[49] Ruffin took his first outing as an agricultural traveler in early December 1832, when he rode through familiar terrain of James City County, an account he published in 1833. In the next ten years he extended his range: to Charles City County (1833), Albemarle (1834), North-ampton (1835), York and Elizabeth City (1835), Charlotte, Prince Edward, and Nottoway (1836), Nansemond (1836), Goochland, Chesterfield, and Powhatan (1837), Gloucester and Mathews (1838), Southampton (1839), Prince George (a return inspection in 1840), Hanover, New Kent, and King William (1840). He wrote accounts of twenty Virginia counties. In seventeen of them he was seeing the land for the first time: all but five of them were in the Tidewater.[50]

A moment emblematic of change came in May 1838, when Ruffin undertook an inspection of Gloucester County, at the tip of the Middle Peninsula, which juts into Chesapeake Bay between the York and Rappahannock rivers. Then and there he experienced his first optical illusion. Apparently he left home in Petersburg on 9 May and rode down the James River as far as Williamsburg. Then he crossed the Peninsula by stagecoach to Yorktown, where he sailed across to Gloucester Point. At Gloucester he was seventy miles from home. Between 11 and 17 May he toured this flat, sea-level county, lodging with farmers who subscribed to the *Farmers' Register* and who acted as guides and informants.[51]

In Gloucester County he surveyed the farms of at least eight men, starting on 12 May. He dug in fields wet with spring rains, gathering soil samples he would analyze later in Petersburg. His eyes and senses told him that marl lay almost everywhere, just beneath the surface. Here was a discovery to lift the spirits, for Gloucester clearly possessed the natural resources for agricultural reform. At Whitemarsh, the farm of John Tabb, he "rode briskly and easily across many acres without any danger of miring."[52] His informants told him that reform in Gloucester had begun about five years before, around 1833, and that local farmers now used manure in amounts "tenfold greater than a very few years ago." Ruffin named two farmers who had begun to apply marl successfully and indicated that others were following. "This impulse, in part, was said to have been received from the contents of the Farmers' Register."[53] The vagueness of local estimates—"about five years ago," and a "tenfold increase"—were forgotten momentarily in the celebration.

Ruffin's course through Gloucester County took him gradually northward. Near the end of his stay he must have lodged with Warner Taliaferro, a subscriber to the *Register* whose house stood within a few yards of the North River, which formed the border with Mathews County. (Taliaferro had prospered; he had just purchased an addition to his holdings, a rich tract of 500 acres, for fifteen thousand dollars.) After inspecting Taliaferro's estate, Ruffin continued only a few miles onward. "A few minutes' passage, in a beautiful sailing boat, carried us across from the last-mentioned residence to that of Wm. H. Roy, esq. in Matthews." There, at the northern limit of his journey, in Mathews County, Ruffin spent a "clear and bright morning," his senses struck, not by the marl or the clover but by the Chesapeake Bay.[54]

He stood on the shore, "near Mr. Roy's house," facing the Bay. Looking straight in the direction of the Virginia capes and the ocean, he saw "nothing but water and sky" to the horizon. Then his senses deceived him:

> I saw, towards the sea, at such apparent distance as to be not distinct except in shade and in outlines, a very high and large object, nearly square in form. Had I not known that no such thing existed, I should have guessed it to be a castle, or some other enormously large dark building, at more than 20 miles distance.

Reason took hold: he supposed it to be a "thick cluster of very tall pines, on some low island, or point." Confidence failed: he consulted William Roy.

> Upon asking what the object was, I was told that it was a "ship's-head bunch," which is a little brush fastened down by a few low stakes, and which is made as a baiting place for angling for that kind of fish. The actual height above the water was not three feet, and the distance to the bunch was not exceeding three miles.

Ruffin returned his gaze to the object. He confessed that the "deception of the sight was not removed, and scarcely lessened," by Roy's telling him its "true size and distance."[55]

Ruffin was witnessing the phenomenon of "looming," a distortion of vision that occurs under specific atmospheric conditions, involving shapes of objects such as distant volcanoes, or fishing blinds on large bodies of water. Later, he was able to explain to his readers how looming occurred. Doubtless, he concluded, "those who are accustomed to the phenomenon, learn to judge much better than strangers, and therefore cannot be so much deceived." Comforted by that thought, he returned to his narrative-ride with Roy. "As we rode along, another equally large and equally deceptious object came in view. It was nothing larger than a 'blind,' made for baiting and shooting wild-ducks."[56]

These illusions surprised Ruffin. Many other descriptions of landscape appeared in his writings, displaying his fondness for the color and texture of soils, and the beauty of cultivated fields with fences. This passage, unique in his travel accounts (except for two later narratives of journeys to the Dismal Swamp and Lake Scuppernong) disclosed much more than Ruffin's astonishment at confronting sublime illusion. His account of the looming revealed that never before had Ruffin stood on that point in Chesapeake Bay. In all his forty-four years, he never had been in Mathews County, never had met these men—these "strangers"—who hosted him as a celebrity, a mere seventy miles from his own farm at Coggin's Point.[57] For the first time in his life, Edmund Ruffin was seeing parts of Virginia not far distant from scenes of his youth. And now he found cause to mistrust his own eyes.

Down to the year 1833, when he was forty-one years old and began his editorial career, Ruffin was a provincial man. He made at least one annual journey thirty miles down the river to Jamestown, where he had gone to college and where his wife's surviving family lived.[58] In 1811, as a youth of seventeen in the year after his father's death, he visited historic sites at Yorktown; but he did not return to Yorktown for another thirty years.[59] As a youth he must also have visited immediately east and south of Prince George in Surry and Sussex counties, where his father and grandfather had owned property. He had been to Richmond frequently between 1823 and 1826, when he was a state senator. Around 1825 he must have toured the hot springs of western Virginia, digging for samples of earth.[60] In 1827 he escorted his sister Elizabeth on a two-month tour of the North, visiting Philadelphia, New York, Saratoga Springs, Princeton, Bedford Springs, Baltimore, and Washington; in 1828 he made a second, brief northern journey, when he enrolled his eldest son at boarding school in New Haven.[61] Then, having determined not to send the boy to Yale, he traveled with him to in 1831 to Charlottesville.[62] His negotiations to publish his book and the *Register* occasionally took him away from home. By the time Ruffin began to edit the *Farmers' Register*, he had traveled beyond the borders of Virginia twice, though the only records of those journeys were left by others. He knew every creek and ravine and cleared field between Coggin's Point and Evergreen Farm, a distance of five miles; and though he had done some traveling, Ruffin knew little of the world beyond the James River. In the next ten years he changed.

In 1837 he traveled for the first time as an adult into North Carolina, taking notes on Warren and Halifax counties; in 1839 he returned and visited Washington, Tyrrell, Hyde, and Beaufort counties.[63] In 1840, for the first time in his life, Ruffin went to South Carolina, a journey by railway and steamship, stopping in Wilmington, North Carolina, also for the first time. In Charleston he was hosted by "warm-hearted southrons," who were "entire strangers."[64] On this journey Ruffin first met individuals he would join twenty years later in secession.

Ruffin's purpose in the accounts he wrote of country rides was to inspire Virginians to reform their farming. All of his travel accounts had a didactic tone. In his first published account, a narrative of a visit in April 1833 to Fielding Lewis' Wyanoke Plantation on the north side of the James River, he declared his intention to write about "practices and opinions of experienced and successful farmers." He would gather advice "instructive" for farmers facing similar problems, who sought "improvement of their lands."[65] In plain English, he would collect narratives of experiments with crop rotations, farm machinery, horizontal plowing, marling and liming, and putrescent manures. Wherever he went, he would take soil samples, to test for acidity and the presence of calcareous deposits.

Unlike William Cobbett in England, Ruffin did not intend to use his sketches as a medium of social criticism or to deplore conditions of the rural poor.[66] Indeed, Ruffin consistently avoided contact with the poor and the slaves. His writing, burdened by the Latinate words and bloated sentences he probably assumed would give his prose the weight of authority, never did achieve Cobbett's directness or clarity (except in episodes like the looming); but Ruffin did shift toward social criticism by 1835. There grew in his writing that same Cobbett-like tone of anger, of direct talking and arguing with his readers about issues they should decide and changes they should make.

That anger first appeared in his sketch of a journey through the back river lands of York County in 1835. Ruffin had arrived at Williamsburg on 8 July and traveled by stagecoach along the back road from Yorktown to Hampton, where he was to embark by boat for Northampton County. For the last nine miles, he persuaded the driver to take him through an area he had not seen in York and Elizabeth City counties. He was looking for marl, and he found good supplies "along the road." Yet no one was using it: "there is for 20 miles the same general, indeed, almost total neglect and disuse of this manure." He assailed these people:

> It appeared as a striking illustration of the general apathy of the people, and of the small desire for any means of deriving information, that not one post office was on this main mail route for the 24 miles between Yorktown and Hampton—nor did I see the stage driver throw out for any one in this distance, a way newspaper, or other periodical.[67]

That anger remained with Ruffin through the end of his career, particularly when he implored his audience to keep their slaves in Virginia, to demand canals and railroads for shipping marl and crops, or to drain mill ponds (which brought profits to their owners and malaria to their neighbors).[68] Criticism, which had not been his original intention, appeared only after he had extended his range of informants beyond a small circle of old friends along the James River.

Ruffin developed a method in traveling and in writing his narratives that he followed until the time he abandoned the form altogether. He chose counties to visit for specific reasons: Northampton because it had retained its population against a general decline in Virginia; Albemarle because it lay in the Piedmont and presented problems of erosion rather than soil acidity; James City County because it had the oldest continuing use of marl; Charlotte because it needed marl and markets, but its remoteness and lack of a railway presented trans-portation problems; Gloucester because it had a vast, ubiquitous deposit of marl beneath its surface; King William because reform suddenly caught fire there; Prince George because reform had become universal; Nansemond because reform had never started and the county had declined below its level in 1600. Each county would teach his readers something different. In turn, readers of the *Farmers' Register* became Ruffin's informants, his source of intelligence.

Whether the *Register* ever became a financial success or revolutionized agriculture in the South, when Ruffin founded that journal he changed the institutional context of Tidewater Virginia. He created an audience, a defined group of people who had not existed before 1833. Their gathering constituted a significant change, particularly for lower Virginia.[69] His readers lived predominantly in the Tidewater and fall-line counties of Virginia. The list of subscribers Ruffin published in 1834 revealed a total of 1,307 subscriptions, of which 1,121 (85.7 percent) were from Virginia. Of these Virginia subscriptions, 815 (72.7 percent) were from Tidewater, fall-line, and Southside counties; 250 (22.3 percent) were from the Piedmont.[70] The vast majority fell within a sixty-mile radius of Petersburg, providing a dense core of readers the editor could reach easily and quickly.

Whenever Ruffin undertook an agricultural inspection after 1835, he always contacted men whose names appeared on his list of subscribers. He came as a stranger into every county he toured after 1835, knowing only the names and addresses of his readers. It was they who gave him lodging and drove him through the countryside. They told him about their careers, farms, reforms, soil, crops, and neighbors. They gave him facts. They also determined his perceptions of rural Virginia and the South.

This meant that the editor saw farming from the point of view of a specific class. In Goochland County he stayed three days with Richard Sampson, a self-made man who had accumulated and revived 1,050 acres between 1816 and 1837.[71] In Gloucester and Mathews counties he spent a week on farms of the elite. "Even the short time . . . was made shorter," he wrote, "by the urgent claims made on my time by the hospitable attentions of gentlemen to whom before I was personally unknown, and whose kind invitations and attentions there was no resisting."[72] He did not set foot in that part of Gloucester where the poor lived, a district called "Guinea." This was "the only part of the low-ground district which I did not see," he reported. "It is settled exclusively by a number of poor people, who live more by fishing than by tillage." He "was told" about these people by his hosts, the men who also estimated that the quantity of manure used in Gloucester in one year was "tenfold greater than a very few years ago." These were the men who attributed the recent rejuvenation of agriculture in the county to the *Farmers' Register* and explained to Ruffin the phenomenon of looming.[73]

Every Tidewater county had a core of reformers and subscribers.[74] Before he was finished with the *Register*, Ruffin wrote the histories of ninety-two of their farms. Not only did these people form an audience like Cobbett's readers in England—a new social institution—they also led Edmund Ruffin to new facts.

Their willingness to let him dig in their fields and take samples back to Petersburg permitted him to determine the extent of marl deposits throughout Tidewater Virginia—well before William Barton Rogers completed the Virginia geological survey. Ruffin knew by 1835 that calcareous deposits could be found almost everywhere in Tidewater Virginia; he knew also where marl could not be found, an important fact. By 1840, his subscribers in North Carolina and South Carolina had enabled him to form a comparable estimate of the marling resources for the Atlantic South. When he traveled to Wilmington, North Carolina, in 1840, he proceeded as always:

> One of my first objects after reaching Wilmington was to seek out, and make personal acquaintance with Dr. James F. McRee, a gentleman whom I knew merely as the only subscriber to the Farmers' Register in or near Wilmington. I drew the inference, in which I have rarely been mistaken, that a man who had thus appreciated my labors for seven years, would probably be one both able and ready to aid me in acquiring information. I was not mistaken.[75]

McRee drove Ruffin by carriage road out of Wilmington along level lands toward his plantation, Ashemoore. Fifteen miles north of Wilmington, at Rocky Point, they entered what Ruffin perceived at once to be "most valuable calcareous lands." Here was the first evidence gathered by anyone (except a civil engineer for the railroad, whom Ruffin interviewed) that marl deposits lay beneath "a vast region of the state," and probably beneath the entire coastal plain of the South. Here Ruffin made a stunning discovery, his first empirical evidence that Southern seaboard states possessed the natural resources to rejuvenate their agriculture.[76]

The History of Marling Revealed

Other subscribers led Ruffin to his most important discoveries about the history of marling in Tidewater Virginia. Factual information about past experiences with marl became significant for several reasons. Ruffin knew from his own experiments at Coggin's Point that marl created a neutral pH and increased fertility measurably within three years of the first application; he needed to know if others had replicated this finding, involving the element of time. He also had asserted that the effects of marl would last forever: he needed historical evidence, based on the oldest experiments he could locate, to establish this doctrine beyond doubt. He suspected that to most Virginia farmers the doctrine of permanence appeared to be an illusion, and that he had failed to dispel their skepticism.

It was historical evidence gathered from subscribers that enabled Ruffin to see the dimensions of his own role since 1821 in rejuvenating rural Virginia. Ruffin had discovered by that year that other farmers had experimented with calcareous shells in Tidewater Virginia fields before his first experiments in January 1818.[77] His interest did not lie in being first. What Ruffin's journeys into the countryside after 1833 enabled him to uncover was the timing and extent of early reform in rural Virginia. This discovery of the general history of marling and reform was absolutely new; it was made possible by contacts Ruffin made with his subscribers and informants in Tidewater counties. Without the subscription list, without the newly created audience, without the Farmers' Register, Ruffin could not have made the discovery.

Through his rural rides Editor Ruffin confirmed his early thesis that marling began just before the Revolution, when a few young planters who had inherited old estates tried to revive very small portions of tobacco fields by scattering fossil shells over the ground. Apparently they acted alone; and either because they did not allow sufficient time for results or because of interruptions during the Revolution, they abandoned their efforts. Ruffin's contacts pinpointed the times and places of these first efforts: in 1776, in James City and Prince George counties, at least two farmers had applied marl to about two acres apiece.[78] Then they forgot the experiments. This first phase of reform, defined by sporadic, individual efforts, had continued for thirty years.

Until 1815 individual farmers occasionally tried to restore fertility to their fields in this way, following folk methods practiced for centuries on the Continent and in Britain and Ireland. On the ancient assumption that soil could be kept fertile by scattering new earth over their fields, medieval husbandmen routinely mixed soil of different color—particularly clay, sometimes burned—with soil already in their fields.[79]

As soon as Ruffin began to take his rides, he found that Virginia farmers had retained a cultural memory of these ancient methods. In 1834 Ruffin received an inquiry from a "Poor Farmer," concerning the efficacy of mixing "burnt clay" with other soils—the European definition of marling. "That is the only source of manure accessible to myself, and many others around me," the man wrote. Ruffin expressed doubt and explained the origins of the notion. "The burning of clay for manure, extended rapidly from Ireland, where it was begun, through England and Scotland—and was extolled as a cheap and efficacious means for improving land—and then . . . was allowed to go very generally out of use."[80] In North America, where soils along the Atlantic seaboard lacked carbonate of lime, this old method was chemically hopeless. In Virginia the first period of experimenting with soil renewal continued until 1814, characterized by the isolation of the experimenters, their drawing of assumptions from English tradition, and their stopping after one attempt.

Ruffin's rides and his interviews with subscribers revealed a change in the history of marling after 1815, when young men of his generation assumed control of their estates. Reform still began with farmers on newly acquired farms, and it still proceeded in isolation, under ancient assumptions about the mixing of soils. What changed between 1815 and 1821 was the number of young men who began individual experiments in Tidewater Virginia, and their persistence. Any young man with a worn-out Virginia farm had inherited the option either to make his land produce or to emigrate to the West. Those who could not leave had to restore fertility.

Through the *Farmers' Register*, Ruffin located the earliest marlers in Virginia. In 1832, when he was taking his first journey in preparation for the *Register* accounts, Ruffin visited the farm of Archer Hankins. He determined eventually that Hankins and Henley Taylor, "two plain and illiterate farmers, and near neighbors in James City county, were the earliest *successful* and continuing appliers of marl in Virginia." Taylor had died years before. "Mr. Hankins was unable to say when he and his neighbor began to try marl. He was only certain that it was before 1816." Neither man had "the least idea of the true action of marl," and neither had communicated their experiment with others. Ruffin, who passed within fifteen miles of their farms each year on his trips to Williamsburg, "never heard an intimation of their having begun such practice, until some time after my own trials in 1818." They worked alone. "Even after this mode of improvement was commenced by perhaps twenty isolated individuals, each remained ignorant of the success or errors of his fellows, and had to grope alone and unaided through all the difficulties and losses that every experimenter must undergo."[81]

In 1840, during his tour through King William County, Ruffin discovered evidence of one other experiment that had begun at about the time of Hankins'. His host in the county, William Spotswood Fontaine, had heard about an acre of ground that had been marled years before, on the farm once belonging to a farmer named Richard Hill. Fontaine thought Hill had kept records, but since Hill had sold his farm and moved away, the history was lost. Ruffin appealed for information on Richard Hill. Within days his subscribers had located Hill near Richmond. Ruffin wrote to him and reconstructed a classic sequence of events.

Hill said he had purchased the farm as a young man in 1811. The land proved "proverbial in all that time for its *extreme poverty*," so within three years he abandoned the idea of farming.

In 1814, I commenced building a mill, and, in digging out the foundation, to a few feet of the surface struck upon a bed of marl, of which I thought but little, being more intent on the mill at that time than the improvement of land so very poor as to be beyond all hope of recovery.

He carried a wheelbarrow of marl to his corn field nearby, applying it in two rows that crossed one another. He saw no effect in corn that year; but in the spring of 1815 he sowed the field in oats, and could see higher growth where oats had been planted over marl, in the shape of a "cross mark."[82]

Richard Hill, like Archer Hankins and Henley Taylor and all marlers before them, acted on ancient impulses, not chemical theory.[83] He differed from reformers of earlier generations only in that he noticed the effect of marl and continued his trial. These trials, undertaken precisely when Edmund Ruffin was beginning his own experiments at Coggin's Point, verified his results and theory, even though these poor, illiterate farmers knew no chemistry. They proved his findings were not idiosyncratic.

Equally important, they proved that Ruffin was not the first to experiment with soil rejuvenation. Others had succeeded before he started, beginning in 1771 and continuing in the early nineteenth century. With this discovery Ruffin introduced the idea that even in the material life of agriculture there was a history of events, a change that might be impelled by reform. In a Tidewater culture that thought of change only in terms of decline or stasis, this idea represented a significant novelty. To persuade his readers that change was possible, Ruffin traveled in search not only of marl and marling, but also historical evidence. He was attempting to change the way people thought.

Whether Ruffin's essays revolutionized agriculture in the South, or whether the *Register* transformed farming, when Ruffin founded that journal he changed the context of intellectual life in rural Virginia. His early papers on marling and the history of reform, together with his publication of the *Register*, created a new constituency.[84] Once that journal had come into existence, there formed an audience for theory and criticism, for the simple exchange of information. The isolation of experimenters like Richard Hill ended. And incidentally, once the *Register* existed, the impulse for reform shifted away from the poor, illiterate class of farmers who followed folkways of the Middle Ages. Men of Ruffin's class, who could read and comprehend the newest theories, now picked up reform. The journal, unlike Ruffin's democratic original concept of historical change, made reform a class-specific phenomenon. That was something he learned to accept.

Oral testimony about the history of reform at the county level gave Ruffin a kind of evidence beyond what he could see with his own eyes. His very purpose in undertaking the rural rides had been to gather testimony about personal experience and opinion: when had marling begun, how many acres, what effect on soil and crops, why the inspiration to try something new? On the basis of evidence from his travels, Ruffin attempted to reach some judgments concerning the success of reform in Virginia. His assessments assumed a predictable sameness after 1833, simply because the travel account elicited a sameness of information. He had difficulty finding precise facts.

Concerning marl in James City County, he reported in 1833, "The manure is now generally used, and though in such a manner as not to yield half its value, still it has done much for this part of the country."[85] Near Williamsburg, he reported in 1840, "almost every proprietor was marling, to some extent; and most persons near Williamsburg have now marled the greater part, or all, of their cultivated lands."[86] In King William County in 1841, "every body who possesses marl has used it to some extent, and some to great extent."[87] Ruffin was whistling in the dark.

On and on he estimated, guessed, approximated, and reckoned, with no more accurate perception of reality than he had that morning on the beach in Mathews County. What did it mean, after all these travels, to say in 1841 that everybody was engaged "to some extent," and some engaged to great extent? Was this, too, illusion? Was marling really there?

The texts of Ruffin's rides provided evidence primarily of his own perceptions—of Virginia and himself. Like Cobbett, he criticized apathy and error. In 1840 Ruffin turned upon his readers, chiding them for apathy in their reluctance to provide material for the *Register*. He was, he said, "wearied, despondent, and almost ready to cease our long-continued efforts."[88] At the end of 1841 he announced his intention to leave the *Register*, and with the close of the tenth volume in 1842 he carried out this intention. The journal still had between six hundred and a thousand subscribers, about four hundred of whom were original subscribers.[89] This was the size of his core constituency. As late as 1842, however, the travel accounts revealed that despite the demise of the *Register*, Edmund Ruffin by no means defined the effort to rejuvenate rural Virginia as a failure. What did emerge in his later writings of this period was the fact that Ruffin, at age forty-eight, was judging not only the objective history of reform in Virginia, but also the degree of his own success. The questions had become more than merely antiquarian in interest. With stakes this high, he had to find firmer evidence.

The Need for New Evidence

His restiveness with the genre of the travel account led Ruffin to cast about for another way to perceive and measure the reality of change in rural Virginia. He sought a pure perception. At the very time when agricultural writers in America were just discovering the travel account, Ruffin began to reject it. The rides had taught him the need for more precise measurement. In 1837, a year before the looming episode in Mathews, he developed a questionnaire for the farmers he visited, asking them to record precise dates, amounts, and changes.[90] Perhaps if they recorded data directly, without passing through his eyes and brain, he could perceive reality objectively.

Few of his informants, he discovered, took time to answer all his questions. In the end, he gathered only twenty-two questionnaires from volunteer respondents.[91] From these data he received clues about the momentum of marling, together with testimonials to his own importance. From Hanover County, farmers wrote praises of his achievements. Edmund F. Wickham, who had marled 425 acres by 1840, told Ruffin, "I am firmly convinced your Essay is destined to work a vast improvement throughout the whole marl region of the United States." Carter Braxton, who had marled 350 acres since 1832, said the *Essay* "gave birth to a revolution in the agriculture of our country, that will be ever memorable in its annals—and place its author among its greatest benefactors."[92] Here was praise enough to satisfy his vanity. By this time, however, Ruffin no longer found himself convinced by the fervor of disciples. He wanted to know if he had changed reality.

Despite some doubts about evidence gathered on the rural rides, Edmund Ruffin decided late in 1841 to sum up his findings and publish an assessment of the marling revolution before he departed the editorship of the *Farmers' Register*. He proceeded county by county, going over evidence he had gathered on his rides. Two counties emerged most clearly as centers of reform: Prince George and James City, both on the James River, both very familiar to him. Norfolk and Princess Anne, which he had not toured, were "wretched" disasters.[93] When he drew his conclusions, he still just guessed and puffed in the old fashion. "In Prince George county, there is not one farmer having marl on or near his land, who has not applied it to greater or less extent, and always with more or less profit—and, in most cases, largely as well as profitably."[94] In James City there had been "perhaps the next largest as well as the oldest practice." After these two counties came York and ten others:

> In Surry, Isle of Wight, Nansemond, Charles City, New Kent, Hanover, King William, King and Queen, Gloucester, and Middlesex counties, in the middle of the marl region of Virginia, marl has been already extensively applied, and the profits therefrom are annually increasing.[95]

This vague generality betrayed the fact that evidence still eluded Ruffin, and he no longer trusted his wishful impressions. While he had not wavered in his optimism, he needed a new source of knowledge. Rural rides no longer answered the questions he was asking. He needed statistics. He needed a census.

At precisely this point, the subscription list of the *Farmers' Register*—the constituency of the new journal—gave Edmund Ruffin a windfall. William Spotswood Fontaine, his loyal, original subscriber in King William County, had been reading Ruffin closely since 1833 and had detected in the editor's writing a compulsive desire for new, empirical evidence. Fontaine, the owner of Fontainbleau Farm and a marler of 750 acres (out of a total thirteen hundred), was a powerful man in the county. When it came time to take the 1840 Census of the United States, Fontaine summoned the census taker, George N. Powell, and handed him a copy of Ruffin's 1837 questionnaire on marling. He told Ruffin he had asked Powell "to take the census of the marled lands in the county, in consequence of your circular, asking information on the subject." Powell did his best. The county clerk, Hardin B. Littlepage, carelessly recorded the data on acreage without entering the names from Powell's extract—to Fontaine's irritation. Fontaine himself added the names of thirteen farmers whom Powell had forgotten to ask about marling, and then he sent the result in 1842 to an astonished Edmund Ruffin.[96] For the first time, Ruffin knew with certainty the number of marlers and the number of acres marled within a specific area. This was the most precise evidence he had ever seen. While it came indirectly from his agricultural travels, it was evidence of a new kind.[97]

Fontaine's statistics arrived in their original chaos, written down apparently in order of visitation. They disclosed that eighty-eight farmers, including a Mrs. Susan Tuck, had applied marl to their fields.[98] (Ruffin had found an estimated dozen marlers on his ride two years before.) Fontaine counted 9,370 acres marled by 1840.[99]

Ruffin had never calculated a total for any county. Now, thanks to one local informant, he knew exactly the dimensions of the objects he perceived. He could not be fooled by vague estimates that most farmers had started slightly, or a few had begun largely, or that many had made modest attempts, while a few had not. Fontaine's table, brought to order, was clear. One-tenth of the improved, arable land in King William had been marled since 1834—a fact. Nearly one-fourth of the farmers in King William had begun to use marl—a fact.[100] Facts made Ruffin look more successful than did the empty boasting. The rides had not been fruitless. While he was about to abandon them as a method of inquiry, Ruffin still had to thank his travels and his informants for the end of his provincialism, for acquainting him with realities he had never seen, and for a new way of looking at the rural world.

Even as the 1840 census was being taken in King William County, Edmund Ruffin had determined to change the way he gathered information. He decided to exclude descriptions of "splendid mansion houses and beautiful gardens and ornamental grounds," because they were "not proper subjects for farm reports." He devised a form, asking a series of statistical questions to be printed by the State Board of Agriculture. Ruffin proposed to appoint one agent in each county to interview farmers and fill in the form. He himself interviewed his neighbor Harrison at Brandon in 1842, abandoning the travel account. Ruffin became the census taker, asking questions on these categories:

1. Acreages;
2. Best crops;
3. Liming and fertilizing—in acres;
4. Livestock;
5. Cattle;
6. Horses and stable management;
7. Sheep and hogs;
8. Distemper of cattle;
9. Laboring force of teams and hands;
10. Agricultural implements and machines.[101]

Except for the third inquiry (liming and fertilizing) and part of the ninth (hands), these were questions the United States government would ask every farmer in America in the 1850 census, superintended by a man who would become Ruffin's acquaintance, James D. B. De Bow.[102] Whether Ruffin influenced the design of that census of agriculture, the mind of this antebellum Virginian had conceived a new instrument of research into rural society.

The Impact of Marling

Inspired by the power of "statistical fact," Edmund Ruffin went to Richmond to draw his final conclusions about the impact of marling, changes in rural Virginia, and his own role in reform. This ride to the capital was nothing like the old ones. In Richmond, in the state auditor's office, he spent parts of 1851 and 1852 examining quantitative evidence in the state land tax assessment lists for 1781, 1819, 1838, and 1850. He also studied returns of the federal censuses of 1840 and 1850, "notoriously loose and imperfect," their "individual reports" containing obvious, numerous errors he hoped would "balance each other." (He actually may have been examining the original, manuscript returns.) He also examined lists of slaves over twelve years old and of horses and mules. His task, he said, "as a private individual," was enormous.[103] He chose a sample of nine counties to measure the impact of marling. Three he knew were "marling counties": Prince George, Charles City, and James City. Three other Tidewater counties he knew from his travels were not engaged heavily in marling: Southampton, Sussex, and Greensville. Three adjacent counties above the fall-line he chose for comparison.[104]

This research in the auditor's office led Ruffin to draw the most precise and conservative assessments he ever made about the spread of marling. Though there still were no direct "statistics of marling and liming," Ruffin based his estimates upon indirect evidence, particularly on acreages and values of improved land. In Prince George, James City, and Charles City—the leading counties—he apparently already knew the limits of reform. In these counties, marling still had not covered one-third of the arable land or one-eighth of their whole surface. In the rest of the Tidewater, the evidence led him to estimate that the area marled was less than one-twentieth of the total surface.

What Ruffin discovered through indirect evidence in the auditor's office indicated that marling had primarily affected the Tidewater, the very region where most of his subscribers had their farms. The intensity of marling reform varied, spiraling outward from where it began in the three leading (and contiguous) counties along the James; but it extended across the great area of marl deposits. Advertisements for farm sales in 1850 would have sustained Ruffin's impression. The Richmond *Enquirer* that year listed fifty-seven farms for sale in Tidewater and fall-line counties, and another fifty-nine in Piedmont counties. Of the Tidewater farms, sixteen (28 percent) were advertised as having marl deposits; nine (15.8 percent) were advertised specifically as having been marled. A total of 29,447 Tidewater acres were offered for sale; of these acres, farms containing 5,814 acres (19.7 percent of the Tidewater offering) had been marled at least in part. In the

Piedmont, where deposits of fossil shells were not available, none of the fifty-nine advertised farms had been marled; on just ten of these farms had the owners begun to grow clover, apply lime, and begin draining. The Ruffin reforms were phenomena of the Tidewater.[105]

Ruffin also uncovered the precise timing of agricultural decline and recovery, based on documentary evidence. The whole of the Tidewater had declined from 1781 (at the latest) until 1828, the nadir, or "true zero of the general decline of fertility and production." In the tax lists of 1838 he found the first positive results of marling, in rising land values and taxes recorded that year for individual landowners. After 1838, Prince Edward, Charles City, and James City had begun to recover in terms of land values, taxes paid, population, and numbers of slaves and horses.[106]

Precision in quantities, exactness in measurement, scrupulousness in detail, consistency in recording: these skills Ruffin applied to his historical researches in Richmond. He had been thinking about these bureaucratic and scientific methods in 1837, when, while still conducting his rural rides, he developed the questionnaire. As early as 1842 he had called unsuccessfully upon the state to collect agricultural statistics, an appeal he later derided as "the mere illusion of a visionary enthusiast."[107] Actually, this way of thinking had evolved from his earlier career as a farmer at Coggin's Point, where he learned to test soil with Davy's chemical apparatus, to survey precisely the size of experimental fields, to record exact dates of planting and harvesting, and to measure the crop. When he applied this changed way of thinking to the history of reform, it altered his perception. While it reduced the scale of reform to credible proportions, it did not lead Ruffin to despair or to think of himself as having failed. The fact that marling had advanced across only a portion of lower Virginia did not necessarily mean that the world had been left unchanged. For one thing, Ruffin discovered when he addressed his audience—which still existed in 1852—that this new kind of writing gave him certainty and authority. A new kind of power lay in numerical fact.

A Change in Thought

As early as 1821 he knew, too, that he had changed a way of thinking. The response of editor John Skinner of the *American Farmer* to his first experiments told him that. Skinner instantly seized Ruffin's idea that soils could be rendered *"permanently fertile"* as the significant novelty. Reviews of Ruffin's first book had confirmed Skinner's judgment. In 1836 a sixteen-page review in the *American Journal of Science and Arts* made the same point. No longer need anyone believe in "the decreasing fertility of soils which political economists assumed," the reviewer said; soil could be improved, and "nothing in fact except climate would oppose a limit to the approach of agricultural product to the maximum."[108] Gradually, too, Ruffin gathered evidence that proved he had won his neighbors to his theory. He had conquered their ecological fatalism.

In assessing this change, the crucial insight came from the behavior of Thomas Cocke, Ruffin's skeptical old guardian. Slowly, this man had become an advocate of Ruffin's doctrine. As late as 1826 Cocke still was acting as inhibitor, dissuading Ruffin from publishing the manuscript of *An Essay on Calcareous Manures*. When the book did appear in 1832, Cocke then joined reviewers in praising it.

Conclusive evidence about Cocke's change of mind came to Ruffin at the time of Thomas Cocke's suicide in February 1840. After the burial on 25 February, when Ruffin withdrew at night to compose the memoir of his last visits with Cocke, he recorded their customary debates on serious subjects. In raising the issue of suicide, half-revealing his intentions and raising Ruffin's suspicions, Thomas Cocke had revealed his perception of himself as a declining man whose recent apoplectic attack threatened him with senility. When he turned the discussion to burial customs, he joined a debate like those the two men had enjoyed since they became friends in 1810. The issue became the earth and the role of decaying organic matter in rejuvenating the soil. Cocke's scorn for the "folly" of Western burial customs, his ridicule of deep burial in "the attempt to prevent the designed operation of the universal law of nature," conveyed more than one message to Ruffin. There was more than one message in Cocke's advocacy of Chinese burial at eighteen inches (to hasten the return of flesh into grass) and in Cocke's recitation of the now-familiar cycle of the eternal food chain, from living body to grass, to grazing animal or grain, and again to the human body in the "perpetual round of changes."[109]

When Ruffin wrote of this last conversation, he dwelt upon his own failure to dissuade Cocke from killing himself. At the same time, his narrative revealed that he had changed the older man's way of thinking. In terms of their old disputations, Cocke had come to view his own body as part of a natural food chain, as putrescent manure. Nothing should have seemed more natural, rational, or familiar to Edmund Ruffin, who, after all, had been the first to press upon Thomas Cocke this notion of the earth. In a macabre way, Cocke's words measured Ruffin's success in the task to which he had devoted his early career.

After 1840 Ruffin referred infrequently to Cocke, and he appears never to have mentioned the suicide or the legal relationship between himself and Cocke. William Boulware, a friend who lived in King and Queen County, did not discover these facts in 1851 when he prepared for *De Bow's Review* the brief biography that made Ruffin a celebrity.[110] In that year, however, Ruffin's thoughts did return to Cocke, for he wrote a second memoir of his oldest friend, using ideas and language reminiscent of his 1840 sketch.[111]

In both sketches, Ruffin established his former guardian as a model figure who, though lonely and isolated, possessed a mind capable of wisdom and "friendly criticism." He was a venerable figure of congenial opposition. In both sketches, Ruffin noted similarities between himself and Cocke. Like Ruffin, Cocke had spent his youthful years with books, virtually a recluse. His only "companion of equal mind" in later years had been Ruffin. They shared investigations into the problems of farming in their home county. Among the things they both admired was the work of Edmund Ruffin on calcareous manures. One of the last thoughts Ruffin expressed about Cocke concerned a common object of admiration: "Especially he valued my theoretical views of the causes of & means for producing fertility."[112] Here was the important judgment. Ruffin finally inferred it from clues left by Cocke in conversation. In the same setting of family and neighborhood that had influenced his first experiments, Ruffin found that even his most articulate critic had become convinced. Ruffin had changed theory.

3
Family and Reform

In my children it seems to me that my life is renewed & extended. Their well-doing is nearly all that concerns me personally for the short remainder of my life.

EDMUND RUFFIN, 1851

Once Edmund Ruffin had abandoned the *Farmers' Register* and its thousand subscribers, he found himself forced to make other decisions that changed the fortunes and functions of the Ruffin family. He left his printing shop in Petersburg in December 1842, a month before his forty-ninth birthday: the *Register* had proved disappointing as an establishment that might sustain a career in reform and, at the same time, support his family. At forty-nine Ruffin still headed a large household, with his wife and six of their nine children still under his roof. He had lost money in Petersburg, and since he was not rich, he had no choice but to return to the country. After a year of searching, he bought a farm at Old Church, northeast of Richmond, and moved his family there in January 1844, beginning his second period as a full-time farmer. This second period would be even briefer than the first, lasting less than a decade, but it brought significant change.[1] In these years of withdrawal and isolation from public life, he began to transform the Ruffin family itself into an institution that could sustain a career in reform.

When he left Petersburg in late 1842, the notion had not yet occurred to Ruffin that a large family, with members placed on linked Tidewater farms, might become an institution of public influence. Seven years earlier, in 1835, when he left Shellbanks Farm and moved to town, he had hoped never again to be a farmer or to supervise slaves in farming. He even had tried to sell his acreage at Coggin's

57

Point Farm and all of his field slaves, designing to cut all ties with the countryside. At that time he still was thinking conventionally about institutions that could sustain careers in reform and promote the rejuvenation of rural Virginia: universities, agricultural societies, state agricultural surveys, journals. In the *Register* he had tried to create such an institution, one that would support him as an "agricultural writer & publisher." This work he considered "engrossing & delightful as had formerly been my farming labors."[2]

Ruffin abandoned the *Register* after a series of specific disappointments. In addition to the difficulty of coaxing original articles from his subscribers, he found it hard to get them to pay their subscriptions. His shop did not draw enough printing business to supplement his own writing, a problem he later would see as inherent in Southern publishing. The *Register* did not gather an audience sufficiently large to make it a secure institution, unlike William Cobbett's writing and publishing enterprises in England. Discouraged after ten years, Ruffin cast about for alternatives. In 1843 he took a one-year appointment in South Carolina as state agricultural surveyor; but an old suspicion of legislatures and governors warned Ruffin that public appointments could not be strung together for a living, not in the American South. When he completed his appointment in South Carolina at the end of 1843, Ruffin withdrew from his public career and concerned himself with his new farm and with the "well-doing" of his children.

At this point, the children of Edmund and Susan Travis Ruffin began to influence his career simply through their numbers—a revolution in family size that represented both novelty and unforeseen opportunity. These nine children were born between 1814 and 1832. (There were no births after 1832, when Ruffin was thirty-eight and his wife thirty-nine.) Until the summer of 1855 all nine would remain alive. Their collective needs forced Ruffin back to the country and impelled him to seek more land. Then, as they matured, he began to think of the family as a corporate institution, or "co-partnership," whose mutual resources would provide a competency for every member.[3] In this view, the large number of survivors eventually became a benefit.

Survival of the Ruffin Children

No male Ruffin since the seventeenth century had nurtured such a large family. Ruffin's great-grandfather had seen only two children

Table 1 Relatives of Edmund Ruffin: Survivors in the Ruffin Family, 1800–1865

	1800	1810	1820	1830	1840	1850	1860	1865
Grandparents	1							
Parents	1	1						
Siblings		3	4	4	4	3	3	3
Children			2	7	9	9	6	3
Nieces & Nephews			3	9	13	15	15	14
Grandchildren					3	13	20	23
Total	2	4	9	20	29	40	44	43

Sources: Published Ruffin genealogies; U.S. Census, Manuscript Schedules for Dinwiddie, Hanover, and Prince George counties, Va., 1850, 1860; Dupuy family Bible records, VHS; Ruffin Papers, VHS; Dorsey and Coupland Papers, CWM.

Note: Figures exclude Edmund Ruffin, Susan Travis Ruffin (his wife), and his stepmother. The table excludes Ruffin's maternal aunt and maternal cousins in Surry County, whose dates of death could not be established and whom Ruffin did not know; he had no paternal cousins. The number for nieces and nephews in 1865 is a maximum figure; the minimum figure is 9. Figures include only people alive on 1 Jan. of each year.

survive infancy, and his grandfather only one. Five of his father's children survived, but his father died before any of them reached adulthood; these five—Edmund Ruffin and his siblings—were the first indications that infant mortality was declining among the Ruffins along the James. Then, among offspring born to Edmund Ruffin and his sisters after 1814, the number reaching adulthood quadrupled.[4] Ruffin's sister Jane brought eight children through infancy and (probably) to maturity, Juliana brought three, and Elizabeth four. The number of their children alive at one time reached twenty-two in 1840.[5] (See Table 1.) This family was witnessing its own miniature demographic revolution.

Ruffin left insufficient evidence to explain fully the causes of this change. He left no account concerning childbirth practices or vaccination against smallpox, though he mentioned no cases of smallpox among his children or slaves.[6] He did provide housing for the white and slave families in separated cabins and dwellings, a conscious effort to reduce contagion (about which he had some understanding) and to improve sanitation. He feared foul and stagnant water, suspecting it caused dysentery and malaria. In the marsh immediately south of the two main houses at Coggin's Point, he felt certain there lay a source of malaria. In 1831, after an experiment of three summers, he deliberately moved his family three miles south of the river, away from the peninsula at Coggin's Point and inland to Shellbanks Farm, hoping to escape malaria. Susan Ruffin left no evidence of the role she must have played in this decision, but Ruffin did. By 1820, after two of their first four infants had perished, he had begun to take measures to control threats to their children.[7] He cannot have seen their survival as accidental; their vitality represented a fulfillment of his desire to see this generation live—a triumph over death itself, reinforcing assumptions about controlling nature that he had acquired by 1818, when he began his experiments in soil rejuvenation.

After they survived, Ruffin experienced a fatherhood like none in the history of his male ancestors. The need to plan rationally for the future was thrust on him by his children. None of his direct ancestors born after 1700 had planned a vocation for more than one son or had considered placing a son in a vocation other than farming.[8] None of them had needed to provide education for so many children. Ruffin was the first male in his family line in a century to plan for a daughter's marriage, the first in more than a century to determine property inheritance for more than one heir, and the first since 1700 to deal with a possible division of the family estate into portions. No male ancestor had found himself entangled in family diplomacy involving more than two households or dealing with many-sided family quarrels. None of his ancestors came to know their children so well as he, since none of them experienced Ruffin's span of years with offspring. From the time the family first settled in Prince George County, only his great-grandfather had known more than one grandchild. None had needed to devise new arrangements for old age. Not one of his progenitors could have prepared him for his fatherhood.

By the time Ruffin turned fifty in 1844, his three eldest children had moved to their own households. Edmund, Jr. (1814–1875), the first-born, was nearly thirty. The closeness in age between Ruffin and this son created a closeness in their relationship. Edmund, Jr., became Ruffin's partner in farming, his best critic, his most frequent correspondent. Ruffin had devoted himself to the education of young Edmund: teaching him geometry at home, taking him to New England in 1828 for secondary schooling, and fetching him back to Richmond to complete that schooling. In September 1831 Ruffin enrolled Edmund, Jr., at the University of Virginia, where he finished his education in 1833.[9] Young Edmund became a civil engineer on three different railroad projects; he rose by 1837, his father noted, "to the highest grade, that of Principal Assistant Engineer." Ruffin invested in these railroads and considered engineering a modernizing profession appropriate for his sons, whom he prepared not for farming, but for versatility and new careers. "It had been my purpose to give my sons good educations, & to fit them for working men, in such professions or business as they might prefer," Ruffin wrote in 1851. "I was entirely opposed to following the *universal* practice in Virginia, of every gentleman's son, who cannot inherit a sufficient patrimonial estate, (& many who do,) studying for either the profession of law or medicine."[10]

After the Panic of 1837 Edmund returned to Coggin's Point, became his father's resident partner there, and began to buy the farm, permitting Ruffin to continue editing the *Farmers' Register*. In 1836, at twenty-two, Edmund, Jr., married Mary C. Smith (1816–1857), an orphaned only child, and heiress of Bellevue, a farm with thirty-nine slaves in King and Queen County, thirty miles northeast of Richmond. "By this marriage, in addition to many other & far greater acquisitions & sources of happiness, my son obtained considerable property, & very much more than I could expect to give to him as a sharer of my own property."[11] Marriage, in fact, made Edmund, Jr., a wealthy man, enabling him to purchase Coggin's Point Farm. West of the Point, on the river bluff above Tar Bay, Edmund, Jr., first built a cottage named "Beechwood"; then, in 1848 and 1849, he built a large house with the same name. Ruffin later would describe Edmund as "the only wealthy member of my family"; this son became "by very far the richest of all the family."[12] No longer did Ruffin worry about the welfare of Edmund, Jr. Through the end of the Civil War, this son remained Ruffin's most valued ally, more powerful in family affairs than any of his brothers and sisters.

Agnes Ruffin Beckwith (1817–1865), the second child, presented difficulties. After early schooling at home, Agnes went to private school in Richmond. Then, in 1838, at age twenty-one, she married Dr. Thomas Stanly Beckwith (b. 1813) of Petersburg, apparently with Ruffin's consent but without his blessing. Beckwith pursued a controversial medical practice from which he helped support his brother and parents. (Beckwith's mother took in boarders to provide income.) The number of Beckwith children grew quickly, draining the family's finances: Agnes eventually gave birth to thirteen children, ten of whom reached adulthood. By 1844 Ruffin already regarded Beckwith as an improvident failure, a threat not only to Agnes but to the domestic economy of the entire Ruffin family. Beset by poverty and dependence the rest of her life, Agnes never gained her father's approval or affection.[13]

The third child, Julian Calx Ruffin (1821–1864), had established his own household in 1843 at Ruthven, a small farm in Prince George County, leaving Petersburg just before Ruffin himself moved from the city. Sweet-tempered Julian was a pious, evangelical soul, a dutiful son who worried about Ruffin's health and spirits. Ruffin sent him to Charlottesville to prepare for college and then to the College of William and Mary, where he completed his course in 1839, aged eighteen.[14] For the next three years Julian helped his father produce the *Farmers' Register*. Though Julian appeared to be the one family member who was content with his lot in life, he did share his father's work ethic, confessing once that he had no illusions about success: "I do not expect ever to make any thing but by hard work."[15] Prudently, Julian postponed marriage until he established himself, meanwhile living a bachelor's life at Ruthven. In 1852 he married Charlotte S. Meade of Petersburg, when he was thirty-one (a decade older at marriage than Edmund, Jr., or Agnes). Lottie brought no wealth to the marriage (her mother in 1860 owned just one family of five slaves) but within four years she proved herself a hard-working, efficient planner of domestic economy and thereby won Ruffin's admiration.[16] Compared to his older brother, Julian made slow progress. He began farming with just six slaves and added to his holdings slowly over the next two decades, borrowing field hands regularly from his father. By 1860 he owned twenty-two slaves. Unlike Edmund, Jr., Julian performed the same labor he assigned his slaves. "After breakfast, I rode to Ruthven," his father recorded in his diary in 1862. "Found Julian at work with nearly all his hands, in the garden, & he working with his own hands as hard as any other laborer."[17] Julian was a worker.

Of the six children remaining at home when Ruffin moved to Marlbourne in 1844, five were daughters. Between 1844 and 1850 Marlbourne was home for all of these dependents, who departed slowly, forming their own families at later ages than had Ruffin and his generation. They remained dependents a long time. (See Graph 2.) Rebecca (1823–1855) became an adult in 1844 but remained at home another seven years, until she married in October 1851, when she was twenty-eight. Elizabeth (1824–1860) left Marlbourne in 1850 to live at Ruthven before she married in 1852, also at twenty-eight. Mildred (1827–1862) was still attending school in Richmond when the family moved to Marlbourne; she remained at home until 1859, when she married at thirty-two. Jane (1829–1855), Ruffin's fourth and favorite daughter, married in 1854 at twenty-five. Finally, there were the twins, Ella (1832–1855) and Charles (1832–1870), aged twenty-two when Ruffin declared his retirement in 1854. In that year, when Ruffin was sixty, he still had to regard four of his nine adult children as dependents.

The survival of these children determined policies the family pursued after 1844. They began to buy land and to place members in a network of affiliated households, altering their relationships to one another and to their communities. They withdrew to their own society. Power shifted away from individual members to the collective family, headed by Ruffin and his most trusted adult children; the collective family assumed new legal and economic functions, simply by virtue of its size. And in a family of this size there lay possibilities for new kinds of conflict.

The need to support a large family, which had forced Ruffin back to the country and impelled him to begin buying land, launched the Ruffins into an expansionist phase of their collective life cycle. Their expansion of land holdings was one of the first schemes they undertook as a common enterprise, the germ of a new idea. The purchase of farms for Ruffin and three of his children, together with the colonization and management of those farms, became family ventures, and the Ruffins began to think of themselves as a partnership. When Ruffin left the *Farmers' Register* in 1842, only one farm belonged to a family member, the homestead of 1,582 acres at Coggin's Point. Edmund, Jr., had settled at Coggin's Point in Prince George County in 1839, buying a half-interest in the farm for $10,800, and planning to purchase the second half within a decade.[18] From this one farm in 1842, the family embarked on an expansion that would continue for twenty years, with Ruffin himself acquiring four farms in two counties.

They nearly doubled their holdings in 1843. In January Ruffin bought Ruthven, which became Julian's farm: 351 acres in Prince George County, three miles inland from Coggin's Point.[19] In October Ruffin bought 977 acres in Hanover County, the original plot of land that became Marlbourne.[20] With these two purchases the family acquired 1,328 acres, bringing their total to more than 2,910 acres. In 1849 Ruffin purchased two adjacent tracts at Marlbourne, adding 623 acres to that farm.[21] Between 1849 and 1855 the family acquired two more farms in Prince George County, both probably purchased by Ruffin. One of these became Woodbourne, 260 acres on which his daughter Agnes settled with her family in 1849.[22] The other, containing 241 acres, was settled by his youngest son, Charles.[23] By 1860 family members together would own more than five thousand acres, and their buying would continue into the early years of the Civil War. This expansion represented a dramatic shift in Ruffin's commitments from the period between 1835 and 1841, when he had supervised not one acre of land.

Land purchases in the Tidewater made possible a remarkable gathering of Ruffin family and kin south of Richmond in Prince George County. In terms of numbers, Prince George became the social center of the family, a dramatic change in the 1840s. In 1835, just two farms had been owned there by family descendants, Evergreen and Coggin's Point, and the latter lay virtually abandoned by Ruffin. Evergreen was in the hands of Harrison Cocke, husband of Ruffin's half-sister Elizabeth. After 1844, as Ruffin's children matured, their numbers in Prince George increased.

First came Edmund, Jr., and his wife, Mary, in 1839, followed by Julian in 1843 and by the Beckwiths in 1849. These three households were established near farms already occupied by two of Ruffin's half-sisters: The Glebe, home of his sister Jane Dupuy, and Evergreen, home of his sister Elizabeth Cocke (who died in 1849).[24] At this point, Ruffin's younger daughters finally began to marry and establish households in Prince George. In 1851 Rebecca, the second daughter, married John T. Bland, a son of former neighbors, and moved to Bland's farm. Ruffin's fourth daughter, Jane, married the physician-son of Ruffin's half-sister in 1854 and moved to Cottage Farm, near her sister Rebecca. When Ruffin bought a farm for Charles, the expansion was complete. There were at least eight related households and farms, six of them with living, married couples in the early 1850s, providing a complement of aunts, uncles, cousins, and nearly a full generation of grandparents in Ruffin and his two surviving sisters.[25]

For the first time, these people now could withdraw almost completely into the exclusive society of family and kin, needing few outsiders. Their social life stopped at the boundaries of the family and did not include people from the community at large. This domestic exclusiveness had not been possible as recently as 1810, when Ruffin's father died at Evergreen with no immediate relatives apart from his wife and children. By 1848 the family was outgrowing the capacity of its houses. When Ruffin's sisters Juliana and Elizabeth visited Beechwood Cottage that year, he had to sleep in the dining room.[26] On 30 January 1848, Agnes Beckwith reported that on the first night of a visit by the Beechwood Ruffins there were thirteen children in her Petersburg house. "The next evening we had quite a room full at prayers," Agnes wrote; "12 children are now present under 10 years of age."[27] On one visit to Beechwood in February 1850, Ruffin's daughter Jane saw four of her brothers and sisters and two of her cousins.[28] By 1860 the Ruffins conducted almost no social relations with other white families around them. At Christmas in 1858, Edmund, Jr.'s family celebrated exclusively with immediate relatives and one couple visiting from outside the county.[29] In 1860 Julian confessed that he had only "slight intercourse" with his neighbors.[30] By this time he was totally absorbed in family. For the first time, the Ruffins found themselves a significant white minority amid the population of their black slaves, nearly equalling the number of servants at some family houses. A white family society was forming apart from the black. This degree of family centeredness had not been possible fifty years earlier; there simply had not been enough kin.[31]

The domestic demographic transformation altered relationships within the family, too. The number of survivors made it necessary now to make decisions concerning property and inheritance that seldom presented themselves when survivors were few. By 1850 there were enough members alive to create choices that generated conflict, particularly over marriage, vocation, and inheritance. A shift in power occurred at this point: the collective family, headed by its eldest male, began to exercise greater power, particularly in the distribution of property. Conditions fostering this rise of familial and paternal power had appeared only at the middle of the nineteenth century. In Ruffin's case, this power fell short of absolute patriarchy. He shared it with his eldest sons, and exercised it for a limited period: indeed, he held it only while the distribution of his estate to the next generation was in question. And, as he discovered, he would encounter stiff resistance whenever he tried to exert authority against the wishes of his children. Still, the family did become more powerful.

The source of this change lay in the family's growth, which strengthened its legal and economic functions. Legally, the collective family now had enough adults to protect its children against orphanhood; no longer did the Ruffins need to depend on the county or friends like Thomas Cocke to act as guardians for the next generation. This reduced their dependence on the courts and enhanced their power over children. More significant were their ventures in purchasing land. From those ventures came new notions about the family estate, investments, and the portions allotted to each member. The family became a legal "co-partnership," its financial affairs a tangle of intertwined exchanges, its object being to provide economic independence, or competency, to every man and woman in the family. In exchange, each member became linked to the fortunes and power of the collective family.

This partnership, based on the survival of his children, enabled Ruffin to think of the family as an institution that would support not only the final stage of his life, but a new career for himself. His family had grown large enough to sustain this one member full-time in writing and reform. And while there were precedents for their partnership reaching back into the 1830s, the first real undertaking they made in common was the purchase and colonization of Marlbourne Farm.

Reconstruction at Marlbourne Farm

Marlbourne lay in Hanover County on the south bank of the Pamunkey River, sixteen miles northeast of Richmond. It was thirty miles north of Coggin's Point, a day's drive away. Ruffin paid seventeen dollars an acre for Marlbourne, or $16,611 for all of its 977 original acres,[32] using money from the sale of Shellbanks, his half of Coggin's Point, and the Petersburg printing shop.[33] A new two-story frame house came with the farm, the largest house Ruffin ever owned. Below it, to the north, lay the Pamunkey River valley, three to five miles wide. There were 735 acres of low, level land, stretching below the house northward to the river, and 242 acres of high, poor, table land on the hill above the valley.[34] Altogether, there were 750 arable acres, exactly the number at Coggin's Point.[35] This farm, together with Ruthven, more than doubled the family's productive capacity. Ruffin's slaves moved to the new farm in late December 1843 and were followed by the Ruffin family on 18 January.[36]

The reconstruction of Marlbourne Farm became the crucial family undertaking for the next decade. Upon its successful rejuvenation depended not only Ruffin's fortune, but future support for almost

every member of his family. At various times between 1844 and
1855, eight of his nine children, together with Ruffin and his wife,
derived their entire living from the income of Marlbourne.[37] Beyond
this material significance, reconstruction made Marlbourne a center
in the Tidewater for agricultural reform. Reconstruction involved
tasks that required scientific precision, attention to detail, and innovations in farming techniques. It proceeded on a scale that demanded enormous labor, making Ruffin intent on improving the
efficiency of his slaves and committing him to the preservation of
slavery. This move to the country involved the Ruffin family in major
historical decisions.

Ruffin described his new land in the same stock terms he once had
applied to Coggin's Point. "All had in past times been greatly abused
& as much worn out as the owners could effect," he recalled in 1851.
"The last proprietor was a wretched farmer & manager of his business.
The condition of the farm & its fitness for production had been getting
worse & worse for years before its sale."[38] Old ditches intended to
drain away surface water from the lowlands had filled with sediment.[39]
He saw "shallow ponds of stagnant water," sources of malaria. "It
was with much apprehension that I encountered the still remaining
dangers."[40]

To restore fertility, Marlbourne needed to be marled and drained,
so with those two tasks the reconstruction began. A deposit of marl
underlay the entire farm, but too deep for easy exploitation. On other
Pamunkey River farms the marl beds lay closer to the surface; on
neighbor Carter Braxton's farm, Newcastle, a huge marl pit already
existed. As an inducement to lure Ruffin to Hanover County, Braxton
offered him his marl. On 20 January 1844, two days after moving
his family from Petersburg, Ruffin sent his hands to begin digging
marl from Braxton's pit. On 29 January they completed a road to
Marlbourne, and then, Ruffin reported, "I began to haul the marl."[41]

Marling in Hanover demanded the same precision, routines, and
hard labor that Ruffin had developed twenty-five years earlier at Coggin's Point. He had to measure the pH of soil and the strength of
local marl deposits. As at Coggin's Point, he recorded amounts of
marl carried to the fields in standard-sized mule carts, counting the
heaps his slaves dumped before spreading them in the fields.[42]

The physical labor involved no less a task than moving the earth
from one farm to another. After building roads, Ruffin's slaves dug
the marl from the surface pit at Newcastle, carted it to Marlbourne,

and spread it over the fields. The pit lay nearly half a mile from the nearest fields at Marlbourne and two miles from the most remote. Each round trip covered between one and four miles, each cart carrying eight bushels at the maximum rate. In 1844 Ruffin's slaves carted 67,875 heaped bushels of marl from Newcastle to Marlbourne, making 8,600 round trips in that one year, an average of twenty-eight round trips daily, six days a week. The peak marling year came in 1845, when they carted 75,512 heaped bushels, loading one-mule carts with nine bushels per load and employing new two-mule carts filled with eighteen bushels. In the first five years the mules moved 276,613 bushels of marl, with each animal limited to about twenty-five miles daily. Ruffin directed more labor into marling than into any other farm work in 1848, accounting for 43 percent of his labor costs. That free human labor could have performed this task did not occur to him.[43]

Draining the fields at Marlbourne required two different engineering tasks: the digging of open ditches and the construction of covered drains. On flat lowlands in the valley, rainwater stood in surface ponds; this water had to be drained into the Pamunkey through open ditches. At the southern edge of the valley, just below the house, there were other saturated areas surrounding springs; these springs were fed by water seeping downward between rock strata from the high land above the valley. Water feeding these springs had to be diverted beneath the lowland fields to the river through a system of covered drains. Ruffin had taught himself the elements of draining in reclaiming a marsh at Coggin's Point in the early 1820s. From European authors (Thaer, Johnston, and Stephens) and the *American Agriculturalist*, he had grasped pertinent geological theory: once again, he turned for crucial ideas to scientific and technological writings.[44]

The tasks in digging open drains demanded precision and technical skill. First, the contours of the entire farm had to be surveyed with leveling instruments. "The eye," Ruffin warned, "is an uncertain guide to indicate levels, or degrees of slope in lines."[45] In digging large ditches, a four-mule team plowed a strip twelve feet wide. Then slaves used shovels to remove the loosened clay, carting it away to "manure the nearest sandy land.".[46] After another measurement with leveling instruments, a second layer of earth was cut by plough and removed. Finally, when the new ditch became too deep for ploughs, two and a half feet more were "marked off accurately," and the laborers dug to the bottom using spades.[47]

Slaves began digging open ditches immediately after marling early in 1844. In cold weather, he said, "when laborers could not stand in mud and water," he had them draw mud from the ditches with broad hoes, "the laborers standing on the dry margins of the ditches." Since there were tasks all hands could do, "& there was a vast quantity to be done," he assigned almost everyone to clearing ditches, completing an imperfect job before spring. "Then men were put to deepening & completing the ditches with spades & shovels," he said. He measured these ditches by the mile. The greatest project involved straightening, deepening, and lengthening the main ditch, which crossed the entire width of Marlbourne.[48]

Construction of more complicated, covered drains began in the spring of 1845. They were a novelty in Hanover County: "No covered draining had ever been thought of," Ruffin noted.[49] The task required skill, precision, and heavy labor. First, laborers dug ditches between three and six feet deep and from twenty to twenty-four inches wide, allowing themselves room to move while digging. Then Ruffin measured the ditch for its rate of fall, to be certain that no part of it was level. Slaves then cut slender poles from second-growth pine saplings. They placed two saplings (2.5 to 3.5 inches wide, 12 to 20 feet long) on either side of the ditch bottom and covered the sapling poles with rough, green, pine boards cut half an inch thick with hand mauls or mallets. This created a wooden "pipe." Above the boards they placed a thin layer of straw, pine needles, or coarse grass, creating a filter through which water, but not dirt, could pass. Finally, they shoveled as much of the dirt as possible back into the ditch, ramming the initial shovelings slightly to "close all hollows." Excess dirt they carted away.[50]

By 1850 Ruffin and his slaves had constructed three miles of covered drains at Marlbourne.[51] By November 1853 they had deepened the main ditch to between five and six feet throughout its entire length, about two miles.[52] In addition, they completed thousands of yards of smaller ditches. With his slave force Ruffin changed the entire drainage system of the farm, altering its natural water courses and removing the most obvious sources of malaria.

Reconstruction of the soil and drainage system enabled Ruffin to transform Marlbourne into a wheat farm that began immediately to generate significant new wealth for the family. No wheat was sown in 1844, the year he moved there. By 1848 Ruffin had planted 256 acres in wheat; in 1851 Marlbourne yielded a vast crop of wheat,

6,072 bushels, an average of 22.74 per acre. As wheat crops got thicker, his scythe-men took notice: they "complained loudly" about the lightness of ordinary harvesting cradles. Marling and draining had generated a Tidewater crop rivaling some in the West. In 1844 Marlbourne yielded 18.14 bushels of corn per acre; in 1848, 28.12; and in 1852 it was reached an astonishing 43.85. Ruffin sold 91 percent of his wheat and 63 percent of his corn between 1844 and 1853, committing himself profitably to Richmond and northern markets. After a first-year loss of $74.23 in 1844, his profits rose: $2,236.94 in 1845, $3,545.39 in 1846, $6,391.24 in 1847, $5,810.06 in 1848. At the end of five years at Marlbourne, Ruffin announced an annual average profit of 12.87 percent on the capital invested, not including gains in the value of slaves or in the market value of the land.[53] Reconstruction had established a secure source of material support for his family.

Marlbourne also regained for Ruffin the attention of reforming farmers, beginning with a core of neighbors in Hanover County. The circle widened in 1849 when he published an essay on Marlbourne's profits. This article, Ruffin's first signed piece in four years, became his best-known short essay, attracting attention throughout Tidewater Virginia and Chesapeake Maryland, adding subscriptions for the *American Farmer*, especially in Virginia.[54] Reform began to widen its appeal exactly as it had at Coggin's Point in the 1820s, spiraling outward from its original center at a single, "pattern" farm.[55]

Ruffin's reforms in Hanover County were influenced by certain habits of mind he had manifested early in his career. His narrative accounts of Marlbourne reveal the significance of his reading, as well as his familiarity with chemical apparatus. From his library, Ruffin acquired his book-knowledge of soil chemistry, hydrology, and geology; and from his surveying, soil testing, and farming experiments, he trained himself to focus on detail, to divide tasks into parts, to devise methods of repetition, to mark time, to keep records, and to plan according to statistical probabilities.[56] Reform at Marlbourne had its origins not only in the objective decline of the soil, but also in ideas, books, and the tools of intellectual life made available by the Ruffin family.

As his work proceeded, Ruffin began to apply this way of thinking not only to soil and crops, but to people who worked for him. The campaign to increase production at Marlbourne turned his thinking toward the efficiency of his slaves. All through the second half of the

1840s he experimented with new ways to use slaves efficiently in growing crops, particularly in planting and harvesting clover, corn, and wheat. He introduced methods of cultivation that required laborers to pay attention to detail and to heighten their consciousness of time. He also introduced simple tools and devices that made it possible to use larger portions of the slave colony at Marlbourne.

Ruffin had read Boussingault's experiments on clover and understood the theory of nitrogen fixation; he was among the first to demonstrate that clover could be grown on neutral Tidewater soils.[57] There remained technical difficulties, however. Sowing clover by hand was causing problems as late as 1850, before mechanization. March winds, sometimes halting sowing completely, scattered the seeds in irregular clusters, a flaw no one could detect until the clover was "well up." Few farms, Ruffin noted, had even one "competent sower," white or black.[58] Simple geometry and applied physics led Ruffin to an innovation. He gave each sower an apron, "one end of which is tied around his neck, or waist, as found most convenient." The sower held the other end in the left hand, along with a light paddle made from old barrel heads or shingles, "of which the broad part may be about 7 inches wide, and 8 or 9 inches long." The sower then walked through the field with a group of four other sowers (along plotted lines between 5 and 5.5 feet wide for each person) holding the paddle breast-high in the left hand, broad end outward, using the thumb and finger tips of the right hand to grasp the seeds from the apron and throw them "with some force against the paddle." For each step, one throw. The advantage for owners of unskilled or truculent hands was clear: "If the board is only held in a proper and uniform position, and the seeds taken up as directed, and thrown with sufficient force, any totally inexperienced laborer can sow well, and indeed cannot avoid distributing the seeds equally."[59] The paddle made it possible for Ruffin to employ women and young slaves in sowing clover, allowing men more time for heavy marling and draining. Ruffin routinized and simplified a task of considerable scale and difficulty, expanding the role of slaves formerly considered insufficiently skilled for sowing.

He introduced a discipline of timing and attention to detail in harvesting clover, wheat, and corn. He wanted to harvest and cure clover so that it lost a minimum of moisture, becoming the kind of hay "eagerly preferred by horses and mules," an objective that Tidewater farmers of his youth had considered impossible because in June the heat would dry cut clover to a crisp. Heat, wind, and rain were enemies he attempted to overcome with a prescribed routine of clover harvesting. Mowing began with hand tools between 9:00 a.m. and 2:00 p.m., when no dew remained on the plants. The swaths of cut clover were left on the ground until next morning, when other hands with iron forks threw swaths into small heaps. Then they gathered the wilted grass, "still full of sap, or juices," into hay-cocks constructed according to precise specifications. Slaves made pine stakes between 5 or 6 feet long and 1.5 to 2 inches thick at the large end, 1 inch at the small, sharpened end. Men then drove stakes into the ground in rows. Workers heaped clover grass around each stake until the heap stood six feet tall and four feet wide. The grass then settled, preventing excess rain from penetrating beyond the outer layer of grass, which, being exposed to the sun, was the only layer of grass that dried crisp. These were Ruffin's hay cocks, preserved by the stakes from being scattered by high winds and rain. After the cocks had cured from four to seven days, "loaders" passed through the field "half an hour or an hour" before carting them to shelter, pulling out the stakes, turning the cocks "nearly upside down, but leaving the old bottom somewhat facing the sun," to remove all dampness. Then they carted the crop into the barn, "moderate dew still remaining on the cocks." Finally, they gathered the stakes and returned them to shelter for use again.[60]

Identical precision accompanied the harvesting of wheat in June and corn fodder in September, with timed routines and prescribed methods for constructing shocks of wheat and corn. By 1851 Ruffin began pleading with Virginia and Maryland farmers to use clover in place of corn fodder, seeking to end the outdoor exposure of workers in the malaria season, thereby reducing illness and mortality rates and increasing production.[61] His motive in all of these reforms at Marlbourne was to increase production.

Rejuvenation at Marlbourne came through Ruffin's application of science and slave labor, not through introducing new machines or new schemes of bureaucratic organization. Marlbourne was not a factory-in-the-field. Machinery represented only a small portion of investment at Marlbourne, far smaller than the value of Ruffin's slave colony.[62] Nor did Ruffin devise a perfectly bureaucratic system at the farm. He did establish rules for planting and harvesting, and he did train slaves for specific tasks, introducing some division of labor. But he always wanted farm work to be supervised by himself or a family member, with no managerial level between owners and laborers. For the first year and a half at Marlbourne he did hire an overseer who had worked in marling at Coggin's Point, but he dismissed that man in 1846, replacing him temporarily with a white youth; then he appointed a slave, Jem Sykes, as farm foreman.[63] To the end of his days at Marlbourne Ruffin relied on himself, his sons, his sons-in-law, and his daughters to manage Marlbourne. The organization at Marlbourne was personal and familial, not bureaucratic.[64]

This insistence on management by himself and his family originated in an old belief Ruffin had held since his youth in the days of Thomas Jefferson. There were limits to the size of a productive farm. A farmer, Ruffin thought, "cannot extend his operations profitably much beyond the space and objects that he can personally supervise and direct." The farmer could operate only to the limit his own eyes could see. "If farming beyond this limit, his operations would become less and less profitable the farther they were extended; until the most remote or most neglected parts of his business would be attended with absolute loss."[65]

Here an idea had consequences. The idea of limited scale would lead Ruffin to oppose buying farms on which he himself or a member of his family could not reside or supervise; he refused to be an absentee owner.[66] The idea led him to invest profits not in endless accumulations of land and slaves, but in bonds and stocks. The idea of limited scale released him from yet another form of dependence, for it freed him from the need to hire outsiders to manage his lands. Yet absolute independence eluded him. In ways that became clearer every year, he discovered that success depended upon the Ruffin family. And the enormous scale of the rebuilding had one other significant consequence that cannot have escaped Ruffin's attention.

By 1847, a year in which he completed more than a mile of covered drains in one field, he must have realized that the prosperity of his family depended upon his slave force. With every step in the reconstruction of Marlbourne, he linked farm and family to slavery. By 1851, when he began to conceptualize the significance of changes at Marlbourne, he assumed without question that scientific agriculture in Virginia demanded the labor of slaves and that slavery must be carried into the second half of the nineteenth century.

Slavery and the Ruffin Family

Five years at Marlbourne fixed in Ruffin's mind a commitment to slavery that had not been absolutely firm when he moved to Petersburg in 1835. When he moved to the city from Shellbanks that year, he had tried to sell all of his "landed estate & nearly all other property," assuming he would never return to the country. He refused, however, to sell his slaves to "any other person than to the purchaser of the farm, who would keep them together, & by which arrangement my negroes would not suffer in their change of ownership."[67] He failed, therefore, to sell the farm in 1835 or to deliver himself from slaveholding.

Ruffin's sense of his own dependence on slavery changed in the course of reconstructing Marlbourne Farm. Crucial changes in his thinking came between 1848 and 1850 as he began to write essays about his Marlbourne experience. Clearly, the labor in reconstructing the farm had surpassed the capacity of himself and his family. This gave him two options. One he rejected immediately: the hiring of free labor, with which he had almost no experience. In rural Hanover County, he claimed, he could find no hired laborers who met his standards.[68] Ruffin was instituting a regime of work discipline that he assumed would have no appeal to hirelings; he forbade preindustrial habits of drinking, resting, and casual working without concern for time. What counted most, he insisted, was discipline:

> No laborers, either reapers or binders, worth having, can be hired here; and all who seek for such employment in harvest, studiously avoid all farms where there is any heavy growth to reap, and no whiskey is permitted to be used by the laborers. I have ceased to seek for or to obtain any aid of harvest hirelings."[69]

The alternative was slave labor. On his own farm, slaves had performed the physical labor of reconstruction successfully, and the lesson began to seem clear.[70] After six years his new covered drains still were working; they might last, he estimated, between twenty years and "centuries" or "forever."[71] Reconstruction had provided tasks for almost the entire slave community at Marlbourne—men, women, young, old.[72] With slaves under his own direction, he did not need to worry about whether his labor force would appear for daily work. Slavery made it possible for him to control the supply and routines of labor. Ruffin in 1850 was approaching a broader notion that the

Table 2   Marlbourne Slave Colony, 1844

	Males	Females	Unknown	Total
Laboring slaves				
Skilled and Disabled				
Ages 48–54	2	0		2
Field Hands				
Ages 24–40	8	2		10
Ages 12–23	5	1		6
Ages 10–12	0	4		4
Subtotal				22
Household Slaves				
Ages 32–43	0	5		5
Under Age 16	1	1		2
Subtotal				7
Unaffiliated Children				
Ages 1–13	6	2	4	12
Total	22	15	4	41

Sources: Edmund Ruffin, Marlbourne Farm Journal, 1844–1851, pp. 12, 82 (1844), VSL; Edmund Ruffin, "Farming Profits in Eastern Virginia: The Value of Marl," *American Farmer*, 5 (1849): 2–9; U.S. Census, Slave Schedules, Hanover County, Va., 1850, p. 151.

Note: In the Marlbourne Farm Journal in 1844 Ruffin named all of his laboring slaves: Jem Sykes, Joe, John, Harry, Zack, Titus, Erasmus, Tom, Dick, Jesse, Lewis, Burwell, Edmund, Daniel Byrd, Anthony, Amos, Betsy, Nancy, Rhoda, Esther, Phillis, Maria, and Phoebe. As household slaves he named Esther, Isabel, Sukey, Anaca, Sally, and Daniel Scott. Three unaffiliated children were Martha (age 13, disabled), Charles, and Isaac (the latter two being mentioned in a sick list). He did not mention in 1844 the other unaffiliated children.

scientific reconstruction of Virginia and the entire South could be founded upon slavery. Confirmation of this idea lay in his first five years at Marlbourne and in the slaves he brought there.

The forty-one slaves who colonized Marlbourne in December 1843 constituted a labor force that functioned on the scale of a large, single-family farm, rather than a vast plantation. (See Table 2.) Ruffin selected the colony both to perform the heavy work of reconstruction and to serve in the household. They came from two sources: Ruffin's household in Petersburg and Edmund, Jr.'s farm at Beechwood (the former Coggin's Point). The latter people Ruffin considered a remnant of his patrimonial slaves, though in fact only four of them were old enough for him to have inherited. All the skilled and field slaves came from Beechwood, accounting for twenty-two laborers between the ages of ten and fifty-four. Two of these were disabled but had skills that made Marlbourne self-sufficient in work like blacksmithing. Thus, twenty of the group from Prince George County (eight adult men, three adult women, five males in their teens, and four females aged ten to twelve) had field experience on a farm where marling was a routine task. Ruffin selected these twenty to be the labor corps for rebuilding Marlbourne.[73]

Six females (five of them adults) and one young male came to Marlbourne as house servants in 1844 to perform domestic work for eight Ruffins. Finally, Ruffin brought a group of twelve young slaves "under working age or otherwise unfit for labor, and not belonging either to farm hands or house servants."[74] Within the next five years most of these unaffiliated children, whose presence Ruffin must have calculated as a future source of labor, moved into the working force. Though some of the forty-one were shifted occasionally to other family farms, all of the permanent colonists survived the first six years at Marlbourne. In 1849 Ruffin noted the whereabouts of these individuals (mentioning no names), and in 1850 the census taker recorded the presence still of forty-one slaves at Marlbourne, though a few had left the farm and others had arrived.[75] Reconstruction did not exact a toll in human life.

The Marlbourne slave colony probably came entirely from the current holdings of the Ruffin family itself, underscoring the family's significance in this undertaking.[76] Ruffin purchased not one adult slave for the colony, and he could have drawn even the unaffiliated children from Beechwood.[77] In assembling this colony he disregarded the impact of the migration upon family ties among the slaves, indicating his awareness of the need for labor. Thus, not every adult slave who came to Marlbourne moved with a family. Six adult males had wives at Beechwood in 1845 and could return there only during long holidays or when Ruffin sent them to deliver messages or to work on Julian's farm. Of the slaves under age nineteen, nine might have moved with parents. There remained, however, a dozen children in 1844 who belonged to no one but Edmund Ruffin.[78]

Ruffin felt no need to explain whether these twelve were orphans being sent to surrogate families at Marlbourne or whether they were children being separated from parents. Sixteen years later, on the eve of the Civil War, most of these people were still alive, having matured into experienced workers who would make it clear during the war that they felt scant loyalty to their old master.[79] What mattered most in 1844 was their potential fitness as laborers, for these children would be trained as workers on a reforming farm; they represented the Ruffin family's investment in a future supply of disciplined labor.

By 1860, after Ruffin had given up Marlbourne, the original slave colony had grown from forty-one to fifty, almost certainly through natural increase.[80] Consistent with his assumptions about the limits of scale, he at no point aspired to climb higher than this into the class of great Southern planters who owned more than fifty slaves. In 1830, when he was farming Coggin's Point and reconstructing Shellbanks, he had owned sixty-six slaves, his largest holding; after 1830 he held fifty-two or fewer. Of all members in this branch of the Ruffin family, only Edmund, Jr., ascended permanently into that elite group with more than one hundred slaves. Collectively the family owned about 176 slaves in 1850 and 216 in 1860.[81] (See Table 3.)

Ruffin's growing commitment to slavery, therefore, did not derive simply from an aspiration to increase the number of his own slaves after 1844, though the expansion of his sons' holdings may have figured in his thinking. More precisely, his commitment stemmed from dependence on slaves he already owned, through their significant role in rejuvenating Marlbourne and in helping his children develop their farms in Prince George County between 1839 and 1860. The order of events played a significant role in his decision: once he failed to sell his slaves in 1835, he sealed his commitment to slavery. By 1844 slaves still represented 31 percent of Ruffin's personal property; the buildings and land those slaves sustained accounted for 63 percent.[82] By 1850 Ruffin viewed his slaves not only as a necessary source of labor but as the human capital sustaining his estate. It was not until slaves deserted the family's farms along the Pamunkey and James rivers after 1862 that he began to imagine he once had stood in a paternal relationship to these people, whose loyalty and affection he briefly conceived in terms almost feudal. That sentimental notion, however, did not develop until the war years.

Before 1858 Ruffin considered slaves not as dependents who defined his superior social position, but as part of his "capital invested." That capital included four kinds of property: the farm (including land and buildings), working animals and livestock, machines, and farm laborers. (In his farm journal he considered house servants not as invested capital but as family expenses, along with carriages, clothing, food, and costs of entertaining guests.)[83] In the spirit of this rational, calculating idea, he figured that between 1844 and 1848 he spent

Table 3 Ruffin Family Slaveholdings, 1782–1860

	1782–1790	1810	1820	1830	1840	1850	1860
Edmund Ruffin 1 (1713–1790)							
Evergreen	58						
Charlotte County	41						
Edmund Ruffin 2 (1745–1807)							
Coggin's Point	30						
George Ruffin (1765–1810)							
Prince George (estate)		143	39	53			
Sussex (estate)		26					
Edmund Ruffin 3							
Coggin's Point			52	66			2
Petersburg					12		
Marlbourne						41	50
Edmund Ruffin, Jr.							
Beechwood (Coggin's)					94	86	95
Bellevue					39		
Evelynton						29	43
Julian C. Ruffin							
Ruthven						13	22
Agnes Ruffin Beckwith						7	1
Charles L. Ruffin							3
Total	129	169	91	119	145	176	216

Sources: 1780–1790: *Heads of Families at the First Census . . . : Virginia* (1908; reprint, Baltimore: Genealogical Publishing Co., 1986), p. 14; Augusta B. Fothergill and John Mark Naugle, *Virginia Tax Payers, 1782–87* (1940; Baltimore: Genealogical Publishing Co., 1986), p. 108; Edmund Ruffin I, Inventory, 17 June 1791, Prince George County Deed Book, Part 2, 1787–1792, pp. 588–91, VSL (microfilm).

1810–1840: U.S. Census, Manuscript Returns for Dinwiddie, King and Queen, Prince George, and Sussex counties, Va.

1850, 1860: U.S. Census, Slave Schedules for Charles City (1850 listing for Beverly Walker), Dinwiddie, Hanover, and Prince George counties, Va.

Notes: Slaves in George Ruffin's estate in Prince George were listed for Rebecca Ruffin in 1810 and Rebecca Woodlief in 1820. Totals for 1840–1860 do not include slaves in the residue of this estate held by Ruffin's half-siblings.

nine hundred dollars annually to feed family members and house servants (about seventy dollars per person), counting food grown on the farm as well as food purchased. He budgeted just seven dollars a year in food for the twelve young, unaffiliated slaves during their unproductive years, allowing pork and bacon only to field hands and house servants. Medical bills in these early years of good community health totalled just sixteen dollars for all slaves. His budget for buying

clothes for working slaves varied between $6.00 and $6.50 a year[84]
His point was that through planning and budgeting for the slaves'
material life, he had found a profitable way to incorporate slavery
into the domestic economy of his own family.

Ruffin did not yet see his slaves as part of a design to demonstrate
mastery, power, or racial superiority.[85] These were not people whose
welfare and affection he viewed as evidence of his own ascent, he-
gemony, or position; he viewed them in worldly terms of income and
expense. His commitment to slavery, growing firmer as he reclaimed
Marlbourne, developed from necessities within the Ruffin family at
mid-century. The connection between vital events in this white family
and their dependence on slavery had its origin far back in the early
nineteenth century, when the Ruffins began to survive in large numbers. Awareness of this connection dawned on Ruffin between 1844
and 1850. In that brief period he made decisions that caught him in
a chain of cause and effect. It was not for the sake of mastering others
or restoring a feudal world that Ruffin took up the cause of slavery,
secession, and war. A man of the nineteenth century, he did it for
the family and reform.

The Family Fortune and Reform

Success at Marlbourne restored Ruffin's prosperity. Significant new
income from the farm permitted him to recoup losses suffered in
Petersburg and to replenish the family estate he had been husbanding
since 1813. Ruffin knew men far richer than he, but by 1850 his
estate had grown and assumed a new function in his life.[86] (See Table
4.) By that year it was large enough to permit him to plan a second
retirement from farming. At this point, suspecting nothing of what
was about to befall his children, he announced an ingenious plan.
He would turn his property over to them and transform the family
into an institution that would support not only the final stage of his
life, but a new career in Southern reform.

After the Panic of 1837 Ruffin had lost $30,000 in stocks, in
Petersburg properties, and in the *Farmers' Register*. This left him in
1842 with assets worth $70,000.[87] By the end of 1850, after six good
years at Marlbourne, he estimated his worth at $81,000.[88] In 1857
he noted his estate was worth $140,000, seven times greater than
the face value of his original inheritance.[89] Marlbourne increased in

Table 4   Growth of Ruffin's Estate

1813	$ 18,000
1827	40,000
1836	100,000
1842	70,000
1850	81,000
1856	128,500
1857	140,000

Sources: Ruffin to Charles L. Ruffin, 19 Oct. 1857, Ruffin Papers, VHS; Ruffin, "Incidents," 2: 102, 158, 216; Ruffin, *Diary*, 1: 43–45 (10 Mar. 1857), 2: 552 (23 Jan. 1863); Ruffin, Distribution of Estate, 1 Mar. 1856 (Typescript copy in possession of Marion Ruffin Jones, Walkerton, Va.); Ruffin, Will, 20 Oct. 1862 (Typescript copy in possession of M. R. Jones); U.S. Census, Population Schedules, Hanover County, Va., 1850, p. 391. Ruffin apparently placed a value of $37,100 on his real estate in the 1850 census, though the figure was not written clearly. Joseph F. Inman and Isobel B. Inman, comps., *Hanover County, Virginia: 1850 United States Census*, Typescript copy of census returns, Mar. 1974, p. 119, NA; Ruffin, diary (manuscript), p. 4093 (16, 17, 18 June 1865), Library of Congress, Washington, D.C.

Note: All figures represent Ruffin's own estimates except that for 1813. Ruffin claimed his inheritance in 1813 was worth less than the $9,000 he had given to Charles L. Ruffin by 1857, probably an underestimation. If his claim were true, Coggin's Point was worth only about $2 per acre that year and its fifty slaves, $100 apiece. The figure for 1813 represents an estimate based on a price of $5 per acre and an average $200 per slave. Estate figures are not adjusted for inflation.

value rapidly between 1843 and 1860. In 1843 the farm was worth $16,611 ($17 an acre). In 1850 Ruffin reported its value at $37,100, more than double the purchase price. In 1860 the Ruffin family reported the value of the farm at $58,200, three and a half times the purchase price.[90] Ruffin calculated in 1858 that the farm produced a net income of $8,000, almost four times its profit in 1845.[91]

The scheme to retire a second time from farming began to form in Ruffin's mind as early as 1845, within two years of his arrival in Hanover County, when he was approaching his fifty-second birthday. Late that year he attempted to persuade Julian to join him in a partnership in Marlbourne, an offer Ruffin's daughters opposed and which Julian eventually declined.[92] Seven years later he tried to install twenty-year-old Charles as farm manager. In 1852, after Charles had studied a year at Virginia Military Institute, Ruffin persuaded this youngest son to "take upon himself my whole farming business." Then, within months, Charles quit the farm to pursue civil engineering and railroad construction.[93] Ruffin was compelled to remain unhappily at the farm. After forty years, too, the charm of overseeing the affairs of offspring—six of them still unmarried and dependent adults—had begun to fade.

Finally, he persuaded Julian and Lottie to move to Marlbourne in 1854 and at that point declared himself retired. In a formal memorandum of agreement with Julian, Ruffin repeated his desire "to be relieved from the labor & care required by the management of his farm & other property." Julian agreed to be sole manager of the farm, to occupy the house, and provide housekeeping for his own family, "his father, & his unmarried sisters." He agreed to pay annual allowances to his father and unmarried siblings. In return he was promised an annual salary of $1,000 and an equal division of farm profits.[94] The agreement lasted almost two years, until Lottie's father died and Julian returned to Ruthven, where he could also manage his mother-in-law's small farm. In desperation, by September 1857 Ruffin turned Marlbourne over to William Sayre, husband of his daughter Elizabeth.[95] With the arrival of Sayre the problem of finding a family member to act as manager appeared to be solved. Ruffin then launched a scheme to transform his family into a legal business entity, or "co-partnership."

This scheme had occurred to him in 1850, when he began to think of ways to link the distribution of his estate with an early escape from farming. (Here was no patriarch clinging to vestiges of paternal power, but a man seeking release for a different line of work.) He confronted a series of difficulties. Ruffin's primary objective was to secure an independent income he could control completely. He also wanted to give equal portions of his wealth to each heir without destroying the revenue generated by the greatest single assets in the estate, Marlbourne and its slaves. Certain options, therefore, were unthinkable. He could not deed the farm to one child in return for support and shelter, since that would have made Ruffin himself a dependent upon the chosen heir. Nor could he divide Marlbourne into equal parts, conveying equal acreage to each heir, since this would have destroyed Marlbourne as a single, profitable farm and forced a separation of the slaves.[96] These options he rejected.

Ruffin devised an arrangement in 1850 that involved provisions very different from those in wills left by old men of the eighteenth century, with their demands for widow's or widower's rights, provisions for the best room, sustenance, and the comfort of a cow. Ruffin found a way to convey his estate while retaining control of its capital; he found a way to divide his estate equally while keeping it intact. He said his new scheme was "yet very unusual," indicating that he followed no known family precedents and no examples among his contemporaries.[97] He would refine the provisions at least three times—in 1856, 1862, and again in 1864; but the original concept of 1850 remained, defined precisely in indentures and wills recorded in Prince George and Hanover counties.

Marlbourne he sold as a single piece of property to his children as a group, creating in them a collective legal partnership. They agreed to pay him the full value of the farm, but not in cash, which only Edmund, Jr., might have raised. They gave Ruffin bonds (or mortgages) equal to the value of their portions in Marlbourne, secured by signatures and property they already owned. In exchange for these bonds, each of Ruffin's nine children in 1850 acquired title to a share of Marlbourne worth $9,000, and thus a share in its annual income. Ruffin reserved for himself a share in Marlbourne worth $25,000 (and later a share of $7,500 for a granddaughter). To compensate their father for these shares, the heirs agreed to provide him a home at Marlbourne or in Prince George, space for his library and chemical apparatus, and semiannual interest payments on his reserved fund at a rate between 5 and 6 percent a year.[98] This provided him with a predictable income of $1,500 a year.

Ruffin's scheme originated in assumptions he had carried forward from an earlier time in the nineteenth century. He began to follow a policy of dividing his estate equally among all sons and daughters in 1836 and 1838, when Edmund, Jr., and Agnes married. Ruffin made them marriage gifts of $4,000 as part of their shares of the estate. The idea of distributing his estate while he was still alive appeared at the same time, and, as he well knew, it fit nicely with his desire to have a living without farming:

> It had always been my designed policy to distribute to my children, as they arrived at sufficient age & discretion, such portion of capital of their designed patrimony, as I could spare without injury to the general farming capital, & the future benefit of all my children.[99]

Above all, the scheme expressed his old assumption that economic independence was necessary for himself and for each of his children, daughters as well as sons. He dreaded dependence for himself, and he sought to spare his children the horrors of dependence and poverty. The portions he offered would establish their independence, and the partnership would secure the same for himself. He acknowledged that he was prompted to give each heir "his or her respective portion" not only for the child's welfare, but for his own "ease & relief from labor & care."[100]

While Ruffin knew of no precedents for his scheme, similar ideas had occurred elsewhere in the nineteenth century, and they did not distinguish him as peculiarly Southern in his thinking. Like the heads of merchant families in Massachusetts after the Revolution, Ruffin was creating a family partnership—in a farming enterprise. He was pooling his family's slaves, work animals, carts, and capital, to undertake a venture that no single member could have funded. Like wealthy men in New England, he took pains to keep the estate in one holding, beyond the control of any individual except himself, preserving a permanent fund in which all family members could share. It became important in Virginia as well as in New England that all partners be responsible, trustworthy members of the partnership.[101]

The partnership became therefore not only an economic arrangement but also a moral tool. It promoted virtues of self-reliance, judgment, industry, and economy. Here was no design for the leisure of aristocratic sons:

> In this way, when it can be done, each son is put to work to nurse & increase his own share of capital—instead of drawing the income from the father's annual gifts or allowances. The first course, if the son is trustworthy, is the surest to make him industrious & economical—& the latter to make him idle, & prodigal, if not worse in his habits founded upon idleness.[102]

Here was no effort to retain patriarchal authority over the affairs of frivolous daughters:

> Thus, I was at last freed from my care about disbursements for their expenses, or having to exercise my judgment or direction in regard to their expenses. This procedure worked well; & in leaving them all, even when just having left school, to use their own income at will, in no case has either of my daughters exceeded the amount, or been wanting in proper prudence in expenditures.[103]

The patrimonial portion became a goad to industry, not an instrument to preserve privilege and luxury. The portion would provide a competency upon which his children would start equally in life; then they could race ahead by expanding their own capital. This was no *seigneur*, concerned merely to pass the family fortune down the line to the next generation; here was a man with the values of Franklin, using inheritance to instill the virtues of industry and hard work.[104]

The concept of the portion as a moral device became a kind of devil in Ruffin's brain, hurting relations with some of his children; particularly was this true after 1850, when their behavior became increasingly significant to his own welfare. Constantly he reminded them of what he had provided in their portions. (Eventually Elizabeth would protest against this obsession.) Always he judged them in terms of the portion he had improved as a youth. In their portions he included a test of character, and an assumption that self-discipline would lead to success. This assumption made Ruffin a harsh judge of conduct and poisoned his relations with those who did not prosper.

Still, the portions became the most significant devices in creating the family co-partnership. Through them, each heir developed an interest in the success of Marlbourne. Through their shares in Marlbourne, the Ruffin children found their individual affairs linked together in economic relations that cemented older bonds of sentiment and affection.[105] They discovered, too, that this linkage altered relations within the family: once the partnership began, the collective family began to exercise great power over individual members, creating for the children an institution that Ruffin as a youth had never known.

There were, finally, two other consequences. With his retirement arrangements Ruffin implicated his children in the survival of slavery, since his estate was founded to a significant degree upon investments in slaves, who were also the source of labor on the farm. In this period of Ruffin's retirement, then, there originated a connection between the domestic, financial affairs of this white family and their commitment to slavery. At the same time, Ruffin implicated all members of the family in supporting his career in retirement. Through his careful calculation and planning at Marlbourne, Ruffin created the material basis for an intellectual life in the antebellum South. He needed no institutional support from patrons, no large audience of subscribers like Cobbett's in England, no agricultural societies or universities, no state libraries or laboratories to sustain him in material or intellectual life. Only one institution was necessary to launch him back into a career in antebellum Southern reform: the Ruffin family itself.

4

Crises in the Ruffin Family

It would have been much better if . . . freedom of communication had always been used by all my children with me.

EDMUND RUFFIN, 1860

Absolute control over his own future lay in Edmund Ruffin's hands, it appeared, once he had devised the concepts of the portions and the partnership. He had succeeded in entwining his support with the fortunes of his family. The only prerequisites for his career lay in the family's prosperity and survival. Then, just as he was perfecting his plan, there arose the unforeseen, uncontrollable specters of death and conflict.

The Deaths of the Ruffin Women

Of the eight women most closely related to Edmund Ruffin, seven died between 1846 and 1862, including his wife, a beloved daughter-in-law, and five daughters. His daughters died between 1855 and 1862, removing almost an entire generation of the family's women in seven years, just as Ruffin completed the transfer of property to his children. Their deaths had a profound psychological and philosophical impact on Ruffin; the accounts Ruffin wrote of their passing revealed his dismay over a sequence of miseries common to all of the deaths. Only the large size of the family prevented their deaths from becoming a total material disaster as well.

Susan Travis Ruffin died first. In the spring of 1845, after sixteen years of good health, she noticed "a slight pain in one of her wrists," which physicians diagnosed as a "rheumatic affection." The disease

85

spread "until resulting in great pain, & a privation of almost all use of her limbs, & growing prostration of every bodily power." Her illness lasted almost a year. "This state of increased suffering was closed by death, on the 21st of February 1846."¹ Here, for the first time, Ruffin adopted an attitude similar to that of Thomas Cocke six years earlier, seeing horror in prolonged dying. For five of his six daughters and for his daughter-in-law, this horror would be repeated.

Unlike his father, who did not live to see a child older than sixteen, Ruffin knew all of his daughters as young adults, a new experience for a male in the family history. After the death of Susan Ruffin he formed close bonds with these women, particularly with daughters Jane and Mildred. His single daughters stepped into their mother's place as keepers of the household. Then, as they advanced into their twenties and thirties, he saw them taken away. Having crossed the ancient, early barriers of childhood diseases, his daughters succumbed to unconquered mortal dangers awaiting young women in epidemic disease and childbirth.

The first three died within five shocking months of each other in 1855. Ruffin's favorite daughter, Jane Ruffin Dupuy, became ill on 6 April 1855, gave birth to a daughter on 8 April, and then "continued for some days longer in great peril of life" before improving, deceptively, for "intervals."² Jane's physicians, including her husband, could not diagnose the illness; her most noteworthy symptoms were recurrent chills and pain.³ Jane's sisters attended her constantly, changing her posture frequently, to give "temporary rest & relief," and her husband administered opium for pain.⁴ She died 27 July at Beechwood, fifteen weeks after the onset of her illness, aged twenty-five. Few men, Ruffin said, could have "borne this trial," knowing death would come at an almost definable moment.⁵

The youngest daughter, Ella, died a month later, unmarried at twenty-three. In early summer Ella had been "indisposed," but not "seriously sick," until she traveled to Beechwood to help care for Jane. She became fatigued and "was very soon placed under medical care, for continued slow fever, which was pronounced to be typhoid," her father reported. After Jane died, Ella's physician told Ruffin that Ella had incurable heart disease; the doctors at Beechwood advised him to take her to the Virginia springs. At Red Sweet Springs in August Ella declined. A physician urged Ruffin to take her home quickly. By stagecoach they reached Fincastle, north of Roanoke, where she was "struck by paralysis, which rendered her whole left side incapable of motion." She died at a hotel on 24 August. Ruffin felt the "most horrible" aspect of her disease was "paralysis, (when the sufferer still continues to live,) threatening, & usually producing, total helplessness & prostration of body & mind."[6]

A third daughter, Rebecca Ruffin Bland, died three months later, 28 November 1855, at her home near Beechwood. She died at thirty-two, during the final days of her second pregnancy, without giving birth to the child. Her sister Agnes, who nursed Rebecca, reported that the illness had lasted three weeks, and she clearly attributed the death to childbirth: "The feet & limbs swelled very much & she suffered a good deal, but no more than many women under the same circumstances."[7] In fact, all three deaths in 1855 may have involved typhoid fever, an epidemic of which was present that year among slaves at Beechwood. Edmund, Jr., reported a slave child was near death on 7 December, "the 6th case this year, indeed since 1st July, of a strange disease, all of which we have lost, and which Dr. Harrison pronounces typhoid fever and I reckon he is right."[8]

The response of family members to Rebecca's death revealed that they already had become concerned about Ruffin's state of mind. Agnes asked Edmund, Jr., to notify Ruffin. "Good God I am almost beside myself," she told her brother. "My poor father!"[9] The family's depression after Rebecca's funeral was evident in the account Edmund, Jr., sent to his father, who did not attend the services. Just three or four days before Rebecca's death Edmund, Jr., had enlarged the family cemetery at Coggin's Point, bringing the new grave of Jane Ruffin Dupuy within the enclosure; thus there was room for another grave. "A few more years & its enclosure will be well filled—Thomas asked me on seeing how the carriages drove across the field why I did not make a road to it?"[10] Young Edmund attempted to console his father with the thought that the entire family would be reunited in heaven, but Ruffin did not believe in heaven and the idea failed to comfort him.[11]

Two years later, in 1857, young Edmund's wife, Mary Cooke Smith Ruffin, died of consumption at age forty-one, removing a woman Ruffin had come to love as much as his own daughter Jane.[12] At the end of 1860 his daughter Elizabeth Sayre died in childbirth at Marlbourne, the victim, according to Ruffin, of a tumor that proved fatal in pregnancy.[13] Finally, in 1862, his daughter Mildred Sayre died in Kentucky after giving birth to a daughter. At the arrival of this news Ruffin declared himself perplexed by his inability to grieve. Had age, he wondered, "paralysed my affections, & dried up the sources of parental love . . . , that I scarcely grieve for the death of her who was my best beloved remaining child?"[14] Of the women most closely tied to Ruffin in 1844, only Agnes Beckwith survived this time of sorrows.

These deaths had one aspect that would have profound consequences for Ruffin's thinking and for his state of mind. All the women suffered long periods in helplessness and pain, and all knew that death was approaching. Ruffin came quickly to reject the idea of such a death and moved much closer to the position taken in 1840 by Thomas Cocke. He also became depressed and began talking about his own death, to the alarm of his family. As early as August 1845, during his wife's illness, Ruffin had begun to worry about the decay of his mind, at age fifty-one; Edmund, Jr., assured him that no one had "discovered any decay of your mental powers."[15] One month before Susan Ruffin died, Edmund, Jr., again admonished his father. "I regret exceedingly to see your own low spirits, so plainly stamped in your letter," he wrote. "There is nothing like complete happiness in this world."[16] Julian repeated this admonition two years later: "It gives me much pain, my dear father, to hear you speak so often now of the decay of yr. mental powers, of dotage, &c.," Julian wrote. "I do wish you wd cheer up, & not allow yr. mind to dwell upon such an idea—for I think you are giving yourself unnecessary pain."[17]

This sense of decay remained in Ruffin's thinking. In late 1851 he closed his autobiography with complaints about memory loss and "infirmities" of old age, still influenced by the deaths of Susan Ruffin and Thomas Cocke. He dreaded illness, senility, and dependence: "May God protect me, even if early death be the means, from my living through an old age of great infirmity of body & imbecility of mind!"[18] Ruffin's view of his early life as a history of achievement through self-reliance now began to hinder him in coming to terms with the natural end of his life. He dreaded losing control over his body, given the deaths he witnessed after 1845.[19]

None of the deaths entailed disastrous economic consequences for Ruffin or the family, nor did they destroy the idea of the family as an economic partnership. When Ella died, her portion of the estate was added to those of the survivors. The deaths of Jane, Rebecca, Elizabeth, and Mildred removed insignificant amounts of their portions. Since there were four surviving children through 1862 (three of whom were sons), the mere size of the Ruffin family blunted any material or economic consequences. In these terms, only the deaths of the Ruffin men would have mattered.

Loss of the women did entail social consequences. Susan Ruffin's death altered Ruffin's social situation in one significant way: he became dependent upon his daughters to assume his wife's domestic duties.[20] While those duties were diminishing as the family matured, the tasks women performed were crucial. Most of them worked hard in both productive and reproductive labor, even though black women did the washing and cooking for most of the family's households. Ruffin women either cultivated or oversaw family vegetable gardens; Rebecca Bland oversaw her own poultry and dairy; Mary C. Ruffin made clothing for slaves; Mildred at times acted as overseer at Marlbourne. Susan T. Ruffin, Agnes Ruffin Beckwith, Mary C. Ruffin, and Lottie Ruffin had charge of rearing children; and all but Jane Ruffin Dupuy had to devote themselves to the significant tasks of nursing the sick. These women also provided amusement (in music and discussion) and acted as diplomatic agents between different houses of the family, conducting extensive visits and correspondence. They were not women of leisure.[21]

The deaths of the daughters completed a social change for Ruffin, removing all seven of the women who had managed his household. The marriages of Agnes, Jane, Rebecca, Elizabeth, and Mildred played a role in this removal, but death took all of them with finality.[22] No single death brought about this social change, but all of them together did. Together, they removed the possibility of Ruffin's maintaining a household on his own, when he was between age sixty-one and sixty-eight. For all his assumptions about self-reliance, the collective passing of the Ruffin women was a disaster, revealing the real sense in which Ruffin had been dependent upon them.

As a result, Ruffin assumed a life almost totally independent of women. By 1860 he had had no sexual partner for at least fifteen years.[23] By 1862 he had determined never again to marry, and he was dependent in no material way upon any woman.[24] The deaths of the Ruffin women had finally forced him into independence in this part of his life. He would live alone. As long as he remained healthy, he had no need for the help of the women around him. Though others in the family still lived, these deaths sealed Ruffin's isolation.

Conflict in the Ruffin Family

What death could not undo, quarrels nearly demolished. Conflict erupted after 1850 within the Ruffin family, involving decisions that now affected the partnership. By joining his children in a common enterprise that determined his own welfare, Ruffin had opened possibilities for conflict he had not anticipated. The family's prosperity now depended on the judgment and self-discipline of its younger members, and decisions about marriage and vocation became matters of common interest. Recklessness by anyone could threaten all. In the decade after 1850, three serious quarrels nearly broke up the partnership. Two of them involved the marriage relationships of daughters, Agnes Ruffin Beckwith and Elizabeth Ruffin Sayre. The third involved the indecisiveness of the youngest son, Charles L. Ruffin, about a vocation. These three conflicts involved children whose behavior raised questions about their judgment, competence, self-control, and ability to plan for the future. In response to conflict, Ruffin found himself changing ideas about the family and inheritance.

Ruffin's feud with his eldest daughter, Agnes, and her husband, Dr. T. Stanly Beckwith, had been simmering since 1838, when Agnes married Beckwith.[25] Ruffin had given Agnes $4,000 at her maturity as an initial share of her portion, but that money quickly disappeared.[26] In Agnes, Ruffin perceived a recklessness that could threaten everyone. The Beckwiths began to sink into poverty, threatening to burden the collective family with their obligations.

Opportunities for conflict appeared at once. For a time between their marriage and 1841 the Beckwiths lived as neighbors of Ruffin in Petersburg, while Beckwith pursued a controversial medical practice.[27] As the number of Beckwith children grew (eventually reaching thirteen, of whom ten survived infancy), Beckwith's income became less adequate for their support. In 1845 Beckwith's parents moved to Petersburg from Raleigh, leaving behind the scandal of a duel in which the senior Mrs. Beckwith's brother was killed. These parents, too, became dependents of Beckwith.[28] At about that time Beckwith's furniture was sold at public auction in the city. Ruffin was witnessing the collapse of his daughter's competency and independence.[29]

In 1847 Beckwith himself became a figure of scandal when another doctor, according to Agnes, "interfered in a case of his." Beckwith confronted his rival in the other man's office, where a fistfight ensued, Dr. Beckwith taking a blow in one eye. "I trust it may come to nothing more than fist fighting," Agnes wrote to her father, stifling (if she could) all memory of the duel in Raleigh.[30] This public humiliation was the last straw.

That same year Ruffin addressed to Agnes a list of grievances against Beckwith. The significance of their quarrel emerged now, revealing not only a widening alienation but the terms in which Ruffin now judged his children and their spouses. The mere fact that children were heirs of a family line, fruits of one's body, creatures of the same blood, almost did not matter. What mattered to Ruffin were the tests of ambition, competence, and self-reliance. Beckwith failed. Her father's judgment stung Agnes, who turned against him in defense of Beckwith. Her assumptions became as clear as her father's. She had adopted other standards, closer to those of her brother Julian and sister Elizabeth, who, under the influence of local religious revivals in 1847, had embraced sentiments of benevolence and charity. Agnes did not deny Beckwith's failings. "If he had committed some crime it would be different," she wrote, "but I can't see that poverty is a crime." Then she struck at the heart of Ruffin's judgment: "You don't know how quick your sentiments toward him would change if his fortunes were changed. I know you are not conscious of this."

Agnes accused her father of judging Beckwith simply by his ability to sustain himself. That, she felt, was too harsh. "I know that he stretches every nerve to get himself out of difficulties, but the sin of improvidence & consequent difficulty is on him & he has to bear it," she said. Then she attempted to change her father's way of thinking. "I trust he will yet show what he is," she wrote, "but when a man gets in difficulties, it is hard to get out without the aid of others— and I am fully convinced that it is intended for us to help one another."[31]

This declaration may have persuaded Ruffin for a short time. In the winter of 1848–49 a farm was purchased for Agnes in Prince George County (probably by Ruffin himself, who probably kept the actual deed in his own hands), and Beckwith left Petersburg to start farming.[32] This farm, eventually called Woodbourne, contained 260 acres and was worth $1,950 in 1850.[33] Ruffin then loaned money to Agnes, provided a mule and other animals, and paid $250 for carpenters who worked on the house at Woodbourne in 1849.[34] For the next five years Beckwith tended the farm and pursued a country medical practice, presenting no apparent threat to the Ruffin estate.

Word reached Ruffin in 1854, however, that Beckwith had begun

to slide once more into debt, bringing this experiment in benevolence
to a halt and ending the peace. Beckwith denied rumors that Agnes
had sought credit from Petersburg merchants, or that he himself had
contracted new debts "without her knowledge." He admitted opening
an account for groceries in Petersburg. "When I came to the country,
I had no money, having paid away all I could collect," he protested.
"My losses on my books were large. My family was large & must be
fed & clad." The grocer, moreover, knew that he "owned no property," so the farm cannot have been endangered. He confessed he
might have told other creditors that Agnes might agree to endorse
another debt, "the property being hers." He simply had overlooked
this one instance in which Agnes and her estate had been tied to his
own debts, and then he had forgotten it. Reports reaching Ruffin
were unfounded and "calculated to injure my reputation (the only
legacy I have for my children)." Finally, Beckwith denied that he
had appropriated for himself "such little presents of money as you
have occasionally given your daughter." If Beckwith anticipated this
accounting would allay his father-in-law's fears, he had miscalculated;
his account revealed too much.

Ruffin drafted an apology to Beckwith, conceding the rumors to
be unfounded, but reasserting the propriety of his concern for Agnes.
Then he chose not to send the apology, the tone of which made it
clear that he had noticed the new debt tied to Agnes. He vowed that
so long as he and Beckwith lived he would "claim & exercise a father's
right to inform & defend" his daughter. As for Beckwith's assurances
about the "little presents of money," Ruffin revealed that they
amounted in 1854 to more than he had distributed to all but one of
his children. "But all, & much more than can ever be hoped for,
cannot save my daughter & her children from the severe privations
of poverty."[35]

Here was the danger for Agnes—this slipping into poverty and
dependence. Beckwith cannot have realized the significance family
history played in this conflict with his father-in-law. He certainly did
not comprehend an analogy Ruffin must have drawn immediately
between this young Petersburg doctor and an identical figure from
the 1820s, Carter Coupland, whose marriage to Ruffin's sister Juliana
left her in almost hopeless dependency. Ruffin saw in Coupland (who
by chance also practiced medicine in Petersburg) an incompetent
opportunist. As Juliana's legal guardian in 1823, Ruffin had opposed
the marriage. She defied him, appointed another guardian, and then

watched Coupland claim her estate (including slaves who had once belonged to the whole family) and fall into debt.[36] At his death in 1833 Coupland revealed bitterness in his will; he forbade Ruffin to care for the Couplands' three young sons and left no bequest for Juliana other than some land of unknown value in Mississippi.[37] Juliana lived to regret her mistake. Her brother savored his role as protector, knowing these events had given him an aura of wisdom. From Mississippi, where she went to assess Coupland's estate in December 1833, Juliana wrote Ruffin of her shock on learning that her remaining property was in jeopardy. "Do I understand you to say in your letter that Dr. Coupland was trying to get it to pay the creditors?" She felt indignant at Coupland's meanness in wishing to take her last "pittance," and she felt trapped, too. "I am like the man in the bramble bush. I cannot turn but a brier scratches."[38]

Beckwith represented an old threat that other members of the family recognized at once, and if he got hold of Agnes's share of their estate he would menace their welfare, too. Over the decade of quarreling between 1847 and 1857, the Beckwith-Ruffin feud became a cause of change in family inheritance policy. To combat the menace, Ruffin resorted to a legal device other Virginia families employed increasingly in the antebellum period to protect their married daughters and estates: the trust fund.[39] In a formal indenture filed in 1857, he designed a trust for Agnes that closed every avenue Beckwith might have taken to abscond with his wife's property. First, Ruffin transferred legal ownership of Agnes' portion to Edmund, Jr., and Julian on condition that they spend income from her funds to support her and her children, "free from the control, debts or liabilities of her husband T. S. Beckwith." This clause was intended to prevent Edmund, Jr., and Julian from paying Beckwith's debts. Second, Ruffin required that, should Agnes survive her husband, the trustees must give to her "the whole of the property herein conveyed in fee simple." In short, he did not oppose his daughter's ownership of property once her husband was dead. Finally, he provided that if Agnes died before Beckwith, the trustees could not convey portions to Agnes' daughters if there was a danger that their father might lay claim to their inheritances. This prevented Beckwith from seizing their money and throwing them on the family dole.[40]

With these provisions Ruffin completed a transformation that had begun in 1846 in his thinking about inheritance. In that year, when Agnes's dilemma had become clear, Ruffin decided he would never again transfer portions to the possession of each child in fee-simple. Instead, he began to devise rudimentary forms of the trust fund for other daughters who were coming of age; until he felt confident in the judgment of his heirs, he would keep their capital in special funds, giving beneficiaries only the annual interest. In 1857, for Agnes, he made this arrangement permanent.

Ruffin was not demanding patriarchal power for its own sake. In his mind he was the father protecting his other children—including his daughters—and securing his own retirement funds. Under common law in Virginia and elsewhere in antebellum America, husbands gained rights to the property of their wives.[41] Ruffin was attempting to raise a barrier against that law, keeping Agnes's capital in control of the Ruffin family, beyond Beckwith's reach. Her capital included assets worth nearly $16,000 in 1857, and by 1860 her portion had become larger than any of the others.[42] Agnes's predicament forced her father to think in different terms. Instead of leaving her penniless, Ruffin had found a way to assure Agnes and her children of "a competent support and maintenance." In this instance, one man resorted to legal tactics to prevent another man's seizing the property of a woman—a woman whom state law did not protect and about whose decisions in domestic matters there was some doubt. He also was attempting to let responsible heirs manage the estate and to free himself from a paternal care.

With the indenture of 1857 another consequence emerged from Ruffin's feud with the Beckwiths. Significant legal and economic power shifted away from the family of generation, or the family composed of spouses and their children. That power was seized by the family of origin, or the family composed of parents, brothers, and sisters.[43] The demographic transformation in the Ruffin family made this transfer possible. In Ruffin's youth his own family of generation had held power over property by default: the family of origin simply did not exist, so youngsters in their teens and twenties acquired property at marriage or maturity because their parents' cohort survived only in remnants. By 1850 the older cohort, representing the family of origin, survived in sufficient numbers to enforce their decisions concerning property distribution, not leaving this matter to chance and death.

Ruffin denied appeals for Agnes based on sentimental love, though he did offer sums that eventually gave her the largest portion of all. Julian appealed to his father in 1855. "My poor dear Sister! I can scarcely refrain from shedding tears whenever I think upon her sad fate," he declared.

> How much she has borne in her poverty, how much as the wife of one evidently disliked & ill treated by her own family upon whom she is nevertheless dependent for the necessities of life, how much as the mother of children whose actual physical wants, to say nothing of their education & success in life she has no means of supplying—how much she has to bear in these & numerous other matters of minor importance none of us can fully know.

Julian conceded that Beckwith could not inspire Agnes' children to "success in life," but he urged his father not to vent his anger on Agnes, who suffered "poverty & misery" and "wretchedness." Julian invoked an idea of marriage more strict even than Ruffin's own prim view; he pressed his father to acknowledge that Beckwith was "an affectionate husband" and that Agnes was "bound to him by a tie as strong as that which holds together soul & body, & which can only be severed by death." He appealed not only for aid, but for charity and sympathy. "Pecuniary aid is all important, of course I admit, to those in actual want," he said, "but the human heart cannot be happy without an interchange of love & kindly feelings between it & those whom nature & circumstance have bound together."[44] Julian's plea got no response; Ruffin probably did not believe in such bonds.[45] He did not change course.

Immediately after the indenture was drawn in early 1857, Beckwith returned to his Petersburg medical practice, leaving Agnes and all but one child on the farm. A year later Agnes abandoned the farm and followed her husband. At that point others in the family (including Julian, Edmund, Jr., and Elizabeth Sayre) began to share their father's contempt for Beckwith and to express it discreetly.[46] Ruffin did not stand alone in his view of Beckwith, but he did become more angry than others. He began to use terms of abuse: Beckwith became Agnes' "despicable husband," her "spendthrift and worthless husband," "lazy & heedless of the future," a "worthless son-in-law."[47] He resolved in May 1857 to shun Beckwith, declaring in his diary, "I shall hereafter, if ever again meeting him, pass him as a stranger." Ruffin acted on this resolution for the first time in February 1858.[48]

Agnes attempted to restore relations with her father early in 1863, when news of Mildred's death arrived from Kentucky. Ruffin was living at Julian's farm, during his early days as a Civil War refugee.

Agnes cast her appeal in terms of family love. "I did not know how much I loved you until I heard of your heavy affliction," she wrote from Petersburg. Her heart yearned "for the love that I need to have from you." She sought reconciliation. "Dear father you have no other daughter left you. Will you not receive me and love me as of old?" Agnes saw the family as an institution of affection, of comfort in "sad, sad times." Now, when she was forty-six and Ruffin sixty-nine, she asked him to forgive and forget.[49]

Ruffin claimed he had forgiven Agnes years before. "But '*forget*' what has occurred, I cannot, while life & memory remain to me." He revealed that he did not view familial relationships simply in terms of sentiment or affection inspired at occasions like the death of a daughter. "It is not my disposition, nor in my nature, to put off & put on love, according to my changes of temper, or of expediency." Implicit in his response to Agnes was a concept of family that also considered "prospects of prosperity," and an affection between parent and child that observed the due authority of the parent. Agnes now paid for her defiance and her decision to be a fool for love. Ruffin refused to put aside his anger over the Beckwiths' improvidence and the crisis it had raised. "I have *no daughter* left alive."[50] When Agnes herself exploded in anger and pressed Ruffin to reveal which of her brothers and sisters had conspired against her to gain his favor (suspecting Julian and Elizabeth), Ruffin determined to shun this daughter. "If another letter should come to me, it will be returned unread—& not opened, unless by mistake."[51] Thus, although he maintained her trust fund, Ruffin banished Agnes from the family of affection she treasured, heightening with the same stroke his own isolation.

If the Beckwith quarrel resulted in a transfer of power to the Ruffin family over its individual members (who now had equal rights to its resources), then his quarrel with daughter Elizabeth and her husband William Sayre established a new and narrow definition of family membership. As a result of conflict with Sayre, the conviction grew that only immediate relatives could belong to the family partnership. After William Sayre's attempt to seize Marlbourne, the entire family learned a lesson: outsiders could not be trusted. This shift in belief was reinforced by demographic conditions that already disposed the Ruffins to withdraw into a private world of immediate family relations.

William Sayre began his relationship with Ruffin as an outsider and never lost that status. Born in 1814, Sayre was ten years older than Elizabeth Ruffin.[52] His origins were different. He began his adult life as a merchant seaman and as petty officer on a New Bedford whaling ship, and by the time he married at age thirty-eight, he owned only a small market farm on the Elizabeth River near Norfolk.[53] He probably met Elizabeth at Marlbourne through his sister, wife of Ruffin's neighbor Carter Braxton.[54] (By this time Ruffin was feuding with Braxton over the latter's marl pit, as well as the new state constitution.)[55] Though Ruffin disapproved of Sayre, Elizabeth determined to marry. She moved to Julian's farm in 1850 and prepared for her wedding in October 1852. Julian urged Ruffin to attend the ceremony. "I wish very much, Father, that you would be present on that occasion," he wrote in September. "Her marriage will be very private. None but our immediate family & relatives will be invited."[56]

Ruffin refused to attend, so Julian wrote him about the event and revealed that the rest of the family shared Ruffin's unhappiness. "The match is, I believe, displeasing to all of us." Still, since Elizabeth was of "mature age," Julian argued, "we should not embitter her life by showing a useless opposition & disapproval of it." He predicted Sayre would prove an "industrious & upright man," who would provide Elizabeth a "comfortable support."[57] The couple moved to Sayre's farm near Norfolk for four years; apparently Ruffin and Elizabeth then reconciled their differences during Jane's illness in 1855. By December 1856 Ruffin had named Sayre manager of Marlbourne, placing his greatest investment in the hands of this son-in-law.

The problem with Sayre did not lie in the smallness of his estate or in his humble origin, but in his ambition. Sayre's presence as the new son-in-law at Marlbourne presented a classic, historical threat to the family.[58] He wanted Marlbourne. The Ruffin family adopted two tactics to secure their farm against seizure by this outsider. First, at the time of the marriage, Ruffin and Julian forced Sayre to abandon some claims to Elizabeth's property by establishing a trust fund to protect her in case of Sayre's death. "He has brought with him a deed (already written but which has to be signed & acknowledged before a magistrate)," Julian reported in October 1852, "by which he conveys to a trustee, for Sister E's sole benefit, the property which she had at the time of her marriage—so that in case of accident she will still at least have her own."[59] Neither Sayre nor his relatives could get hold of Elizabeth's portion now. (Concurrent difficulties with T. Stanly Beckwith were undoubtedly influencing these decisions.)[60]

Their second tactic developed in 1856. As part of Ruffin's retirement agreement, the Ruffins incorporated William Sayre as a member of the family, admitting him as one of five partners in Marlbourne Farm. Ruffin sold Sayre one share of the partnership on the same terms he had given his children, taking Sayre's personal bonds as payment. Sayre thus replaced Elizabeth as a full partner, joining Edmund, Jr., Julian, Charles, and Mildred.[61]

Sayre blundered twice at Marlbourne, threatening the greatest Ruffin asset. His first mistake stemmed from innocence: he had no experience in managing a large-scale grain farm, nor had he supervised slaves. Within a year Elizabeth was begging her brothers and father to help her husband. Sayre was in a "peck of trouble"; he had confessed to her that he was "entirely inexperienced & knows not what to do" about plowing.[62] Sayre himself appealed for help with the 1858 wheat crop. "As I have no experience I do not know how much injury the rust can do." Ruffin later blamed Sayre for neglecting maintenance on the drainage ditches and for failing to establish his authority among the slaves, who viewed him as "a stranger whom they first disliked, & subsequently hated heartily."[63]

When Sayre's difficulties became apparent, Mildred Ruffin came to his rescue. It was she who really began to oversee "plantation matters" at Marlbourne, permitting her father to leave the farm and travel. Mildred was twenty-nine years old in 1856, when the decision to admit Sayre was made. As a single woman she continued to live at Marlbourne after the Sayres arrived. She had learned much from Ruffin, had read his books and articles, and she knew his farm.[64] Mildred made regular reports to her father on plowing, relations with neighbors, the contents of Ruffin's mail, and on the progress of brickmaking for a new barn. "I have ventured down twice to see them at work," she wrote in 1858. "I rode down yesterday afternoon to look at the wheat. It is beautiful now. I never saw any-thing improve so much in so short a time."[65] In managing Marlbourne between 1856 and 1859, Ruffin depended on Mildred.

Sayre blundered with less innocence in attempting to take possession of Marlbourne. Ruffin began to suspect his motive when Mildred, at age thirty-two, married William Sayre's brother, Burwell, a widower with one daughter. Mildred arranged the entire match herself, surprising her father and giving him no role except to consent.[66] The Sayre brothers now represented a threat more serious than Beckwith, for they seemed bent upon taking control of the farm, threatening to ruin Ruffin's retirement arrangements and break up the family partnership. Ruffin immediately took steps with young Edmund and Julian to remove the Sayres.

They easily disposed of Burwell Sayre. Edmund, Jr., bought from Mildred her share of Marlbourne. Then, without complaint or hesitation, the Ruffin men simply executed a marriage settlement that transferred Mildred's cash proceeds to Burwell, a concession they had denied to Agnes and Elizabeth. (In 1861 Mildred's share of the estate included bonds and securities that were still worth $8,000, perhaps half their value 1859.)[67] Proceeds in hand, Burwell determined not to try farming but to return to teaching at a "large & profitable school" in Kentucky. Ruffin concurred with this decision.[68] Burwell Sayre thus removed himself from Marlbourne, taking with him Mildred and the proceeds of her estate, and leaving his brother William alone to confront the Ruffins.

William Sayre remained a threat and a source of conflict. He and Ruffin argued audibly—apparently over the partnership—before and after Mildred's wedding at Marlbourne in October 1859. "Each of us deemed himself very badly treated by the other," Ruffin noted. "I soon put an end to what was becoming on W. S.'s part a very angry as well as insulting course of complaint & remark—& as soon as I could, after the marriage, & the leaving of the married pair, I went away."[69] Ruffin concluded that Sayre and Elizabeth wanted him to leave Marlbourne permanently, so he moved at once to Beechwood.[70]

Conflict with Sayre confirmed the Ruffins in their narrowing definition of themselves as a family. Ruffin mused to himself in 1859 that it had been impossible to admit both Sayre brothers to the partnership because "two whole families cannot assimilate."[71] For the next three years he and his sons sought to eliminate Sayre and the threat he posed to the efficient management of Marlbourne. As long as Sayre held a full share in the partnership, he held their asset hostage. Finally, in the winter of 1862–63, they agreed to Sayre's terms. Edmund, Jr., and Julian together bought Sayre's share for $22,000, one-fifth the total value of the farm, its slaves, stock, and equipment. "Thus," Ruffin wrote, "at last—& much too late—has been gotten rid of this great evil of a foreign partner in this property—but at a very heavy cost to the purchasers."[72] The estate now returned completely to the control of the family, rescuing it from an outsider whose admission Ruffin termed the "worst blunder" of his life.[73] Once the quarrel was ended, the Ruffin family consciously closed its circle of membership.

The Problem of the Youngest Son

The third quarrel within the Ruffin circle saw the family emerge as an institution of individual discipline and reform. This conflict between Ruffin and his youngest child, Charles L. Ruffin, demonstrated that even a blood son who failed to demonstrate industriousness did so at his own peril. The quarrel also revealed that this particular Southern family sought to rear no Hotspur, that it would indulge no period of devil-may-care idleness, that it wanted no impulsive defender of archaic notions of honor.[74] The virtues Ruffin sought to instill in Charles—industry, self-reliance, discipline—were intended to secure not family honor, but family estate.

The nub of the conflict was Charles's inability to settle himself into a profession. He appeared to lack ambition. His brothers and sisters suspected he suffered from depression, and he appears to have been stricken more frequently and violently than the others by malaria.[75] Late in 1850 or early in 1851, when Charles was eighteen and Ruffin fifty-seven, the two had a talk at Marlbourne about Charles's shortcomings. In a letter he wrote a short time later, Charles owned the faults Ruffin had enumerated. He seemed unable to "think of the future." He vowed to pursue engineering and embraced, hesitantly, the prospect of hard work and professional advancement. "I admit the wrong I am doing and shall endeavor to correct it, or rather I say I will."[76] His thoughts drifted to his childhood, where he thought their conflict originated. "Father, I confess I have never felt towards you as a son should do toward his parent," he wrote. "Even in my childhood, fear of you always kept me distant. Whether it is that that has grown into coldness, I cannot say." Cleverly, he played on Ruffin's fears, claiming to feel a love that strengthened as he saw "the hair whitening around thy honoured brow—showing thereby the shortening span of life, as well as the feebleness that may be expected in after years." Tears came to his eyes not for the possible loss of his portion, but for "the sad fact of which you spoke, viz. your life drawing to a close."[77]

After leaving Virginia Military Institute without a degree in 1852, Charles did not find paying work.[78] He failed both trials as manager at Marlbourne, "by inattention and carelessness," his father said.[79] In 1856 Ruffin bought him 241 acres in Prince George County, deeming it "prudent for me to retain the legal title."[80] Charles was feeling the influence of a paternal power that Ruffin himself as a young man had never imagined.

Their quarrel lasted the rest of Ruffin's life, reaching a crisis in 1857, the year Ruffin parted with the Beckwiths. By then Ruffin, too, believed the difficulties had begun in Charles's childhood. "As boy and youth, you were idle & heedless, made no use of all your opportunities for learning, & have continued idle, neglectful of all duties, improvident & wasteful of your time, money, & latterly of your credit in more senses than one." The object was not to be dashing and sociable, but rather to become a hard worker. "I have tried my best, & all in vain, to give you education, & afterwards business & business habits—to induce you to be an industrious & worthy man, even though I despaired of having any comfort in you as a dutiful & good son." Once, when Charles had shown signs of "reformation," Ruffin had given him capital worth $9,000, part of his portion. Now, having incurred debt, Charles was threatening the security of the whole family. "I am now hopeless," Ruffin declared. "I see that every dollar of income you have above a bare competency, & not contingent on your own exertion, industry, & economy, will do you harm by encouraging your evil propensities." His only recourse was to "stint" Charles to a minimum income before the young man fell into dependence by his "improvidence, wastefulness of time & means." History came back to haunt Charles, just as it had Dr. Beckwith. "You show to me your beginning of a course like Dr. Beckwith's—& I do not mean by my aid to let it go on to the like deplorable & shameful consequences." He demanded that Charles pay all debts and offered to buy Charles's share of Marlbourne, fearing the creditors would demand it.[81] Ruffin was expressing a rational fear.

Debate within the family over Charles' difficulties revealed not only a history of Ruffin's relationship to his children, but the moral role of the family and its estate. In 1860 Elizabeth Ruffin Sayre initiated an exchange with her father about Charles, who was always a great favorite of his sisters, cousins, nieces, and nephews. Only Elizabeth's fear that her pregnancy might prove fatal emboldened her to address Ruffin on 14 July.[82] "I have longed to write or speak to you," she wrote, "but never could summon the courage to do so." She hoped to see her brother a "useful member of society, a comfort to his

family." Admittedly, Charles was in trouble. From what she had seen
and "something" she had heard, she feared he was "fast falling into
bad habits." Charles had spoken freely to her about his unhappiness,
his feeling that "a great difference has been shown him & your other
sons." He felt "like an alien—almost an outcast."[83]

Elizabeth compared the lives of her brothers, revealing things she
had noticed but concealed for years. Their order of birth seemed
significant. Had Charles been brought up in the place of Edmund,
Jr., or Julian, he would have been "a better Son—a worthier Man."
Edmund was the first born. "You were proud of him. You made a
companion of him, treated him as he grew up as a man—& this made
a man of him," she said. "Brother J. was from childhood staid &
sober—you gave him your confidence—& confidence begets confidence." Both the older boys had the "training & prayers" of their
mother. "Charles was deprived of this great blessing when a child—
& God only knows what a loss to a child the loss of a Mother is."[84]
Early in his boyhood Charles "showed a greater fondness for play than
study," which had displeased Ruffin, "& I think you hastily judged
his future by the then present." Then Elizabeth appealed to higher
authority. "I know that the Bible teaches as plainly as any other lesson
that of obedience from Children to their Parents," she said, "but it
also warns Fathers against provoking their children lest they be
discouraged."[85]

She begged her father to reason with Charles about his troubles.
"I fear he owes money which he cannot pay." Ruffin should persuade
Charles to reveal the amount. Then she tried to put Ruffin's estate
to another use. "Take some of what you call his portion & pay back
what he owes. Start him again." Ruffin had aided "an alien & a
stranger (Dr. Beckwith)," she noted. "Can you not do it for your
own son?" The power to save Charles lay in Ruffin's hands. "Father,
you are the author of his being—& it is in your power with God's
blessing to reclaim him & make him more worthy to be called your
son."[86] The idea of reforming an individual was not new to Ruffin,
for he had conquered his own drinking habit as a youth and he had
also tried in 1857 to reclaim at least one friend from intemperance.[87]
Elizabeth, however, appeared to have in mind not reform, but rescue.

Ruffin did not dismiss her appeal as an affront to paternal prerog-
ative. Within six days he responded reassuringly. "So far from of-
fending me, I heartily thank you for your opinions being thus
expressed—however painful the subject is to me," he wrote. "It would

have been much better if the like freedom of communication had always been used by all my children with me."[88]

Certain facts about Charles needed clarification. Charles's portion was equal to the others' except that of Agnes, so Charles had no grounds for ill-feeling. True enough, Ruffin had retained title to this property in 1857, except for three thousand dollars already given, "which I fear he has spent—& as you fear, gone in debt still more." Ruffin rejected her proposal to give Charles his entire portion to pay debts; Charles must reduce spending and repay debts with an allowance. "If I had given up all to him, all would now be going, if not already gone, in the same way," he said. "Therefore, it was fortunate for him, as well as for the safety of the secured property, that I took this course." Ruffin declined to use his own capital to pay these debts; such a course would threaten his own security and dash all hope for Charles's reform.[89]

They agreed on this last need. "At 28 or 9 years old, Charles seems not to have reached the years of discretion—or to be more trustworthy for his own guidance than a boy of 16." Ruffin hoped Charles would acquire "industry & discretion," with "prospect of success" that might lead him to the western frontier, where he could triple his worth. "But this is beyond my hopes. I despair of his ever acting prudently or worthily."[90] They disagreed only on how to bring Charles to heel.

In Charles's case Ruffin made clear his assumptions about inheritance. Not only did he believe in equal portions and in distributing them before he died, but he believed in their moral function. His children did not receive their shares by virtue of being his offspring or by belonging to a family line. Portions, like a father's love, had to be earned and deserved. For that reason, Ruffin did not deny he found Charles difficult to love. "I cannot pretend that long continued misconduct & disobedience would not lessen or in extreme cases destroy, the respect & esteem, & next the love which I had felt, & trust I should equally feel for all equally deserving children." Ruffin prayed daily, he confided, asking God to bless his children and grandchildren "in health of body & of mind, in their conduct & condition."[91] Elizabeth probably had not realized before 1857 the extent to which Ruffin's portions functioned as moral levers, or instruments of reform.

They were not yet dealing with a reprobate, but Ruffin feared Charles might succumb to vice. "For it is very rare—indeed almost impossible—for the idler & spendthrift not to become also a drunkard

& a gamester." Thus far, the inheritance policy had failed. Abundance seemed to corrupt. If Charles did not reform, Ruffin would seize his capital and let him have only the interest on "safe monied stocks, yielding 6 percent." If Charles remained a "worthless idler," the income would be enough for the "comfortable & genteel support of any single man" not addicted to gambling or drink. "If this should prevent his making an imprudent & very improper marriage, (as I think it has done in one case,) it will be an additional benefit." Charles would not have enough in his pocket to gamble, drink, and marry all at once. If he failed to develop self-control, he would find himself confronting the kind of discipline imposed by insufficient funds.[92]

Ruffin had assigned $16,000 to Charles by 1860, primarily in land, slaves, and railroad stocks and dividends. In 1862 Ruffin revoked Charles's fee-simple title to the remainder of his forthcoming inheritance, creating a trust fund for this young man.[93] The device used for two daughters he now employed for a rudderless son. The issue was not gender but competence.

More was involved in Ruffin's policy toward Charles than the stock criticisms of a father. Charles's behavior did affect the welfare of Ruffin and his other children. His behavior was also being judged according to standards Ruffin defined early in his life, involving success, hard work, and self-control—all of which remained powerful ideas in Ruffin's thinking. He refused to embrace the prodigal son. In viewing the conduct of his children in terms of reform and family welfare, he left himself no ease in dealing with a wayward son or daughter.[94]

Ruffin met these threats from Beckwith, the Sayres, and Charles by consolidating ownership of Marlbourne into the hands of his two most industrious sons, Edmund and Julian. In 1859 Edmund, Jr., bought Burwell Sayre's share; in 1862 Julian bought Charles's share, and Ruffin separated his affairs from those of Charles.[95] In 1863 came the joint purchase of William Sayre's share.[96] Ruffin then withdrew to the company of his two eldest sons. Preservation of the estate, along with the death of his daughters, led him into an ever-smaller circle, isolating him increasingly from the troublesome affairs of others.

By retaining an allowance from profits on the farm, Ruffin freed himself from farming and from acting as a father in daily life to his grown children. At the same time, he created in the family an institution that would support his second career in writing and reform.

In this sense, too, the Ruffin family became a reform institution. And Ruffin relied on some members of his family to sustain his interest in agricultural reform. Edmund, Jr., read his manuscripts, provided criticism, and helped his father conduct surveys of farming in Prince George, circulating questionnaires among neighbors. Julian conducted soil tests on Ruffin's samples and explored Prince George County for layers of marl. Both sons joined Ruffin's effort to change Virginia fence laws and both aided his effort for secession. Mildred helped conduct his correspondence and, after her marriage, offered appreciation of his geological writings and teachings. Even Agnes and T. Stanly Beckwith, at the farm they named "Woodbourne," kept a library and a mineral cabinet; Agnes wrote Ruffin dutifully about Beckwith's discoveries of marl. The Ruffins were not a reform family like the Tappans, Beechers, Grimkes, or Welds, with several members taking public roles. Ruffin always was the primary reformer, with others supporting him; but without the institution of the family, he could not have had that career. He did not suffer, therefore, from the absence of institutions to sustain intellectual life. For Ruffin, the central institution for such activity in the antebellum South was his own family.

By resting his career on the family, Ruffin made himself independent (except for intrusions by Charles and Agnes). His annual allowance did provide about $1,500 between 1856 and 1862, giving him free time. There were almost no reins on his freedom, for he controlled the very institution that supported him. He freed himself from William Cobbett's dependence on a large audience of fickle readers, and he worried no longer about offending his subscribers. He freed himself from institutional restraints imposed by state agricultural societies, colleges and governments. Indeed, in the opinion of his eldest sons, he became too independent, too isolated.[97] He knew no restraints beyond those he had instilled in himself from the past. He was in command of his own fortune, his own welfare, and his own thoughts. He had achieved his antebellum dream of competency and self-reliance.

5

The Southerner as Reformer

In this, I will not pretend to restrain my pen.

EDMUND RUFFIN, 1859

One old difficulty reappeared during Edmund Ruffin's years at Marl-bourne, a difficulty of his own making: he did not like farming. Not even experimental farming held its appeal. Within four years of his arrival in Hanover County he was trying to free himself for another vocation he had wanted to devise since starting the *Farmers' Register* in 1833, a life devoted to writing and reform.[1] His change in career would alter the role of the Ruffin family, for at this point the family became the crucial institution of his intellectual career. From the family he obtained the support and freedom he needed for this new life in the Old South.

The plan to escape from Marlbourne began when Ruffin determined to find someone who would take his place as manager of the farm. Late in 1845, when he was still only fifty-one years old, he made the first attempt to lure Julian to Marlbourne as partner and manager.[2] In 1846 he dismissed the overseer and replaced him with Jem Sykes, his "most trust-worthy negro." In 1848 Ruffin astonished the neigh-bors by leaving Sykes in charge of the farm (and the threshing and delivering of wheat) while he slipped away to the springs of western Virginia for August and September. In 1850 he did it again. That same year he first announced his intention to divide the property among his children.[3] Two years later he devised the scheme to install twenty-year-old Charles as farm manager, an opportunity Charles failed to seize.[4]

Ruffin was forced to remain in charge, but he fixed his attention on writing. This change of focus had its origin in 1849, when he published his first signed essay in four years, a history of the rejuvenation of Marlbourne.[5] "The act of writing," he said, "brought back something of my old habit of & fondness for treating agricultural subjects—& the continuance was strongly invited by the extensive notice & favor with which my late publication had been received."[6] He devoted "the leisure hours of a few months" in 1851 to the first two volumes of his memoirs, filling 220 pages.[7] That year really marked his withdrawal from the farm; thereafter he passed the time writing new essays on farming and helping to found the Virginia State Agricultural Society, continuing all the while to search for a manager for Marlbourne. By the time he sat down to complete his memoirs in November 1853, his impatience had peaked. He needed relief from "labors & perplexities" that became "more onerous & disagreeable" every year. At fifty-nine he had farmed more years than he could stand, and even Marlbourne was suffering. "My attention to my work has been much withdrawn," he confessed, "until but slight & general personal attention is given to the farm operations."[8]

He declared himself retired in 1854, insisting that his children take title to the farm and responsibility for its management. "I had desired this long before, & had made vain efforts for the purpose, which were always discouraged by my children," he said. "But now I was determined." He divided the property among his heirs, submitted the division to them, and "required of them the execution."[9] The terms in which he described his departure revealed his attitude toward Marlbourne. In his new will of 1856 he continued to complain, affirming his wish to be "released from the cares & difficulties of managing my estate."[10] A few months later, in the first entry of his new diary, he expressed relief at being freed from "the harassing claims" of the farm, even though it had been several years since he had suffered any real harassment.[11]

For a man who had made his reputation through practical farming and agricultural reform, Ruffin spent remarkably few years of his life farming. His entire career—including both farming and writing—lasted from 1813 to 1862, a span of fifty years. He owned farms during two periods, between 1813 and 1839 in Prince George County, and from 1844 through 1854 in Hanover County, a total of about thirty-six years. Of these he devoted only twenty to full-time farming. At Coggin's Point he began to drift away from daily work as early as 1822, and by 1826 he was teaching himself French

and writing his first book. He devoted his total attention to Coggin's
Point for about thirteen years. To Marlbourne he committed only the
seven years between 1844 and 1851. Altogether, his career in farming
occupied fewer than half his working years and less than a third of
his lifetime, evidence of a persistent aversion.

He had in mind a different line of work. If his behavior after 1850
made this motive apparent, the diary he began to keep in 1856 made
it explicit. He began the diary to hone his style. "Writing, & especially to describe or discuss agricultural subjects, was designed to
be made one of the means of passing my time."[12] He would devote
himself first to agricultural reform, and then to another, decidedly
more dangerous, cause.[13]

Obstacles confronted anyone seeking a writing career in the antebellum South. Ruffin reflected on these obstacles in the summer of
1859, when he warned Charles Campbell, an aspiring historian from
Petersburg, not to deceive himself. He warned Campbell (whose first
book was in press in Philadelphia) that writers could not publish in
the South without losing money. "A few great publishing houses in
the northern cities have a virtual monopoly of the business, & they
only can sell a book to any profit," he said. Later that summer he
noted that books "written for pay & support of the writer" had
appeared only in the North. "Writing for gain is a business not yet
begun in the southern states."[14] Ruffin had discovered these obstacles
in the 1830s through editing and publishing the *Farmers' Register* and
producing the first edition of his *Essay on Calcareous Manures*. In the
kind of writing he now proposed to do and in his arrangements to
support himself, Ruffin apparently calculated that he could surmount
all the difficulties.

The Role of the Ruffin Family

The family provided nearly everything Ruffin needed to sustain his
new public venture. Since he could pay for necessities with dividends
from his share of family investments, he did not have to use his pen
actually to support himself. Food, rooms, clothing—the necessities
of material existence—came from his "reserved fund." All he needed
initially were specific resources for research, a quiet place for study,
and absolute control over time. He found these necessities of intellectual life at home.

Since Edmund Ruffin did not write purely polemical or imaginative works, the nature of his subjects usually required him to do research. This he performed by either consulting sources in a library, conducting experiments in the field, or traveling to specific sites throughout Virginia and the South where he could collect samples of rock and soil or inspect the farms of other experimenters. The family made all of this possible.

The Ruffin family maintained two large libraries between 1850 and 1862, one at Marlbourne and one at Beechwood (the latter belonging to Edmund, Jr.). No inventory of their libraries survived the Civil War, but Ruffin estimated in 1862 that together they had "some thousands of volumes & valuable pamphlets." His diary preserved a record of his daily reading and indicated what the family libraries contained. Between January 1857 and December 1860 he mentioned 195 books and other publications in these libraries, most of them new purchases. He was acquiring about thirty-eight new titles a year for his own collection, almost one a week.[15] A letter written by a Union soldier during the occupation of Beechwood in 1862 revealed the nature of the Ruffin library, which at that point represented a combination of the two collections. "His library was very large and valuable, mostly of agricultural works, but containing a great number of scientific and classical books," the soldier wrote. "Thousands of books were carried off by our men."[16] The Ruffins also subscribed to a wide range of British and American periodicals, including *Harper's* and *De Bow's Review*, as well as newspapers from Richmond, Charleston, New Orleans, Washington, and New York. In May 1860 Ruffin said they subscribed to so many newspapers at Beechwood that it took him "from 6 to 10 hours to look through all the papers brought by each tri-weekly mail."[17] He preserved as part of this collection all of his manuscript farm journals, consulting them whenever he prepared essays on agricultural reform. These libraries provided a crucial resource that permitted Ruffin to perform intellectual work at home, in the country.[18]

At home, too, he conducted experiments that provided subjects for most of his reform writing between 1849 and 1855. In his own fields he experimented with clover, corn harvesting, and drainage— subjects he addressed at length in those years, using the manuscript journals in which he had recorded observations since 1813. In 1857 he determined to write for the Virginia State Agricultural Society an account of the drainage system at Marlbourne as a guide for other

Tidewater farmers. To prepare this memoir he and Charles gathered their instruments and during the first week of May left the house each day to map the farm, conducting an engineer's survey of its slopes, ditches, and fields.[19] The farms themselves provided material for his new career.

Income from his family funds provided secure resources to pay for travel, permitting him to gather evidence and begin speaking on agricultural reform. Like reformers in the North, he became an itinerant advocate between 1850 and 1862, traveling by carriage, steamboat, and railroad into regions of the South he had not seen, venturing west beyond Atlanta for the first time in 1858. The proportion of his time devoted to travel would increase, reflecting not so much his leisure as his increasing engagement in Southern reform causes. In 1857 he spent 38 percent of the year away from home; in 1858, 45 percent; in 1859, 36 percent; in 1860, 50 percent; and in 1861, 56 percent. Between 1857 and 1862 he made six trips to Charleston and South Carolina, passed eight times through North Carolina, and appeared twice in Florida and Georgia. He made two long journeys to the new Southwest—in 1858 to Alabama (where he first saw a prairie) and in 1860 to Tennessee and Kentucky.

In North Carolina he gathered materials for his first articles and a later book on swampland.[20] In Florida and Alabama he took soil samples in order to analyze the content of calcareous earth; in South Carolina and North Carolina he inspected farming practices and new machines, and surveyed land for agricultural resources. He addressed farmers' meetings and led discussions on practical subjects throughout Virginia and North Carolina. He assumed the role of a traveling reformer, and focused on agriculture until the summer of 1858, when, after attending a convention at Montgomery, his attention shifted irresistibly to secession. These journeys across the South provided Ruffin with the kind of inspiration he had found when he was editing the *Farmers' Register* and riding through rural Virginia. His travels provided him with evidence and suggested schemes for reconstructing rural society throughout the seaboard South.

How Ruffin Worked

Ruffin did most of his writing at home.[21] Gradually, beginning in 1850, he gained control over his daily work routines until he could

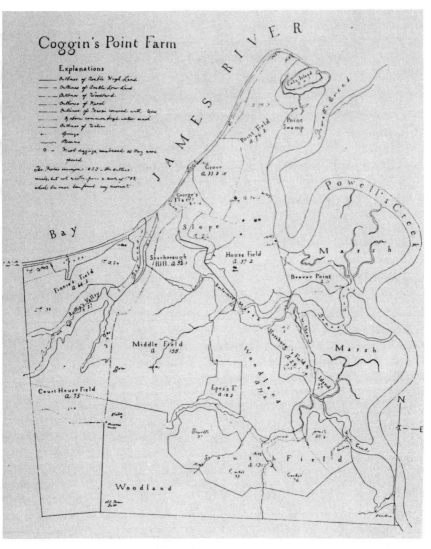

Ruffin's Survey of Coggin's Point Farm, 1823 The two small, frame houses in which Ruffin began his married life in 1813 appear as blocks above the label for House Field, west of Powell's Creek. Beechwood was built near the river bluff in Finnie's Field, west of the small stream entering Tar Bay. The first marl pit is identified below the label for Middle Field. *(Copy of survey courtesy of James S. Gilliam)*

Shellbanks Shellbanks, three miles south of Coggin's Point, was the second farm Ruffin owned. Here, in 1833, he began editing the *Farmers' Register*. He bought the farm in 1828 and made it his permanent home between 1831 and 1835, when he moved to Petersburg. (*Virginia State Library and Archives*)

Marlbourne The finest house Ruffin ever owned, Marlbourne stands on the southern rim of the Pamunkey River Valley in Hanover County. The house was new when he moved his family here from Petersburg early in 1844.

Surviving Drainage Ditch at Marlbourne, 1988 Slaves dug this open ditch between 1845 and 1851 according to Ruffin's design. Drainage of low ground in the Pamunkey River Valley was a crucial project in the reclamation of Marlbourne.

Cottage and House at Beechwood When the Civil War began, Ruffin had a room for himself and his library in the cottage (*left*), built by Edmund Ruffin, Jr., about 1839. Edmund, Jr.'s family lived in Beechwood House (*right*), completed in 1849. Immediately behind the house and to the right is the bluff leading down to the James River.

Evergreen Ruffin's childhood home was the largest house in which he ever resided. It was built by his father some time between 1795 and 1808.

Ruffin and Four of His Children Julian (*left*), Ella, Charles, and Mildred posed with their father for this family portrait in about 1851. (*Virginia Historical Society*)

Ruffin in Charleston   Ruffin became a favorite subject for photographers at the start of the Civil War. Quinby of Charleston circulated this portrait, taken probably in December 1860. *(Southern Historical Collection, Library of the University of North Carolina at Chapel Hill)*

Redmoor   Ruffin committed suicide in the room to the right of the porch on the main floor. (*Virginia State Library and Archives*)

Family Burial Plot at Marlbourne   In the valley below the plot are the Marlbourne low grounds. The line of trees behind the barn roof (*center*) marks the course of the main drainage ditch. Ruffin's grave is second from the right.

determine absolutely the way he passed the time. He must have spent half the year 1850 preparing essays on clover, corn-fodder, wheat harvesting, marl digging, and draining. In 1851 he devoted at least three months to writing the first two volumes of his memoirs; that same year he wrote two long communications to the Virginia State Agricultural Society and completed an enlarged edition of the *Essay on Calcareous Manures*. The number of his publications in these two years indicates that this was the point at which he ceased to be a farmer. He really had no duties other than self-imposed intellectual tasks after 1854, when Julian and Lottie arrived at Marlbourne to manage the farm, to be followed shortly by William Sayre at the end of 1856.[22] Even before these replacements arrived, Ruffin could write at home because there were others to work in the fields and care for the house. After 1856 he was seldom distracted by domestic duties, though he did run small errands in connection with his own work, as in September of 1857, when he went to Richmond to consult with the secretary of the Agricultural Society and then took time to confer with millers about his son-in-law's wheat crop. At Marlbourne he could withdraw to the large library on the west end of the house, or to his room upstairs, and command his own time.

Often he worked all day on drafts of essays and correspondence, or on research and reading. Hours in seclusion at the writing desk or with books and papers became part of his daily life and led to his productivity.[23] Though routines might vary wildly when he was traveling (rising hours before dawn to board a train or coach), at home he maintained a regime of regular self-discipline.[24] Usually he rose by 7:00 a.m., had breakfast, and then withdrew to work until the afternoon. After the main meal at midday he would return to his desk until the evening meal. After conversation with the family he would withdraw to his room at about nine and go to bed by eleven.

Before writing he might spend weeks or months assembling evidence.[25] There was, therefore, a cyclical pattern to his intellectual activity, and there were long periods when he had not yet assembled the evidence or formed the opinions that would draw him to his writing desk. In those periods, after 1856, he used his diary to stay in practice. When starting to write he would compose a first draft and, when finished, copy it in a clearer hand, revising its expression. He revised almost everything he wrote—he would begin to rewrite long pieces before completing the first draft.[26] Thus he labored toward a comprehensible, expository prose, thickened always with the parenthetical insertions he considered his worst writing flaw, but which he never could resist.[27]

He wrote for hours at a stretch. "When so employed, I can with pleasure write rapidly for 12 or more hours in the day & night—& until it is necessary to rest my cramped right hand."[28] On 25 September 1858 he worked all day on an article concerning the American Colonization Society, producing sixteen manuscript pages, tiring "before sunset." The next day, a Sunday, he again wrote all day and produced twenty pages more.[29] Diary entries for March 1857 recorded his progress on an essay about the lowlands between Albemarle Sound and Chesapeake Bay, the research for which he had completed in 1856 with a field visit: here was the record of a working month, most of it passed at Marlbourne. He was writing from field notes gathered in the Dismal Swamp of Virginia and North Carolina. During the morning of 2 March (a Monday), he copied into final form seven pages from an early, partial draft of the essay. At 12:30 p.m. he stopped and went to dinner at a neighbor's farm. By 5 March (Thursday), he finished copying and revising the whole essay, now forty-two pages long. On 17 March—despite a heavy cold—he was still engaged in a routine of rising early for breakfast, taking a walk, then writing until 2:00 p.m., continuing to copy and correct this work. He declared it finished on 20 March, entering his production as forty-three pages, "ready for the press." On the twenty-first he experienced what would become a recurring depression after finishing long pieces: "Am at a loss what next to prepare, from my rough drafts—& did nothing."[30]

This had become his only work, and he always was working. He worked on Sundays and holidays, and during vacations.[31] The pleasure of trips to Richmond lay in conducting the business of the Agricultural Society, buying books, and gathering evidence at the Virginia State Library. Visits with his kinsman Thomas Ruffin in North Carolina were never mere vacations: each of these two Ruffins continued to work through the weeks of their visits in Alamance County, halting labor only at mealtime and in the early evening for family conversation.[32] Ruffin's annual vacations in July and August at Old Point Comfort (across from Norfolk on Chesapeake Bay) or in August and September at the Virginia springs, were times of tedium. He carried books to the hotel at Old Point Comfort, and he suffered if he ran out of work or could not strike up profitable conversation. "This place is especially tiresome after dark," he complained in 1860, "to those who, like myself, do not dance, or drink, or play cards."[33] In July 1860, when he stayed nineteen days at Beechwood, he devoted at least twelve of them completely to intellectual work. On 21 July he wrote all day, copying and revising the text of his already-published pamphlet, *African Colonization Unveiled*, and producing twenty-two pages. "Did not finish until after dark," he wrote. There were moments of idyllic rest that month, pleasures apparently permitted when work was in progress; but work was never far away. On 19 July 1860 he sat "some hours" in the woods at Beechwood, where Edmund, Jr., found him at 1:00 p.m., napping on the river bank, a copy of *De Bow's Review* at hand.[34] This retired slaveholder worked as hard as any Yankee, and he measured his progress by the page.

After moving to Marlbourne in 1844 Ruffin produced almost nothing for a public audience until 1850.[35] In 1844 he completed a short supplement to his survey of South Carolina agriculture and in 1845 he wrote one short article on putrescent manures.[36] Nothing more appeared under his name until the 1849 history of Marlbourne.[37] At this point a change occurred. The essay on Marlbourne marked the start of a decade that approached his years at the *Farmers' Register* in productivity. A five-part essay on draining appeared in 1850 in the *American Farmer*, followed immediately by five long articles on other innovations at Marlbourne and two petitions to the legislature.[38] His productivity continued until the early years of the Civil War, when events would force him into his final seclusion.

For an author whose writing required research, Ruffin's publications appeared at a fairly regular pace, though there were peaks and valleys. In 1856 he credited himself with 170 pages, not counting a report for the Agricultural Society and "argumentative" newspaper pieces "published anonymously."[39] In the single month of March 1857 he copied, revised, or wrote a total of 198 pages, including essays on peat bogs, the agricultural features of lands bordering Albemarle Sound and Chesapeake Bay, the reefs and landlocked waters of North Carolina, swamps, and the pine trees of lower Virginia and North Carolina.[40] At least one other peak of production came in early 1860, when, shortly after his sixty-sixth birthday, he attempted his only work in a semi-fictional genre, *Anticipations of the Future*.[41] He began *Anticipations* at Beechwood on 29 February, writing seven pages that day. Through March and April he consulted maps and an occasional reference book, but he wrote primarily from imagination, delighted by the ease of composing without evidence. By 20 April he had completed 230 pages and was adding as many as fifteen a day. He finished on the first of May, two months after starting a book that contained nearly 350 printed pages of new material, demonstrating that he had found a setting in which he could devote himself to this task with unbridled freedom.[42]

The Ruffin Reforms

Ruffin returned to public life with schemes in mind for new institutions and new ways of organizing rural society. Some of his schemes resembled those of Northern benevolent societies. Taken together, they indicated that by 1850 Ruffin had begun to think about a "reconstruction" of the Atlantic seaboard of the South even before the Civil War, one based upon the institution of slavery.

The pace of his reform activity quickened after the appearance of his 1849 Marlbourne essay; the first signs were his rapid publication of essays on practical farming. In November 1850, at a fair in Easton, Maryland, he delivered his first public address in seven years, on agricultural reform.[43] A year later he delivered a similar speech in Macon, Georgia, followed by others in Charleston and Richmond in 1852, and another in Richmond in 1853.[44]

Reforms Ruffin proposed revealed the scope of his imagination and ambition. He wanted nothing less than to alter institutions and rejuvenate agriculture throughout the entire southeastern United States. He assumed quite consciously that without this rejuvenation, Virginia, Maryland, North Carolina, and South Carolina would soon confront a Malthusian crisis, with a growing slave population consuming a declining supply of food, leading in turn to an exodus by whites and the end of slavery. He assumed that the power to stave off that crisis lay in state governments, to which he assigned new tasks. He did not intend to do away with slavery, nor did he envision a pre-capitalist, pre-bureaucratic South. Nor did he fail effect everything he imagined.

By the time he delivered his 1850 Easton address, Ruffin had devised a scheme to organize Southern farmers so that reformers could instruct them in scientific agriculture and help them increase food production. Farmers' clubs like those in Britain would be formed, through the agency of a state agricultural commissioner; these clubs would diffuse new research and permit farmers to learn "knowledge already possessed by scattered individuals." State commissioners, heading small bureaus, would survey changes in farming and issue reports. Agricultural fairs would exhibit inventions and farming innovations. States would establish agricultural professorships at universities and publish the results of research. They would also operate farms that would become centers for experiments, making "trials of new or doubtful manures, implements, particular methods or processes in farming," to "test their respective merits."[45] These schemes all anticipated a shift of power from individuals and local communities to the state.[46]

The most ambitious expression of Ruffin's reform imagination came in his 1852 address in Charleston, where he proposed to reconstruct rural South Carolina on a scale approaching the reclamation of Holland from the sea, or of the "worthless and pestilential swamps" along "the celebrated borders of the Po." The entire seaboard river system of the state would be dredged and controlled with levees and dams. A new system of canals would connect these rivers, creating a vast system of drainage to reclaim marshes for agriculture; the canals would do away with malaria and bilious diseases and create a transportation system to carry farm products to world markets and to bring fertilizers (in the form of lime and marl) to reclaimed fields. The state, through "wise legislation," would create the legal setting in which this reclamation would advance, taking as a model the South Carolina agricultural survey of 1843 in which Ruffin himself had located deposits of marl. What he proposed in Charleston in 1852 he assumed to be possible also for eastern North Carolina, Virginia, and Maryland.[47] Reclamation would revive agriculture and preserve the value of farmlands in the Southeast, enabling the region to feed a growing population and stem the tide of emigration to the West.[48] This reclamation would require vast amounts of labor—demanding the preservation of slavery.

Promoting these reforms made Ruffin a prominent figure once again and brought him back into the company of the farming elite. In 1852 he played a crucial role in founding a new institution, the Virginia State Agricultural Society. He became its first president that year and returned as president in 1857, 1858, and 1859. In 1854 he became the Society's first agricultural commissioner, and throughout the decade he sat on its executive committee.[49] He positioned himself thereby at a new center of power.

During his first term as president, his concept dominated the Society's first fair in November 1853. The mere scale of the event made obvious its dramatic potential as an agent of change, creating a huge new audience for agricultural reform. Twenty thousand fair-goers, including General Winfield Scott and former President John Tyler, crowded Richmond on the first public day. Such a "concourse," Ruffin said, "was never seen, nor imagined." Comparable crowds arrived on each of the succeeding two days. "And every night the Metropolitan Hall was packed full of people, who remained in session & discussion to 10 or 11 o'clock, with untiring attention."[50] Ruffin perceived the significance of the crowds.

Some of his work for the Society harked back to the days of his rural rides for the *Farmers' Register*. In 1854, as agricultural commissioner, he traveled through Prince George, Gloucester, Nottoway, Amelia, Powhatan, Prince Edward, Cumberland, Mont-gomery, and Pulaski counties, visiting ninety farmers and gathering minutes of "agricultural facts and observations," all of which the Society published. He collected testimony on distemper in cattle, on hillside terraces, on the condition of emancipated blacks. The only official duty he deliberately neglected was soliciting donations and new memberships, a task William H. Richardson had performed admirably in 1853.[51] In seeking out farmers under auspices of the Society, Ruffin had begun to act as its traveling agent, exactly in the manner of agents for benevolent societies in the North.

He even began to deliver speeches; this was a task he dreaded at first, apologizing for awkwardness, suffering from the shyness he had felt as a young man. The six speeches he delivered between 1850 and 1855 dealt primarily with agricultural reform. Between 1856 and 1859 he also began to lead informal discussions with farmers, a form of meeting in which he learned to speak extemporaneously. In July 1859, while passing through New Bern, North Carolina, he was pressed to conduct a "farmer's talk." Ruffin's own remarks (before fifty to sixty people) concerned draining. "I had a blackboard, & drew diagrams thereon to illustrate my views." He apparently talked with-out notes. "After speaking an hour, & forgetting perhaps half of all the points I had intended to present, I closed." The assembly did not disperse, "& another hour was spent in my answering questions which some of the most intelligent farmers asked, in further expla-nation of draining, or other connected subjects of improvement."[52]

By the time he appeared in New Bern, Ruffin had become a speaker crowds wanted to hear.

In Richmond he became a tireless petitioner. His petitions, reports, and drafts of proposed legislation appeared on desks in the capitol, at city council, and in the office of the Agricultural Society. He wanted to reform Virginia by law, and the terms in which he expressed that desire disclosed his image of the existing order. State laws requiring inspection of wheat flour he ridiculed as "remnants" of the Dark Ages. They restrained "the law of free competition." While he failed to win the Agricultural Society to this view in 1854, he did convince the city council in 1857.[53] He had influence.

Virginia reformed its fence law in 1858 according to a scheme he put forth. Ruffin's proposal called for fencing animals (particularly hogs) within enclosures, thereby preserving a ban on an ancient custom of open grazing. He knew the prohibition against grazing worked against the very poorest farmers, who needed to let their animals forage; these people he did not try to help.[54] Instead, his concern focused on the fear that the existing law would lead to great accumulations of land by wealthy farmers, who alone could afford the timber for boundary fences around their farms. He therefore lobbied for a system of common, or "ring," fences. The legislature adopted this idea. In Prince George, farms in a large section of the county were no longer required to be fenced individually, but were defined as one unit, "severally under common & single surrounding fences."[55] When he learned the proposal had become law, Ruffin knew he had put his imprint on the landscape. "This will be the commencement of a reform & revolution in this heretofore fixed policy of Va, & which, by other means, I have been laboring to produce, for 20 years."[56]

On the eve of the Civil War, Ruffin was still working on laws, noting with pride that his proposals to alter the status of blacks—admitting their evidence in courts (when their testimony obviously could be crucial to the state), enslaving or banishing free blacks from the state, restricting the hiring of slaves in towns, banning manumission in wills, and banning entry of free blacks on northern vessels—had been referred to committees of the legislature.[57] This influence, this access to power, would never have come to Ruffin had he remained on the farm.

Intellectual Life in Southern Cities

At the midpoint of his second intellectual career, late in 1856, a change appeared in Ruffin's routines. After William Sayre moved to Marlbourne and became its full-time manager, Ruffin began to travel more frequently and extensively through the South. The change began as early as 1851, when he went to Macon, Georgia, taking his first trip beyond Virginia in seven years. (On his return through Charleston he submitted a letter to the *Mercury* about tensions between the North and South.)[58] Another trip to Charleston came in 1852, when he addressed the South Carolina Institute on the subject of manures and reminisced about his work there in 1843.[59] From Marlbourne it had always been easy to ride the sixteen miles into Richmond for short periods. After 1856, however, he spent longer periods away from home, in Washington, Charleston, and Richmond. At about this time, too, the character of his work changed. He widened his interests beyond agricultural reform and began to address issues of slavery, secession, and race. As this shift occurred, he would spend less time gathering evidence in the field or in libraries, and more of his time talking. In these years and in these cities, the opportunities for talk were endless.

After Marlbourne and Beechwood (where he still did the bulk of his writing), the most important settings for his reform career became these three Southern cities—Washington, Charleston, and Richmond—each a center of the growing controversy over secession. Never did Ruffin find in the antebellum South an institution that provided so much material support for intellectual work as his own family.[60] In these three cities, however, he did find crucial institutions of intellectual life, where could he inspect document collections, purchase new books, publish his work, and conduct the business of agricultural reform. Each city provided social circles and places where he could meet thinkers and men of power, and where his speculations drifted effortlessly from practical farming to the politics of slavery.

The importance of Washington, Charleston, and Richmond for Ruffin emerged in the frequency of his visits to them after 1857. In that year he made what may have been his first trip to Washington since 1827, staying eleven days.[61] In the next four years he made six more sojourns there, all of them lasting between one and two weeks.[62] Charleston he visited ten times between 1851 and 1861, the longest stay of fifty-one days coming in the secession spring of 1861.[63] Richmond became his second home. He made seventeen extended stays there between 1857 and 1862; in October 1861 he leased a room in a house on Clay Street near the state capitol, calling it his "temporary home."[64]

Richmond, with nearly forty thousand people in 1860, assumed particular significance for Ruffin's work. There he devised a career like that of Benjamin Franklin in eighteenth-century Philadelphia, inventing institutions and conducting his affairs in places of public business.[65] In antebellum Richmond, Ruffin created the life of a nineteenth-century *philosophe*. His days in the city were not filled with abstract theorizing, tending as he did to practical matters, but Ruffin did not feel that he lacked support or important things to do in the capital of Virginia; it was a place of excitement and stimulation where he went to work.

In Richmond he stopped regularly at the office of the Agricultural Society, as he did on 23 October 1857, when he arrived in town with daughters Mildred and Elizabeth and with William Sayre.[66] The Society office became a place of socializing; there he would meet with officers from around the state and discuss the fair (and its gate receipts), fencing laws, the agricultural professorship, and farming.[67] Quite apart from the fair, the rise of the Agricultural Society itself changed the institutional setting of the city. Its *Journal of Transactions*, annual reports, and official communications provided a means to publish even the most technical, applied writings.[68] Between fairs, the Society's office was a significant center of reform activity.

Richmond provided an array of publishing houses and newspapers that offered options in publishing his work. There were four major political newspapers, and the *Southern Literary Messenger* and the *Southern Planter* were published in the city (the latter sharing its office with P. D. Bernard, who printed works for the Society). Among the eight booksellers and publishers was J. W. Randolph, Ruffin's favorite.[69] Ruffin frequented the shops of printers and engravers, overseeing jobs for the Society as well his own work. He visited a printer on 6 November 1857, correcting engraver's errors on maps of Marlbourne (for his forthcoming essay on drainage of the farm) and giving directions about Society publications.[70]

Along with a publishing house, J. W. Randolph operated a bookstore on Main Street, where Ruffin became a subscriber to the lending library and where he could read the newspapers. Nearby was the Library and Reading Room Association, where he also found new books and newspapers.[71] For serious research he worked in the Virginia State Library and the state auditor's office; here he found manuscript records for essays on land values, population, and free blacks.[72] In the capitol itself there were debates in the legislature. The city provided rich resources for research and engagement in questions of state policy.

Finally, there were the hotels and restaurants. Except during a period in 1861 and 1862, when he lived in the rooming house, Ruffin nearly always stayed at the Exchange Hotel, one block from the southeast corner of the capitol square, at the center of the district containing the city's hotels, newspapers, banks, telegraph office, and train stations. Hotels became places to find morning papers, meet friends, and talk. "As usual here," he wrote in January 1860, "much of the day consumed in reading newspapers & chatting with acquaintances (mostly members of the legislature) in the public halls."[73] Like the Agricultural Society and the libraries, these places of socializing were important, given Ruffin's decision about the last stage of his working life. "I am anxious to keep employed," he wrote in 1859, "& writing is my only employment."[74] Richmond would sustain that employment through the end of 1862.

Washington and Charleston were exciting cities in 1857, when Ruffin began to make frequent trips beyond Richmond. He went to these two cities primarily for amusement, not business. He stayed at the famous hotels, at Brown's in Washington and at the Charleston (though on his third trip to Washington he moved to a boarding house).[75] In Washington he studied at the Library of Congress, attended debates in the House and Senate, and observed meetings of the Colonization Society. He passed most of his time meeting influential Southerners; James D. B. De Bow agreed to publish some speculative essays on agriculture and one piece on secession.[76] In Charleston he inspected the new water supply and drainage system (which demonstrated the truth of his theories about Marlbourne), and attended Lutheran and Jewish religious services. In Charleston, too, he met radical southerners; editors John Heart and Robert Barnwell Rhett, Jr., sought Ruffin's most outspoken pieces on secession for their *Charleston Mercury*.[77] As in Richmond, he enjoyed the incessant talk.

Conversation became Ruffin's greatest pleasure, and a useful one, too. He relished practical talk. He was not a sophisticated social theorist. Most of what he knew about social and economic thought he acquired early in life from T. R. Malthus and Adam Smith, and most of his notions about slavery before 1850 derived from Thomas R. Dew. He especially liked to read agricultural memoirs, "descriptive and narrative of actual labors, & their effects." His own gifts lay in this kind of description, and these were the subjects he most liked to discuss with friends in Richmond.[78] He relished meetings of the Agricultural Society and its executive committee, like the one on the night of 29 April 1857, when they disposed of Society business and then held "a meeting for agricultural conversation & discussion—& next in social conversation to 11."[79] In July of that year Ruffin took a tour as Society president to Albemarle and Orange counties, where he met with farmers' clubs of the two counties for practical talk. "An interesting discussion was held on the preparation for & seeding of the wheat crop," he reported. "When called on, I described the construction & operation of my pegged roller—which was the only new information I had to offer that could be advantageous here." The session lasted into the late afternoon, and some remained through the night.[80] During the state fair in October 1857, Ruffin presided for two nights over a discussion in which at least fifteen men narrated their experiences in growing wheat: Ruffin gave a history of his own wheat farming, beginning with his decision in 1821 or 1822 to cut wheat in the "dough state," which could be determined by mashing grains "between the finger and thumb without producing milk." Ruffin later remembered discussing the subject for three nights, "until 11 o'clock, without being exhausted, or the interest of the attendants flagging."[81] Here he found eager listeners.

The Problem of Audience: Writing for Oneself

Neither in Southern cities nor in the rural South after 1850 did Ruffin find a reading audience to support his career as a writer. Unlike William Cobbett in England, with his permanent readership of fifty thousand, Ruffin did not generate a large following who would pay to read his work. In fact he found it difficult to give away his later writings. When he explained to Charles Campbell in 1859 that it was difficult for Southern writers to make a living, he was speaking from experience. This difficulty did not stop him from writing, for he found agencies other than Northern publishing houses to publish

and circulate his work. The difficulty lay elsewhere, in the consequence of writing in isolation. He did not find himself in dialogue
with critical minds.

This difficulty had begun to bother Ruffin by 1857, even though
he had won wide attention between 1849 and 1852 with his earlier
essays on practical farming. By 1857, when he undertook an essay
on the draining of Marlbourne, he was depressed at the thought that
"the public would treat this with even more neglect than I have been
accustomed to have shown to my publications, so as to subject me
to mortification of my pride, as well as pecuniary loss."[82] At the end
of that year he noted he had finished some work on pines that filled
214 pages, "if there was any demand for them—which there is not."[83]
In April 1858, momentarily without a book to read, he began to
examine some of his own unpublished manuscripts, "which produc-
tions it seems will not soon (if ever) have any other reader."[84] He
sensed that he was writing for himself.

His audience after 1850 resembled in some ways the one he had
written for twenty years earlier. That early audience, too, was small.
In 1832 his publisher issued only 750 copies of the first edition of
the *Essay on Calcareous Manures*. (The manuscript had lain in a drawer
for six years, having been criticized only by Thomas Cocke.)[85] The
second edition of the *Essay*, appearing as a supplement to the *Farmers'
Register*, reached no more than fifteen hundred readers. The *Register*
audience was equally small, beginning in 1833–34 with thirteen
hundred subscribers, moving toward fourteen hundred in 1835, and
then falling below one thousand by 1843.[86] There was just one difference: at the *Register* Ruffin did create a group of regular readers he
knew well and who responded—often critically—to what he produced, both in their farming and in their communications to him as
an editor. After 1850, however, he found it difficult to recreate this
relationship with his readers. His audience was disappearing.

Circulation of Ruffin's articles and books fluctuated wildly. He
placed five articles in *De Bow's Review* between 1857 and 1860, and
De Bow paid him for a series on abolition in 1857, but Ruffin valued
the journal less for the money than for its wide circulation.[87] Ruffin's
pamphlet *The Political Economy of Slavery* (1858) was printed in an
edition of five thousand; and his pamphlet attacking the American
Colonization Society, *African Colonization Unveiled* (1859), probably
had a pressrun of the same size.[88] These numbers seemed feeble
compared to those cited for the cheap edition of Hinton Helper's *The*

Impending Crisis (1857), which, Ruffin noted, was "exhausted" after a publication of 100,000 copies.[89] He could not command such numbers.

Twice between 1850 and 1860 Ruffin's work did reach audiences of this scale. His Charleston lecture on Southern agriculture (seventeen pages assailing "northern aggressions") was republished—to his astonishment—in the U. S. Patent Office report for 1853, with "more than 100,000 copies printed & bound at government expense, for gratuitous distribution throughout all the land."[90] His 1859 article, "Slavery and Free Labor Defined and Compared," reached twenty thousand new readers when it appeared in the *New York Weekly Day Book*, edited by John H. Van Evrie, a proslavery northerner.[91] Yet neither essay signaled success in creating the kind of audience Harriet Beecher Stowe or Hinton Helper had gathered—a large readership with a continuing demand for their work. The pieces in the Patent Office report and the New York paper saw print only through the personal influence of De Bow and Van Evrie, who acted as Ruffin's patrons. These publications did not gather a group of readers he could expect to address with each new work.

The problem was never solved. When Ruffin settled his accounts in Richmond with J. W. Randolph in 1862, the evidence showed clearly that he had failed to find readers. In three years (1859, 1860, and 1861) Randolph had sold almost nothing by Ruffin: the fifth edition of the *Essay on Calcareous Manures* (1852), twenty copies; *Essays and Notes on Agriculture* (1855), thirty-one copies; *Anticipations of the Future* (1860), a few more than four hundred copies, "issued in sales & gifts." Even his four pamphlets on slavery and colonization cannot have sold more than a thousand copies altogether. His net income after deducting his own purchases was seventy-five dollars.[92]

This indeed was failure. When he stopped at Randolph's office in October 1860 he discovered exactly how small was the demand for *Anticipations of the Future*—"much less than I should have supposed that curiosity would have induced." One thousand copies had been printed, and Ruffin had paid $113.04 to cover his share of the production cost.[93] There were few readers and no reviews until 1861—in New York. "It is to me a mortifying truth, that, instead of being thus welcomed, my book has been scarcely noticed, & its very existence seems to be ignored by the public, even in the more southern states, where, if no where else, I expected notice & approval."[94]

These difficulties in the market of the antebellum South forced

Ruffin to resort to irregular, antiquated arrangements for publishing, always in the hope that he could catch the public eye. Between 1850 and 1855 he had found a demand for essays on practical farming in the *American Farmer* and the *Southern Planter*. His speculative pieces in the middle of the decade found their way into *De Bow's Review*, and his polemical pieces appeared in newspapers. The real difficulties had begun after 1855, particularly when he attempted to publish long pamphlets and book-length manuscripts. He turned to friends and agencies in federal and state governments, who began to act as his patrons. In this way he published *The Political Economy of Slavery* in 1858; half of its pressrun of five thousand was subscribed by Southern congressmen, half by himself. His pamphlet on colonization was published through the same arrangements in 1859. Ruffin oversaw the printing of these works himself. He distributed them in part through the mail (addressing them himself), using the franking privileges of Senator James M. Mason and Congressmen William O. Goode and Thomas Ruffin. He also acted as his own distributor; in 1860 he left for the springs with his "usual travelling supply of pamphlets (for gratuitous distribution abroad)."[95]

State governments and agencies also were useful. He relied on the State Agricultural Society between 1853 and 1857 to publish six of his most scholarly essays on agricultural reform in its *Journal of Transactions*. His final book, *Agricultural, Geological, and Descriptive Sketches of Lower North Carolina* (1861), was published by the state of North Carolina through the influence of Governor John W. Ellis and Judge Thomas Ruffin. In Ruffin's view, this was "government bounty."[96] In relying on subvention, Ruffin must have known he was doomed to a circulation of a few hundred. He noted with envy in 1860 that C. G. Memminger's address on secession was the largest publishing project ever undertaken by the state of Virginia; it reached ten thousand copies, "a number larger by 6000, than any document ever before."[97] Yet this did not deter him.

Even the disgraceful prospect of publishing his own work did not deter him. The terms under which Randolph agreed to publish *Anticipations of the Future* required Ruffin to pay for two-thirds of the cost. In return Randolph agreed to keep only one-third of the receipts.[98] There were precedents for this in Ruffin's recent career; he had paid for half the costs of his slavery and colonization pamphlets, and he paid for all two thousand copies of the pamphlet version of his article on free blacks, published first in the *Southern Planter*. These arrangements were not those of an author writing to meet demand. In fact, Ruffin sustained his writing career through money from his reserved fund, the income from Marlbourne. His real patron in this last stage of his career, therefore, was the Ruffin family.

Certain consequences followed from this manner of publishing, eventually leading Ruffin to withdraw from public writing altogether. "Last winter," he wrote in 1861, "I determined to write & publish nothing more—or to be known as mine—under the mortifying belief that my writings neither attracted attention of or benefit to the public, nor added anything to my own reputation or appreciation."[99] Until he withdrew, however, there were other consequences. For one thing, he began to write primarily with the intention of influencing politicians in Washington and Richmond and a few wealthy personages at the springs. His tone became polemical, rather than expository. He became less concerned with evidence than with pleasing the powerful; he delighted in seeing his Liberia pamphlet on the desks of congressmen in 1859, just before a debate on funds for the Colonization Society. He was chagrined at first to observe those congressmen neglecting the pamphlet, then relieved to hear his phrases in their speeches.[100]

Then, as he grew less concerned about reaching beyond a few hundred men, he became reckless. When he composed his virulent essay on reforming laws governing free blacks he made a vow: "In this, I will not pretend to restrain my pen, nor to attempt to be correct in plan or expression—as is more or less the case usually in my writing, designed for publication."[101] He began to throw thoughts on paper without concern for what a critical reader might think; an author who could pay his own publishing bills or had wealthy patrons was immune to criticism. And there was one other consequence. Before the final confirmation came that he had lost his readers, Ruffin would find himself in demand by an alternative audience. All through the South after 1856 crowds would demand to hear him speak. In this new setting the normal demands of critical judgment ceased to exist. From those restraints, too, he felt totally free.

6
Secession and Slavery

We soon got upon the all-absorbing topic.

EDMUND RUFFIN, 1860

Ruffin freed himself at a time coinciding with the rise in the South of a new cause. True enough, he had intended to address agricultural reform. "I had however in design another writing," he admitted in 1856, "requiring much deliberation & unusual care." This writing would deal with another cause he began to consider as early as 1850: the movement for secession. During an 1855 vacation at the Virginia springs he aired his opinion "that the slave-holding states should speedily separate from the others, & form a separate confederacy" in order to save slavery. He felt a "zeal" to publish these views. "But I wished to be a worthy & efficient advocate of the cause—& for its sake, & my own reputation, not to appear to disadvantage as a writer."[1] In the beginning, then, there was more than just the changing of careers and more than just coincidence. He was not drawn down this path unwittingly or against his will. As he prepared for a life given totally to writing and reform, he had this motive of supporting the secessionist cause. His deed would have consequences for members of the family, who found their lives entangled now in public causes. In taking this course, Ruffin led his family into the bramble bush.

The two movements of agricultural reform and secession intertwined. Secession became for him the great reform cause of the antebellum South, a catastrophic success, attracting him irresistibly. The record he left of his involvement with secession revealed what it did to his thinking, particularly on slavery. He also left clues about why this one white man resisted the appeals of antislavery and why, late in his life, he hardened his heart on the question of race.

The timing of Ruffin's commitment to secession revealed how

closely he linked the rejuvenation of the rural South to the survival of slavery. Early in 1850, disguising his identity with a pseudonym, he published three letters in the *Richmond Enquirer* calling for secession if Congress moved further against slavery.[2] He entered the slavery controversy at the same moment Harriet Beecher Stowe found herself drawn into the conflict on the other side; both were responding immediately to arguments over the forthcoming Compromise of 1850. Ruffin's first warnings in the *Enquirer* expressed merely a reactive, negative fear that antislavery forces in Congress would attempt to confine slavery to the southeastern states and abolish it in the District of Columbia, thereby threatening slave property in northern Virginia. Behind this fear lay the yet-unspoken assumption that by preserving slavery, secession would secure the human labor needed to rejuvenate agriculture in the Southeast. Thus his first call for disunion appeared amid the flood of his 1850 articles on practical farming, and just six months after his history of Marlbourne, in which he came to realize the significance of slavery in that farm's revival. In all of these pieces he assumed the necessity of slave labor: agricultural reform, slavery, and secession joined in his mind. For this one ardent secessionist, the cause involved no desire to preserve mastery over slaves for its own sake, nor to save some paternalistic rural lordship. Rather, it involved calculations of what he would lose materially if deprived of slave property and slave labor.[3]

Other circumstances may have established an emotional setting in which Ruffin felt obliged to make some dramatic declaration. He committed himself for the first time to secession in the very weeks other members of his family were experiencing religious conversions in the local Episcopal church.[4] At a moment when his children were professing their faith and urging him to do the same, he became one of the first Virginians to decide for disunion. To the end of his life he resisted appeals from his children that he make a formal profession of faith; and though he was a religious man who said daily private prayers, he viewed both the revivals of religion and the rise of abolition through the eyes of a man who felt himself besieged by uprisings of irrational, fanatical fundamentalism.

And there was one other significant circumstance. It was only in the second half of the 1850s that Ruffin devoted significant portions of his time to secession and became an agent for that movement. The turning point came late in 1856, when he knew for certain that he was rid of Marlbourne. Until that time, although he wrote occasional pieces on disunion and brought the subject into his talks, his focus remained on farming reform. His involvement, therefore, came late in his life. It was a phenomenon of four intense years. After 1857 all of his writing dealt with secession, slavery, and race—three long pamphlets, two significant articles on race and the slave trade, a book-length tract foretelling the consequences of secession, and dozens of newspaper pieces. Between the spring of 1858 and the spring of 1861 he delivered at least fifteen speeches (some prepared, some extemporaneous) on secession.[5] These were the years Ruffin sensed he had lost his readership and when he got responses only by pleasing a few powerful men or a crowd. These were years in which he encountered almost no rigorous criticism, not even in the cities.

The Absence of Criticism

As the decade advanced he spent most of his time with companions whose thoughts agreed with his own.[6] Among these were his six closest friends, three of them from Virginia. Willoughby Newton (1802–1874) he met often in Richmond, through their common involvement with the Agricultural Society. Newton owned a farm in Westmoreland County and had been a congressman from 1843 to 1845. In the summer of 1858 Ruffin visited Newton's farm for four days of confidential talk about a strategy to promote secession.[7] William Boulware (1810–1870) was a Ruffin companion in Richmond, in Washington, and at the Virginia resorts. A Princeton graduate and former minister to Naples in Tyler's administration, he lived at his farm in King and Queen County, a few miles from Marlbourne. He became a close friend when Ruffin moved to Hanover County; it was Boulware to whom Ruffin entrusted the biographical sketch for De Bow's Review.[8] Another close Virginia friend was William H. Harrison (b. 1810), who conducted an academy for boys at his home, the Wigwam, on a farm in Amelia County. The fathers of Harrison and Ruffin were first cousins; but distance had separated the kin, and Harrison did not become a fast friend until 1839, when Ruffin "learned to love him, & still more to esteem him."[9] Harrison proved to be a friend and companion to the end.

The fourth crony was James Henry Hammond (1807–1864), senator from South Carolina between 1857 and 1860 and the former governor who had appointed Ruffin to conduct the South Carolina agricultural survey in 1843. The pair met frequently in Washington, and Ruffin paid two visits to Hammond's plantation, Silver Bluff.[10] Another companion in South Carolina was Dr. John Bachman (1790–1874), whom Ruffin described as "my valued and revered friend." Bachman, a New York-born Lutheran minister and naturalist, had moved to Charleston in 1815. Ruffin visited him regularly and exchanged letters with him all through the 1850s. Bachman's book, *The Doctrine of the Unity of the Human Race* (1850), would have a significant impact on Ruffin.[11] Finally, there was Judge Thomas Ruffin (1787–1870), chief justice of the North Carolina Supreme Court and an authority on the law of slavery, whom Ruffin often visited when passing between Richmond and South Carolina.[12] Relations between these two distant cousins became closer in 1860, when Thomas Ruffin's daughter married Edmund Ruffin's son. Bachman and Judge Ruffin would become the only two of these companions to disagree with Ruffin in any significant way.

Ruffin moved among influential men who loved to talk as much as he. On his arrival for ten days in Washington in January 1858 he immediately encountered "among the crowd in the hall of the hotel" old acquaintances, M. R. H. Garnett, Charles J. Faulkner, and William Smith, all congressmen from Virginia (the last also twice governor), and the congressman from North Carolina, Thomas Ruffin. He also met Congressmen Lawrence O. Branch and Thomas L. Clingman of North Carolina, and Senator Robert M. T. Hunter of Virginia, who became his guide to the city. At Senator Hammond's home he met Senator James M. Mason of Virginia. He conversed with Alexander Stephens and Robert Toombs, senator from Georgia, in Stephens' room. In Congressman John Letcher's room he talked about Kansas with Hunter and Letcher (who would soon become governor of Virginia). With politicians the conversation drifted inevitably to slavery and expansion. Senator Hunter told Ruffin about "the population & condition of Dominica," whose inhabitants Ruffin knew were of "mixed blood," presenting a difficulty if the island were to be annexed by the United States.[13]

Ruffin did meet influential men outside the Congress, but they were interested in the same subjects. He saw De Bow, from whom he collected a debt, and encountered "accidentally" Philip Slaughter, general agent of the Virginia Colonization Society. With Slaughter he had a "long conversation" about the Society, one of the few times Ruffin crossed paths with anyone who disagreed with him candidly.

"We went through our arguments in perfect good temper."[14] Twice in early 1858 he encountered Elwood Fisher, whose lecture and essay "The North and the South," had created a national sensation in 1849. On the previous year's trip to Washington, Fisher actually came to Ruffin's room with Boulware, and the three men talked for two hours, with Fisher the "main talker." "I referred, with due & high commendation to his celebrated lecture on the 'North & South,' & our conversation was on its subject, & that of my own former Address on the social results of slavery & of its absence."[15] Fisher became a great favorite; they agreed on everything. At Fisher's house in April 1858 they talked about the races of Central America and then turned to the common schools of Ohio. "We discussed this subject, with entire agreement of his with my views, taken up without any knowledge of the practical working of the system, but merely from reasoning *opinion.*"[16] In Washington the topics and methods of conversation became predictable.

In Charleston and Richmond and at summer resorts, in lobbies and rooms and around tables, the conversation continued. It was as if the talkers adjourned to ride the trains before reconvening to open their mouths again, and Ruffin was keeping minutes of their meetings. In Charleston on 16 May 1857 Ruffin dined with ten guests at the home of William M. Lawton, "a prominent & wealthy & very intelligent merchant." Among the guests were Richard Yeadon, editor of the *Courier*, and Isaac Hayne, state attorney general. They talked from 4:00 p.m. to 9:30 p.m. Yeadon, a believer in mesmerism and spiritualism, introduced some examples of these "miracles" to the discussion, "as table-moving, &c." The rest of their agenda included familiar subjects, apparently inexhaustible in their appeal: "Much of our conversation on the subjects of slavery, & of secession of the southern states." Two days later at Yeadon's home Ruffin joined a dinner party of twenty, including two former governors "& sundry other intelligent country gentlemen, then visiting Charleston." He sat between Yeadon and a Mr. Cutler of New York City, who informed him that most native Cubans were of mixed blood. "This I was not aware of—& it will be a serious objection to our receiving Cuba as a sister state, & its highest class as fellow-citizens & equals."[17] One learned facts.

At Old Point Comfort in 1858 Ruffin arrived on 11 July to find himself registered with more than seven hundred guests. "A conversation begun with Boulware on African character & the slave trade, attracted others, & among them an intelligent gentleman of Louisiana, whom I afterwards learned was named Hayden." At the Exchange Hotel in July 1859 he continued this discussion with a group that included Boulware again and Governor J. L. Manning of South Carolina. "Gov. Manning is strongly opposed to the reopening of the African slave-trade—but thinks that the advocates of that measure are gaining strength in S.C."[18] Three weeks later he resumed the conversation with Boulware and Manning at the springs.[19] On that same vacation he had a "long conversation" with Barney Reybold, a peach farmer from Delaware who filled Ruffin's ear with talk about the free black population of that state.[20] "He deems them a bad population, & their faults & vices very much as they are here," Ruffin reported. "But at the same time, they supply so much of the present amount of labor, that this class could not be dispensed with." Ruffin, apparently having lost all critical faculties, found such talk useful in his current writing: the very next day he finished an essay containing a plan for the Virginia legislature to remove "the nuisance of free negroes" from the state, essentially by re-enslaving or banishing them. He had mentioned this reform to "sundry intelligent gentlemen" other than Reybold since leaving home, and none had denied its novelty or questioned its usefulness.[21]

Conversation became a ritual, affirming the goodness of what he and his friends already believed. No one wanted anything but confirmation and comfort. The exchange of thought stopped once the parties affirmed their agreement, though the talk continued. Ruffin's minutes reveal that he and his colleagues avoided controversy among themselves. They sought consensus. Occasionally he did argue with Hammond or Newton about reopening the slave trade, or the price of slaves, but rarely did he encounter anyone who would argue about the existence of slavery or the wisdom of secession; nor could it have been said that he sought out people who might have challenged him.

In all the years between 1830 and 1860 Ruffin appears never to have met an abolitionist, though he read Harriet Beecher Stowe and Hinton Helper. The only people he brushed against whose views on racial policy differed from his own were colonizationists. Of these, his most open exchanges were with Bishop Atkinson of North Carolina in 1857 (they had "entirely different opinions") and with Philip Slaughter during their accidental meeting in Washington in 1858.[22] In December 1858 he met Ralph R. Gurley, corresponding secretary of the American Colonization Society and editor of the *African Re-*

pository, who offered Ruffin factual information on Liberia (but too late for inclusion in Ruffin's new pamphlet on that country). "I found him very polite," Ruffin said, "& agreeable in conversation."[23] These were all polite meetings where the issue involved a defense of colonization, not Ruffin's views on slavery. The only person who acted to moderate Ruffin's thinking about race was his friend John Bachman of Charleston, whose *Doctrine of the Unity of the Human Race* stopped him from embracing the theory of separate origins of the races.[24]

On secession he did encounter some argument.[25] On the train to Charleston in May 1858 he was opposed by William C. Wickham, a fellow Virginian. At Charles Town (now West Virginia) before John Brown's execution, an incident may have occurred in which an angry unionist shouted that Ruffin's remarks to a crowd were treasonous, though Ruffin denied having made a such a speech.[26] In Columbia, South Carolina, in 1860, Ruffin was nearly trapped into a public debate with the Roman Catholic Bishop of Charleston, Patrick N. Lynch. "He was in the public hall of the hotel, like any other visitor," Ruffin explained. "We soon got upon the all-absorbing topic." Lynch opposed any move by South Carolina to secede alone, fearing the United States could isolate the state simply by refraining from an attack. "I opposed his views, & our argument soon drew a dense crowd around us, which made me anxious to get out of it—especially as the bishop reasoned fluently & forcibly, & I felt him to be an able antagonist—greatly my superior in the manner of argument." Ruffin asserted the greater dangers of submission, drawing "a storm of applause" from the surrounding crowd of students, which permitted him to retire from the contest.[27]

In Richmond he encountered little criticism of his secession views from other writers or from journals of inquiry and debate.[28] Though Ruffin complained by turns about the city's newspapers, those papers did publish his articles; the literary and agricultural journals, on the other hand, either neglected his work or judged it by the disastrous standard of conformity with their opinions.[29] Resistance to secession did arise in Virginia, but the opposition Ruffin encountered did not come from the expected quarter. Until the start of the Civil War, the most stubborn criticism of his views came from within the Ruffin family itself. The memory of their resistance cannot have been forgotten. It must have salted his final humiliation, adding a sting to the pain of having been wrong.

The Ruffins of North Carolina resisted his effort to recruit them to the cause all through the decade. During a visit to Alamance County in June 1858, he tried "in vain" to persuade Judge Ruffin to lend his name to a "scheme of an association to agitate & maintain the rights of the Southern States." The Judge favored staying in the Union. "He is too cautious—perhaps too wise—to go with me," Ruffin wrote. "He does not admit the doctrine of the right of secession (except as a revolutionary right,) & believes that its exercise never can be peaceful."[30] Here Ruffin heard one of the pithiest criticisms anyone ever offered him. Two years later, in October 1860, he discovered that the Judge's son, William, had read *Anticipations of the Future* and now favored secession. The Judge remained a unionist, but avoided talking politics or arguing. "Therefore we rarely discuss points, as on union & secession, in regard to which we differ widely." In light, jocular, family conversations they did touch on these "exciting subjects," and the Ruffin women took part. They were "all unionists."[31] In March 1861 Thomas Ruffin attended the peace conference in Washington as a delegate from North Carolina. At the end of March, on the way to Charleston, Edmund Ruffin stopped in Alamance County to test family political opinion. While the Judge still avoided argument, he at last was a secessionist, "& so is every member of his family."[32] Events had converted the Alamance Ruffins to the cause.

Among Edmund Ruffin's own children there were two who appear to have withheld enthusiasm for secession. Young Charles Ruffin certainly did not become an ardent Confederate and clearly dreaded going to war, though if he disagreed with his father he expressed himself only through his behavior.[33] His sister Mildred, Ruffin's favorite surviving daughter, told her father precisely what she thought. "I fear that S. C. and some of the other Southern States are hurrying our whole country into civil war," she wrote from Kentucky in February 1861. She favored waiting until the Washington conference revealed Northern attitudes toward Southern rights. "I fear if S. C. takes Fort Sumter, by force, and fires the first shot, then the *South* will commence the war, and if there is any war, I want the North to have all the blame." More could be done "before we plunge into a war, which will be the more violent for being between brothers, and the end of which we may never see," she said. "Oh! it is perfectly awful to think of what we may all have to suffer."[34]

Ruffin's response apparently was designed to allay Mildred's anxiety that a war would occur. She then admitted that newspaper accounts and "the warlike threats of the Mercury," had heightened her fear that the capture of Sumter would mean war. She denied Ruffin's apparent suggestion that her sympathies for the South might have been "injured" in Kentucky, insisting that she maintained her loyalty. "But I have a perfect horror of war in any form."[35] In April, Ruffin wrote Mildred from Charleston and told her he was returning to Virginia, now that the state had left the Union. She responded by expressing her gladness that his exile had ended, but anxiety remained. "I know the South can never be conquered, but do you think it can ever be victorious." Her thinking had advanced beyond his. She was asking questions no critic had forced Ruffin to consider:

> I feel so anxious though when I see in the papers talk of making eastern Va. the battle ground—and I don't know but even now that you & my brothers are exposed to danger, and even their houses and families may ere long be exposed to our Northern enemies. They seem to have a particular spite against dear old Virginia.[36]

In May 1861 she retreated, professing joy at the news of Virginia's secession; but she stood firm in her belief that war was coming, an idea Ruffin still dismissed.[37] "Oh, how mistaken the idea of a peaceful secession—and our having so many friends at the North," she declared. "I see in the Mercury notice of your being in Richmond at the time of the arrival of the S. Carolina Volunteers," she noted without comment. "And that you were called for, and you made a short speech congratulating Va on joining the South."[38] She expressed surprise at her father's expectation that she might visit Virginia that summer. "I should feel as though I were jumping out of the frying-pan into the fire." She expected violence in Virginia. "It looks to me as if eastern Va is to be made the battle ground, and though there is prospect of Ky being the same, yet it does seem farther off."[39] In her final letter to Ruffin, Mildred informed him of her expected confinement and her hope for peace. "While every thing in nature is so smiling," she wondered, "why should man, sinful man destroy our happiness. Oh that I could rule for a month or two. I would soon put all things straight."[40]

Ruffin must have dismissed these sentiments as womanish, yet he continued to try to persuade her, even after he lost hope that she might receive his letters. He wanted to reassure her about the early battles, to win her support with comforting words. Through her dissent Mildred had assumed an importance beyond her status or power. In her letters this daughter favored her father with challenges he neither sought nor experienced among his cronies at the resorts and in the cities of the antebellum South. Her challenges came too late, and his responses disappeared into the West, many never reaching their destination; but Ruffin finally was confronted by one person who set forth the plain truth. He kept her letters and stitched them into his manuscript volumes. He was prepared, therefore, for what happened.

Agent for Secession

After 1858, when he attended the commercial convention at Montgomery, Ruffin began to act as a self-appointed traveling agent for secession, working particularly to convert Southern legislators and members of Congress.[41] By 1858 the subversive nature of his behavior became apparent. This was why he and his closest collaborator, Willoughby Newton, met secretly at Newton's farm that August to plot, and why they abandoned Ruffin's scheme of organizing Southerners openly in support secession, knowing that many would fear to join.[42] In 1859 the report by the *New York Herald* of his "treasonable harangue" in Charles Town gave more proof that he had launched a dangerous enterprise. Yet Ruffin continued to speak, winning the notoriety that would make him a symbol of secession and the Old South. In 1860 he appeared in Charleston at a meeting to select delegates to the state secession convention, where he was called upon to address the hall. "I spoke, & without embarrassment, after the beginning, for about three-quarters of an hour—& then stopped, having forgotten to bring in some of my main points," he reported in his diary. "I referred to no notes." The assembly's warm response was tempting to a man who had lost his reading audience. "I was greatly applauded, & I believe, from what I was told afterwards that my remarks, & my plain manner of delivering them, gave much satisfaction."[43] In Tallahassee he addressed the Florida secession convention.[44] In April 1861, while making his triumphal return to Virginia after that state's formal secession, Ruffin was called from the train by crowds in at least three North Carolina towns.[45] In Richmond on 25 April 1861, he was called from his hotel by "an immense crowd" for a short speech. (This was the speech about which Mildred read in Kentucky.) "I was heard with marked attention & respect."[46] Here at last was an audience.

Ruffin worked for secession as a pamphleteer, debater, and occasional orator. He did lead the small Virginia delegation at the Montgomery convention in 1858, but he did not become a crucial political figure in the maneuvers that led Virginia or any other state to secede. In no sense did he become the leader of an organized movement. At secession conventions in South Carolina and Florida he appeared as an elder, lending respectability to the cause. With regard to decisions that took Virginia out of the Union, he was an outsider who only later discovered with fascination "the secret history of this revolution."[47] His speeches and writings were significant, not as statements of a powerful politician, but as expressions of a significant Southern thinker's case for secession. On this subject Ruffin held ideas common in the South after 1857.

His argument hinged on assumptions he began to articulate as early as 1850. Secession was constitutional. (The memory of his Revolutionary grandfather, for whom he felt a growing reverence after 1850, sustained this belief against the opposition of his contemporary kinsman Thomas Ruffin, who denied the doctrine until 1861.) Antislavery forces would soon enhance their power in the United States Senate by admitting only free states to the Union and by partitioning older free states; such power would permit them to amend the Constitution, exclude slavery from the territories, and abolish slavery in the District of Columbia. This change in law would devalue slave property in the Southeast.[48] Eventually, antislavery forces would attempt to seize and abolish slave property everywhere. If slaveholding states were to dissolve the Union, no hostile regime in Washington could carry abolition forward. A new international border would seal the South safely from abolition agents, who no longer would be able to travel through the region as citizens; the new border would become a barrier that runaways would find impassable. Finally, after secession there would be no war.[49] These deductions involved no appeal to preserve an idealized precapitalist social order or seigneurial planter identity: secession would save property in slaves, thereby keeping the laborers without whom Ruffin could not imagine rejuvenating the rural South.

Slavery and Race

In arguing for secession Ruffin revealed opinions about slavery and race he had kept to himself most of his life. Now he expressed his opinions in print. Neither on slavery nor on race did he develop original ideas. He borrowed eclectically from different theorists of slavery, ensnaring himself in their contradictions with no evident concern. He did try to find his own evidence for conclusions on race; but here again he drew his notions from others and from racial lore. His writings about bondage and human types, unlike his essays about soil and farming, did not present discoveries. They simply revealed, chronologically, his changing thought.

At some point between 1844 and 1849, during the period at Marlbourne when he withdrew from public writing, Ruffin must have experienced a conversion in his beliefs, for he emerged in 1852 with ideas he never before had expressed.[50] After 1852 this man betrayed no hesitation about owning slaves, no doubt about the goodness or usefulness of slavery. If he had not always believed firmly in slavery, he did so now. If he had never expressed in print the thought that black people constituted an inferior race, he did now. His tracts of the 1850s not only established the timing of this development, but they made it clear that Edmund Ruffin was conscious of the change. He expressed these ideas later than some proslavery writers in the South and rather late in his career; but in that decade, when he entered his sixties, Ruffin left a trail of evidence showing how he deliberately fixed his mind. His late tracts indicated precisely why this one Southern reformer, in an era of benevolence, rejected all appeals for abolition.

Anyone who had followed Ruffin's writing after 1832 could have perceived the turning of his thought. In that year he began to publish a flurry of seven short essays about slavery, starting with an appendix (possibly written as early as 1826) to *An Essay on Calcareous Manures*. The rest appeared in the *Farmers' Register*. He discussed slavery in mildly critical terms, in the tone of a man who was still making up his mind. For him, the great issue had personal implications.

On three occasions before 1850 Ruffin had experienced specific difficulties in owning slaves. Early in his career at Coggin's Point, while he still was having trouble sustaining his family and slaves, he considered selling the farm and probably its slaves, hoping to escape to the West. This was in 1816 and 1817, before he discovered marl.[51] He encountered the difficulty of selling such property again between 1835 and 1838, when for four years he tried to sell Coggin's Point to a buyer who would keep his slaves together on the farm.[52] Ruffin wanted to quit being an owner of slaves—at least of farm slaves. Finally, in 1839 he was able to shake himself out of the business, but only by selling an initial half-share of the property to his son. For ten years, between the time he moved to Petersburg and the time he arrived at Marlbourne, he successfully withdrew from the supervision of farm slaves.

The second difficulty occurred between 1828 and 1833, when the quarrel erupted between Ruffin and his sister Juliana Coupland over the disposition of house servants (eventually five in number) who had been part of Juliana's inheritance. The five included two women, Esther and Tilla, and Esther's child and Tilla's two children. At Juliana's marriage in 1823, Esther and Tilla became the property of Juliana's husband, Carter Coupland, and any of the women's children also would have fallen into his possession. When Coupland sank into debt in about 1828 the slaves were seized to meet his obligations. To prevent their separation Ruffin purchased them at a sheriff's sale and returned them to Juliana. Coupland continued to incur debts, leading Ruffin to fear the slaves again would be seized, sold, and separated. He tried therefore to keep legal control over them either by conveying the servants as gifts to Juliana and her heirs or by hiring them to his sister. The strategy produced discord. The fates of Esther and Tilla hinged on negotiations between Ruffin and the Couplands.[53] Ruffin's fears proved to be well-founded, for when Coupland died in 1833 he left Juliana only his debts and the land in Mississippi.[54] The slaves appear to have been lost; but throughout the ordeal Ruffin kept two objectives in view. First, he tried to keep the five in the family; then he tried merely to keep them together at sale.

Ruffin's sister Elizabeth, who had acted several times as intermediary between Ruffin and the Couplands, at some point before her marriage found herself confronting a similar difficulty concerning the disposition of slaves (who may have included the same Esther, Tilla, and children). Elizabeth apparently needed money; and in considering the sale of some slaves she had to choose between selling an entire group of slaves or selling just a portion of them, which would have separated at least one family. The uncertainty of the situation also created anxiety among the slaves. Elizabeth favored selling the smallest number possible, a consoling compromise that would have kept some of them with the Ruffins; but she was troubled by the issue of separation.

She turned to her brother for advice, which he offered in consistent fashion. He favored selling them all. Elizabeth hesitated. "I admit with you that the most prudent and merciful measure would be to sell them all," she wrote, though she still favored the minimum sale. She gave in hesitantly. "I say brother it would be best to sell them; to keep them in such a situation is cruel, I know," she conceded; "but in selling them would I not be doing the thing which now perplexes me and be obliged to endure the unpleasant reflection of having caused general unhappiness among them, by the same means—Separation?" If she sold them all in accord with Ruffin's principle, not even he could guarantee they would stay together.

To placate her conscience, Elizabeth proposed alternatives whose terms remain unclear. At the minimum she must have proposed to let the slaves themselves determine who would go and who would remain. "Poor creatures! I really think they ought to have a voice in the matter, in as much as their own individual happiness is concerned." Perhaps—and this may have been the nub of her proposal—the slaves would agree to "endure present hardships" until the family could redeem them (by which she probably meant they might agree to be hired or sold temporarily). Elizabeth may even have proposed some form of manumission: she was distressed at not being able "to do a deed which would give me as much heart felt pleasure as any thing else." In the end, she agreed it was necessary to be cautious, for slaves in the future certainly would make "similar applications," and the Ruffins themselves certainly would experience "the return of similar feelings in their behalf." Her brother apparently convinced Elizabeth that such important decisions must not be handed over to the slaves. A carefully managed sale offered the best chance to keep the group together without pecuniary loss. "The truth of your reasons against the expediency and propriety of my proposal, is clear and satisfactory," she said. "You have taken a deeper, juster and more deliberate view of the matter than I did, who acted unhesitatingly from the feelings of the moment." Still, she was unhappy, noting, "for my part, I hardly know what is the best plan; the evils and advantages appear to be nearly balanced."[55]

Elizabeth's proposals revealed that by 1832 Ruffin had established some clear principles about the selling of slaves. First, he would not separate slave families. Second, he would try to prevent the selling of slaves outside the Ruffin family. If slaves had to be sold, whole families would go. Third, he opposed the strategy of easing one's way out of debt by hiring or selling servants while vowing to redeem them soon. Nor would he—the son, grandson, and great-grandson of slaveholders—consider manumission as a way of cutting losses or avoiding conflict between evil and advantage. Within his own family Ruffin had been forced to resolve issues of this kind before he reached the age of forty and before he began to react to criticism of slavery from abolitionists.

A Change on Slavery

In negotiations with his sisters Ruffin revealed his early, implicit assumptions about slavery. His public writings after 1832 made those assumptions explicit. In the course of his adult life this slaveholder changed his mind about slavery and, particularly in the 1850s, expressed ideas that occasionally contradicted one another. If he displayed any consistency, it was in two constant themes that ran through all of his thinking: slaves were personal property that could not be seized without the owner's consent, and black people would not work or survive except in slavery. He was not an original thinker about slavery or race, but within the limits of these constant ideas he did change his thinking in significant ways.

Between 1826 and 1836, when Ruffin was leaning toward rejecting the ownership of slaves, he wavered on slavery itself. His writings in these ten years proved his later claim of having passed through a period "in the early part" of his life when he became a "speculative abolitionist."[56] By that, he meant he once had been willing to entertain ideas about abolition. Late in 1831 and again in 1832, at about the time of Nat Turner's rebellion and the Virginia debate on slavery, Ruffin calculated the costs of rearing slaves to adulthood and balanced them against the profits of working or hiring slaves for a lifetime. He published these calculations in 1834 in the *Farmer's Register*, apologizing for approaching the subject in a "disgusting" and "repulsive" way. After establishing his credentials as a slave owner whose income was "derived almost entirely from their labor," he reckoned the enterprise a loss. A female slave kept exclusively for labor would yield barely six percent of her cost a year, a return inferior to profits from lending money. "It requires no farther detail to show that holding such property must be attended with certain loss." If the same female were kept for the value of her children, there would be "certain loss." Even in rearing slaves for hire, "the profits of ownership are commonly and greatly overrated."[57]

Something more troubling than profits and losses was worrying Ruffin at this time—the very time his sister Juliana found her slaves imperiled. He aired his more serious worries in 1832, in *An Essay on Calcareous Manures*. There, in an appendix he may have written as early as 1826, he expressed doubts about the domestic slave trade. Some "cultivators," he wrote, derived income from "a source distinct from tillage." Then he named it. "This source of income is the breeding and selling of slaves." He charged no one with calculated, intentional breeding as a business, "but whether we wish it or not, from the nature of existing circumstances, we are all acting some part in aid of a general system, which taken altogether, is precisely what I have named." He acknowledged that no one was so "inhuman as to breed and raise slaves" and then sell them off in the manner of a cattle drover. "But sooner or later the general result is the same."[58] His words—"a general system," "inhuman"—revealed the difficulty: Edmund Ruffin was troubled by a particular problem in the morality of slavery.

"The sale of slaves is always a severe trial to their owner," he said; "obstacles are opposed to it, not only sentiments of humanity, and of regard for those who have passed their lives in his service—but every feeling he has of false shame comes to aid—and such sales are generally postponed, until compelled by creditors, and are carried into effect by the sheriff, or by the administrator of the debtor." When the sale finally came, its "magnitude" was greater for the delay.[59] This thought hardened Ruffin momentarily against "false shame," but he had defined a dilemma difficult to escape. Slaves lived in the only possible circumstance in which individuals had no motive to check their own reproduction through an "opposing check, either prudential, moral, or physical." Reliant upon whites for material life, slaves could drag down their masters through reproductive power. Thus there arose the need and the function for a domestic slave trade, to carry off the multiplying slaves of impoverished masters. "The slave first almost starves his master, and at last, is eaten by him—at least he is exchanged for his value in food." Only by rejuvenating the soil and increasing food production could Virginia end this Malthusian nightmare.[60] The alternative was to abolish slavery.

Until 1833 at least, Ruffin was willing to entertain arguments for colonization. In that year he devoted twelve pages of the *Farmers' Register* to a debate on colonization, printing opposing excerpts from pamphlets by Jesse Burton Harrison (for the Virginia Colonization Society) and by Thomas Dew (whose arguments against colonization became most influential for Ruffin).[61] Ruffin took a neutral stance in his preface to the excerpts; he introduced the subject, he said, in the "spirit of toleration and of compromise." He noted "strong points of their opposing arguments," and hoped actually to open a discussion of slavery in Virginia.[62]

The exchange Ruffin printed certainly did not represent a wide range of views on slavery in 1833. Harrison criticized the institution in terms congenial to Ruffin: slavery could not be profitable in Virginia; it led to depopulation and economic decline; the increase in black population should be colonized, by the state, outside Virginia, using revenues from the sale of western lands; slaveholders, far from being guilty of "moral turpitude," suffered most under slavery.[63] Yet Harrison, Ruffin said, proved "beyond dispute, that the existence of slavery in Virginia, is a great and increasing evil." In summarizing the debate, Ruffin himself repeatedly used "evil" to describe slavery. "The *abolitionist* can scarcely fail, when attempting to prove that negro slavery in Virginia is attended with enormous evils," he wrote. "Undoubtedly the condition of a slave is deplorable, and it must ever be afflicting that such a state should exist, and be extended so widely over the globe, as to seem to be the inevitable lot of a large portion of mankind."[64] In his conclusions, however, he drew away from these concessions. Afflictions were unavoidable in society, and emancipation would bring disastrous demographic consequences for blacks, leading to a decline into "want, wretchedness and disease," and at no remote period, "the extinction of the race."[65] Concessions of the evils of slavery were difficult for him to make, and—apart from an occasional use of the word *evil*—he would not repeat them many more times.[66]

In 1835 he turned away slightly from this toleration of debate and compromise. The moderate editor issued a warning both to abolitionists and to anti-abolitionists among his Virginia readers. Abolitionists received a reminder that others still considered slavery an evil: "The detestation of slavery, in the abstract, is a feeling almost inseparable from man's best feelings." There were "thousands of slave holders" who would make greater efforts "to mitigate the evils, or remove, if possible, the existence of slavery, than those who condemn and denounce them." To other readers he addressed a disapproving notice that public meetings in Richmond and Petersburg recently had demanded suppression of abolition activities, "perhaps rather exceeding the legal limit." He wanted the public to calm its temper. At the same time he warned Northerners not to foment rebellion: this would produce "misery, if not destruction" of the slaves, "without there being a semblance of hope for effecting, by any of their efforts, the object of a peaceable extinction of slavery, and elevation of the condition of the blacks to equality of right and power with the whites."[67] He was nearing the limits of tolerance. In his 1836 address to the Historical and Philosophical Society of Virginia he spoke once more in moderately critical terms about slavery, treating its evil impact on slave owners and interpreting it as a survival from a rude stage of frontier agriculture.[68] When he next addressed the public on the issue of slavery, after 1849, he had changed his way of thinking.

Edmund Ruffin committed himself to slavery and to ideas of racial inferiority between 1849 and 1852. After withdrawing to farming at Marlbourne in 1844, he returned to public writing and experienced a kind of conversion. In those years he reversed his old attitude toward slavery and published thoughts about blacks he had never expressed. Even the tone of his writing changed as he turned from descriptions of farming experiments to polemical tracts defending slavery. Between 1850 and 1860 he ceased to consider the arguments of anyone opposed to slavery, except to refute them. In that decade he displayed a heightened consciousness of skin color and a vicious antipathy toward blacks. A transformation began, and apparently there was nothing to stop it. Old barriers against certain thoughts and expression collapsed.

A shift appeared first in Ruffin's new emphasis on the profitability of slavery. He had always believed slavery was necessary to rejuvenate agriculture in Virginia, so his thinking displayed some continuity with past ideas. In that spirit he continued to urge Virginians not to sell slaves outside the state and thereby shrink the pool of labor, "already deficient on almost every farm." Virginia needed more slaves—ten times more in some places—for "improvement and tillage of the fields."[69] This change in Ruffin came after the pivotal first five years in reconstructing Marlbourne; his 1849 account of the farm demonstrated not only that slave labor had been crucial, but that a young, working slave force could increase in value. There was some profit in rearing slaves after all.[70] By the end of 1852, when he delivered his presidential address to the Virginia State Agricultural Society in the capitol at Richmond, he no longer believed the rearing of slaves to be a dead loss. He now presumed "as granted and unquestionable" that slave labor was profitable and cheap.[71]

That same address in 1852 marked Ruffin's conversion to the doctrine of slavery as a positive, moral good. There was some continuity with his views of the 1830s, for he still was willing to use "evil" in connection with slavery. In 1852 he conceded the slave trade had been horrible (though he blamed Rhode Islanders). Southern slavery fostered "minor evils" of waste in production (which proved how mild it was) and poor education among farmers. As late as 1858 he still spoke in terms of evil, but by 1859 the evil lay not in slavery but in its abolition. He reversed meaning.[72] Even Ruffin knew the idea of evil had changed and faded, particularly when he considered the good. In 1852 he embraced for the first time the argument that slavery made possible a superior culture among Southern whites by sparing them the "drudgery and brutalizing effects of continued toil."[73] By 1858 he was extolling slavery for the "intimate association" it produced between master and slaves, whose years together from childhood to death produced "mutual feelings of personal regard and attachment."[74] By 1859 he would call slavery a "one of our chief blessings," and declared its removal would be "an unmixed evil and a curse to the whole community."[75]

The concept of reserved lines of work for blacks did not originate with Edmund Ruffin and did not die with him. Ruffin acquired the idea from Elwood Fisher in 1849, when he first read Fisher's famous pamphlet, *The North and the South*.[76] The image of the South and of work implicit in these arguments for slavery, if not original, did represent a departure in Ruffin's own thinking. Never had he admired the notion of an elite devoted to "mind, taste, and manners."[77] Never had he held up a life of leisured refinement as an ideal to his children. To the end of his life he expected Ruffins to work hard at tasks anyone might consider drudgery. Nor had he felt a close bond with his slaves or imagined that he lived in some organic community with mutual obligations fulfilled by the different orders. Rarely did he mention a slave in his correspondence or diary; only Jem Sykes was named in his memoirs. He had begun to write and speak this way only at a particular time, between 1852 and 1858, and for a particular audience outside his family. The open expression of racial assumptions implicit in the notion of reserved lines of work—drudgery for blacks, intellectual culture for whites—was equally the product of a particular time. Though he may have thought such thoughts long before 1852, he had not spoken them. Now, at the time of the first state fair in Richmond and in Thomas Jefferson's capitol building, Ruffin passed the point of no return.

In reserving some lines of work for blacks and some for whites, Ruffin employed for the first time the terms *inferior race* and *superior race*.[78] Over the next six years he let the evil spirit out, expressing ideas that would fix forever his association with racist ideology of the nineteenth century.[79] By 1858 he had arrived at a fully developed doctrine of fixed racial differences. No "unprejudiced mind," he declared that year, "can now admit the equality of intellect of the two races, or even the capacity of the black race either to become or remain industrious, civilized, when in a state of freedom and under self-government—or, indeed, in any other condition than when held enslaved and directed by white men."[80] He dismissed the possibility of change through social influence, asserting his belief in the innate inferiority of blacks. Again, there were continuities with his ideas in the 1830s, particularly with the idea that blacks would not work unless enslaved to white men. Ruffin derived this idea in 1832 from Thomas Dew.[81] After 1852, however, he developed more elaborate notions about race, based on evidence he found in travelers' accounts, Colonization Society reports, and in documents he gathered on free blacks in Virginia, Haiti, Liberia, and Jamaica.

Competence and Inferiority

In the experience of free blacks Ruffin found evidence of racial inferiority. In Virginia and the South they were "noted for ignorance, indolence, improvidence, and poverty." They failed biologically; he found statistics demonstrating their inability to replenish their numbers "by procreation." The decline of the Haitian and Jamaican economies and the collapse of those islands into anarchy proved the incapacity of blacks to work for and govern themselves.[82] His researches on Liberia led to the same conclusions.[83] A few free blacks in the northern United States had accumulated property, he conceded; but their children would not inherit the ability to keep it. Evidence of intellectual inferiority appeared in the history of free blacks in the United States over two centuries. "In all this long time of freedom, and with great facilities for improvement, there has not appeared among all these free negroes a single individual showing remarkable, or even more than ordinary, power of intellect—or any power of mind that would be deemed worth notice in any individual of the white race." His research revealed that "the only truly great man yet known of the negro race" was Toussaint L'Ouverture, the illiterate slave who made himself great. "Is not this alone, sufficient to prove the natural and great inferiority of the negro mind?"[84]

Fragments of other evidence and old arguments from the 1830s and 1840s shored up his case. Blacks themselves acknowledged the inferiority of their race and were unwilling to be governed by other blacks. To bolster this claim he alluded in 1852 to his own experience: "It is well known to every slaveholder, who has made an overseer of one of his slaves, that the greatest difficulty was because of the discontent of the negroes to be so governed."[85] Africa itself was a land of slavery, ruled by masters in "savage ignorance." Africans had no history other than "darkest ignorance, with savage ferocity and cruelty."[86] At the Virginia springs in 1859, a freeborn mulatto named Joseph Mackintosh arrived providentially with direct evidence. Once a judge in Liberia, Mackintosh returned happily to Virginia to work as a bath attendant.[87] Ruffin's rhetoric alone revealed the trend in his thinking: increasingly he justified slavery on grounds of racial inferiority.[88]

As he grasped at explanations of inferiority, his consciousness of race became more acute than in the past. He and his companions at hotels and on trains and steamboats talked constantly about race. In Charleston in 1857 he first heard church music performed on "a chime of bells" at St. Philip's Church. In November 1860 he returned to this favorite church and heard the chime, noting for the first time that, "[i]t is played by a negro."[89] In July 1860 he went sailing on Core Sound in North Carolina, noting with criticism the performance of "the negro captain."[90] An extreme expression of racial antipathy—unique for Ruffin—came forth in his 1860 tract, *Anticipations of the Future*. One chapter was a burlesque of a reception in post-secession Washington for the minister from Haiti. The "Duke of Marmalade" was a "stout, burly negro, of clumsy frame and awkward mein; of features intensely African, in shape and color." Lower classes in the capital stared at this duke and major-general "in the person of an ugly negro."[91] This acute consciousness of color—and of situations in which blacks played significant roles—was not typical of Ruffin's early writing about slaves, either in his public essays or his private diary and correspondence. (The diary was almost universally temperate on matters of race and religion and mild in its prejudicial statements about blacks.) They appear to have been expressions confined largely to the last two years before the Civil War.

In those final two years Ruffin dragged out divinity, biology, and geography to explain racial inferiority. For a time he attributed racial inferiority to divine origin, to "nothing but the immutable decree of God, fixing on them mental inferiority."[92] He also attributed it to biological inheritance, explaining small successes of blacks by the presence of "white" blood.[93] Finally, he used the argument that God had designed blacks to be inferior in intellect, but to possess "ability to endure the heat and miasmatic air of tropical climates."[94] In falling upon racial inferiority as a defense for slavery, this Southerner who possessed a world of practical experience was resorting to the abstraction of all abstractions in antebellum thought. Abstraction was not a characteristic confined to Northern abolitionists.[95]

Now Ruffin was asserting notions he once knew to be flimsy. He always had rejected scriptural justifications for African slavery. What did it mean to declare God the author of slavery while denying the Bible sustained such a doctrine? In his diary in the spring of 1859 he rehearsed and rejected again the familiar scriptural arguments. "Further—I would utterly reject the belief that the just & merciful God would sanction & consummate the curse of Noah, by which . . . perhaps a third of all the human family, were doomed to live in degradation & misery!"[96] Three months before this confession he had become convinced that his Charleston friend, Dr. John Bachman, was correct in insisting that human races had a common origin.[97] Ruffin, too, rejected polygenesis. His new proslavery justifications also contradicted his experience. Much earlier in his career, in 1834, he had noted that "particular slaves" did have exceptional "moral or mental qualities," which made it difficult to calculate the costs of rearing them. He knew, too, that slaves at Marlbourne had worked effectively under Jem Sykes and had become unhappy only under the administration of William Sayre.[98] His opinion that blacks had a different ability to endure tropical climates drew on no solid evidence of his own.[99] Nevertheless, he became eager to express these unoriginal ideas in turgid, repetitious tracts written quickly and carelessly. Some of his willingness to change positions on slavery and race might have resulted from a desire to keep pace with the audience, to capture its attention. So eager was he to cast this writing before the public that he published much of it himself and imposed upon uncritical friends assist him. This was one fact he should have noted when he began to suspect he had published too much.[100]

Other influences were at work, too. Ruffin's decision to turn away from colonization and "speculative abolition" and toward slavery and secession came at a pivotal point between 1836 and 1850. The most significant influences leading him to make that decision were evident in the trail of writings he left behind. During one period between 1826 and 1832, Ruffin came so close to rejecting slavery—by himself, through his own reasoning—that conceivably a powerful impulse from sympathetic opponents at that very moment might have sent him down the path of other Southerners who took the course of abolition or colonization. That did not happen. And while he apparently never met any abolitionists, he did know their work. He knew well the thinking of Wilberforce, Clarkson, Bigelow, Bledsoe, Carey, Tappan, Garrison, Birney, Sumner, and Greeley. After the rise of Garrison, Ruffin felt insulted by what he perceived to be their arrogance toward the white South. If abolitionists had intended to convert a man like Edmund Ruffin, the terms in which they characterized the slaveholders were tactical blunders. Yet less threatening people failed, too.

He did meet the colonizationists face-to-face; Slaughter and Gurley, for example. He knew well Bishop William Meade of Virginia, who occasionally stayed at Beechwood and was a supporter of the American Colonization Society. In his travels through the South he met other agents of colonization. He must have known of John Hartwell Cocke's experiment in educating and manumitting slaves at Bremo in Virginia and Hopewell in Alabama, and he certainly knew about Richard Randolph's emancipation of slaves in Prince Edward County.[101] He thought all of these men were naïve; Meade's intellect he considered "not more than ordinary."[102]

He found colonizationists and their cause impossible to take seriously because, by the time he encountered them, he had already acquired an unshakable idea from Thomas R. Malthus. Not only did Malthus explain for Ruffin the behavior of the poor in England, but he explained the behavior of black slaves in the South. Malthus gave Ruffin a consistent way of viewing slavery throughout the antebellum period. Outside slavery, blacks would work only if pressed to the point of starvation and extinction. He added his own corollary: given their inferiority, they would perish before working.[103] Given this fixed notion, Ruffin's thinking was simply closed to social ideas that assumed a gentle, environmental influence over human behavior.

Isolated as he was, books were a critical influence in shaping his thinking on slavery, particularly if they could be made to fit with a fundamentally Malthusian frame of mind. Though Ruffin read almost every proslavery book, pamphlet, article, and leaflet he could lay his hands on between 1832 and 1860, his thinking was influenced most by Thomas Dew, Elwood Fisher, and the seventeenth-century Scottish theorist Andrew Fletcher. From Dew's 1832 critique of the Virginia debates he first learned that colonization was a demographic impossibility, and that free blacks would not labor. "Never," said Ruffin, "has any work, of mere reasoning on previously known facts, had such great effect."[104] Ruffin read Dew's pamphlet at least three times; in his diary in 1858 he said it was still "the best that has yet appeared."[105] From Elwood Fisher's *The North and the South* (1849) Ruffin derived the idea that slavery had produced a superior civilization among whites in the South.[106] And in Andrew Fletcher's *Two Discourses on the Affairs of Scotland* (1698) Ruffin first discovered the argument, however ironic, that in "personal slavery" the laboring poor would find security against "poverty, idleness, and misery." Ruffin read Fletcher almost twenty years before George Fitzhugh published his first book, which contained a similar analysis of the solution to evils of free society.[107]

Though Ruffin had read Malthus sometime around 1816, and though he continued to lead a bookish life, these books by Malthus, Fletcher, and the rest merely gave him a way of interpreting actual experiences with slavery and the daily behavior of his own slaves. The evidence for all of his conclusions about slavery ultimately came from his own slaves, who may have displayed insufficient enthusiasm for the herculean tasks he assigned them, and who now got little credit from their master for perseverance or skill.

The assumption that black people would not work to sustain themselves may have had no definable beginning in Ruffin's mind. He must always have believed this central idea about racial difference.[108] He must have incorporated it as a boy at Evergreen and at Coggin's Point. There is no evidence that his father, grandfather, or stepmother imparted it to him, but this single individual's interpretation of racial behavior must have risen from experiences on the farms of his ancestors and on his own first farm. Slavery itself may have given him the idea, by inference. In *An Essay on Calcareous Manures*, where he revealed some of his earliest thoughts on race, he described slaves at Coggin's Point and Shellbanks as awkward, careless, and unskilled.[109] He came to see them as lacking the very quality he admired most in himself: self-discipline. Slaves were lazy. If freed, they would not work, but would become a dependent, impoverished, starving population. This assumption could have come from Malthus's writing about the poor, but it also must have been one of the circular, self-reinforcing consequences of slavery itself on the thinking of an individual master of slaves.

The core idea must have come from his perception of himself and his own slaves. Ruffin cannot have known many free blacks in Prince George County. They were indeed twelve percent of the black population there in 1820, but none of them lived on his farm.[110] Had he traveled back and forth to Williamsburg by way of the Peninsula, he might have encountered free blacks at the mouth of the Chickahominy, but he appears to have traveled usually on the James itself.[111] Though he must have known free blacks in Petersburg, he recorded no personal memories of any free black other than Mackintosh at the springs. He always had to ask others to seek out evidence on them. His experiences with Jem Sykes and Zack, his two most trusted and responsible slaves, came late in his life, after 1844. If these two men provided his evidence on black behavior, then ironies abounded. They got credit only for dutifulness and for amusing Ruffin, as when Sykes remembered precise events about farming in the past.[112]

One final influence was at work in determining Ruffin's course on slavery. This was his view of his own past. Once he assumed that the origin of slavery lay in an aversion to labor and that black people of the world were naturally vulnerable to this aversion, certain contrasts between these people and himself were thrown into high relief. As he said in 1858, the willingness of blacks to "forego all intellectual and moral improvement for themselves and their families" or even to "furnish the means for comfortable subsistence" made these people dependent. In Ruffin's interpretation of personal experience, this lack of ambition made them very different from himself, though a good deal like his son Charles. Having no competence, they enjoyed no independence. In his reasoning it followed that a "good and proper remedy for this evil, if it could be applied, would be the enslaving of those reckless, wretched drones and cumberers of the earth."[113]

This harsh assessment of the worthlessness of human beings who could not achieve a competence, or "comfortable subsistence," through their own labor—this assessment was the very one Ruffin $\vee$ applied to his children and to himself. His use of it in criticizing black people near the end of his life revealed a consistency of thought about his career that led him from an interpretation of his own success to a condemnation of dependent people and a justification for slavery. Then it led to the ultimately fatal judgment that all cumberers of the earth are worthless. Seldom has one man's harsh judgment of other human beings circled back so precisely upon himself as would this particular judgment in the life and death of Edmund Ruffin.

7

The Death of Edmund Ruffin

I am now merely a cumberer of the earth, & a useless consumer of its fruits, earned by the exertions of others.

EDMUND RUFFIN, 1865

Arguments Edmund Ruffin assembled for the final entry of his diary—a defense of suicide—took him two or three days to put on paper. He wrote, he said, almost to his last breath, literally putting down his pen and picking up the gun. He ended the diary in a soliloquy of seven thousand words that revealed he did not kill himself impulsively or merely in response to the collapse of the Confederacy. For months he had made calculations concerning the end of his life, drawing on ideas he had encountered in the early years of his career.

Ruffin shot himself shortly after noon on Saturday, 17 June 1865, in his room on the main floor of the house at Redmoor, the small Amelia County farm his son had purchased in 1862 as a refuge from the Civil War.[1] His behavior, along with documents he left in his room, gave evidence of preparation. He had known for at least two days precisely when he would act: weeks before this, his son began to suspect his intentions, particularly in April, after the fall of Richmond. "Two months ago, or a little more," Edmund, Jr., wrote on 20 June, "when there was danger of his being captured by the Yankees I feared that he contemplated such a step rather than to allow himself to fall into their hands, but latterly my fears have been completely allayed." Ruffin took care, therefore, to arouse no suspicions in his son or daughter-in-law Jane when he appeared for breakfast Saturday morning. "Nothing unusual was noticed in his manner on Saturday," his son said. After breakfast the senior Ruffin returned to his room, "where lately he was in the habit of staying and writing." In that room, one of three on the main floor of the house, he had hidden the musket that Edmund, Jr., and grandson George had loaded for use against horse thieves.[2] As a precaution against its misfiring, he also had secured at least two percussion caps. He bathed himself and, as a reporter for the *Richmond Whig* noted, he put on "clean under and outer clothing."[3] He worked on the long, final entry in the diary until it was finished. He noted the hour (ten o'clock) and then wrote, "The End."[4]

Finally, he completed two pages of "Memoranda" instructing Edmund, Jr., about his burial, the care of his manuscripts, and his watch. Thus he added a coda to the soliloquy.[5] In a note at the bottom of the second page he instructed his son to examine five passages in the diary beginning on 5 January, giving page numbers. Each passage explained his motives.[6]

There were two moments after Ruffin began writing these memoranda when chance gave him opportunities to change his mind. A neighbor, Mr. Marshall, arrived downstairs for a visit, and so apparently did Ruffin's friend and distant cousin, William H. Harrison, with his son Hartwell. Ruffin paused. At noon the last visitor left the house. Edmund, Jr., walked outside, beyond the barns into the cornfield, leaving Jane with his two daughters, Susan and Mary, on the porch, near Ruffin's door. Ruffin made a final notation: "Kept waiting by successive visitors to my son, until their departure at 12:15 P.M."[7] Then he proceeded. "He was in a sitting position in a chair," his son later reported, "braced against the arms of the back and no doubt put the mussle of the gun in his mouth. The butt of the gun rested on a trunk before him and he pulled the trigger with a forked stick."[8]

The musket misfired, though the cap did explode. On the porch, ten feet from Ruffin's window, Jane Ruffin and the two granddaughters heard this explosion. Jane, who "immediately suspected the cause," ran from the porch, but not toward the door. She ran toward the cornfield, calling to her husband. Edmund, Jr., later explained that "the girls were very much alarmed, and in the midst of their alarm and doubt, did not know what to do." Ruffin therefore had time to reset the cap and reposition the musket and forked stick, "before they could well collect their thoughts."[9] For a third time that morning he proceeded.

In their alarm the Ruffin women revealed what they had perceived in the mere sounding of a cap: they knew what he was doing and that he had chosen a lethal weapon. Jane Ruffin must have believed, moreover, that she alone could not dissuade him: she assumed he was determined. The diary later confirmed that Ruffin had calculated his timing for weeks, not hours. By 5 January at the latest, he had decided upon suicide, fearing calamities in the imminent end of the war.[10] In April, after the war, he had waited for Charlotte Meade Ruffin and her children (the last of the family refugees sheltered at Redmoor) to depart for their home; these were the widow and surviving children of Ruffin's second son Julian, killed the previous year at Drewry's Bluff, and Ruffin wanted to spare them another shock. Next he had waited for a nephew's wedding to take place, not wanting to spoil that occasion. Finally, he had waited for Edmund, Jr., to return from an inspection trip of Beechwood, sixty-six miles away on the James, so that his son would be present to dispose of the corpse. At noon on 17 June, conjuncture arrived. He found the visitors gone, his son home and in the field, and himself at Redmoor house with only two infants and three young women. On his second attempt, according to the *Whig*, the musket fired properly, "the charge of ball and buck blowing off the crown of the venerable old gentleman's head and scattering his brains and snowy hair against the ceiling of the room."[11]

Interpreting the Suicide

The deceased himself offered what seemed to be the most plausible explanation of his motives. Ruffin's soliloquy and coda—fifteen pages long—contained two almost identical concluding paragraphs, each declaring "unmitigated hatred to Yankee rule," and to the "Yankee race."[12] By their position at the end of the diary, these two passages gained persuasiveness. Furthermore, on the eighth page of the suicide entry, Ruffin confessed that after the fall of Richmond his thoughts had been possessed "every day & night" by the "calamities" of the Confederacy, whose defeat had "wrecked all my hopes for my country's defence & independence."[13]

Edmund, Jr., discovered these short paragraphs immediately, and within three days they dominated his interpretation. He acknowledged that his father had been "weary of life" for many years, and that a recent loss of hearing, together with an "utter inability to enjoy social life," had increased that weariness. Edmund, however, emphasized the effect of the war. "The subjugation of our country has weighed heavily on his mind and determined him to take the fatal step," he wrote to his own sons at Beechwood. "In his journal he denounces to the last the Yankee despotism under which our country labors and I feel that the Yankees have just as certainly killed your Grandfather as they did your beloved uncle who fell gloriously on the field of battle."[14] The *Richmond Whig*, in an account republished by the *New York Tribune*, cited speculation that "Mr. Ruffin's mind had been very perceptibly affected since the evacuation of Richmond, and the surrender of the Confederate armies." The *Whig* also quoted from a letter Ruffin reportedly left his family in which he said, "I cannot survive the loss of the liberties of my country."[15] Within three days, contemporaries, drawing on the very last words in the diary, had found a link between the defeat of the Confederacy and the death of Edmund Ruffin.

They decided quickly that Ruffin killed himself in despair over the outcome of the Civil War. The *Whig* saw momentary insanity in the suicide, speculating that his "brooding over the troubles of the times, the war and its results, no doubt unhinged his mind and caused a derangement of his once strong and vigorous faculties." On 19 June the Richmond correspondent of the *New York Times* determined the cause at once: "The collapse of the rebellion and the utter prostration of his schemes, drove him mad."[16] The *Richmond Republic* and the *New York Tribune* embellished this interpretation. According to the first report in the *Tribune*, Ruffin declared that "he could not live under the Government of the United States—that he preferred death to doing so."[17] His suicide became an act of honor, a refusal to accept life in defeat.[18]

Ruffin's engagement in secession and the war prepared contemporaries to view his death in these terms. In the spring of 1861, he took part in two of the great early engagements of the Civil War at Fort Sumter and First Manassas (Bull Run). His bravado at the age of sixty-seven made him a celebrity. In Charleston in April he joined the Palmetto Guard, winning the ceremonial honor of firing the legendary first shot.[19] At Manassas in June he slept in a tent, took mess with officers, and was issued a rifled musket. He helped dig trenches but did not take part in drill or guard duties, "for want of bodily ability." Yet he did march with Confederate troops during the battle, advancing and then retreating from Blackburn's Ford "for

nearly two miles," carrying his musket. Realizing he "could not hold
out in such a rapid march for another mile," he accepted a ride on a
caisson, noting that other, younger men, also were lagging behind
in exhaustion. On the old turnpike to Alexandria he won another
ceremonial honor, this time firing a first cannon shot that killed as
many as eight Union soldiers.[20]

In the spring of 1862 Ruffin inspected ships in the Portsmouth
Navy Yard, then visited in the Navy Hospital with the injured captain
of the *Virginia*. In Norfolk he secured a pass to visit nearby camps
and batteries.[21] On 1 April he traveled to Sewell's Point, five miles
north of Norfolk, taking a Confederate steamer to the landing at
Tanner's Creek. Then he proceeded to the point, where he had a
sweeping view westward across the bay, toward Union-held Fortress
Monroe. There, with his own eyes, he saw the U.S. fleet, "a forest
of masts, stretching almost continuously from above the Chesapeake
College, to below Fortress Monroe." The apparent size of the fleet
took him by surprise. "It was impossible to count the vessels, though
aided by a spy-glass. But, at a rough guess, I supposed there were
nearly 100 still there." Next day he took tea with the new commander
of the *Virginia*. "When I mentioned to Com. Tatnall the great number
of Yankee vessels that I had seen yesterday off Fortress Monroe, &
which I supposed to be as many as 100, he answered that there were
about 150."[22] The eyes had deceived.

More action followed in 1862, when Ruffin guided six batteries
of Confederate artillery to the bluff on his old farm at Coggin's Point,
where they launched a night cannonade against Union ships and
McClellan's camp at Berkeley across the James. Ruffin extracted a
promise of firing the first shot here, too, but did not actually perform
the honor.[23] By seeking action during the first two war years, Ruffin
became a mythic figure of the defeated South.[24]

Ruffin invited this wartime interpretation of his death in the diary,
particularly in condemning Yankee oppression of "aged men & help-
less women." In his birthday entry on 5 January 1865, he expressed
his hope for an honorable death, and at the end of that entry he
confessed his depression over the outcome of the war. Yet he did not
actually say he was killing himself to protest Yankee oppression; nor
did he see honor in suicide. And both Ruffin and his son knew that
real crisis passed in April, not in June. He had waited more than
two months beyond the end of the war; more was involved than the
military defeat of the South. Before he wrote the soliloquy and coda,

he revealed that he was impelled by motives older than the immediate historical dilemma. The war did generate motives for suicide; in fact, it had consequences greater than his contemporaries realized.[25] Ruffin's arguments revealed that his career in farming, writing, and reform in the antebellum South had depended on historical conditions that the Civil War demolished.

The soliloquy offered justifications. Ruffin began by addressing religious objections against self-murder; this section had required several years of preparation. He had done research in Biblical history and exegesis, drawing on sources he began to read in 1862.[26] He analyzed Christian and Jewish doctrine on suicide, using evidence from the Pentateuch. Ruffin emphasized Biblical precedents: ancient Jews had killed themselves after military defeats, as in the fall of Jerusalem. Jews in Rome and in Christian Europe during the Middle Ages had followed this practice.[27] Ruffin found these examples of defeated people persuasive: the fall of Richmond was on his mind. He discovered that neither the Old nor the New Testament forbade suicide and that its condemnation came only from theologians.

Dismissing church authorities, he turned to Biblical injunctions concerning the duty of a father to support his children and serve his country before leaving the earth. He assessed what he had provided: to his children he had transmitted thousands of dollars before the war, and to Virginia, millions of dollars through the rejuvenation of fields. Midway through the entry Ruffin declared that he had performed his duty. He had not failed his children or Virginia, and he felt free now to depart.[28]

Finally, he took account of personal difficulties that had mounted during the Civil War. He had lost his accumulated capital and with it all material support for an independent old age. Though he no longer feared he would be punished physically by the Federal government, he did fear the onus of his treason would harm his son. He thought mournfully of deaths in his family during the previous ten years, and of his declining health: the loss of hearing, blindness at night, forgetfulness, and two recent periods of apparent incontinence. (Of these disorders, Edmund, Jr., discreetly mentioned only the loss of hearing.) Ruffin foresaw a protracted, isolated, dependent old age in the care of women who were not his daughters. The problem, he feared, was that he might go on for years in a body that would not die. Only after he had said all this, after ten and a half pages, did he express his hatred of all Yankees.

More was involved than Yankees and humiliating defeat, but the end of the Civil War combined with other causes, remote in time, to make Ruffin wish for death.

Consequences of the Civil War

In his whole diary, beginning in 1856, he left a record of losses explaining how and when the Civil War became a personal and family calamity. Ruffin, who had devised arrangements for his late career that depended upon the family, experienced the war as a barrage of disasters that entirely changed his material and intellectual life. When the Civil War began, Ruffin's livelihood derived primarily from four farms owned by his children. Edmund, Jr., the eldest child, owned Ruffin's old farm at Coggin's Point; in 1849, on the western side of that farm and just above the river at Tar Bay, he completed the large frame dwelling that became Beechwood House.[29] In 1860 the farm was listed as comprising 1,200 acres.[30] Edmund also owned Evelynton, 860 acres on the north side of the James River in Charles City County, a farm he acquired with funds derived from his first wife's estate. Edmund, Jr., who held 138 slaves at Beechwood and Evelynton in 1860, was the only member of the family Ruffin said he could describe as "wealthy."[31] At the start of the Civil War he was living at Beechwood with six surviving children by his first marriage, devoting himself to his farms. In April 1861, shortly after the war began, he married Jane Minerva Ruffin (1829–1898), a distant cousin fifteen years younger than he and the daughter of Thomas Ruffin, chief justice of the North Carolina Supreme Court. Edmund married well and brought property to the family.

The third farm was Ruthven, which Ruffin had helped to purchase for his second son, Julian Calx Ruffin. It was five miles south of Coggin's Point, away from the river. Here Julian had enlarged his landholding to eight hundred acres and had accumulated twenty-two slaves by 1860.[32] Julian's wife, Lottie, did not have wealthy parents, and after her father died in 1855 her mother shared the small house at Ruthven.[33] As the war progressed, Ruffin's affection grew for Julian and Lottie, whose start in life must have reminded him of his own early years with Susan Travis Ruffin at Coggin's Point.

Finally, there was the magnificent Marlbourne, with its sixteen hundred acres and large frame house in Hanover County, northeast of Richmond. This was the key property for Ruffin's endowment. Edmund and Julian emerged as the major partners in Marlbourne, dominating the family partnership, sustaining their father. William Sayre, widower of Ruffin's deceased daughter Elizabeth, remained as manager at Marlbourne at the start of the war. Having quarreled with Sayre in 1859, Ruffin had made his permanent home at Beechwood. In 1861 he was living in Edmund, Jr.'s original, four-room cottage in the Beechwood yard, where he had his bedroom, furniture (including a writing table), manuscripts, and library."[34] As late as June 1861, neither deaths nor quarrels had disturbed his careful arrangements.

In addition to Edmund, Jr., and Julian, three other children were still alive in 1861, but they no longer figured in Ruffin's support. Agnes lived in Petersburg, shunned by Ruffin (because of her spendthrift husband): she was not a partner in Marlbourne. Mildred, in marrying Burwell Sayre, had withdrawn from the partnership and moved to Kentucky. Charles Ruffin was twenty-nine in 1861, still single and living on his own small farm, but not yet blessed with firm plans for a career and not enjoying good relations with his father.

The consequences of warfare—the Union blockade, the battles and movement of armies around Richmond—did not enter Ruffin's calculations in the winter of 1860–61, for he anticipated neither a war after secession nor danger for his estate. Experience demonstrated, in fact, that his family arrangements were succeeding brilliantly. He could afford to take train journeys to Charleston and spend seven weeks at hotels and restaurants.[35] He could afford to outfit himself in Richmond before the battle at Manassas and then spend twenty-two days with the army.[36] Income from his reserved fund bought him freedom of movement, liberty from farming duties, free time, and total engagement in reform.

War changed the routines of Ruffin's life almost immediately. After July 1862 he was forced to spend almost all of his time at his children's farms, a dramatic change in his life routines. From 1857 through the end of 1861, Ruffin had spent as much as half of each year traveling to Washington, Richmond, and through the South. After 1863 he rarely ventured from his sons' homes. As early as April 1861 the war began to affect Ruffin's role at the farms. Given his prominence in the secession movement, the family felt an obligation to offer males for war duty. In 1861, Edmund, Jr., was forty-seven years old, and his eldest boy, Thomas, was seventeen. Julian Ruffin was forty years old, the father of four young children. Charles Ruffin, at twenty-nine, was not eager for battle. Eventually, all three sons and four grandsons went to war, as well as all the family's white overseers. This created a crisis. As a first consequence of the Civil War, Edmund Ruffin was forced to return to farming.

He spent June 1861 at Beechwood, acting as protector for the females in Edmund's family. Between 1862 and 1864, when his sons were in Confederate military service at various times, Ruffin oversaw farm work at Beechwood, Ruthven, and Marlbourne. While he continued to keep his diary, he read little in the most active months. The war isolated him from his intellectual circle in Southern cities; it was one reason Ruffin stopped writing for the public. Simply by reviving a demand within the Ruffin family for his labor as an overseer, the war effectively ended his intellectual life. Beyond this, there would be material losses.

All four Ruffin family farms lay in the path of armies that contended for Richmond and Petersburg, beginning in 1862. Beechwood and Evelynton, on the James River, and Marlbourne, at the head of navigation on the Pamunkey River, were exposed to assaults both by land and by water. Marlbourne stood in the defensive perimeter around Richmond, close to the armies and coming battles. Ruthven, five miles south of the river, had only a small buffer of security. To save these farms, the Ruffin family resorted to three tactics.

Initially they attempted to continue occupying their properties and to keep the farms in production, relying heavily on Ruffin as manager. By this tactic they hoped to provide themselves and their slaves with a common source of food and income during the emergency, and to protect their property. This attempt began to fail within a year. Ruffin's most energetic effort, at Marlbourne in the spring of 1863, was defeated by weeks of heavy rains that delayed planting and ruined seedlings, even though the rain slowed military action. Ruffin's choice lay between the devils of weather or war, for as soon as the rains stopped, the Union armies arrived. As Ruffin wrote in one of his most astute analyses of the impact of the war, one raid—or mere threat of a raid—by an army through an agricultural county could disrupt farming for a year: the slaves would leave, and the crops would be appropriated or fail to reach markets. Farmers then would decline to invest capital in planting next year's crop.[37] This is what happened at Marlbourne, Beechwood, and Evelynton.

In the spring of 1862, with McClellan advancing up the Peninsula

toward Richmond, the Ruffins decided to abandon three farms, keeping only Ruthven in production. First, they gave up Marlbourne.
With Union forces approaching from the east along the Pamunkey
River, William Sayre fled on 24 May 1862. Mary Custis Lee, wife
of General Robert E. Lee, had taken refuge at Marlbourne that spring
with her daughters and remained there two weeks after Sayre fled.[38]
Though the Ruffins would reoccupy Marlbourne briefly, the time was
approaching when they would have to abandon it for the rest of the
war. Beechwood and Evelynton they abandoned in June 1862. Ruffin
had begun to move his "most valued manuscripts, private family
letters, & copies of some published articles," to Ruthven as early as
22 March. On 23 June, with Union gunboats moving freely up the
James and Union troops across the river at Harrison's Landing, Edmund, Jr., ordered the slaves, livestock, and most valuable possessions
moved to Ruthven.[39] This move they completed at night on 25 June.
They would not resettle Beechwood until after the war.

Now they were forced into a second tactic, seeking refuge away
from the Union army. At this point, Ruffin became a refugee, his
initial such experience lasting for six months. After that, he and his
family were refugees for three years, moving from farm to farm,
country to city, attempting to keep their households and slaves away
from the war. At first, all members of the family and their remaining
slaves gathered together in Julian's small farmhouse. Edmund, Jr.,
then rented a house for his family in Petersburg, where they moved
in late July, Ruffin himself electing to remain in the country. When
Federal troops actually landed near Coggin's Point on 3 August, the
remaining members of the family, including Ruffin, fled to Petersburg, where everyone lived in temporary quarters until 17 August,
when McClellan's forces withdrew and Julian reoccupied Ruthven.[40]
This second tactic of moving to places of refuge was designed to give
Edmund, Jr., time to effect a more permanent solution, the purchase
of a new farm in a safer part of Virginia. Temporary though it was,
life as a refugee brought significant changes in the life routines of
Edmund Ruffin.

Ruffin always had maintained his privacy and seclusion, whether
traveling or at Marlbourne or in the cottage at Beechwood, which
enabled him to study and write. This privacy ended forever in June
1862. During his first month as a refugee at Ruthven, Ruffin lived
in that small house with eighteen other occupants—Julian and Lottie
Ruffin and their four children; Edmund, Jr., and his seven children

(one with typhoid) and new wife Jane; Mrs. Meade (Lottie's mother), Mrs. Lorraine (a permanent lady-resident with Edmund's family), and William Sayre. In Petersburg, when the family finally succeeded in renting its own house on High Street, Ruffin noted, "the sitting room is so filled with a pile of beds & mattresses that it can scarcely be entered." He boasted that the outhouses afforded "plenty of accommodation for the unusually large number of servants, & especially of mothers & young children."[41] Ruffin had never lived in such crowds or in close proximity to servants. Conditions improved. At Marlbourne from October 1862 to May 1863 he shared that large house with just nine other people, and at Ruthven in 1863 he lived with just seven.[42] Occasionally he had his own room, as in the final week of his life; but his last four years would be spent without privacy, in cramped quarters with large numbers of relatives who were constantly moving as the war disrupted their lives in turn.

In October 1862, Edmund, Jr., purchased the small farm in Amelia County that he intended to occupy as a redoubt, making plans to move his remaining slaves there at once. This was Redmoor. Since Edmund could not take possession of the farm until 1 January 1863, he elected to move his family temporarily back to Marlbourne, which was safe for the moment. Ruffin joined him there from late October 1862 until 9 May 1863, when he fled again, resuming the refugee existence that would last the rest of his life, moving between Ruthven, Richmond, and Redmoor.

This flight in search of refuge began in fear. In the spring of 1862 the women at Beechwood—Mrs. Lorraine and Ruffin's granddaughter Nanny—began to view his presence as a danger to the family and saw, too, that he was in danger himself. Union troops were near. Ruffin's role in secession and at Fort Sumter, they feared, had made him a wanted man across the James. On a day's journey to Richmond that spring he talked to his old friend Willoughby Newton and his son-in-law William Sayre, both of whom expressed the same concern. As events of 1862 progressed, Ruffin became convinced these people were right, and for the first time in his life he began to perceive himself seriously as an outlaw.

Evidence accumulated that Ruffin was in danger for having committed treason. General George McClellan had the neighboring house at Maycox burned, thinking it was Ruffin's.[43] When McClellan withdrew from Prince George on 16 August 1862, Ruffin returned to Beechwood for inspection and found all the evidence he needed to fuel his fear of capture. On the walls of the mansion and in his own cottage the Yankees left graffiti addressing the point: "You did fire the first gun on Sumter, you traitor son of a bitch," wrote one of the invaders.[44] A year later, when Stoneman's cavalry appeared suddenly at Marlbourne, Union officers demanded to know Ruffin's whereabouts; his family and slaves revealed nothing. Five days after the raid, Ruffin fled.[45] Thereafter he saw himself as a liability to his children, his presence endangering the very property on which he and they survived.

Ruffin began to keep an inventory of damage to that property early in 1862, when the farms passed for the first time under Union control. Only Ruthven escaped damage to buildings and fields early in the war, and its crops kept the family and slaves in food. At Marlbourne in July 1862, after the first Union occupation, the inventory showed Union forces had appropriated corn and wheat stored in the barns, fodder, and all mules and horses, "except two, which Mrs. Lee was permitted to use to convey her to Richmond." All carts and wagons had been seized, but no cattle. The fields at Marlbourne were trampled, having become pasture for Union horses, and fences were burned for firewood.[46] Contrary to Ruffin's expectations, the house survived, though its doors had been broken and Ruffin's two cabinets of fossil shells—holding invaluable specimens—had their contents either stolen or scattered.[47] At Evelynton, near the site McClellan had made his headquarters, Edmund, Jr., found every farm building "completely torn down, & the timbers used, except a piece of the overseer's house."[48]

At Beechwood came the heaviest losses, in two different occupations. In 1862, when the Ruffins returned after the first Union advance into Prince George County, they found the corn crop gone to feed McClellan's army, and the wheat lost to the advanced season. Their reaping and threshing machines were broken and two excellent farm wagons appropriated, along with "every valuable farm utensil & tool." Furniture the family left behind was broken. (The most valuable pieces, however, had been secured in Petersburg.) The mansion, to Ruffin's amazement, had not been burned, but windows and doors were broken, both in the main house and in the cottage in the yard. Ruffin's own furniture lay broken and strewn around the yard. The overseer's house and other farm buildings were damaged by "tearing off the boarding, breaking of windows, doors &c."[49] More damage occurred to buildings at Beechwood during a second Union occupation, near the end of the war in 1864 and 1865. On 9 June 1865, Edmund, Jr., reported the houses had been pulled to pieces, particularly the large dwelling. "To repair it probably would cost more than the original charge for building," he said.[50]

Union soldiers did not cause all the damage to the farms, as Ruffin knew all through the war.[51] He pointed to the neighbors' animals and the neighbors' slaves as culprits, and sometimes to the neighbors themselves.[52] Even Confederate troops began to seem lawless and threatening. By April 1863, Ruffin was referring to new Confederate companies and regiments as "sturdy & shameless beggars," and "as unscrupulous robbers as the Yankees."[53] Ruffin found his family caught between the two armies, victimized by warfare itself.

One other loss of property occurred during the first occupation at Beechwood, the result of looting by Union troops: the libraries were destroyed. Ruffin had no inventory of his books. In his cottage he had only three book cases with doors (which he purposely had left open), but he owned many books more than those cases contained. He suspected at first that most of the volumes had been sent by the Union commander to New York for sale.[54] A Union soldier's letter, which eventually fell into the family's hands, explained that the libraries had been the objects of looting by Union troops.[55]

Loss of the libraries meant a change would follow at once in Ruffin's vocation. His family libraries had permitted him to conduct intellectual work; through them, the family itself had sustained his research and writing, as well as his only pastime of reading history, fiction, and current periodicals. In destroying his books the Union soldiers undermined a crucial function of Ruffin's family and, with the same stroke, removed his most important scholarly apparatus. In the destruction of his shell cabinet at Marlbourne, Ruffin suffered a comparable loss, plainly making it impossible for him ever again to make the kind of identification of fossils that had proved so significant in his soil research. The loss of these collections left him without two of the resources that had made him an independent thinker. A crucial link between family and reform disappeared with his books and shells.

Loss of family slaves destroyed another of those links. Slaves began "absconding" from Marlbourne, Beechwood, and Evelynton very early in the war, just as they did from farms all along the Pamunkey and lower James rivers once McClellan occupied the Peninsula. The level of desertions around Marlbourne astonished Ruffin. "The number, & general spreading of such abscondings of slaves are far beyond any previous conceptions," he confessed. After Marlbourne fell behind Union lines for the first time, Ruffin simply wrote off that entire group of slaves as a loss, accusing them of having joined an "open & avowed rebellion." Beechwood suffered heaviest losses from slave defections between May and June 1862, when sixty-nine of the slaves still held there fled. "Not a single man is left belonging to the farm," he noted on 11 June.[56] (One of the absconders, a man Ruffin knew as William and described as "an uncommonly intelligent negro," would return in August 1862 to guide Union forces landing in Prince George.)[57] Losses at Marlbourne were shared by all partners in the farm, but Edmund, Jr., was the heaviest loser through abscondings from his James River farms.[58] Julian had lost none of his small group at this point.[59] By midsummer of 1862, however, the significant holdings at Marlbourne, Beechwood, and Evelynton had been greatly reduced.

At the start of 1862 there had been two hundred slaves at those three farms. By early summer the Ruffins remained in control of about eighty-one of these, including eleven men impressed into labor by the Confederate government. At the end of the summer, they held only about sixty, scattered at houses and holding farms and at government works around Petersburg.[60] Though these losses fell upon his children, they also produced reverses for Ruffin, both for his state of mind and for his financial position. Within a matter of weeks, he was forced to confront a revolution in relations between his family and black people, with both sides precipitating changes.

Events in June 1862 that broke up the slave community at Beechwood and Evelynton demolished Ruffin's assumptions about slaves and their relationship to his family. As a result of this breaking up, Ruffin attempted to amend ideas he had held in the 1830s about the slave family; he decided the notion that black people felt a commitment to their own families was just a false sentiment. At Beechwood and Evelynton individual slaves had absconded with no apparent concern for their families left behind—evidence, Ruffin surmised, that they had no such commitment. He began to revise his old ideas in the early summer of 1862, trying to justify Edmund's astonishing, sudden decision to sell twenty-nine troublesome slaves. That sale, Ruffin said, was an ordeal for the Ruffins; their slaves had forced them to "a painful necessity thus to sever more family ties, & also those before subsisting, (& supposed to be strong on both sides,) between the master & his family & the slaves."[61]

Yet his behavior on the day of the sale at Beechwood was that of a troubled man. Julian helped Edmund load the people headed for sale on June 23. "As I could render no aid to my son in this disagreeable business, I left at 10 A.M. for Ruthven," Ruffin noted. "The wagons did not leave until 2 P.M., after which Julian returned home." His diary entry that day was a mixture of contradictory statements, asserting that slaves cared nothing for family ties, yet noting that he had found himself unable to witness the departure from Beechwood. And despite his new view of the black family, he found it necessary to console himself with protestations that Edmund had done everything, even for these troublemakers, to consider family ties: he had sold to just one buyer, who represented only two plantations; he had tried to break no family tie except those already broken by the slaves themselves.[62] For some reason, Ruffin was unable to observe a scene in which he might have tested the accuracy of his new ideas.

Another revolution in relations between the Ruffins and their slaves occurred at Marlbourne when the family reoccupied that farm for six months in the winter of 1862–63. Ruffin arrived at the farm dreading to confront those slaves, fearing it would be impossible to "preserve towards them the same manner as if they had not offended." They had broken the old bonds by their absconding and by their appropriation of the product of the farm during the recent Yankee occupation. When Edmund, Jr., and Julian announced their intention to sell the farm, Ruffin expressed regret at "this unfortunate close of the service of my patrimonial slaves." Edmund, Jr., offered the absconders an "amnesty" (which was rejected) and that winter Ruffin duly noted each of the four occasions when a slave returned and professed penitence. He noted, too, that it was the coldest winter in memory.[63] He did not imagine, however, that he was witnessing a severing of feudal ties. Immediate matters of the Ruffin family estate were at stake. The Ruffins were simply weighing their chances of needing a labor supply in the spring against the danger of losing their investment if the Yankees returned with warm weather.

As Ruffin perceived, the balance of power had shifted in 1862 in favor of the slaves. He knew then that if the Union army returned, the slaves would abscond again; and, based on the experience at Beechwood earlier that year, he knew that in another occupation of Hanover County the Ruffin family was powerless to remove the Marlbourne slaves to Petersburg or Amelia County. "They could not be removed to any other place of more security, if against their will, at a moment's warning."[64] Having no illusions—certainly not now—about mastery or power, he endorsed his sons' sensible effort to sell, even in a buyer's market. In the face of facts, the Ruffins were moving rapidly out of the business of farming with slaves.

In all his adult life Edmund Ruffin never had cultivated relations with his slaves that placed him in anything but an impersonal, managerial role. Toward his slaves he did not play the role of patriarch, nor did he really imagine himself in a paternal role toward them until the slave communities at Marlbourne and Beechwood began to seize their freedom.[65] Never did he have a body servant. Except for the winter of 1857, when he suffered from poor circulation, no servant slept in his room or cared for his fire.[66] In the journal he kept at Marlbourne he seldom referred to individual slaves, and after 1855 he could summon the names of only a few people belonging to his family; those he did name were either members his generation, or household and livery servants, or his two black foremen.[67] In 1862, when he rode south of Richmond to the fortification project at Drewry's Bluff, in search of Edmund's slaves who had been impressed into construction work, he did not recognize or know those men when he chanced upon them: it was they who identified themselves to him.[68] At the end of June 1862, after the evacuation of Beechwood, Ruffin took a ride over to the farm. "About the mansion, & elsewhere on all the farm, I saw no human being, except an old negro woman in the dairy, churning (at her discretion,) & a negro child sitting in the door of one of the few houses now occupied by the remaining old or infirm slaves." These had been Edmund, Jr.'s slaves; as Ruffin himself admitted, he did not know these people.[69] His own identity never had been secured by an image of himself exercising benevolent, paternal power over slaves. These people were simply a necessary source of labor.

The one significant change Edmund Ruffin experienced in his relations with individual blacks as a result of the Civil War involved his own sense of physical security. He had spent his entire life as a member of a white minority among a black slave majority without displaying fear for his personal safety. As late as 1861 he boasted of sleeping without a gun and without locking his doors or windows. His servants had keys to the houses.[70] By May of 1862 his behavior changed abruptly as the Union army approached Beechwood. He knew that slaves might seize this opportunity to advance their own cause. "We prepared & loaded our fire-arms—& for the first time I even locked my room door (which is also an out-door,) & closed & fastened the very frail window shutters, when I went to bed."[71] With this gesture he acknowledged a simple shift of power between masters and slaves, with one side losing significantly. There would be other, more material losses concerning the slaves.

The most immediate losses affected investments linked to the labor supply at Beechwood, Evelynton, and Marlbourne. These farms ceased production in the spring of 1862 for the duration of that year, entailing a loss of at least $35,000 in gross annual income, equivalent to perhaps 10 percent of their entire capital.[72] By 1865 the family had lost most of their income for three years. Only Ruthven and Redmoor sustained the Ruffins and their remaining slaves with food; neither of these minor farms produced significant amounts for the Petersburg and Richmond markets. This loss of production alone threatened the family with financial ruin as early as 1862. Above this, Ruffin's sons lost about one-third of their estate by 1863 through the defection of slaves.[73]

For Ruffin himself, this brought a financial disaster he foresaw as early as May 1862, when Marlbourne and its slaves were abandoned for the first time in the war. "My own reserved fund, principal & interest, was secured on the Marlbourne farm & property," he noted then.[74] The family did reoccupy Marlbourne between October 1862 and May 1863, but eventually Ruffin lost almost his entire endowment at Marlbourne, a farm valued at $109,600 (Confederate dollars) in January 1863, including forty-three slaves at $700 each.[75] These remaining Marlbourne slaves alone—temporarily in the family's possession that month—were worth $30,100. It was upon the labor of these slaves that Ruffin's "reserved fund" of $25,000 was grounded.[76] This was the fund on which he had counted for his modest annual competency of $1,500 in interest payments.[77] The property was lost finally in May 1864, when it fell behind Union army lines for the duration of the war.[78] In these years Ruffin's income and competency began to disappear. He became, for the first time in his life, dependent on his children, who themselves had suffered in their fortunes. If not penniless, he had very little money, a situation made worse by general scarcities in Virginia. Paper became so expensive that he broke up quires once intended for the *Farmers' Register* and made his own envelopes.[79] In March 1863 he owned only one pair of shoes.[80] If board and room could be found in the crowded hotels of Richmond or Petersburg, Ruffin now had to calculate whether he could afford the expense.[81] In the summer of 1864 Ruffin wrote to his sister that his capital "would not now serve to buy me a full suit of decent clothing with my total income from a year."[82] The war demolished the ingenious arrangements he had devised for investing in family farms, which made his own family and its slaves the institution of support for his late career in writing and reform. With the collapse of the economic underpinnings of that institution, he lost any material basis for aspiring to lead an active career to the end of his natural life. By 1864 his income had declined to less than half its former value, and he had signed most of his capital away.[83] In the spring of 1865 he owned no real estate, no house, and all of his income and capital were "annihilated."[84] He was totally dependent upon his sons for his support. This was what he meant in that final entry of his diary when he wrote, "I am now merely a cumberer of the earth, & a useless consumer of its fruits, earned by the exertions of others."[85]

Final Misfortunes

The war years also brought to Ruffin's family a series of deaths, which made Ruffin despondent long before the collapse of the Confederacy. These tragedies he found simply unspeakable. People beyond the circle of his family and a few friends, therefore, did not know about this accumulating grief and melancholy; newspaper accounts of Ruffin's death did not mention the others, and awareness of them disappeared. Between 1844 and the end of 1860, eight members of Ruffin's immediate family died: his wife, two grandchildren, a beloved daughter-in-law, and four daughters. During the war itself, five more members died, including his daughter Mildred, granddaughters Nanny and Jane (to whom Ruffin had been devoted) and grandson Julian Beckwith, killed instantly by gunshot to the head in 1862 at the Battle of Seven Pines.[86]

Most traumatic of these deaths for Ruffin was that of his son Julian, killed in action on 16 May 1864, a year before Ruffin took his own life. By this time Ruffin was living with Edmund, Jr., at Redmoor. Julian was commanding an artillery company when he died at Drewry's Bluff, seven miles south of Richmond. Ruffin's granddaughter, Margaret Stanly Beckwith, recalled years later that the Petersburg family tried to suppress details of the death, to spare his survivors.

Ruffin's son-in-law, Dr. T. Stanly Beckwith, was a volunteer surgeon that day at Drewry's Bluff, and it was he who brought the body to Petersburg for burial. Beckwith's daughter Margaret heard the news within two days. "Uncle Julian had just aimed the gun & stood to see the effect of shot—when a shell took off his head," she wrote. "His family never knew this."[87] Though news of Julian's death did not reach Amelia County until 23 May, days after the funeral, Ruffin did learn what young Margaret Beckwith had heard, and in accurate detail. His grandson George, who had been on duty near Julian, provided facts that Ruffin entered in his diary. "He was leaning against & looking over the top of the earthwork, when he was struck by a minnie ball over the right eye, which penetrated the brain, & caused his instant death."[88] When Ruffin wrote to his sister in June, he took consolation in the fact that Julian had led a just life and had died in "brave performance of his military duties." Amid these comforting words he interjected the now-familiar thought: "his death blow was instantaneous & painless."[89]

Julian's death was particularly hard to bear. He was then forty-three years old, the father of five young children. Ruffin had spent much of 1863 and 1864 at Julian's farm, apparently deciding finally that Julian was the son reserved for himself. When Julian was born in 1821, Ruffin had chosen his middle name, "Calx," referring to the crumbly residue remaining after a metal or mineral has been subjected to intense heat; the name also is related to the word *calcium*, referring to the element of the earth's crust formed by leaves, bones, and shells. Julian returned the honor in 1861, a week after Fort Sumter, by naming his fourth child Edmund Sumter.[90] While Ruffin had acquiesced when Edmund, Jr., and grandson Thomas volunteered for war duty, and while he had absolutely insisted that the reluctant Charles serve the Confederacy, he had begged Julian to stay home. Julian hesitated two weeks, joined the Prince George militia in 1862, and then was conscripted into the Confederate army in July 1863.[91]

In its implications for Ruffin's future, Julian's death was a disaster. All of Julian's estate went to Lottie, and Ruffin would not enforce obligations upon a widow's estate for payments toward his own support. While Ruffin expected no other disposition of Julian's estate, he plainly understood a harsh fact: there would be no more interest from Julian's obligations.[92] This changed his relationship to Edmund, Jr., for Ruffin now was utterly dependent upon this one son—who was himself the father of seven living children, whose farms lay in ruins, and who said he could not afford the price of a train ticket to North Carolina.[93] Three years had brought a transformation in Ruffin's social situation, from competence to dependence. The partnership, the investments in the family's farms, the endowment and the income that promised an independent, competent old age—these had expired with Julian, instantly.

These private griefs accompanied other losses that only Ruffin knew fully and that he discussed only in his diary. Contemporaries knew very little, therefore, about the decline of his body between 1862 and 1865, or the exact chronology of that decline. When the war began, Ruffin was sixty-seven years old. His behavior in 1861 and 1862 at Fort Sumter, First Manassas, and Seven Pines demonstrated his vigor. He still could walk across Richmond and from Ruthven to Coggin's Point, regardless of the weather. The description of him on his 1862 military pass (permitting him to inspect the fortifications around Norfolk) listed his height as 5 feet 8 inches and his weight as 140 pounds. He never had enjoyed better health. The Confederate clerk in Norfolk noticed only the one ominous sign, that his complexion was "florid."[94]

Yet by 1861 Ruffin himself was beginning to detect signs of declining health. Between 1857 and 1865 he would experience an almost total loss of hearing, a loss of eyesight, incontinence, loss of motor skills (noticeable, he said, in the trembling when he grasped a pen), and the onset of dizziness that would lead to falls.[95] At this point, too, Ruffin knew he had survived longer than any of his ancestors except for his great-grandfather. He began to think of himself as old.

The first clues that he was losing his hearing appeared in January 1858, in Washington, as he attempted to follow debates in the Senate and House chambers. "I could hear but badly," he complained. The same difficulty occurred in 1859, but Ruffin did not yet see that he was deaf.[96] His complaints multiplied. By September 1860, he realized he could not hear other passengers on trains, "so that, generally, I prefer not to converse when moving on a railway."[97] In January 1861, at the Florida secession convention, Ruffin acknowledged his deafness for the first time.[98]

One major cause of his deafness, ironically, occurred in the action against Fort Sumter. On 9 April 1861 Ruffin waded ashore through the surf on Morris Island, slept in a tent, and took arms with the Palmetto Guard; on 12 April he fired the first shot.[99] This activity fatigued him. On 13 April, after breakfast on Morris Island, Ruffin sat down and leaned back against the wall of a mortar battery. "Without intending it, I fell asleep," he wrote, "& remained so until the first 10 inch mortar was fired."

> This was the one not far from my seat, & of which I was obliquely in front. Thus placed, the sound & concussion were unusually powerful, & I was roused not only by the loud & close report, but by a great shock to my ears & sense of hearing. My previous slight deafness was greatly increased.[100]

In fact, he never did recover. At Manassas in 1861 he was able to hear cannon and musket fire, and he could see clearly in the brilliant sunlight; but his account of that battle revealed an uncertainty about his hearing.[101] In Richmond in May 1862, during the Battle of Seven Pines just east of the city, he could not hear cannon reports until mid-afternoon, when he did hear "many of the louder reports." At Marlbourne in the spring of 1863, after a morning of heavy rain on 30 April, members of the family and small work force listened as cannons began firing late in the day near Chancellorsville (fifty miles to the north); Ruffin heard nothing until the others called his attention to the sound.[102]

The consequence of deafness was isolation. Though he could hear an individual who spoke while facing him, he could no longer hear general conversation. "And when two or more are talking or making any other noise at once, I can hear nothing clearly, no matter how loud the talking may be."[103] This removed him increasingly from his family and from the kind of intellectual activities he had always relished. In Richmond, Washington, and Charleston, Ruffin's intellectual life had depended on the ability to hear other men talk, no matter how vapid the talk. He had used conversation to gather thoughts—in churches, legislative chambers, lobbies, and hotel rooms, on porches, steamboats, and trains. As early as March 1863 he knew his loss of hearing would isolate him from this kind of exchange.[104] People at the time did know the significance of this loss; no one apparently persuaded him to take it in stride.

By the summer of 1862 Ruffin knew also that he was becoming at least partially blind, the first symptom being "night blindness." He discovered this first at Manassas in 1861, during the retreat in darkness from Centreville to Bull Run.[105] A year later, in June 1862, while the nighttime encounters of the Seven Days' Battles were in progress around the eastern perimeter of Richmond, Ruffin joined his family outdoors at Ruthven to witness the flashing of artillery fire twenty-five miles to the north. "While I was standing in the yard to listen for the reports, & to note the direction, I observed many very faint flashes of light, like the faintest of sheet lightning, all seeming to rise from the horizon, & in different points, but from the same general direction."[106] The next month, however, during the night cannonade against McClellan from Coggin's Point, he again experienced almost total sensory isolation. "When passing on the road through a part of the Grove, amidst large oaks, I could not see (except the sky above,) any more than if I had been totally blind." Since the Confederate force moved that night in strict silence, little sound reached his "deaf ears." After the cannonade, whose first discharges "startled and agitated" him, he was led home by his grandson.[107]

Ruffin's night blindness was a symptom of either chronic simple glaucoma or cataracts. As either of his two sons-in-law who were physicians could have told him, there was no cure. Night-blind people in the nineteenth century progressively lost their vision. For Ruffin this meant his reading and writing would be confined soon to hours of bright daylight; if lights, too, became expensive, evening would become a period of killing time. Although he continued to read and to keep his diary, the day was nearing when he no longer would be able to spend sixteen hours with books and papers. Few people outside the family knew about this imminent loss, since he retained his vision during the day; no one beyond the family, therefore, perceived the consequences.[108] Ruffin knew by 1862 what those consequences would be. Not only was he headed for physical dependency, but the senses necessary for his life's work were simply failing. His isolation, as on that night at Coggin's Point, would become complete.

Other afflictions began to compound his physical misery in 1862. Early that year in Richmond he suffered an attack of "disordered bowels," an affliction so prolonged that "the habit seemed fixed." A second attack began in May of 1863, becoming prolonged and severe by the first of June. "I had before (when at the worst) believed, & now again suspect, that this change is the indication of the breaking down of my constitution, & bodily powers," he wrote, "& the precursor of death not far off." Regarding the possible onset of incontinence with horror, he attempted to conceal his condition from the family, thus heightening his isolation.[109]

The chronology of family events was significant in determining his response to his troubles. By the summer of 1863, Ruffin had been a widower nearly twenty years. The daughters who had cared for his physical welfare had all died—Jane, Ella, Rebecca, Elizabeth, and Mildred. In 1863 Nanny, the only granddaughter who could have taken such a role, died.[110] The idea of assigning a servant to care for him did not suggest itself, for by 1863 there were few slaves remaining who might have taken that role. Assigning a slave to such a task, moreover, would have required a decision by Edmund and Julian. Ruffin was trapped. Having been cast into a situation in which he might be forced to depend upon attention and care from white women (his shirts, his diet), he now found that events had removed all but two such women from his family, and they were daughters-in-law: Julian's Lottie, and Edmund's new wife, Jane Minerva Ruffin, daughter of the chief justice of the Supreme Court of the state of North Carolina.

At about this time, it was Jane Minerva Ruffin who began to espouse the principle that elderly people might find liquor beneficial in aiding the digestion. (She knew Ruffin's secret.) Her father had favored the remedy for years. Ruffin complied with her suggestion, and the family maintained its discreet silence. "Not on account of my frequent disease, (which indeed has not been known fully except to myself,) [Ruffin assured himself] but because of my age & weakness, my children at whose houses I have latterly remained, & especially their wives, have urged me to abandon my general habit of abstinence from all intoxicating liquors, & to drink a glass of toddy every day." Ruffin knew all about the origins of this family remedy and its reputed beneficial effect: "I do not believe it."[111]

The other afflictions were minor (a persistent pneumonia in 1863 and 1864, loss of appetite, sleeplessness, and forgetfulness), though Ruffin did not suffer these afflictions in silence.[112] The family heard much about his weakness. From Redmoor on 18 May 1864, Ruffin (still unaware of Julian's death) wrote to Lottie that he felt "extreme feebleness" and pain. "I have barely made out to write the concise daily entries in my diary, necessary to preserve its connection." He still felt pain in his right shoulder, the result of a recent fall. "I do not think you have realized my past extreme illness & prostration," he complained. "I must now rest," he said, interrupting the letter for a day.[113] He probably had not suffered a stroke, though he knew the symptoms of apoplexy through his experience in 1840 with his neighbor, Thomas Cocke. The fall probably resulted from weakness of pneumonia fever. If his trembling, feebleness, forgetfulness, and florid complexion suggested apoplexy, his handwriting did not. He retained a consistent, readable hand to the end.[114] The physical afflictions he suffered during the years of the Civil War were those of a man whose body was aging, a fact about Ruffin that contemporaries certainly did perceive: the *Richmond Whig* estimated his age at eighty. Ruffin also experienced depression over the fate of the Confederacy; this began not in 1865, however, but in 1862, when he understood the first effects of the Union blockade. As early as March 1862— three years before Appomattox—he foresaw defeat and referred to himself as "gloomy & depressed."[115]

These feelings remained throughout the war, as his family knew. When the armies of Lee and Grant passed south of Redmoor after the fall of Richmond, the Ruffins felt panic, fearing another of their farms would be overrun; they worked "several nights," harder than they had worked in their lives, concealing and burying provisions and valuables. But, as Edmund, Jr., reported to North Carolina in-laws, "we had the blessed good fortune, for which I shall ever be profoundly grateful, to escape both armies—they passed a few miles (from 6 to 10) south of us." They saw not a single Yankee. Confederate stragglers did pass Redmoor, "all of whom we were glad to feed, and all of whom refrained from interfering with or molesting us in any-way."[116] (Still, he loaded the musket against horse thieves.) This was the moment, Edmund said later, when he had feared his father might commit suicide.[117] After that moment, the time for suicide impelled simply by fear, honor, or shame had passed.

The end of the war brought some surprises to Ruffin, one of which was an evident release from anxiety. He first heard about Lee's evacuation of Richmond—"the worst of news"—immediately after breakfast on 3 April, within hours of the event. After a long day of hiding valuables (including volumes of the diary, which he carried to Harrison's house) and hearing more reports about the fall of Richmond, Ruffin went to bed. "Strange—I slept last night from very soon after lying down (before 10) & with less than my accustomed comforts of lodging, & did not wake once, until after day-break," he said the next day. "It is very rare for me not to wake once, & generally oftener, & to lie awake for disagreeable lengths of time."[118]

He did continue to imagine he would be taken prisoner and subjected to treatment "compared to which the infliction of immediate death, by shot or halter, would be merciful." He feared, too, that his sons' families would be "stripped of everything" because of his role in secession.[119] These concerns lasted into early June, though they abated and changed form. Evidence concerning the treatment of Jefferson Davis made it plain by 5 June that Ruffin would not be subjected to physical punishment.[120] He continued to worry that his presence at Redmoor was placing the family's property in danger of seizure, though that concern should have passed by the middle of May, when Edmund, Jr., Lottie, and Ruffin's grandson Thomas took the oath of allegiance in Petersburg and secured protection for their property. "When giving his name in the Provost Marshal's office, an officer asked Edmund if he was the son of the 'Ruffin of Sumter notoriety'?" Ruffin reported. "He answered 'I am,' & no further remark was made."[121]

There was at least one final surprise associated with the status and attitude of blacks in the South immediately after the war. In early May, clinging to the belief that blacks would not work in freedom, Ruffin predicted that the South would decline to "the industrial conditions of Jamaica & Liberia." Under emancipation, blacks would suffer a Malthusian disaster, with their numbers decreasing rapidly— a view he held to the end.[122] In the Richmond newspapers, however, he did see one straw in the wind: astonishingly low wages for freedmen were being established, at rates between three and six dollars a month. "If labor could have been hired & commanded at the highest of these rates, I would, for economy, have ceased to be a slaveowner fifty years ago."[123]

Had Ruffin allowed time for these particular fears of disaster to subside completely after the war, he still would have been a troubled man. His family's economic ruin remained. He must have had a clear sense then of his own role in that ruination, a sense that he had been wrong at least in having drawn them down a thorny path. And there remained the problems of dreary boredom, physical complaints, and the humiliating dependence suffered by a "cumberer of the earth."

Lessons from the Past

The most important influences on Ruffin's last decision were two controlling ideas that had governed his thinking for years. These old ideas were still powerful in 1865, establishing the context that permitted him to make the decision. Both were implicit—present as assumptions—in the final entry of his diary.

Beginning in 1813 and continuing thereafter, Ruffin's notion of an acceptable life involved personal independence based on adequate financial resources. This was his notion of competency. His entire plan for retirement and a career in reform had been invented with this idea in mind, for he could not have imagined living upon the patronage of others. Even his relationship to his family was designed to sustain a material independence. The depth of his commitment to this idea was always somewhat ironic, based as it was upon slavery and the compliance of women. Ruffin seldom thought in ironic terms, however. He simply adhered to the old idea and never tolerated dependence. In his concept of his own past, all his achievements were results of his own effort. The idea of competency had formed the philosophical underpinning of his plan for reviving rural Virginia with farmers who would restore their own farms. It was present throughout the final entry in his diary, particularly in the middle section where he reviewed his life history and expressed his horror at living as a dependent upon his son and two daughters-in-law. Now, competency clearly was gone. For Ruffin the conditions of an acceptable life had ended.

There was also in the final passage a specific idea of death that Ruffin began to conceive as early as 1821 and that he developed fully after 1840. Death was the final link in the natural food cycle, when the body returned to the earth, restoring fertility. Bones formed calcareous manure, flesh formed putrescent manure. This notion obviously came from his early work in soil rejuvenation. He articulated the idea fully for the first time in 1840, on the occasion of the suicide of Thomas Cocke.

This idea became a dominating image in Ruffin's perception of nature. Animals in the field would lie down and rejuvenate the earth. Trees would fall and yield their matter. When plans were afoot to bring the long-buried remains of James Monroe from New York for reinterment in Virginia, Ruffin agreed with the comment of former Governor Tazewell, "Where the tree falls, there let it lie."[24] By 1858 Monroe had performed his function, in New York. The idea was a common Ruffin metaphor. Between 1853 and 1865 his ideas about death advanced beyond simple metaphor, reaching new levels of detail and sophistication that only perusers of the diary could have discovered. Events and pressures in those ten years prompted changes in thought, long before the collapse of the Confederacy. Long before that, he became inured to death.

During the succession of family tragedies after 1853, Ruffin's response to death changed in one discernible aspect. After each of the six deaths occurring between 1853 and 1860, he experienced classic, Victorian shock and grief; he spent months in mourning, noting frequently in his diary the anniversary of a death. After the deaths of his granddaughter Virginia (1844), grandson Edmund Quintus (1853), and daughters Jane (1855), Ella (1855), and Elizabeth (1860), he wrote long, private prayers for each. He concluded his prayer after Jane's death with a supplication: "And if it shall be thy will that death shall strike down another of the dearly loved remaining props of my old age . . . , Oh God! in thy mercy spare me this sorrow, by my being first called & removed by death."[125] Most of these deaths occurred after lingering pain and illness, which Ruffin witnessed.

For deaths occurring after 1860 he found himself grieving less deeply, a fact he found interesting and upon which he speculated. The grandson killed at Seven Pines he did not know very well; his daughter Mildred died at a distance, in Kentucky. No explanation offered itself, however, for his emotional failures at the death of Julian Calx. "I have not shed a tear."[126] Edmund, Jr., noticed the same peculiarity in his father. "Julian's death is a severe shock to him, but he stands it better than you would think, but it is simply because he doesn't realize it," he wrote his wife in North Carolina. "He will feel it more sensibly as time wears on."[127] But he did not. There had been too many of these events, and not merely among the Ruffins. Situated as his family's farms were, in a crescent around three sides of Richmond and Petersburg, Ruffin was surrounded by death between 1862 and 1865. The scale of violence he witnessed simply by living in that zone struck no one as unusual, and probably it was not. Ruffin set himself apart from his contemporaries, however, by keeping a daily record of his responses; he referred occasionally to this record, thereby keeping himself aware of change.

The first human being Ruffin saw actually being killed was John Brown. Late in 1859, having been outraged by Brown's raid, Ruffin took the train to Harpers Ferry to see if he could witness the execution. By joining the Virginia Military Institute cadet corps and marching with them, he gained access on 2 December to the execution grounds. There he wrote one of the longest pieces of pure narrative he ever produced, beginning with descriptions of the excitement in the town. Rumors that abolitionists were descending to rescue Brown were fired by what appeared to be rockets in the mountains at night (which, it developed, were simply sparks from chimneys in the town, distorted by the phenomenon of looming). Then Ruffin recorded details of the hanging, centering his attention on Brown. "His movements & manner gave no evidence of his being either terrified or concerned, & he went through what was required of him apparently with as little agitation as if he had been the willing assistant, instead of the victim." Once the hood and "halter" were around Brown's neck, there was a five-minute delay, a "cruel & most trying infliction" through which Brown stood, "erect, & as motionless as if he had been a statue." Finally, the platform dropped.

> The fall was not more than 12 or 15 inches. I could not perceive the least movement of the body or limbs, for about a minute of time after the fall. But after about a minute, the hands were moved convulsively, but still only slightly, for a short time. Then again the whole frame seemed motionless. But I might possibly have been deceived in this, as the wind caused the suspended body to swing like a pendulum during all the time. After some 5 minutes or more of real or apparent entire absence of motion, I perceived slight convulsive motions of the legs, which also soon ceased, & all was still, & so remained, except the swaying of the body to & fro by the wind.[128]

Brown astonished Ruffin by displaying physical courage, "one quality that is more highly esteemed by the world than the most rare & perfect virtues." Brown showed "the most complete fearlessness of & insensibility to danger & death." Ruffin had seen now an episode of death both prolonged and sudden; he had seen an image of what Thomas Cocke must have experienced alone in 1840. The episode exhausted Ruffin. "The fatigue of the forenoon & my loss of sleep last night made me very tired," he wrote. He went to bed "earlier than usual."[129]

During the war he saw many more episodes of violent death. After the battle at Manassas in 1861, he inspected part of the battlefield near the Stone Bridge. "It was a horrible sight." The Union dead lay scattered in an open field of thirty acres, many of them from a Zouave regiment dressed in red trousers. "Clotted blood, in what had been pools, were under or by almost every corpse," he observed. "From bullet holes in the heads of some, the brains had partly oozed out. The white froth covering the mouths of others was scarcely less shocking in appearance." About half a dozen Union soldiers still were alive. Ruffin offered a cup to one and tried to encourage the others, aston-

ished by "this long continued & wretched state of suffering."[130] He
was not yet inured.

In late October 1862, when he and his son's family were moving
temporarily back to Marlbourne, Ruffin began to accept the scale of
these calamities. He ceased to respond with sentiment and began to
think of battles as events in nature. On that journey to Marlbourne,
in order to save the strength of the carriage horses, Ruffin walked
ahead of the family party for two hours from the center of Richmond
toward Mechanicsville. The party overtook him near the town, where
a battle had occurred in June; then they rode together through the
battleground. "I saw the marks of the passage of cannon balls through
houses at Mechanicsville, of limbs & trunks of trees cut down, & the
graves of sundry of our killed, & the bones of horses killed near the
road, & which had been suffered to rot, & all the flesh to disappear."
At Manassas, he recalled, people from the Tidewater had noticed that
no buzzards appeared after the battle, "though thousands of carcasses
of men & horses were exposed over miles, & for days together, &
many for weeks, contaminating the air with the odor of putrefaction
which is so grateful & attractive to these obscene birds." The same
phenomenon occurred at Mechanicsville, where twenty thousand bodies of men and horses had lain exposed to the elements. The buzzards
disappeared, "frightened & driven off by the noise of the artillery,"
he supposed.

> This explanation would be incredible, but for the certain fact that not
> a buzzard was seen, though many bodies, either left unburied, or not
> entirely covered by the slight burying, were exposed to both the senses
> of sight & smell, for weeks, or until nothing was left except the bones.[131]

Here, with this image of nature disturbed but proceeding irresistibly,
he succeeded for the first time in detaching sentiment from surrounding events.

This development in 1862 came seven years after Ruffin began
expressing his own death wish. Beginning in 1855, at every bereave-
ment and at nearly every one of his own birthdays, Ruffin expressed
the wish to die. On his birthday in 1859 he said he did not desire
old age, "if accompanied by great infirmity of body, or much less of
mind."[132] In October of that year, after the wedding of his daughter,
he wrote, "I have lived long enough—& a little more time of such
unused & wearisome passage of time will make my life too long."[133]
In May 1861, after the triumph of secession, he wrote again, "I have

now lived long enough."[134] At some point between 1861 and 1865, this wish must have begun to manifest itself in conversation and in letters like that Ruffin sent to Lottie in 1863, for the family was aware of his thoughts.[135]

By that time Ruffin had defined an ideal death. The horror, for him, was the kind of death experienced by his daughter Jane, who knew she was dying and lingered in pain for weeks, preparing for heaven while she comforted and commanded the soon-to-be-bereaved. Edmund, Jr.'s first wife, the consumptive Mary Cooke Smith Ruffin, died in accordance with the same plan of exquisite suffering, embellishing the sequence only by insisting that Ruffin himself, as father-in-law, come lie on her deathbed, just before the end. None of this would do for Ruffin.

His idea of the perfect death emerged clearly on his sixty-fifth birthday, 5 January 1859. In his entry that day he said he no longer dreaded death, but it must be "sudden & unexpected, & without suffering." Four years later he observed the start of his seventieth year with the same idea. "I only & earnestly desire that when it comes, it shall be unexpected, & immediately obeyed in sudden & painless death."[136] The wish and the idea appeared repeatedly in his diary after 1859: sudden, unexpected, and painless death.[137] If his family knew the lengths of his speculation on the subject, the temptation must have finally been strong to dismiss it as morose self-pity in an old man who was indeed terrified of pain and death.

Yet Ruffin had grounds for defining what he preferred in this idea, based on experiences he never connected explicitly but that did influence his thinking at crucial points late in his life. In 1857, while grubbing roots to clear scenic pathways through the woods at Beechwood, he injured his left hand, raising blisters by handling tools and possibly by touching poison oak. (Being right-handed, he continued to write in his diary.) An infection deep in the hand ensued, necessitating surgery by his nephew and former son-in-law, Dr. John Dupuy. Dupuy used ether.

Under the influence of ether Ruffin experienced the nineteenth-century miracle of painlessness. "I was perfectly conscious of gradual coming over me of the stupifying & also soothing & grateful operation of the gas—& soon after, knew nothing more until I came to, in my clear sense, & with but little feeling of pain."[138] In subsequent years, as he read about the lives of famous authors like Scott and De Quincey, Ruffin's thoughts must have returned to the effects of this soothing gas. He did not believe De Quincey's claim, in the Appendix to *Confessions of an Opium Eater*, that the author had given up using opium. The whole book seemed inspired by opium, and was "far from a dissuader."

> If I could believe that the author's sensations & experience would be mine—& I looked merely to my own feelings & present interest— without regard to the opinions of my family or the world, or the shame & sin of the habit—I would at once commence the practice of opium-eating.[139]

He became fascinated by ether, opium, and the stupefying of the senses. This fascination would lead him to a motive for self-murder. Painless, sudden, unexpected death became Ruffin's standard of the perfect death after he witnessed John Brown's execution. This was one major change in his thinking. The war years fixed this idea in his mind by producing an abundance of similar deaths—many by gunshot wounds to the head, and not all of them on the battlefields at Manassas, Seven Pines, or Mechanicsville.

These assaulted Ruffin in a grotesque, bizarre pattern. In 1861, the seventeen-year-old neighbor boy at Tarbay, Nathaniel Cocke, shot himself (almost certainly by accident) in the head, from below the chin, with a shotgun. Ruffin's granddaughter Nanny was first on the scene, entering the kitchen where Martha Cocke sat on the floor, cradling her son's head in her lap and crying for help.[140] Later in 1861, Ruffin's former associate at the Agricultural Society, Philip St. George Cocke, left the Confederate service and returned to his farm, Belmead, where he killed himself by gunshot to the head.[141] There followed in 1862 and 1864 the instantaneous deaths of the two Julians.

In this context Ruffin first heard about the assassination of Abraham Lincoln. He professed to rejoice in the slaying, though he recorded the news almost dispassionately.[142] As details accumulated in newspapers, Ruffin noticed the striking similarities between the deaths of Lincoln and assassin John Wilkes Booth. Lincoln had been shot from behind, the bullet passing through his head without damaging the brain enough to kill him instantly. "Lincoln lived some 12 hours, but insensible throughout." The bullet that killed Booth followed a comparable course. "Booth lived two or three hours, sensible, & in great agony most of the time." Given the terms in which Ruffin discussed the assassination, he must have drawn a practical lesson from it. "Strange! that, in either case, a ball should have passed quite through the main body of the brain, as I infer, without causing instant death!!"[143]

Ruffin did record one final, significant shift in his thinking about death. As late as July 1859, he still considered suicide in simple, orthodox terms: if not a sin, it certainly was a sign of insanity.[144] When the war began he still held this old view, but by 1865 he had changed. He knew the State of Virginia placed suicide in the category of crimes subject to inquest, but in the context of events in the spring of 1865, he dismissed that definition.[145]

Books and reading, again, became the crucial means for conceptualizing these experiences, just as they had during those troubled early years at Coggin's Point Farm when Ruffin first read Sir Humphry Davy on soil chemistry and began to suspect what was wrong with his fields. Beginning in November 1862, he read Adam Clarke's commentaries, one of his first approaches to scholarly works on the Bible. From Clarke he proceeded to other works on religious thought, Christianity, and the history of the Jews.[146] After losing his library at Beechwood he turned to other reading matter, including the Bible itself, where he found no sweeping condemnation of suicide.[147] As the war progressed, he turned for diversion to whatever lay at hand, including his own manuscripts. There he found crucial material for new ideas.

In the summer of 1863 Ruffin discovered the delight of reading his own diary, and he read long sections of its account of Manassas. He quite loved being his own audience, so he dipped into other sections of the diary. In 1864 he turned to other manuscripts, including his "Incidents of my Life," relishing its account of triumphs at Coggin's Point, of editing the *Farmers' Register*, and rejuvenating the fields at Marlbourne. By 1865, as his writing in the coda to his final entry suggests, he must have turned also to his unpublished 1840 narrative, "Statement of the closing scenes of the life of Thomas Cocke."

There he must have read his debate with Cocke. There was his own argument that suicide was a sign of insanity, followed by Cocke's reply, "In that, you are *altogether* mistaken!" Then came the account of his retracing Cocke's path to the woods at Tarbay and what he saw when he reached the oak. He must have read about Cocke's notion favoring the Chinese custom of simple burial at eighteen inches, and followed again Cocke's recitation of the eternal cycle of the food chain.[148] Some of this last he borrowed for his coda:

> Let my remains be buried in the clothes in which I shall die, & with merely the additional over-wrapping in an old sheet or blanket. The sooner a dead body is enveloped & in contact with the earth to which it is to return, & the more speedy its inevitable decomposition, & the disappearance of the corruptible portion, so much the better. I much prefer, & earnestly request, that there may be no coffin of any kind.[149]

There would be no need for a coroner's inquest, given the evidence in his final handwritten memoranda. (Near the end he gave his manuscripts to Edmund, Jr., requesting that none of them be lost or destroyed.) He wanted no company of mourners assembled for the burial, no ceremonies.[150] Once again, as in 1840 when Ruffin first realized he had taught Cocke a new way of thinking about the earth, the circle of ideas returned to the mind of Thomas Cocke. This time it was Thomas Cocke who played the role of teacher, planting the ideas.

The timing of events sustained reports that Edmund Ruffin killed himself on Saturday, the seventeenth of June.[151] This was two months after his son first suspected he was contemplating suicide—two months after the fall of Richmond, when the family feared he might be captured by the Yankees. That danger passed, however, and Edmund, Jr.'s fears had been completely allayed.[152] Perhaps Edmund's frequent absences from Redmoor that spring prevented him from sensing his father's intention, or perhaps Ruffin was cleverer at deception than Thomas Cocke. In any event, suspicions were put aside.

If Ruffin thought of his death as a final act of self-control, he was overlooking the way he would depend even in death upon his son. He assigned to Edmund, Jr., the management of his affairs, which included that afternoon the disposition of a body (a task Ruffin always had considered revolting) and the cleaning of a room.[153] (Edmund, Jr., after all, had assisted in the aftermath of the suicide in 1840.) Neighbor Marshall, who had been visiting at Redmoor that morning, rushed back to the farm with the Harrisons to help Edmund, Jr., with the calamity. "We procured a coffin that evening at Wilkerson's shop," Edmund reported to his sons at Beechwood, "and early next morning Mr. Harrison and I started with the remains for Marlbourne." That was Sunday morning. Probably they rode on Harrison's farm wagon drawn by mules.[154] Their shortest route from Redmoor would have taken them along Genito Road through Powhatan and Chesterfield counties. They must have crossed the James on the Union army pontoon bridge, passed through Richmond in the night, and then continued through Mechanicsville to Old Church. The journey covered about fifty-two miles. At three miles an hour it would have required about twenty-two hours, allowing five hours to refresh the animals along the way. "We reached here about 5 o'clock Monday morning," Edmund said, "and before breakfast he rested under the sod."[155]

Notes

In citing works in the notes short titles have generally been used. Works frequently cited have been identified by the following abbreviations:

CWM   College Archives; and Manuscripts and Rare Books
       Department, Swem Library, College of William and Mary,
       Williamsburg, Va.

LC   Library of Congress, Washington, D.C.

NA   National Archives, Washington, D.C.

SHC   Southern Historical Collection, University of North
       Carolina Library, Chapel Hill

UVA   Manuscripts Department, University of Virginia Library,
       Charlottesville

VHS   Virginia Historical Society, Richmond

VMHB   *Virginia Magazine of History and Biography*

VSL   Archives Division, Virginia State Library, Richmond

Notes to Preface

1. Christopher Lasch, *The New Radicalism in America {1889–1963}: The Intellectual as a Social Type* (New York: Alfred A. Knopf, 1965), xvii–xviii.

Notes to Prologue

1. Edmund Ruffin, "Statement of the closing scenes of the life of Thomas Cocke," 25 Feb. 1840, 8–11, Edmund Ruffin Papers, Virginia Historical

Society, Richmond. "Tarbay" was the neighboring farm; "Tar Bay" is part of the James River north of the farm.

2. Ibid., 2, 8. Ruffin misspelled "skull."

3. Ibid., 7–10.

4. Ibid., 7, 8, 10.

5. Ibid., 1–2, 4.

6. Ibid., 4.

7. Ibid., 7, 8.

8. Ibid., 3–4. Ruffin gave Cocke's age as sixty-four, though modern authorities give his birthdate as 31 July 1774. He was approaching sixty-six. See Claiborne Thweatt Smith, Jr., *Smith of Scotland Neck: Planters on the Roanoke* (Baltimore: Gateway Press, 1976), 197; John Bennett Boddie, *Southside Virginia Families*, 2 vols. (Redwood City, Calif.: Pacific Coast Publishers, 1955–56), 1:151.

9. Ruffin, "Closing scenes," 5–6.

10. Ibid., 4–6.

11. Ibid., 1, 8–9.

12. Ibid., 2, 11.

Notes to Chapter One

1. For recent studies of death in the Chesapeake Bay region, see Darrett B. Rutman and Anita H. Rutman, "Of Agues and Fevers: Malaria in the Early Chesapeake," *William and Mary Quarterly*, 3d ser., 33 (1976): 31–60. See also the following articles in Thad W. Tate and David L. Ammerman, eds., *The Chesapeake in the Seventeenth Century: Essays on Anglo-American Society & Politics* (New York: W. W. Norton & Co., 1979): Carville V. Earle, "Environment, Disease, and Mortality in Early Virginia," 96–125; Lorena S. Walsh, " 'Till Death Us Do Part': Marriage and Family in Seventeenth-Century Maryland," 126–52; and Darrett B. Rutman and Anita H. Rutman, " 'Now-Wives and Sons-in-Law': Parental Death in a Seventeenth-Century Virginia County," 153–82. See also Lois Green Carr and Lorena S. Walsh, "The Planter's Wife: The Experience of White Women in Seventeenth-Century Maryland," *William and Mary Quarterly*, 3d ser., 34 (1977): 542–71; Lorena S. Walsh and Russell R. Menard, "Death in the Chesapeake: Two Life Tables for Men in Early Colonial Maryland," *Maryland Historical Magazine*, 69 (1974): 211–27; Karen Kupperman, "Apathy and Death in Early Jamestown," *Journal of American History*, 66 (1979): 24–40; and Daniel Blake Smith, "Mortality and Family in the Colonial Chesapeake," *Journal of Interdisciplinary History*, 8 (1978): 403–27. See also observations based on the research of other scholars in Peter Uhlenberg, "Death and the Family,"

Journal of Family History, 5 (1980): 313–20; and Robert V. Wells, *Uncle Sam's Family: Issues in and Perspectives on American Demographic History* (Albany: State Univ. of New York Press, 1985), 65–71.

2. Edmund Ruffin, *The Diary of Edmund Ruffin*, ed. William K. Scarborough, 2 vols. to date (Baton Rouge: Louisiana State University Press, 1972–), 1:262 (5 Jan. 1859); [William Boulware], "Edwin [*sic*] Ruffin, of Virginia, Agriculturist," *De Bow's Review*, 11 (1851): 431. Boulware's sketch was based on information supplied by Ruffin. Ruffin complained of poor and failing health throughout his adult life. His complaints should not be dismissed as mere hypochondria, given his family's constant battle with malaria and their experience with fatal diseases after 1850. See Edmund Ruffin, "Address to the Virginia State Agricultural Society, on the Effects of Domestic Slavery on the Manners, Habits and Welfare of the Agricultural Population of the Southern States," supplement to the *Southern Planter*, 13 (1853): 8; "The State Agricultural Society," *Southern Planter*, 13 (1853): 16. (Ruffin's 1852 "Address" appears after the February 1852 issue of the *Southern Planter* in the American Periodical Series microfilm.)

3. Apparently he became more healthy as he matured. At sixty-four, in 1858, he reached 152 pounds, his greatest known weight; four years later he gave his weight as 140 pounds. See Ruffin, *Diary*, 1:107, 227 (21 Sept. 1857, 28 Aug. 1858); Provost marshal's pass issued to Ruffin on 28 March 1862, Edmund Ruffin Papers, Manuscripts Department, University of Virginia Library, Charlottesville (hereafter cited as UVA).

4. The first wife and youngest child of Edmund I died in Sussex County in 1749, making 1750 the earliest year he might have removed to Prince George; Albemarle Parish Register, 1721–87, p. 162, Virginia Historical Society, Richmond (hereafter cited as VHS). Advertisements by Edmund Ruffin II indicated the Ruffins were established in Prince George before the Revolution: *Virginia Gazette* (Rind), 12 Mar. 1772; *Virginia Gazette* (Purdie), 25 Oct. 1776. The nine Ruffins who had lived on the farm were: Edmund Ruffin I, his daughter Mary and his second wife, Elizabeth Cocke Ruffin; Edmund Ruffin II and possibly his wife, Jane Skipwith Ruffin; George Ruffin and his first wife, Jane Lucas Ruffin, and second wife, Rebecca Cocke Ruffin Woodlief; and Edmund Ruffin III, the subject of this study.

5. George Ruffin was listed for the first time as owner of the farm that became Evergreen in 1795; Prince George County, Va., Land Tax Book, 1795, Archives Division, Virginia State Library, Richmond (hereafter cited as VSL) (microfilm). For a sound judgment about the age of the house, dating its construction at about 1807–08, see Calder Loth, ed., *The Virginia Landmarks Register* (Charlottesville: Univ. Press of Virginia, 1986), 346; and National Register of Historical Places Inventory, Nomination Form for Evergreen, 1979, Virginia Historic Landmarks Division, Richmond.

6. Dimensions of Evergreen appear in Mutual Assurance Society of Vir-

ginia, Policy 343, Prince George County, 1808, VSL (microfilm). The main
house at Evergreen contained 3,630 square feet. The house insured by John
Edloe at Brandon had 4,048 square feet, and Tarbay, 3,538; Mutual Assurance Society of Virginia, Revaluations 2182 and 2184, Prince George
County, 1816, VSL (microfilm). Evergreen Farm must have assumed its
name when George Ruffin built the house some time between 1795 and
1808. Ruffin indicated that Evergreen was not the name by which his
grandfather had known the farm at the close of the Revolution; Edmund
Ruffin, "The Blackwater Guerilla [sic]: A Tradition of Revolutionary Times,"
1851, 12, Edmund Ruffin Papers, VHS.

7. The plan of the house was described in Harrison Henry Cocke, Notes
on Evergreen, c. 1866, Cocke Family Papers, VHS.

8. Genealogical sources for Ruffin's ancestors include the following:
"Ruffin Family," William and Mary Quarterly, 1st ser., 18 (1910): 251–54;
E. Lorraine Ruffin, "Descendants of Edmund Ruffin, the Great Agricultur-
ist . . . ," Tyler's Quarterly Historical and Genealogical Magazine (hereafter cited
as Tyler's), 22 (1941): 242–56; Media Research Bureau, Washington, D.C.,
comp., "The Name and Family of Ruffin," typescript, 1950, 5–8, in the
Southern Historical Collection, University of North Carolina Library, Chapel
Hill (hereafter cited as SHC); John Bennett Boddie, Virginia Historical Genealogies (Redwood City, Calif.: Pacific Coast Publishers, 1954), 262–68;
"Notes from the Records of Prince George County," Virginia Will Records
(Baltimore: Genealogical Publishing Co., 1982), 268–71; and Philip Slaugh-
ter, A History of Bristol Parish, Va., with Genealogies of Families Connected
Therewith, 2d ed. (Richmond: J. W. Randolph, 1879), 225–31. The most
accurate source for the earliest ancestors is David Ruffin, Genealogical history
of the Ruffin family (untitled), 1984, unpublished manuscript in possession
of David Ruffin, Statesboro, Ga. See also Edmund Ruffin, "Ruffin Family
Genealogy, Compiled May 1, 1856 at Beechwood, Prince George Co.,
Va.," VHS.

9. Captain Edmund's first child was born in 1739. His first wife, Anne
Simmons Edmunds (d. 1749), was from Southampton County. Their five
children (two of whom survived into adulthood) were born in Albemarle
Parish, Sussex County, between 1739 and 1744. Captain Edmund's second
wife, Elizabeth Cocke of Surry County, survived him until about 1795. This
evidence suggests that Captain Edmund moved first to Southampton County,
then to Sussex, and then to Prince George after 1750: Albemarle Parish
Register, 28, 162, VHS; Boddie, Virginia Historical Genealogies, 268; John
Bennett Boddie, comp., Births, Deaths and Sponsors 1717–1778 from the
Albemarle Parish Register of Surry and Sussex Counties, Virginia (Redwood City,
Calif.: Pacific Coast Publishers, 1958), 125; E. L. Ruffin, "Descendants of
Edmund Ruffin," 250; "Ruffin Family," 253.

10. About half of Ruffin's ancestors who left wills indicated they knew

they were dying. This was true of his grandfather Samuel Lucas and his step-uncle Walter Cocke, though his step-grandfather, John Cocke, appears to have been in good health. Of Ruffin's Surry County relatives, only his uncle Samuel Lucas seems to have been taken by surprise. See Samuel Lucas (grandfather), Will, 17 Feb. 1770, Surry County, Va., Will Book 10a, 1768–79, 70–74, VSL (microfilm); Samuel Lucas (uncle), Inventory of estate, 4 March 1795, Surry County Will Book 1, 194–95, Surry County Court House, Surry, Va.; John Cocke, Will, 1 Apr. 1795, Surry County Will Book 1, 248, Surry County Court House; and Walter Cocke, Will, 26 Oct. 1801, in Pauline Pearce Warner, *Benjamin Harrison of Berkeley, Walter Cocke of Surry: Family Records I* (Tappahannock, Va., 1962), 85–88. While the will of Ruffin's paternal grandfather, Edmund II, does not survive, the listing of his property as an estate between 1807 and 1814 indicates that he had arranged to leave his farm to his grandson: Prince George County, Va., Land Tax Book, 1809, 5; 1810, 15; 1814, 40–41, VSL (microfilm). Surviving portions of his father's will indicate that George Ruffin knew he was dying: George H. Ruffin, Deed to H. H. Cocke, 1831, Cocke Family Papers, VHS. A distant cousin of Ruffin indicated that Edmund II and George Ruffin both died of gout at forty-three (though the age was wrong in both cases): Frank G. Ruffin to Paul C. Cameron, 1 June 1870, in J. G. de Roulhac Hamilton, ed., *The Papers of Thomas Ruffin*, 4 vols. (1918–20; repr., New York: AMS Press, 1973), 4:236. Ruffin's grandmother thought she was dying of consumption in 1783; Jane Skipwith Ruffin to Sir Peyton Skipwith, 14 Apr. 1783, Skipwith Family Papers, VHS.

11. This was Mary Ruffin Harrison (1739–1767), who married Nathaniel Harrison and settled near Evergreen. Had she lived until 1794 she would have been Edmund Ruffin's great aunt. See Albemarle Parish Register, 16, 24, 28, 160–62, VHS; W. G. Stanard, "Harrison of James River," *Virginia Magazine of History and Biography* (hereafter cited as *VMHB*), 34 (1926): 187. This woman was mistakenly identified as Elizabeth in "Ruffin Family," 253.

12. William Meade, *Old Churches, Ministers and Families of Virginia,* 2 vols. (Philadelphia: J. B. Lippincott Co., [1857]), 1:283, 294. Meade gave an account of his family's ownership of Coggin's Point down to the time his father, R. K. Meade, sold it to Ruffin's grandfather "during" the Revolution.

13. Jane S. Ruffin to Peyton Skipwith, 14 Apr. 1783; George Ruffin to Peyton Skipwith, 3 Aug. 1785, Skipwith Family Papers, VHS; "Ruffin Family," 253. George Ruffin did not mention his mother in the 1785 letter.

14. Thomas Lucas et al. v. Samuel Lucas and John Watkins, Sr., Surry County Order Book, 1789–94, 29 May 1794, 492, VSL (microfilm); Henry Lucas v. Travis Harris, Surry County Order Book, 1804–07, 28 May 1805, 194, VSL (microfilm); Thomas Lucas v. Samuel Lucas, 26 Mar. 1795, Surry

County Order Book, 1795–1800, 22, VSL (microfilm); Samuel Lucas, Will, 1770, Surry County Will Book 10a, 70–74, VSL (microfilm). Jane Lucas signed as a witness on the will of Captain Edmund Ruffin in 1789, though she was not identified. She also gave oath under her maiden name when the will was proved in 1791: Edmund Ruffin, Will, 28 Nov. 1789 (proved 14 June 1791), Prince George County Deed Book, 1787–92, Part 2, 530–32, Prince George County Court House, Prince George, Va.

15. Ruffin, "Ruffin Family Genealogy," VHS. His chart contained no information on the Lucas family.

16. Ruffin's twentieth-century biographers have identified Jane Lucas by name but have not discovered her family history. Avery Craven, *Edmund Ruffin, Southerner: A Study in Secession* (1932; repr., Hamden, Conn.: Archon Books, 1964), 3; Betty L. Mitchell, *Edmund Ruffin: A Biography* (Bloomington: Indiana Univ. Press, 1981), 3.

17. Charles Lucas, Will, 18 July 1758, Surry County Order Book, 1757–63, 100–111, VSL (microfilm); Mary Lucas, Will, 12 Jan. 1760, abstract in Lyndon H. Hart III, *Surry County, Virginia, Wills, Estate Accounts and Inventories, 1730–1800* (Easley, S.C.: Southern Historical Press, 1983), 79; Samuel Lucas, Will, 1770, Surry County Will Book 10a, 72, VSL (microfilm). Samuel Lucas, father of Jane Lucas, can be traced from infancy to death in the Surry County order books, both at the Virginia State Library in Richmond and at Surry Court House, Va.

18. H. Lucas v. Harris, 28 May 1805, 194; Samuel Lucas, Account of estate, 5 March 1795, Surry County Will Book 1, 194–95, 249, Surry County Court House, Surry, Va.; Hart, *Surry County Wills*, 143; T. Lucas v. S. Lucas, 26 March 1795, 22.

19. H. Lucas v. Harris, 28 May 1805, 194, VSL (microfilm). Samuel II had five children, of whom only Thomas was named in this suit; earlier Surry court records also listed Samuel, Lemuel, Jenny, and Sally as his children, though Lemuel disappeared by 1801. The children of Jane Lucas Ruffin's brother Thomas were not named in the suit, nor were those of her sister, Sarah Lucas Burgess. These children would have been cousins of Edmund Ruffin.

20. Dupuy family Bible records, VHS. For George Ruffin's second marriage, see Surry County, Marriage Register, 1768–1853, 29 Aug. 1799, 19 Sept. 1799, 54, Surry County Court House, Surry, Va. The record is published in Catherine Lindsay Knorr, comp., *Marriage Bonds and Ministers' Returns of Surry County, Virginia, 1768–1825* (Pine Bluff, Ark.: The Perdue Company Duplicating Service, 1960), 72.

21. In 1860, at sixty-six, Ruffin knew of only two white men older than himself in Prince George County; Ruffin, *Diary*, 1:389 (6 Jan. 1860).

22. Death notice of Edmund Ruffin II, *Petersburg Intelligencer*, 19 May 1807; Edmund Ruffin, Will, 28 Nov. 1789, Prince George County Deed

Book, Part 2, 530–32, Prince George Court House, Va.; Edmund Ruffin, Inventory, 17 June 1791, Deed Book, Part 2, 588–59, Prince George Court House; "Ruffin Family," 253.

23. Ruffin, *Diary*, 2:531 (5 Jan. 1863).

24. These statements are based on published genealogies and archival records on the Ruffin family. When Ruffin prepared his own genealogy, using records in the Land Office at Richmond, he realized his evidence was slim on the female lines: Ruffin, *Diary*, 1:204, 259 (23 June, 27 Dec. 1858). George Ruffin did know his grandfather's second wife, Elizabeth, who lived until about 1795. She and Captain Edmund were described as elderly and "the only white residents of his mansion" at the end of the Revolution; Ruffin, "Blackwater Guerila," 12, Ruffin Papers, VHS.

25. In 1857 Ruffin encountered in North Carolina his "companion & fellow-lodger at school," Col. James H. Ruffin. This man was the brother of Judge Thomas Ruffin of the North Carolina Supreme Court and descended from the Virginia branch of the family that had settled in King William County, Va., in the eighteenth century. James H. Ruffin left no record of where he attended secondary school, but his older brother attended an academy at Warrenton, N.C. It is possible that Edmund Ruffin and James H. Ruffin followed the same path. The tradition of sending children away for schooling was in the family. Edmund Ruffin's father was tutored at a Methodist minister's school in Sussex County, and Ruffin sent his own sons to such boarding schools (Edmund went for a time to school in New Haven). Ruffin's grandchildren were sent away to schools in Richmond and in Amelia County. Ruffin, *Diary*, 1:108 (23 Sept. 1857); Hamilton, *Papers of Thomas Ruffin*, 1:5, 274, 605; Daniel Lindsey Grant, ed., *Alumni History of the University of North Carolina*, 2d ed. (Durham, N.C.: Christian & King Printing Co., 1924), 540; a record of payments for George Ruffin's tuition is in D. Sturrock, Account book, 1781–83, Mrs. Maria Parker Papers, UVA (microfilm).

26. Surry County, Marriage Register, 1768–1853, p. 54; Knorr, *Marriage Bonds*, 72; Surry County Marriage Bonds, in "Virginia Council Journals, 1726–1753," *VMHB*), 37 (1929): 324.

27. John Cocke, Will, Surry County Will Book 1, 1 Apr. 1795 (proved 23 Jan. 1798), 248; Walter Cocke, Will, Surry County Will Book 1, 27 Oct. 1801 (proved 4 July 1804), 729–30; Warner, *Benjamin Harrison*, 85–88; John Bennett Boddie, *Southside Virginia Families* 2 vols. (Redwood City, Calif.: Pacific Coast Publishers, 1955–56) 1:158.

28. The farm was given to George Ruffin's step-grandmother first, for the remainder of her life; he acquired it at her death, sometime around 1795: Prince George, Land Tax Book, 1795, VSL.

29. Ruffin's half-sister Jane married at sixteen; Dupuy family Bible records, VHS.

30. The half-sisters were Jane S. Ruffin Dupuy (1800–1870), Juliana Ruffin Coupland Dorsey (1806?–1876?), and Elizabeth Ruffin Cocke (1807–1849); Dupuy family Bible records, VHS; Juliana Dorsey, Will (extracts), 20 June 1876, Dorsey and Coupland Papers, Manuscripts and Rare Books Department, Swem Library, College of William and Mary, Williamsburg, Va. (hereafter cited as CWM); Warner, *Benjamin Harrison*, p. 44; Edmund Ruffin to Rebecca Cocke Ruffin Woodlief, 23 Mar. 1823 and fall of 1823, Ruffin Papers, VHS; Elizabeth Ruffin to Edmund Ruffin, 18 Feb. 1828, Ruffin Papers, VHS. Ruffin's half-brother, George Henry Ruffin, survived into the Civil War and lived for a time in 1862 at Beechwood: his year of birth is confirmed in U.S. Census, Population Schedules, Prince George County, Va., 1850, 61a, National Archives, Washington, D.C. (hereafter cited as NA) (microfilm); Ruffin, *Diary*, 2:301 (11 May 1862). Two other half-siblings, George R. (b. 1801) and Rebecca S. (b. 1803) were not mentioned in court records concerning their father's estate: Abstracts of court records for 1812 in Benjamin B. Weisiger III, comp., *Prince George County, Virginia, Miscellany: 1711–1814* (Richmond, 1986), 68, 74; "Notes from the Records of Prince George," 271.

31. *Petersburg Intelligencer*, 19 May 1807.

32. *Richmond Visitor*, 19 May 1810; "Marriage and Death Notices from 'The Visitor,' " *Virginia Genealogical Society Quarterly*, 7 (1969): 61; George Ruffin, Will (quoted portions), c. 1810, in Deed, George H. Ruffin to H. H. Cocke, 1831, Cocke Family Papers, VHS. Genealogies list the date of George Ruffin's death as 12 May 1810.

33. For a different image, of children surrounded by loving, extended families in the Chesapeake after the early eighteenth century, see Daniel Blake Smith, *Inside the Great House: Planter Family Life in Eighteenth-Century Chesapeake Society* (Ithaca: Cornell Univ. Press, 1980), 25–54. Smith's image does not hold for families affiliated with the Ruffins along the James River. For a skeptical treatment of the view that mortality rates improved in the eighteenth century, see Anita H. Rutman, "Still Planting the Seeds of Hope: The Recent Literature of the Early Chesapeake Region," *VMHB*, 95 (1987): 7–8.

34. [Boulware], "Edwin Ruffin," 431.

35. Weisiger, *Prince George Miscellany*, 68, 74. Ruffin also inherited other slaves with the farm at Coggin's Point.

36. Edmund Ruffin, "First Views Which Led to Marling in Prince George County," *Farmers' Register*, 7 (1839): 659, 660; Edmund Ruffin, "Incidents of my Life," 2 vols. (1851–53), 2:110, Ruffin Papers, VHS; Weisiger, *Prince George Miscellany*, 74.

37. The best source on Ruffin's early years at Evergreen has disappeared. The first volume of Ruffin's manuscript memoirs, containing almost one hundred pages about his life prior to 1820, has not been seen by historians

in the twentieth century. The entire manuscript apparently was in his hands as late as 1863; Ruffin, *Diary*, 2:585 (22 Feb. 1863). It appears to have been missing when his daughter-in-law had his papers appraised after the Civil War: Frank G. Ruffin to Jane M. Ruffin, 4 Jan. 1889, typescript copy in possession of Marion Ruffin Jones, Walkerton, Va. One modern biographer of Ruffin has interpreted Ruffin's silence about these early years in psychoanalytic terms, as a withdrawal after rejection by his father: Mitchell, *Edmund Ruffin*, 4. Mitchell wrote that "not once in all his future writing and voluminous correspondence would he refer to his father or to his childhood family experiences." Ruffin's diary does contain some references to his childhood, most of them involving books. He did also refer to his father; see, for example, Edmund Ruffin, Introduction to a fragment of a petition, 1858, Ruffin Papers, UVA; Edmund Ruffin, Prefatory note to extracts copied for Hugh B. Grigsby, 1858, Hugh Blair Grigsby Papers, VHS; Ruffin, *Diary*, 1: 298 (15 Apr. 1859); Ruffin, "Ruffin Family Genealogy," VHS.

38. Ruffin, *Diary*, 1:169, 298–99; 2:136, 151, 195, 205, 408, 604, 656 (20 Mar. 1858, 22 Apr. 1859, 23 Sept. 1861, 22 Oct. 1861, 21 Dec. 1861, 12 Jan. 1862, 7 Aug. 1862, 17 Mar. 1863, 14 May 1863).

39. Ruffin, "First Views," 659; [Boulware], "Edwin Ruffin," 431–32. Ruffin influenced the writing of the Boulware sketch, in which his father figured prominently.

40. Published records of alumni place Ruffin at the college in 1810, but his diary indicates that he was enrolled during more than one year. In 1860 he encountered a former college acquaintance, Charles S. Todd: Ruffin, *Diary*, 1:460 (7 Sept. 1860). Ruffin reported in 1861 that he and William C. Rives were "fellow-lodgers" in Williamsburg: ibid., 2:10–11 (26 Apr. 1861). Both Todd and Rives were members of the class of 1809, though Todd could have been present early in 1810, and Rives may have returned in 1812. These acquaintanceships indicate that Ruffin might have been at the college in 1809 and 1812; *A Provisional List of Alumni . . . of the College of William and Mary in Virginia, from 1693 to 1888* (Richmond: Division of Purchase and Printing, 1941), 34, 35, 40. College account books contain no record of Ruffin, probably because he lived in town: College of William and Mary, Account of Receipts and Expenditures of William & Mary College, 1808, 1809, 1810, 1811, College Archives, Swem Library, CWM. William Boulware, who followed Ruffin's evidence closely in his sketch, said that Ruffin was sent to William and Mary "in the sixteenth year of his age." That would have been 1809: [Boulware], "Edwin Ruffin," 431.

41. Ruffin, *Diary*, 2:10–11 (26 Apr. 1861).

42. [Boulware], "Edwin Ruffin," 431; on his regimen leading toward abstinence, see Ruffin, *Diary*, 2:674 (2 June 1863). In a letter of 1857 Ruffin recalled his youthful decision to adopt total abstinence. He said he had become accustomed to drinking "every day to the extent of intemper-

ance," though he admitted that no one would have deemed him "intemperate." The only means he had to stop drinking, he recalled, was rigorous self-control: Ruffin to unnamed correspondent, 1 June 1857, Ruffin Papers, VHS.

43. College of William and Mary, Bursar's Book, 1754–70, 12, 42, 43, 45 (16 June 1762, 16 June 1763), College Archives, CWM.

44. [Boulware], "Edwin Ruffin," 431. Ruffin's exact whereabouts between June 1810 and March 1812 are uncertain. This chronology is based in part on the order of events in Boulware's sketch, which makes it clear that Ruffin first left the college, then entered the militia, and then took over his farm; after that he married. This was the necessary and customary order of vital events. Ruffin was present in Petersburg in 1811, when he first met his lifelong friend Mildred W. Campbell. That same year he also was in the Williamsburg area, where he toured the ruins of Rosewell House in Gloucester County. See Ruffin, *Diary*, 1:42 (1 Mar. 1857); Suzanne Lebsock, *The Free Women of Petersburg: Status and Culture in a Southern Town, 1784–1860* (New York: W. W. Norton & Co., 1984), 206; Edmund Ruffin, "Remarks on the Soils and Agriculture of Gloucester County," *Farmers' Register*, 6 (1838): 193–94. In turning the farm over to his ward, Thomas Cocke allowed Ruffin to marry Susan Travis.

45. Ruffin, "Blackwater Guerilla," 11, Ruffin Papers, VHS. In 1778 Edmund II advertised for an overseer at Coggin's Point; in 1780 he had established his horse, Stately, at the farm and was advertising the animal's service as a stud: *Virginia Gazette* (Purdie), 30 Oct. 1778; *Virginia Gazette* (Dixon & Nicolson), 18 Mar. 1780. Advertisements for land sales by the grandfather before 1778 did not locate him at Coggin's Point. A survey of the farm was made in 1783, according to a later survey of 1823 now in possession of James S. Gilliam, Hopewell, Va.; for a copy of the 1823 survey see Illustrations.

46. Mutual Assurance Company of Virginia, Policies 343, 346, Prince George, 1808, and Revaluations 2185, 2186, Prince George, 1816, VSL (microfilm); H. H. Cocke, Notes on Evergreen, Cocke Papers, VHS. Ruffin described this site twice in 1862, when the buildings were gone: see Ruffin, *Diary*, 2:358, 422 (30 June, 18 Aug. 1862). Sketches of the two houses appear on Ruffin's 1823 survey of Coggin's Point Farm; see Illustrations.

47. After lending the manuscripts to a Virginia historian in 1858, he retrieved them in 1861 and preserved them through the Civil War: Ruffin to Hugh Blair Grigsby, 16 June, 21 July 1858; 12 Feb., 11 Oct. 1861, Grigsby Papers, VHS. Ruffin copied excerpts from some of his grandfather's manuscripts for Grigsby, making portions of them more legible than the originals deposited in the Ruffin Papers, University of Virginia Library.

48. Augusta B. Fothergill and John Mark Naugle, comps., *Virginia Tax Payers, 1782–87, Other Than Those Published by the United States Census Bureau*

(1940; repr., Baltimore: Genealogical Publishing Co., 1986), 108; U.S. Census Bureau, *Heads of Families at the First Census of the United States Taken in the Year 1790, Records of Enumerations: 1782 to 1785, Virginia* (Washington, D.C.: Government Printing Office, 1908), 14.

49. U.S. Census, Manuscript Schedules, Prince George County, Va., 1820, 54, NA (microfilm). In the earliest account of his farming at Coggin's Point, Ruffin composed a tabular summary of his operations; he had sixteen able-bodied laborers in 1813, and twenty-two in 1823: Edmund Ruffin, "Table of Crops made on Coggin's Point Farm," 1823, Blow Family Papers, CWM. In 1815 he owned thirty slaves aged nine and older: Prince George County, Va., Personal Property Tax List, 1815, 22, VSL (microfilm). These figures indicate that the whole group numbered about fifty. In 1814, his first full year at the farm, Ruffin was taxed for twenty-seven slaves over age twelve, placing him in a tie with one other man as the eighth-largest slaveholder in the county, among 435 slaveholders: Prince George County, Va., Personal Property Tax List, 1814, VSL (microfilm). That year 414 people taxed in the county did not own a slave over twelve years old. In 1810 his father's estate included 143 slaves in Prince George County and twenty-six slaves in Sussex County: U.S. Census, Manuscript Schedules, Prince George County, Va., 1810, 547, NA (microfilm); U.S. Census, Manuscript Schedules, Sussex County, Va., 1810, 661, NA (microfilm). In 1812 George Ruffin's estate was taxed for ninety-nine slaves over age twelve, the second-largest holding in the county. This figure was consistent with his rank in the 1810 census, taken after his death: Prince George County, Va., Personal Property Tax List, 1812, VSL (microfilm).

50. In the accounts of his settlement at Coggin's Point, Ruffin indicated that there may have been a white overseer at that farm in 1813 and 1814: Ruffin, "Incidents," 2:132.

51. In 1859, on a rare visit to Evergreen to see his deceased half-sister's former husband, he went to the kitchen to find Ritter, "the former cook." Ritter's name appeared among the slaves on the 1791 inventory of his great-grandfather's estate. "She is the only one left there of my father's slaves who is older than myself," he said. "She seemed, & no doubt was, very much gratified with my attention in going to see & talk with her—more so probably than by receiving a half dollar which I gave her, when shaking hands with her." Edmund Ruffin, Inventory, 1791, Prince George County Deed Book, Part 2, 588; Ruffin, *Diary*, 1: 298 (15 Apr. 1859). He once was amazed when his black overseer at Marlbourne, Jem Sykes, demonstrated the ability to remember remote causes and perceive gradual changes: Ruffin, *Diary*, 1:87 (4 July 1857).

52. "Travis Family," *William and Mary Quarterly*, 1st ser., 18 (1910): 141–44; "Marlbourne," Hanover Historical Society, *Bulletin*, no. 7 (Nov. 1972), 3; Mary A. Stephenson, "Block 14, Colonial Lots I [J] & K (Travis

House)," typescript research report, 1959, 1–9, Colonial Williamsburg Foundation Library, Williamsburg, Va.; Robert J. Travis, *The Travis (Travers) Family and Its Allies* (Savannah: Bowen Press of Decatur, Ga., 1954), 68–69; James City County, Va., Land Tax Book, 1810, VSL (microfilm); James City County, Personal Property Tax List, 1810, 8, VSL (microfilm).

53. *Richmond Enquirer*, 4 Sept. 1810; death notice reprinted in *Marriages and Deaths from Richmond, Virginia, Newspapers, 1780–1820* (Richmond: Virginia Genealogical Society, 1983), 154.

54. Samuel Travis, Will (abstract), 1 July 1821 (proved 23 July 1821), in William Armstrong Crozier, ed., *Williamsburg Wills* (Baltimore: Southern Book Co., 1954), 58.

55. University of Virginia, Matriculation Book, 1831, 38, UVA (microfilm). No record of their marriage date has been found.

56. William K. Scarborough, "The Ruffin Family: Children and Grandchildren of Edmund Ruffin," in Ruffin, *Diary*, ed. Scarborough, 2:xiii–xxvi.

57. Edmund Ruffin to Thomas Ruffin, 5 May 1834, Thomas Ruffin Papers, SHC.

58. Ruffin, "Incidents," 104.

59. The Ruffin idea of family conforms to that described in Jane Turner Censer, *North Carolina Planters and Their Children, 1800–1860* (Baton Rouge: Louisiana State Univ. Press, 1984), xii, 32–33, 62–64, 152. Neither his idea nor his behavior matched the concept of patriarchy as developed by anthropologists Lewis Henry Morgan and Henry Maine in the nineteenth century: a system of social relations in which a male elder held absolute authority over family members, often including power to govern members of the extended family. A cogent argument that patriarchy did characterize Southern planter families appears in Michael P. Johnson, "Planters and Patriarchy: Charleston, 1800–1860," *Journal of Southern History*, 46 (1980): 45–72; see also James Oakes, *The Ruling Race: A History of American Slaveholders* (New York: Alfred A. Knopf, 1982), 201–4; Steven V. Ash, *Middle Tennessee Society Transformed, 1860–1870* (Baton Rouge: Louisiana State Univ. Press, 1988), 40–51; and Bertram Wyatt-Brown, "The Ideal Typology and Ante-Bellum Southern History: A Testing of a New Approach," *Societas*, 5 (1975): 1–29. Wyatt-Brown's essay has stimulated much of the discussion in this book, though I obviously have not applied his typology of the Southern family to Ruffin. Ruffin's case matched the Northern model as well as it did the Southern. For a skeptical treatment of the patriarchal family, see Lawrence Stone, "The Rise of the Nuclear Family in Early Modern England: The Patriarchal Stage," in Charles E. Rosenberg, ed., *The Family in History* (Philadelphia: Univ. of Pennsylvania Press, 1975), 34–35.

60. Ruffin's ancestors in Prince George County appear to have been no more patriarchal than he. His great-grandfather, grandfather, and father were all able to marry in their twenties. All sought higher education for

their sons (though the Revolution prevented George Ruffin from attending college). Long before they died, Edmund I and Edmund II transferred large portions of their property to their only sons. (George Ruffin probably was prevented from acting similarly only by his early death.) Thus, they attempted to empower their sons with competencies early in life—a necessity, perhaps, in families with few survivors. Given the low survival rate of their children, Ruffin's ancestors did not have the demographic conditions for a meaningful system of patriarchy. These men with few heirs did seem to regard the transfer of culture and property between generations as a matter of custom and legal form; since they had so few choices to make, they appear to have acted without having to examine their assumptions. For Ruffin the situation in this one regard certainly was different. With a greater number of children, he had to be more deliberate about arrangements for transferring property and power. In terms of inheritance and patriarchalism, the Ruffin family experience conformed closely to that described in Smith, *Inside the Great House*, 21–22, 242–46. However, they did not experience the transformation precisely as described in Smith on pages 284–85. The improvement in mortality came only in the nineteenth century, and the father did not become sovereign.

61. His sense of achievement was evident in the opening and closing paragraphs of his first published essay in 1821: Edmund Ruffin, "On the Composition of Soils, and Their Improvement by Calcareous Manures," *American Farmer*, 3 (1821): 313, 319.

62. His writings about malaria stemmed from this assumption: [Edmund Ruffin], "General Remarks on the Causes of, and Means of Preventing the Formation of Malaria, and the Autumnal Diseases Which Are the Effects of It, in Virginia," *Farmers' Register*, 5 (1837): 41–43; [Edmund Ruffin], "Desultory Observations on the Police of Health in Virginia—as It Is, and as It Ought to Be," ibid., 5 (1837): 154–71; [Edmund Ruffin], "On the Sources of Malaria, or of Autumnal Diseases, in Virginia, and the Means of Remedy and Prevention," ibid., 6 (1838): 216–28; [Edmund Ruffin] "Queries in Regard to Prevalent Diseases Produced by Local Causes." ibid., 10 (1842): 68–69; Ruffin, "Incidents," 2:104, 181–82.

63. Ruffin's retrospective account of his youth emphasized what must have been present in his personality in 1810—a passion for self-control and self-reform: Ruffin to unnamed correspondent, 1 June 1857, Ruffin Papers, VHS.

Notes to Chapter Two

1. The interpretation in this chapter differs in particular respects from the thesis in Eugene D. Genovese, *The Political Economy of Slavery: Studies in*

the Economy and Society of the Slave South (New York: Pantheon Books, 1965), 50, 85, 88–90, 92, 99, 124–27, 129–31. Genovese argues that slavery "encouraged ways of thinking antithetical to the spirit of modern science," and that it "rendered futile" attempts to combat soil exhaustion. He properly places Ruffin among thinkers who tried to deny that slavery prevented agricultural reform. While he concedes that the agricultural revival achieved "impressive results" in Virginia and Maryland between 1820 and 1860, he maintains that "on the whole," Southern agricultural reformers failed to change farming practice. The emphasis in this chapter falls on what Ruffin changed at the level of theory, and on his own assessment of change in practice.

2. Ruffin may have ceased farming full-time as early as 1823, when he entered the state senate. By 1826 he was writing his book on calcareous manures. He continued to supervise farming at Shellbanks and at Coggin's Point (the latter with an overseer) until 1835, but his attention clearly had drifted away from farming by 1826. Ruffin's terms in the senate are recorded in Cynthia Millard Leonard, comp., *The General Assembly of Virginia, July 30, 1619–January 11, 1978: A Bicentennial Register of Members* (Richmond: Virginia State Library, 1978), 321, 326, 331, 336.

3. This view of the meaning of Ruffin's despair originated in a letter by Edmund Ruffin, Jr., to his sons, 20 June 1865, in "Death of Edmund Ruffin," *Tyler's*, 5 (1924): 193–95.

4. Ruffin, "First Views," 661–64.

5. The relationship between Ruffin and Cocke has not been discovered in any account of Ruffin's career known to the author. This oversight stems from the fact that crucial modern studies have relied heavily for evidence about Ruffin's early life on an anonymous biographical article, [Boulware], "Edwin Ruffin," 431–36. Ruffin identified Boulware as the author in "Incidents," 3:228–29. Boulware did not mention Cocke's name because Boulware probably did not know the full story himself, relying as he did on documents and information supplied by Ruffin a decade after Cocke's suicide. No scholar in the twentieth century appears to have looked beyond Boulware's account, though Ruffin published documents that provide abundant evidence of the Cocke-Ruffin relationship. Avery Craven included an account of Cocke's suicide and properly identified Cocke as Ruffin's best friend; but Craven missed the early connections between the two men, and he introduced a new confusion by transcribing Boulware's name as "Baulwane." See Craven, *Edmund Ruffin, Southerner*, 6, 89, 93–94. The most recent biography follows Craven's account closely, neglecting the early relationship and perpetuating "Baulwane." See Mitchell, *Edmund Ruffin*, 4, 31, 37–38, 59, 79. The chain of omission passed through J. Carlyle Sitterson, "Edmund Ruffin, Agricultural Reformer and Southern Radical," Introduction to Edmund Ruffin, *An Essay on Calcareous*

Manures, ed. J. Carlyle Sitterson (1832; John Harvard Library ed., Cambridge: Harvard Univ. Press, 1961), vii–ix, xxxi–xxxii. In his essay Sitterson did detect striking similarities in Ruffin and Cocke. The confusion over William Boulware's name finally was ended by William K. Scarborough in his published edition of Ruffin's diary. See Ruffin, *Diary*, 2:11, n. 3.

6. For a study of the importance to Southern intellectuals of friendship as an institution, see Drew Gilpin Faust, *A Sacred Circle: The Dilemma of the Intellectual in the Old South, 1840–1860* (Baltimore: Johns Hopkins Univ. Press, 1977), 2, 6–7, 13, 17, 48, 145. Faust places Ruffin in a circle of Southern intellectuals, described as alienated men who failed to find "any satisfactory intellectual institution." Faust includes in this circle William Gilmore Simms, James Henry Hammond, Nathaniel Beverley Tucker, and George Frederick Holmes. Ruffin did have close ties to Hammond, and Ruffin was among Tucker's correspondents (though the latter died in 1851). See also Mitchell, *Edmund Ruffin*, 261, n. 4.

7. "The Cocke Family of Virginia," *VMHB*, 5 (1897–98): 186–87; Boddie, *Virginia Historical Genealogies*, 268–69; Warner, *Benjamin Harrison*, 80–81, 85–88, 165–69.

8. Ruffin, "First Views," 659–60.

9. Ruffin, "Composition of Soils," 318; Ruffin, "Incidents," 2:100–12; Smith, *Smith of Scotland Neck*, 197–98.

10. Ruffin, "First Views," 660–61.

11. Edmund Ruffin, "The Former Poor and Exhausted Condition, and Earliest Subsequent Improvements, by Marling, of Coggin's Point Farm," *Farmers' Register*, 7 (1839): 113; Prince George County, Va., Land Tax Book, 1814, 41, VSL (microfilm).

12. Edmund Ruffin, "Table of Crops made on Coggin's Point Farm," 1823, Blow Family Papers, CWM; Ruffin, "Former Poor Condition," 114; Lewis C. Gray, *History of Agriculture in the Southern United States to 1860*, 2 vols. (Washington, D.C.: Carnegie Institution of Washington, 1933), 2:915–16.

13. See Chapter 1, nn. 8–11, 14–20, 22, 24. Other historians have reversed the order of vital events in Ruffin's life, placing the marriage before his militia service and inheritance: Craven, *Edmund Ruffin, Southerner*, 3–4; Mitchell, *Edmund Ruffin*, 6–7.

14. Ruffin, "First Views," 659; Ruffin, "Incidents," 2:117, 119.

15. Kathleen Bruce, "Virginian Agricultural Decline to 1860: A Fallacy," *Agricultural History*, 6 (1932): 6–7; Freda F. Stohrer, "*Arator*: A Publishing History," *VMHB*, 88 (1980): 442–45.

16. Ruffin, "Incidents," 2:115–16, 120–21; Ruffin, "First Views," 660–61.

17. Ruffin, "First Views," 661; [Boulware], "Edwin Ruffin," 433.

18. Scarborough, "The Ruffin Family," in Ruffin, *Diary*, 2:xxiii–xxiv; U.S. Census, Manuscript Schedules, Prince George County, Va., 1820, 54, NA (microfilm).

19. Thomas Robert Malthus, *An Essay on the Principle of Population* (1798; repr., New York: St. Martin's Press, 1966), 21–22, 129–30, 193–98, 315–42; Thomas Robert Malthus, *An Essay on the Principle of Population* 2 vols., 6th ed. (London: J. Murray, 1826), 1:458–59; 2:26–34, 118, 156–57, 246–51, 451; Thomas Robert Malthus, *A Summary View of the Principle of Population* (1830; in D. V. Glass, ed., *Introduction to Malthus* [New York: John Wiley & Sons, Inc., 1953]), 138–39, 145–48.

20. Much of the evidence concerning ideas held by Ruffin's neighbors comes from Ruffin himself. The most detailed expression of local ideas about soil appeared in Ruffin's quotations of remarks by Thomas Cocke: see Ruffin, "First Views," 660–61, 664–65. See also Edmund Ruffin, "Observations on the Earliest Marled District of Prince George County," *Farmers' Register*, 8 (1840): 484–97. In this essay Ruffin published responses of ten Prince George County farmers (and himself) to a questionnaire concerning their marling practices. Question twelve asked the farmers about their perceptions of soil fertility "a few years" before applying marl. Originally, none had thought of fertility as increasing, and only two thought fertility was being preserved. All had changed their minds by 1840. A concept of soil barrenness identical to the one Ruffin found in Virginia was discovered in Delaware in 1810 by Thomas Mendenhall, who defined it in an address of 28 Feb. 1810, in "Transactions of the Agricultural Society of New Castle County, Delaware," *American Farmer*, 2 (1820): 75. John Taylor of Caroline expressed his own skepticism about soil rejuvenation through use of minerals or fossils, though he admitted as late as 1818 that the question was yet to be decided: see John Taylor, *Arator: Being a Series of Agricultural Essays, Practical and Political . . .*, ed. M. E. Bradford, 1818 ed.; Liberty Classics ed. (Indianapolis: Liberty Fund, Inc., 1977), 132.

21. Ruffin, *Calcareous Manures*, 18–20, 162–64. Ruffin read Malthus in about 1816; while he regarded Malthus' doctrine as "stern, repulsive, and stubborn," as well as "heart-benumbing" and "hope-stifling," he feared it was true. His earliest reference to Malthus appeared in a note to George Henry Walker, "Extracts from the Manuscript Notes of a Farmer," *Farmers' Register*, 3 (1836): 602; another statement of agreement with Malthusian theory appeared in Ruffin, *Diary*, 1:444–45 (29 July 1860). See also Drew McCoy, "Jefferson and Madison on Malthus: Population Growth in Jeffersonian Political Economy," *VMHB*, 88 (1980): 259–76. Ruffin's critical remarks concerning slavery and population did not appear in the fifth edition of *Calcareous Manures*, issued in 1852.

22. Humphry Davy, *Elements of Agricultural Chemistry* (Fredericksburg, Va.: William F. Gray, 1815); Ruffin, "First Views," 661; Ruffin, "On the Composition of Soils," 314.

23. Ruffin, *Calcareous Manures*, 42–50.

24. Ibid., 72–75, 168–69; Ruffin, "First Views," 662. On the nature and estimation of Ruffin's discoveries in soil chemistry, see W. P. Cutter, "A Pioneer in Agricultural Science," *Yearbook of the United States Department of Agriculture, 1895* (Washington, D. C.: Government Printing Office, 1896), 493–502; Richard C. Sheridan, "Mineral Fertilizers in Southern Agriculture," in James X. Corgan, ed., *The Geological Sciences in the Antebellum South* (University, Ala.: Univ. of Alabama Press, 1982), 73–82; Craven, *Edmund Ruffin, Southerner*, 58–60; and Sitterson, "Edmund Ruffin," xii–xvi.

25. Ruffin, "First Views," 664.

26. Ruffin, "On the Composition of Soils," 318.

27. Ibid.; Ruffin, "Observations on the Earliest Marled District," 490; Ruffin, "On the Composition of Soils," 318; "Cocke Family," 186–87; Francis Earle Lutz, *The Prince George-Hopewell Story* (Richmond: William Byrd Press, 1957), 106.

28. On the general malaise in Virginia during Ruffin's lifetime, see Faust, *Sacred Circle*, 11–14, 46–47, 156–57, n. 19; Robert P. Sutton, "Nostalgia, Pessimism, and Malaise: The Doomed Aristocrat in Late-Jeffersonian Virginia," *VMHB*, 76 (1968): 41–55; Drew McCoy, *The Elusive Republic: Political Economy in Jeffersonian America* (Chapel Hill: Univ. of North Carolina Press, 1980), 190–95; William R. Taylor, *Cavalier and Yankee: The Old South and American National Character* (New York: George Braziller, 1961), 37–65, 145–76; and Avery Craven, *Soil Exhaustion as a Factor in the Agricultural History of Virginia and Maryland, 1606–1860*, (Urbana: Univ. of Illinois, 1926), 72–161. On the Malthusian specter and dilemma in France between 1500 and 1700, see Emmanuel Le Roy Ladurie, *The Peasants of Languedoc*, trans. John Day (Urbana: Univ. of Illinois Press, 1974), 289–311.

29. Ruffin, *Calcareous Manures*, 79, 83–84; Ruffin, "First Views," 662–63, 665.

30. Ruffin, "First Views," 664–65. For accounts of this episode that differ from Ruffin's own version and the one in this passage, see Craven, *Edmund Ruffin, Southerner*, 58–60; and Mitchell, *Edmund Ruffin*, 14–16.

31. Edmund Ruffin, "Ruffin's Agricultural Address," *Farmers' Cabinet*, 8 (1844): 270.

32. Ruffin, *Calcareous Manures*, 87; Ruffin, "Former Poor Condition," 115; Ruffin, "First Views," 667; Ruffin, "Incidents," 2:105. Crop figures for Coggin's Point from 1813 through 1851 appear in Ruffin, *Calcareous Manures*, 5th ed., 184.

33. Ruffin, *Calcareous Manures*, 81, 82–83, 84, 87, 88, 93, 103, 145,

157. On the managerial reform of plantations, see Oakes, *The Ruling Race*, 153–91. Ruffin never did install a thoroughly bureaucratic organization at any of his farms, apparently because he was reluctant to delegate responsibility to supervisors who were not members of his family.

34. Ruffin, *Calcareous Manures*, 128; Ruffin, "Observations on the Earliest Marled District," 488–89; Ruffin, "First Views," 660; Ruffin, "Incidents," 2:103; Edmund Ruffin, "Report to the State Board of Agriculture on the Most Important Recent Improvements of Agriculture in Lower Virginia," *Farmers' Register*, 10 (1842): 258–59; and Ruffin, *Diary*, 1:308 (8 June 1859). Ruffin insisted both that farms in Virginia could be worked by slaves and that landowners should live and work on their own farms. He voiced a fear of a leisured, landowning class. In his hostility to absentee landholders, he expressed a view akin to the Jeffersonian idea defined in Henry Nash Smith, *Virgin Land: The American West as Symbol and Myth* (Cambridge: Harvard Univ. Press, 1950), 133–34, 169–70.

35. Ruffin, *Calcareous Manures*, 40–42, 150–51.

36. Ruffin, "On the Composition of Soils," 319.

37. U.S. Census, Manuscript Schedules, Prince George, 1820, 54; U.S. Census, Manuscript Schedules, Prince George, 1830, 46, NA (microfilm); Ruffin, "Incidents," 2:182; Edmund Ruffin, "Farming Profits in Eastern Virginia: The Value of Marl," *American Farmer*, 5 (1849): 7; Ruffin, *Calcareous Manures*, 157, 193–94; Ruffin, "First Views," 663.

38. Ruffin, "Former Poor Condition," 116; Scarborough, "Ruffin Family," xxiii; Ruffin, "Incidents," 2:140.

39. Ruffin, *Calcareous Manures*, 92, 95, 109, 156–57, 194, 196–97.

40. In his memoirs, Ruffin recalled that he had moved his family permanently to Shellbanks in 1829: Ruffin, "Incidents," 2:96–99, 102, 104–5, 108–9. In a published essay closer to the event, however, he indicated that the move occurred more gradually, with the family spending the summers of 1828, 1829, and 1830 at Shellbanks. In 1831, he said, they finally "abandoned" the homestead at Coggin's Point and made Shellbanks their permanent residence: Ruffin, "Desultory Observations," 159.

41. Ruffin, "Incidents," 106–7.

42. Ibid., 105; Ruffin, "Desultory Observations," 160.

43. Ruffin, "Incidents," 2:104, 112, 131, 139. On plantation bureaucracy, see Oakes, *The Ruling Race*, 154–64.

44. For positive self-assessments, see Ruffin, "First Views," 665; Ruffin, untitled address to the farmers of Prince George County, 1843, in "Mr. Ruffin and the Marling System," offprint from the *Charleston Mercury*, n.d. [5 Feb. 1844], in Ruffin, "Incidents," 2: inserted after p. 162; and Edmund Ruffin, "Southern Agricultural Exhaustion, and Its Remedy," U.S. Congress, Senate, *Report of the Commissioner of Patents for the Year 1852: Part II, Agriculture*, 32d Cong., 2d sess., 1852, Executive Document 55 (Washing-

ton, D.C.: Robert Armstrong, Printer, 1853), 373–89. For negative assessments, see the concluding paragraphs of Ruffin, "Southern Agricultural Exhaustion," 387–89, and Ruffin, "Incidents," 2:160–62. Modern historians have continued to debate Ruffin's influence in terms similar to those he defined, emphasizing his role in changing the reality of farming conditions, rather than his influence in changing theory. See Craven, *Soil Exhaustion*, 133–34; Craven, *Edmund Ruffin, Southerner*, 8, 55–60; Bruce, "Virginian Agricultural Decline," 6–13; Gray, *History of Agriculture*, 2:780–81; Charles W. Turner, "Virginia Agricultural Reform, 1815–1860," *Agricultural History*, 26 (1952): 88–89; Paul W. Gates, *The Farmer's Age: Agriculture, 1815–1860* (New York: Holt, Rinehart and Winston, 1960), pp. 107–10, 341–42; David Donald, "The Proslavery Argument Reconsidered," *Journal of Southern History*, 37 (1971): 10; Genovese, *Political Economy of Slavery*, 88–93, 126–30; Faust, *Sacred Circle*, 33–35; Mitchell, *Edmund Ruffin*, 14–16; W. M. Mathew, "Planter Entrepreneurship and the Ruffin Reforms in the Old South, 1820–60," *Business History*, 27 (1985): 207–21; W. M. Mathew, "Agricultural Adaptation and Race Control in the American South: The Failure of the Ruffin Reforms," *Slavery & Abolition: A Journal of Comparative Studies*, 7 (1986): 129–47. A new work that appeared too late to figure in this study is William Mathew, *Edmund Ruffin and the Crisis of Slavery in the Old South: The Failure of Agricultural Reform* (Athens: Univ. of Georgia Press, 1988). I have profited, however, from Mathew's articles on Ruffin.

45. Ruffin, "Incidents," 2:113.

46. Ruffin, "Incidents," 2:113, 135–36; Ruffin to Thomas Ruffin, 5 May 1834, in Hamilton, *Papers of Thomas Ruffin*, 2:116–17; Ruffin to unnamed correspondent, 10 Apr. 1835, Edmund Ruffin Papers, SHC; Edmund Ruffin, "To Subscribers," *Farmers' Register*, 1 (1834): 767–68; *Farmers' Register*, 3 (1836): 576.

47. Earl G. Swem, *An Analysis of Ruffin's Farmers' Register, with a Bibliography of Edmund Ruffin*, Virginia State Library, *Bulletin*, 11 (Richmond: Davis Bottom, 1919): 42.

48. Edmund Ruffin, "Supplementary Chapter to 'An Essay on Calcareous Manures,' " *Farmers' Register*, 1 (1833): 78.

49. Ruffin had read Arthur Young's accounts of travels through France in about 1818: Edmund Ruffin, "The True and False Doctrines Respecting High Prices of Provisions," *Farmers' Register*, 4 (1837): 759.

50. Evidence that he was paying his first visits appears in each travel account. Ruffin published the earliest of these sketches under the pen name "Gleaner." For evidence that Ruffin himself was the author of the earlier sketches, see Ruffin, "Remarks on Gloucester," 178–79.

51. Ruffin, "Remarks on Gloucester," 188, 191, 181–82, 188–89. Ruffin did not give his itinerary to Gloucester; this route is conjectural, based

on precise accounts he gave of his ride in 1835 to Northampton County, directly across Chesapeake Bay from Gloucester, and on the more detailed account of his return from Gloucester (ibid., 194).

52. Ruffin, "Remarks on Gloucester," 181.

53. Ibid., 183, 182, 188.

54. Ibid., 189. Ruffin misspelled "Mathews."

55. Ibid., 189–190. Ruffin probably meant to write "sheepshead," referring to the fish.

56. Ibid., 190.

57. Ibid., 178, 183, 198.

58. Ruffin, "Most Important Recent Improvements," 258–59. It is possible, too, that Ruffin attended an academy before 1810 in Warrenton, N.C.: see above, Chap. 1, n. 25.

59. Ruffin, "Remarks on Gloucester," 194.

60. Ruffin, Calcareous Manures, 48–49.

61. Elizabeth Ruffin, Diary, (6 vols.) 6:1–170 (29 July–Sept. [1827]), Harrison Henry Cocke Papers, SHC; Edmund Ruffin, Jr., to Susan Travis Ruffin, 6 Sept. 1828, in Mrs. Kirkland Ruffin, ed., "School-Boy Letters of Edmund Ruffin, Jr., 1828–1829," North Carolina Historical Review, 10 (1933): 288–89.

62. University of Virginia, Matriculation Book, 1831, 38, UVA (microfilm).

63. Edmund Ruffin, " 'Jottings Down' in the Swamp," Farmers' Register, 7 (1839): 698–99.

64. Edmund Ruffin, "Notes of a Steam Journey," Farmers' Register, 8 (1840): 244.

65. Edmund Ruffin, "Memoranda of the General System of Cultivation and Improvement Practised by Fielding Lewis, Esq., of Wyanoke," Farmers' Register, 1 (1833): 17.

66. Raymond Williams, Cobbett (New York: Oxford Univ. Press, 1983): 25, 53–56. Cobbett's Rural Rides appeared in 1830.

67. Edmund Ruffin ["A Gleaner," pseud.], "View of Part of York, and the Back River Lands," Farmers' Register, 3 (1835): 414, 416.

68. Edmund Ruffin ["A Gleaner," pseud.], "Rough Notes upon Some of the Agricultural Improvements of Charlotte, and the Adjacent Counties," Farmers' Register, 4 (1836): 376.

69. The interpretation here differs from that in Genovese, Political Economy of Slavery, 124–53. The terms of discussion here also differ from those in Mathew, "Planter Entrepreneurship," 207–21; and W. M. Mathew, "Edmund Ruffin and the Demise of the Farmers' Register," VMHB, 94 (1986): 3–24.

70. The remaining fifty-six Virginia subscriptions went to people in the Shenandoah Valley and western counties. Outside Virginia the largest group

of subscriptions came from North Carolina (eighty-three), all but nine of which were from Tidewater and fall-line counties. Ruffin's list included three individuals who paid for two subscriptions each, and eleven shared subscriptions. Four women (and perhaps a fifth) subscribed. See Edmund Ruffin, "List of Subscribers," *Farmers' Register*, 1 (1834): 769–76. The geographic categories of Virginia counties are illustrated in Roscoe D. Hughes and Henry Leidheiser, Jr., *Exploring Virginia's Human Resources* (Charlottesville: Univ. Press of Virginia, 1965), endpaper map; see also Emily J. Salmon, ed., *A Hornbook of Virginia History*, 3d ed. (Richmond: Virginia State Library, 1983), 3–4; and James Hagemann, *The Heritage of Virginia: The Story of Place Names in the Old Dominion* (Norfolk and Virginia Beach, Va.: Donning Co., Publishers, 1986), 244.

71. Edmund Ruffin, "Notes of a Three-Days Excursion into Goochland, Chesterfield, and Powhatan," no. IV, "Some Account of the Farming of Richard Sampson, Esq., of Goochland," *Farmers' Register*, 5 (1837): 364, 367, 369.

72. Ruffin, "Remarks on Gloucester," 188.

73. Ibid., 181–83, 188–89.

74. Judith Lee Hallock, "The Agricultural Apostle and His Bible: Edmund Ruffin and the *Farmers' Register*," *Southern Studies*, 23 (1984): 205–15.

75. Ruffin, "Notes of a Steam Journey," 246.

76. Ibid., 246, 247.

77. Thomas Cocke had tried this marl as early as 1803, and his father had tried it in 1771, as Ruffin discovered by the time he published his first paper on marling in 1821: Ruffin, "On the Composition of Soils," 318.

78. His first evidence came from Thomas Cocke, Cocke's slave, and the field where Cocke's father had applied marl at Bonaccord, in Prince George. In 1841, H. B. M. Richardson told Ruffin that marl had been used on his farm as early as 1776, and that a second application had been tried in 1829. For the testimony of Richardson, see Edmund Ruffin, "Answers to the General Queries on the Effects of Marl . . . in Regard to Some Farms in James City and Surry Counties," *Farmers' Register*, 9 (1841): 264.

79. H. E. Hallam, *Rural England, 1066–1348*, (Brighton, U.K.: Harvester Press; Atlantic Highlands, N.J., Humanities Press, 1981) 14, 251.

80. A Poor Farmer [pseud.], "Queries and Remarks on the Improvement of Lands," *Farmers' Register*, 2 (1834): 275–76. Ruffin identified individual farmers who carried old assumptions about mixing soils into the nineteenth century, proving English culture of the seventeenth century had not died. In Gloucester County in 1838 he visited the farm of a late Mr. Simcoe, "a good practical farmer," who had declared that yellow earth thrown out of ditches was valuable as fertilizer. Ruffin tested this yellow earth, but

found it worthless and not calcareous at all. See Ruffin, "Remarks on Gloucester," 180.

81. Edmund Ruffin ["A Gleaner," pseud.], "James City Soils, and Resources for their Improvement," *Farmers' Register*, 1 (1833): 108; Ruffin,
"Most Important Recent Improvements," 258–59.

82. Edmund Ruffin, "On the Soils, and Marling Improvements of King
William County," *Farmers' Register*, 9 (1841): 22–25.

83. Ruffin found at least two other farmers who began marling under
ancient assumptions about the beneficial effect of mixing soils. In King
William County, he identified a man named Wesley who had marled about
ten acres in 1820 under these assumptions; and he had known for years
about the experience of Singleton in Talbot County, Maryland, who had
found shells while digging a causeway, and decided to scatter them over his
fields. See Ruffin, "King William," 26; Ruffin, "Most Important Recent
Improvements," 259.

84. This constituency was much smaller than Cobbett's circulation of
forty to fifty thousand a week in England, but it did represent a clear change:
see Williams, *Cobbett*, 16.

85. [Ruffin], "James City Soils," 108.

86. Edmund Ruffin, "The Results of Marling in the County about Williamsburg," *Farmer's Register*, 8 (1840): 416.

87. Ruffin, "King William," 23.

88. Edmund Ruffin, editor's note, *Farmers' Register*, 8 (1840): 446.

89. The figure of one thousand represented Ruffin's estimate in 1851;
Ruffin, "Incidents," 2:157; "Union of the Carolina Planter with the Farmers'
Register," *Farmers' Register*, 9 (1841): 1; "Editorial Notices to Subscribers,"
Farmers' Register, 10 (1842): 504–5. W. M. Mathew estimates there were
between six hundred and seven hundred subscribers in 1842; Mathew, "De-
mise of the *Farmers' Register*," 15–18, 21. In 1835 Ruffin claimed he had
fourteen hundred subscribers: "Remarks on the State and Prospects of the
Farmers' Register," 2 (1835): 765. In 1836 he said he had enlisted sixteen
hundred subscribers to a new edition of the first volume: "Accounts and
Collections," *Farmers' Register*, 4 (1836): 255.

90. Edmund Ruffin, "Plan for Procuring and Publishing a General Report
of the Practical Effects of Marling," *Farmers' Register*, 5 (1837): 509–11.

91. Edmund Ruffin, "Investigating the Effects of Marling," *Farmers'
Register*, 8 (1840): 446–47; Edmund Ruffin, *Report of the Commencement and
Progress of the Agricultural Survey of South Carolina for 1843* (Columbia, S.C.:
A. H. Pemberton, 1843), foldout between pp. 58–59.

92. Edmund Ruffin, "Answers to General Queries on Marling, in Regard
to Green-Sand Marl Used on the Pamunkey River Lands," *Farmers' Register*,
9 (1841): 21; Edmund Ruffin, "Remarks on the Soils and Marling of the
Pamunkey River Lands," *Farmers' Register*, 8 (1840): 689.

93. Ruffin, "Most Important Recent Improvements," 265.

94. Ibid., 259.

95. Ibid., 259.

96. William Spotswood Fontaine, "A Statement of the Number of Acres of Land Which Had Been Marled in the County of King William, at the Time of Taking the Census in 1840," *Farmers' Register*, 10 (1842): 488.

97. Edmund Ruffin, "Estimate of the Increased Value of Property in King William County, Caused by Marling," *Farmers' Register*, 10 (1842): 489–90.

98. Susan Tuck owned of 300 acres, 100 of which were improved in 1850; U.S. Census, Agriculture Schedules, King William County, Va., 1850, 212, VSL (microfilm).

99. Fontaine, "King William," 488.

100. The 1850 census listed 391 farmers and 89,139 improved acres in King William County: U.S. Census, Agriculture Schedules, King William, 1850, 196–214, VSL (microfilm). Thus, about 22.5 percent of the county's farmers had begun to marl by 1842, and about 10.5 percent of its improved acreage had been marled.

101. Edmund Ruffin, "Report to the State Board of Agriculture, on the Brandon Farms," *Farmers' Register*, 10 (1842): 276–82.

102. Carroll D. Wright, *The History and Growth of the United States Census* (Washington, D.C.: Government Printing Office, 1900), 49, 234–36. The 1840 census had sought information on agriculture, but its questions dealt exclusively with the numbers of livestock and production of crops: ibid., 233–34.

103. Edmund Ruffin, "Communication to the Virginia State Agricultural Society: Some of the Results of the Improvements of Land by Calcareous Manures," *Southern Planter*, 12 (1852): 258–64.

104. Ibid., 263.

105. Farm sale advertisements for 1850 in the *Richmond Enquirer*, 1 Jan. 1850–31 Dec. 1850. The total for the Tidewater includes one missing case, an advertisement that did not list the number of acres for sale (4 Jan. 1850). There was no apparent relationship between the size of farms and marling. Farms advertised in the Tidewater ranged between 103 and 2,700 acres. The greatest cluster of marled farms (four) was in the third quartile, a group ranging between 300 and 335 acres. Ruffin was named in one advertisement in 1849 by Ezekiel S. Talley, a neighbor in Hanover County who boasted that the property he was offering bordered "the land of that successful and justly distinguished agriculturalist, Mr. Edmund Ruffin, the rapid improvement and increased value of whose plantation, by the use of marl, within a very few years, are exciting the admiration and wonder of the natives of old Hanover": *Richmond Enquirer*, 24 July 1849. Ruffin himself became the purchaser of at least part of this estate: Ruffin, "Incidents," 2:193–94.

106. Ruffin, "Communication to the Virginia Society," 260–61, 263.
107. Ibid., 259.
108. John Skinner, "Agriculture," *American Farmer*, 3 (1821): 313; Reviews of *An Essay on Calcareous Manures*, by Edmund Ruffin, in *American Journal of Science and Arts*, 30 (1836): 138, and "Calcareous Manures," *Cultivator*, 2 (1835): 66–68.
109. Ruffin, "Closing scenes of the life of Thomas Cocke," 3–6, 11.
110. [Boulware], "Edwin Ruffin," 431–36.
111. Ruffin, "Incidents," 2:110–11.
112. Ibid., 2:110–11.

Notes to Chapter Three

1. The second period of farming really closed after seven years in 1851. While Ruffin continued to manage Marlbourne at different times until 1854, in 1851 and 1852 he turned his attention again to writing. At about the same time he became involved in the state agricultural society and in secession.
2. Ruffin "Incidents," 2:138.
3. Ruffin's commitment to the idea of independence, or a competency, for himself and his children was developed in his wills and estate distributions. Though he took pride in having multiplied his patrimony, he did not seek ever-increasing wealth; he wanted an estate sufficient to provide independence for himself and each of his children. His early retirement—for another form of work—provided the best evidence of his thinking on the issue of wealth. His assumptions about ambition, hard work, debt, and independence fit closely with the analysis in Jan Lewis, *The Pursuit of Happiness: Family and Values in Jefferson's Virginia* (Cambridge, U.K.: Cambridge Univ. Press, 1983), 106–68. Ruffin's embracing of self-reliance and hard work for himself and his children made him less grim in his outlook than Lewis's nineteenth-century Virginians, perhaps because he so thoroughly accepted the consequences of life in the era after tobacco culture. On the concept of competency, for which Lewis uses the term *independence*, see also William L. Barney, *The Passage of the Republic: An Interdisciplinary History of Nineteenth-Century America* (Lexington, Mass. D. C. Heath, 1987), 23. On the self-sustaining individual and the implications of this idea for patriarchy, see Rhys Isaac, *The Transformation of Virginia: 1740–1790* (Chapel Hill: Univ. of North Carolina Press, 1982), 311–12.
4. His half-brother, George Henry Ruffin, did not marry.
5. The total number who survived infancy reached twenty-four, though not all of them were alive at one time. Dupuy family Bible records, VHS; Juliana Coupland Dorsey to Carter Coupland, 10 May, 17 Aug., 1856;

[John R. Coupland] to [Sue H. Coupland], 19 Aug. 1863; Carter Coupland to Tariffa Cocke, 8 Feb. 1840; Juliana Coupland Dorsey, Will (extracts), 20 June 1876, Dorsey and Coupland Papers, CWM; Juliana Dorsey to Edmund Ruffin, 13 May 1849; Julian C. Ruffin to Ruffin, 20 June 1849; Ruffin, "Ruffin Family Genealogy," Ruffin Papers, VHS; U.S. Census, Population Schedules, Prince George County, Va., 1850, 61, NA; U.S. Census, Population Schedules, Prince George County, Va., 1860, 366, NA (microfilm).

6. Ruffin's farm journals did contain such evidence on slaves. In 1847 Edmund Ruffin, Jr., surveyed infant mortality among slaves at Coggin's Point, using Ruffin's journals. From 1813 to 1829, forty-six children had been born: of these, twenty-one died in infancy (five from whooping cough). From 1839 to early 1847, thirty-nine had been born and eighteen died. Edmund, Jr., noted that in both periods nearly half had died, and that the mortality rate was worse at Coggin's Point than at the farm his wife inherited in King and Queen County: Edmund Ruffin, Jr., to Ruffin, Sat., 13 [Mar.] 1847, Ruffin Papers (Section 11), VHS. Ruffin reported in 1865 that his journals had been lost, probably during Union occupations of Beechwood Farm after 1862; Edmund Ruffin, "Account of the Draining of Marlbourne Farm," 1857–65, note following 20 Mar. 1865, 97, Ruffin Papers, VHS. The one for Marlbourne did survive; see Edmund Ruffin, Marlbourne Farm Journal, 1844–1851, VSL.

7. Ruffin, "Desultory Observations" 159; Ruffin, "Incidents," 2:104, 106–7.

8. Ruffin's great-grandfather, the settler of Evergreen, was a carpenter as well as a farmer; his pursuit of dual vocations was not repeated in the next generation.

9. University of Virginia, Matriculation Books, 1825–1880, 38, 44, 50, UVA (microfilm); Maxmilian Schele De Vere, comp., *Students of the University of Virginia: A Semi-centennial Catalogue, with Brief Biographical Sketches* (Baltimore: Charles Harvey & Co., Publishers, 1878), n.p.; *Farmers' Register*, 1 (1833): 192.

10. Ruffin, "Incidents," 2:139.

11. Ibid., 2:140.

12. Ruffin, *Diary*, 2:338, 426 (11 June, 22 Aug. 1862).

13. Margaret Stanly Beckwith, "Personal Reminiscences, 1844–1865," 3 vols., 1:1, front cover, VHS.

14. *The History of the College of William and Mary (Including the General Catalogue.) From Its Foundation, 1660, to 1874* (Richmond: J. W. Randolph & English, 1874), 130; *A Provisional List of Alumni . . . of the College of William and Mary in Virginia, from 1693 to 1888* (Richmond: Division of Purchase and Printing, 1941), 35.

15. Julian C. Ruffin to Ruffin, 30 Mar. 1861, Ruffin Papers, VHS.

16. Ruffin expressed affection for her and satisfaction with their marriage in 1856: Charlotte Meade Ruffin to Ruffin, 4 Jan. 1856, Ruffin Papers, VHS. Ruffin spelled her name "Lotty," though she herself and other family members spelled it "Lottie."

17. Ruffin, *Diary*, 2:340 (13 June 1862).

18. Edmund, Jr., also held a claim to Bellevue, the farm his wife inherited, though his title was not secure in 1843.

19. Julian C. Ruffin, Diary (Farm Journal), 2 vols. (1843–47 1:1–2 (2 Jan. 1843) Ruffin Papers, VHS.

20. Ruffin, "Farming Profits," 4, Table II; Ruffin, "Incidents," 2:162–63. The farm was advertised as having more than one thousand acres; *Richmond Enquirer*, 5 Sept. 1843. Edmund, Jr., purchased Marlbourne at public auction while Ruffin was in South Carolina.

21. Ruffin, "Incidents," 2:193–94; Hanover County, Va., Land Tax Book, 1850, 21, VSL (microfilm); *Richmond Enquirer*, 24 July 1849.

22. U.S. Census, Agriculture Schedules, Prince George County, Va., 1850, 3, VSL (microfilm); Agnes Beckwith to Ruffin, 18 Feb. 1849, Ruffin Papers, VHS.

23. U.S. Census, Agriculture Schedules, Prince George County, Va., 1860, 507, VSL (microfilm); on Ruffin's purchase of Rose Cottage for Charles, see Anne B. Peebles, *Peebles Ante 1600–1962* [Washington, D.C.]: J. Hughlett Peebles, [1962], 80.

24. Juliana Coupland Dorsey to Ruffin, 13 May 1849, Ruffin Papers, VHS.

25. Julian C. Ruffin to Ruffin, 28 June 1846, Ruffin Papers, VHS. Ruffin's half-brother, George, also remained in Prince George. His sister Juliana had moved to Alabama but visited in Virginia frequently. The experience of the Ruffins compares with that of the most persistent settlers of Sangamon County, Ill., in John Mack Faragher, *Sugar Creek: Life on the Illinois Prairie* (New Haven: Yale Univ. Press, 1986), 143–46.

26. Edmund Ruffin, Jr., to Ruffin, 17 Apr. 1848, Ruffin Papers, VHS.

27. Agnes Beckwith to Ruffin, 20 Jan. 1848, Ruffin Papers, VHS.

28. Jane Ruffin to Ruffin, 8 Feb. 1850, Ruffin Papers, VHS. Their sociability contrasted sharply with the isolation of an earlier generation at Coggin's Point, when Ruffin's father could mention only two cousins, one of whom lived in Mecklenburg County: George Ruffin to Sir Peyton Skipwith, 3 Aug. 1785, Skipwith Family Papers, VHS.

29. Edmund Ruffin, Jr., to Ruffin, 29 Dec. 1858, Ruffin Papers, VHS.

30. Julian C. Ruffin to Ruffin, 17 Nov. 1860, Ruffin Papers, VHS.

31. Their relationship with neighbors and the outside world in this period compares closely with that described for the family of Thomas Ruffin and

other planters in Robert C. Kenzer, *Kinship and Neighborhood in a Southern Community: Orange County, North Carolina, 1849–1881* (Knoxville: Univ.of Tennessee Press, 1987), 42–46.

32. Ruffin, "Farming Profits" 4, Table II; Ruffin, "Incidents," 2:162–63; Ruffin, Marlbourne Farm Journal, 1 (1 Jan. 1844). Ruffin's estimates of the distance to Richmond varied between thirteen and sixteen miles: see Edmund Ruffin, "Essays on Various Subjects of Practical Farming: Management of Wheat Harvest," *American Farmer*, 6 (1851): 454; Ruffin to Thomas Ruffin, 7 Apr. 1844, in Hamilton, *Papers of Thomas Ruffin*, 2:226.

33. Ruffin estimated his net worth in 1837 at $100,000, before losses of $30,000 on investments in stocks and bonds of railroads, cotton factories, water-power schemes, and his shop; Ruffin, "Incidents," 2:145–46, 158–59.

34. Ruffin, "Incidents," 2:162–63. By 1857 there were 769 lowland acres; Ruffin, "Account of the Draining of Marlbourne," 8. Ruffin first estimated the lowlands at 684.5 acres. The house was still unfinished when the family occupied it. See Ruffin, Marlbourne Farm Journal, 7–12 (1844).

35. Ruffin, "Farming Profits," 4, Table II; U.S. Census, Agriculture Schedules, Hanover County, Va., 1850, 21, VSL (microfilm); U.S. Census, Agriculture Schedules, Prince George, 1850, 1, VSL (microfilm). The agriculture schedules of 1850 indicate that Julian Ruffin had 160 improved acres and 290 unimproved acres at Ruthven: ibid., 9.

36. Ruffin, Marlbourne Farm Journal, 1 (1, 18 Jan. 1844).

37. Only Edmund, Jr., could rely on his own farms for income. In 1854 and 1855 Julian lived at Marlbourne with Lottie, acting as farm manager: Edmund Ruffin, "Memorandum of agreement & contract between Edmund Ruffin & Julian C. Ruffin," 1854; and Julian C. Ruffin to Ruffin, 31 Jan. 1856, Ruffin Papers, VHS.

38. Ruffin, "Incidents," 2:163.

39. Ruffin, "Account of the Draining of Marlbourne," 7, 11, Ruffin Papers, VHS; Ruffin, "Incidents," 2:164.

40. Ruffin, "Incidents," 2:181.

41. Ibid., 2:167.

42. Ruffin, "Farming Profits," 2. Ruffin recorded these amounts in Marlbourne and Coggin's Point farm journals: Ruffin, "Incidents," 2:175.

43. Ruffin, "Farming Profits," 3, 9, Tables I, V.

44. Edmund Ruffin, "Essays on Various Subjects of Practical Farming: On Draining," *American Farmer*, 6 (1850): 5, 6.

45. Ibid., 91.

46. Here Ruffin and his slaves re-enacted the original European understanding of marling: Ruffin, "Incidents," 2:197.

47. Ruffin, "Essays: Draining," 94; Ruffin, "Incidents," 2:197.

48. Ruffin, "Incidents," 2:164–65, 197–98.

49. Ibid., 2:173.

50. Ruffin, "Essays: Draining," 177–78, 181–82. Ruffin knew that tile pipe was being used in England, but he considered it too expensive for Virginia farmers.

51. Ibid., 181.

52. Ruffin, "Incidents," 3:257.

53. Ruffin, "Farming Profits," 9, Table VI. These were not inflated figures. In 1858 Ruffin estimated privately that Marlbourne profits would be $8,000 in "clear farm income," after paying all expenses: Ruffin, *Diary*, 1:250 (20 Nov. 1858). On complaints of the scythe-men, see Ruffin, "Essays: Wheat," 454. See also Ruffin, "Incidents," 2:213.

54. Ruffin, "Incidents," 2:190; "The New Volume—Mr. Ruffin, of Va.," *American Farmer*, 6 (1850): 16; "To Correspondents," ibid., 49.

55. Newspaper advertisements for farm sales in 1849 and 1850 show the influence of Ruffin in the Tidewater. See especially the *Richmond Enquirer*, 24 July 1849.

56. These characteristics have come to be associated with a Malthusian mentality, devoted to planning of all phases of life. Ruffin had displayed these characteristics at age nineteen when he settled on the peninsula at Coggin's Point. See Philippe Ariès, "An Interpretation to Be Used for a History of Mentalities," in Orest Ranum and Patricia Ranum, eds., *Popular Attitudes toward Birth Control in Pre-Industrial France and England* (New York: Harper & Row, 1972), 110–11.

57. Edmund Ruffin, "Essays on Various Subjects of Practical Farming: On Clover Culture, and the Use and Value of the Products," *American Farmer*, 6 (1851): 257, 259, 293; Arthur H. Bryan et al., *Bacteriology: Principles and Practice*, 6th ed. (New York: Barnes & Noble, 1962), 104–6; Gray, *History of Agriculture,* 2:804.

58. Ruffin, "Essays: Clover," 257, 258.

59. Ibid., 258.

60. Ibid., 292–93.

61. Ruffin, "Essays: Wheat," 454; Edmund Ruffin, "Essays on Various Subjects of Practical Farming: On Harvesting Corn-Fodder—Different Methods Compared," *American Farmer*, 6 (1851): 422, 424–25.

62. Ruffin estimated slaves accounted for 31.7 percent of his investment at Marlbourne; machines, only 1.3 percent. These figures probably did not represent the full value of his machines. See Ruffin, "Farming Profits," 4, Table II; Edmund Ruffin, Jr., to Ruffin, 10 Apr. 1849, Ruffin Papers, VHS; U.S. Census, Agriculture Schedules, Hanover, 1850, 21, VSL (microfilm); U.S. Census, Agriculture Schedules, Hanover County, Va., 1860, 17, VSL (microfilm). In his timing of mechanization, Ruffin was close to farmers in Illinois: Faragher, *Sugar Creek*, 199–203.

63. Ruffin, "Farming Profits," 5, Table III; Ruffin, "Incidents," 2:187–

88, 196. Occasionally Ruffin referred to Sykes as his "overseer": Ruffin, *Diary*, 1:86 (4 July 1857).

64. In this, Marlbourne differed from plantations analyzed generally in Oakes, *The Ruling Race*, 155–56.

65. Ruffin, "Farming Profits," 11.

66. Ruffin, "Incidents," 2:99.

67. Ibid., 2:138–39. This account by Ruffin was written late in 1851, after he could have been sensitized to the issue of separating slave families by Harriet Beecher Stowe and abolitionists. There are no documents of 1835 to sustain Ruffin's later account, but his behavior between 1835 and 1839 was consistent with his later interpretation of his motives.

68. Hanover County census takers in 1850 tallied only 219 free blacks, a small pool of possible hired labor. Free blacks represented 1.4 percent of the 15,120 total population; there were 8,359 slaves and 6,542 whites. Census takers also counted 350 laborers, all but three of whom were white males: U.S. Census, Population Schedules, Hanover County, Va., 1850, NA (microfilm) 341–421, 407b, 421b. For Ruffin's difficulties in hiring laborers, see Ruffin, Marlbourne Farm Journal, pp. 188, 469 (1 June 1846, 25 June 1851).

69. Ruffin, "Essays: Wheat," 457.

70. Ruffin appears not to have supervised slaves closely once routines were established. In marling operations of 1849 he spent not more than half an hour a day inspecting fields. "I did not give any task, nor indicate what work would be expected—nor say a word to stimulate exertion," he reported: Ruffin, Marlbourne Farm Journal, 364 (4 Apr. 1849). For an opposing argument that successful agricultural reform would have spelled the end of slavery, see Genovese, *Political Economy of Slavery*, 99, 124–44.

71. Ruffin, "Essays: Draining," 180.

72. Ibid., 92–93.

73. Ruffin, "Incidents," 2:168; Ruffin, "Farming Profits," 7–8, Table IV; U.S. Census, Slave Schedules, Hanover County, Va., 1850, 151, NA (microfilm).

74. Ruffin, "Farming Profits," Table IV. Ruffin said the average number of family members present at Marlbourne between 1844 and 1849 was five or six, taking into account his children's departures for school and the death of his wife. At some point in these years an eighth servant was added to this household. He never did identify the origins of eleven unaffiliated children. It is possible they were purchased in Petersburg, but more likely that they, too, came from Beechwood. Martha, a disabled thirteen-year-old, was the twelfth member of this group.

75. Ruffin, "Farming Profits," 5, 6, 8, Tables III, IV, and note (o); U.S. Census, Slave Schedules, Hanover, 1850, 151, NA (microfilm). Five of the forty-one slaves present in 1850 were aged five or under, which means they

had been born at Marlbourne. A man named Joe (about fifty-two years old) died of consumption at Marlbourne in 1851, the first field laborer to die there: Ruffin, Marlbourne Farm Journal, 439 (19 Jan. 1851). Four partial lists of slaves appear in the Farm Journal at 12, 82, 364, 420–21 (1844, sick list 1844, 4 Apr. 1849, 20 June 1850).

76. The situation of the Marlbourne slaves was comparable to that of the Cohoon family slaves analyzed in Herbert Gutman, *The Black Family in Slavery and Freedom, 1750–1925* (New York: Pantheon Books, 1976), 123–43.

77. No evidence has survived that Ruffin bought or sold slaves except in 1832, when he attempted to prevent two of his father's former slave women and their children from falling into the possession of his brother-in-law, Carter Coupland: Ruffin to Juliana Coupland, 26 Nov. 1831 (copy in Ruffin's hand); Juliana Coupland to Ruffin, 14 Jan. [1832], 1, 19 Mar., 8 Sept. 1832; Elizabeth Ruffin to Ruffin, Monday night [1832], Ruffin Papers, VHS. Ruffin's sons did purchase slaves, and during the Civil War they sold slaves.

78. Ruffin, Marlbourne Farm Journal, 133, 389 (10 May 1845, 15 Sept. 1849). At different times Ruffin did reveal the names of some of these children. They included Charles, Isaac, and Martha; ibid., 12, 82 (1844; sick list, 1844).

79. Ruffin, "Farming Profits," 6, Table IV. Their presence at Marlbourne can be traced by comparing the table in Ruffin's 1849 article with the ages of slaves at Marlbourne in the 1850 slave schedules of the U.S. census. A group of slaves who could have been comprised largely of these children appeared also in the 1860 slave schedules; U.S. Census, Slave Schedules, Hanover County, Va., 1860, 424, NA (microfilm).

80. U.S. Census, Slave Schedules, Hanover, 1850, 151, NA (microfilm); U.S. Census, Slave Schedules, Hanover, 1860, 424. There were fifteen Ruffin family slaves aged ten or younger at Marlbourne in 1860. Ruffin's son-in-law William Sayre had moved five of his slaves to Marlbourne from Norfolk by 1860, making a total slave population of fifty-five.

81. These figures include slaves owned by Ruffin (52, including 2 in Prince George), Edmund, Jr. (138), Julian (22), Agnes (1), and Charles (3). They exclude slaves at Marlbourne owned by William Sayre (5) and those at Ruthven owned by Julian's mother-in-law (5). The whole family's holding in 1860 (216) had grown by 23 percent (40 slaves) over their total holding in 1850 (176).

82. Ruffin, "Farming Profits," 4, Table II. In 1848 slaves accounted for 32 percent of his wealth. In 1860, when Edmund, Jr., listed his own total worth at $233,000, the younger Ruffin's personal property accounted for $160,000 of that sum. His slaves, who were included in the category of personal property, must have accounted for at least half of his net worth.

U.S. Census, Population Schedules, Prince George County, Va., 1860, 337b, NA (microfilm).

83. Ruffin, "Farming Profits," 2, 4–5.

84. Ibid., 5, 6, Tables III and IV. The expenditures are comparable to those of Thomas B. Chaplin for his slaves in South Carolina: Theodore Rosengarten, *Tombee: Portrait of a Cotton Planter* (New York: William Morrow & Co., 1987), 87.

85. Ruffin presented an apparent contrast to the views of Governor Hammond of South Carolina: see Drew Gilpin Faust, *James Henry Hammond and the Old South: A Design for Mastery* (Baton Rouge: Louisiana State Univ. Press, 1982), 3–4, 69–104.

86. Probably the wealthiest man among Ruffin's acquaintances in Virginia was Philip St. George Cocke of Belmead Farm in Powhatan County. Ten months before this man committed suicide in 1861, his estate was appraised at $1,412,000, ten times greater than Ruffin's; William H. Harrison to Ruffin, 10 Jan. 1862, Ruffin Papers, UVA; Ruffin, *Diary*, 1:8, n. 3. In 1850, when Edmund, Jr., declared real estate worth $20,000 in Prince George County, neighbor William G. Harrison declared $80,000 in real estate; U.S. Census, Population Schedules, Prince George, 1850, 60, 92b, NA (microfilm).

87. Ruffin, "Incidents," 2:158.

88. Ibid., 2:216. Portions for the six children surviving in 1860 eventually rose above $16,000 each, an indication of Ruffin's increasing wealth.

89. Ruffin, *Diary*, 1:43–45 (10 Mar. 1857); Edmund Ruffin, Distribution of Estate, 1 Mar. 1856, with codicil 4 Sept. 1862, typescript copy in possession of Marion Ruffin Jones, Walkerton, Va.; Edmund Ruffin, Will, 20 Oct. 1862, with codicil 18 May 1863, typescript copy in possession of Marion Ruffin Jones. Ruffin's farm journal for 1827 recorded his boast of having doubled his patrimony that year: quotation in Ruffin, "Incidents," 2:102. In the suicide entry of his diary he said he had distributed among his heirs an estate worth six times his original patrimony: Edmund Ruffin, Diary (manuscript), 4093 (16, 17, 18 June, 1865), Library of Congress, Washington, D.C. (hereafter cited as LC). This estimate would be consistent with an original inheritance of about $18,000 in 1813.

90. U.S. Census, Population Schedules, Hanover, 1850, 391, NA (microfilm); U.S. Census, Population Schedules, Hanover County, Va., 1860, 403. In 1863 the Ruffins offered Marlbourne for sale at $75,000 (about $54 an acre), a price reflecting wartime inflation; the remaining forty-three slaves at Marlbourne were valued at $30,100, or an average of $700 each. See Ruffin, *Diary*, 2:552 (23 Jan. 1863). The estimates Ruffin gave to the United States census taker conformed closely to his private estimates of the farm's worth in his various wills and family partnership documents.

91. Ruffin, *Diary*, 1:250 (20 Nov. 1858).

92. Rebecca Ruffin to Julian C. Ruffin, 6 Jan. 1846, Ruffin and Meade Papers, SHC. Julian acted as superintendent at Marlbourne for a time in 1846: Ruffin, Marlbourne Farm Journal, 172 (22 Apr. 1846).

93. Ruffin, "Incidents," 3:255.

94. Ruffin, "Memorandum of agreement & contract between Edmund Ruffin & Julian C. Ruffin," 1854, Ruffin Papers, VHS.

95. Elizabeth Sayre to "Brother," [Julian C. Ruffin], 26 Sept. 1857, Ruffin Papers, VHS. Ruffin briefly considered recruiting John T. Bland, husband of his deceased daughter Rebecca, as manager of Marlbourne in 1856: Edmund Ruffin, Jr., to Ruffin, 10 Jan. 1856, Ruffin Papers, VHS.

96. Ruffin, "Incidents," 3:255.

97. Ibid., 2:215.

98. Ibid., 2:215, 216. The best narrative and analysis of these arrangements is in Edmund Ruffin, Will, 4 Jan. 1864, with codicil 10 June 1864, Prince George County Court House, Prince George, Va.

99. Ruffin, "Incidents," 2:215.

100. Ibid.

101. Peter Dobkin Hall, *The Organization of American Culture, 1700–1900: Private Institutions, Elites, and the Origins of American Nationality* (New York: New York Univ. Press, 1982), 36–42, 53–75; Peter Dobkin Hall, "Marital Selection and Business in Massachusetts Merchant Families, 1700–1900," in Michael Gordon, ed., *The American Family in Social-Historical Perspective*, 2d ed. (New York: St. Martin's Press, 1978), 101–14; Ronald Story, *The Forging of an Aristocracy: Harvard & the Boston Upper Class, 1800-1870* (Middletown, Conn.: Wesleyan Univ. Press, 1980), 4–5. On the rather different policies followed by New England families a century before Ruffin's day, see Philip J. Greven, Jr., *Four Generations: Population, Land, and Family in Colonial Andover, Massachusetts* (Ithaca: Cornell Univ. Press, 1970), 222–58. The notion of the family as a "corporate property group," defined by Theodore Rosengarten in dealing with the Chaplin family of South Carolina, did not have this idea of partnership in a common undertaking: Rosengarten, *Tombee*, 92–93.

102. Ruffin, "Incidents," 2:215.

103. Ibid.

104. Ruffin to Charles L. Ruffin, 19 Oct. 1857 (draft), Ruffin Papers, VHS. The distribution of estate in the Chaplin family of South Carolina, by contrast, apparently emphasized family line rather than individual industry; Rosengarten, *Tombee*, 93, 112.

105. Ruffin's use of his estate as a vehicle to link family members into an economic partnership should not be viewed simply as evidence that Ruffin held an antique, purely economic idea of the family, or that members adhered to his scheme for purely material reasons. The correspondence of the Ruffin family—including the letters of Ruffin himself—are filled with nineteenth-

century notions about the family as a sentimental unit having strong ties of affection and concern for siblings, children, and grandchildren. Indeed, as unprecedented numbers of Ruffins survived in the nineteenth century, they created intense bonds of affection and emotional attachment. Ruffin was merely adding a material dimension to a feeling that already existed, creating an idea of the family as an institution of both emotional and material support. The family (not slavery) was the one institution to which he remained utterly committed.

Notes to Chapter Four

1. Ruffin, "Incidents," 2:182–83; Elizabeth Ruffin to Julian C. Ruffin, 14 June 1845, Ruffin and Meade Papers, SHC.

2. Edmund Ruffin, "In Remembrance of Jane Dupuy, formerly Ruffin," 27 July 1855 (appended to "Incidents," vol. 3), 3, Ruffin Papers, VHS.

3. Ruffin, "Remembrance of Jane," 3–4; Elizabeth Ruffin to Julian C. Ruffin, 26 Apr. 1855, Ruffin and Meade Papers, SHC.

4. Ruffin, "Remembrance of Jane," 10, 15.

5. Ibid., 4.

6. Edmund Ruffin, "In Remembrance of Ella Ruffin," 27 Aug. 1855 (appended to "Incidents," vol. 3), 2–5, Ruffin Papers, VHS. Ruffin entered the cause of Ella's death as heart disease: Hanover County, Register of Deaths, 1853–1871, 10, Hanover Court House, Va.

7. Agnes Beckwith to Ruffin, 2 Dec. 1855, Ruffin Papers, VHS.

8. Edmund Ruffin, Jr., to Ruffin, 7 Dec. 1855, VHS.

9. Agnes Beckwith to Edmund Ruffin, Jr., 29 Nov. [1855], Ruffin Papers, VHS.

10. Edmund Ruffin, Jr., to Ruffin, 3 Dec. 1855, Ruffin Papers, VHS. Thomas was Edmund, Jr.'s son.

11. Edmund Ruffin, Jr., to Ruffin, 3 Dec. 1855; Ruffin, "Remembrance of Jane," 9, Ruffin Papers, VHS.

12. Ruffin, *Diary*, 1:92 (24 July 1857).

13. Ibid., 1:508 (8 Dec. 1860).

14. Ibid., 2:531–32 (5 Jan. 1863).

15. Edmund Ruffin, Jr., to Ruffin, 1 Aug. 1845, Ruffin Papers, VHS.

16. Edmund Ruffin, Jr., to Ruffin, 7 Jan. 1846, Ruffin Papers, VHS.

17. Julian C. Ruffin to Ruffin, 24 Mar. 1848, Ruffin Papers, VHS.

18. Ruffin, "Incidents," 2:217, 218; see also the prayer he wrote on the death of his daughter Jane in Ruffin, "Remembrance of Jane," 31, Ruffin Papers, VHS.

19. The significance of these deaths lay not only in their shaping of Ruffin's family history and late career; they also influenced his idea of death

(already forming in 1840) and eventually his decision to commit suicide. Here the political history of the Confederacy and the vital history of the Ruffin family intertwined.

20. Ruffin, "Incidents," 2:183.

21. Jane Ruffin to Julian C. Ruffin, 7 Mar. 1848, and Ruffin to Charlotte M. Ruffin, 21 May 1863, Ruffin and Meade Papers, SHC; Agnes Beckwith to Ruffin, 18 Feb. 1849; Mary C. Ruffin to Ruffin, 22 May [1849]; Edmund Ruffin, Jr., to Ruffin, 7 July, 3 Nov., 17 Nov., 1849; Rebecca Bland to Ruffin, 24 May 1855; Jane M. Ruffin to Ruffin, 25 Jan. 1858; Mildred Ruffin to Ruffin, 21 Apr. [1858], 21 Nov. 1860; Elizabeth Sayre to Ruffin, 7 Mar. 1860, Ruffin Papers, VHS. On the role of antebellum Southern women, see Anne Firor Scott, *The Southern Lady: From Pedestal to Politics, 1830–1930* (Chicago: Univ. of Chicago Press, 1970), 28–37, and Lebsock, *Free Women of Petersburg*, 146–64. See also Catherine Clinton, *The Plantation Mistress: Woman's World in the Old South* (New York: Pantheon Books, 1982); and Elizabeth Fox-Genovese, *Within the Plantation Household: Black and White Women of the Old South* (Chapel Hill: Univ. of North Carolina Press, 1988). To compare Illinois women at this time, see Faragher, *Sugar Creek*, 207–9, 214–15.

22. By 1862 only Ruffin's granddaughter Anne (Nanny) remained to provide traditional household support for him, once he had moved to Beechwood; Nanny herself would die in 1863.

23. Ruffin's last children were born in 1832, when he was thirty-eight and Susan T. Ruffin was thirty-nine, before their reproductive years normally might have ended. It is possible that the couple determined in that year to have no more children, and that they began a regime of abstinence. Given Ruffin's most emphatic views in favor of marital fidelity and his abhorrence of sexual relations between masters and slaves, it is possible that by 1860 he had abstained from sexual relations for twenty-eight years; Ruffin, *Diary*, 1:120 (7 Nov. 1857). In 1836 he revealed that he had heard only one statement about a practical, "preventive check" to general population growth: "Some Account of the Labors and Improvements Executed by the Marquis de Turbilly," *Farmers' Register*, 3 (1836), 724, editor's note.

24. Charlotte Meade Ruffin, Julian's wife, made his shirts and underclothing, but Ruffin could do some sewing himself and could have relied on other women for this. Lottie and Ruffin did develop a close, affectionate relationship in the 1850s, but events in the Civil War would separate them. See Ruffin to Charlotte M. Ruffin, 21 May 1863, Ruffin and Meade Papers, SHC: on the decision not to remarry, see Ruffin's accounts of his visits with former president John Tyler and with Judge Thomas Ruffin, in Ruffin, *Diary*, 1:123–24, 197 (11 Nov. 1857, 30 May 1858).

25. The date of the marriage was 6 June 1838; Beckwith, "Personal Reminiscences," 1:4, VHS. The year "1836" was written later in pencil

next to the marriage notice on the inside cover of the Beckwith reminiscences. The Beckwiths' first child was born in 1839. Concerning Ruffin's disapproval of the marriage, see Ruffin to Thomas Stanly Beckwith, 25 Sept. 1854, draft (not sent), Ruffin Papers, VHS; Ruffin, *Diary*, 1:121 (8 Nov. 1857).

26. Ruffin asserted that an original gift of $2,500 to Agnes had been "lavishly squandered" after Agnes's marriage; Ruffin, *Diary*, 1:44 (10 Mar. 1857). He gave identical sums to Edmund, Jr., and Julian as they came of age; Ruffin, "Incidents," 1:215.

27. Elizabeth Ruffin to Susan T. Ruffin, [1840?], Ruffin Papers (Section 8), VHS. For an account of the Ruffin-Beckwith feud sympathetic to Agnes Beckwith, see Lebsock, *Free Women of Petersburg*, 61–63. See also Mitchell, *Edmund Ruffin*, 88–89: Mitchell quite properly analyzes Ruffin's view of Beckwith in terms of his earlier experience with Juliana Ruffin and her first marriage. Juliana's first husband was Carter Coupland, however, not William Coupland: "Ruffin Family," *William and Mary Quarterly*, 1st ser., 18 (1910): 253; Stanard, "Harrison of James River," *VMHB*, 39 (1931):177. The original interpretation favorable to Beckwith is in Beckwith, "Personal Reminiscences," 1:1, 23–24.

28. Beckwith, "Personal Reminiscences," 1:1, 11.

29. T. Stanly Beckwith to Ruffin, 21 Aug. 1854, Ruffin Papers, VHS.

30. Agnes Beckwith to Ruffin, 15 Aug. 1847, Ruffin Papers, VHS.

31. Agnes Beckwith to Ruffin, 14 Nov. 1847, Ruffin Papers, VHS.

32. Agnes Beckwith to Ruffin, 18 Feb. 1849; Ruffin to T. Stanly Beckwith, 25 Sept. 1854 (not sent), Ruffin Papers, VHS.

33. U.S. Census, Agriculture Schedules, Prince George County, Va., 1850, 3, VSL (microfilm). The house and farm at Woodbourne were described in Beckwith, "Personal Reminiscences," 1:5–10.

34. Edmund Ruffin, Jr., to Ruffin, 10 Apr. 1849; Agnes Beckwith to Ruffin, Saturday night [23 Nov. 1849] (Section 12); Julian C. Ruffin to Ruffin, 14 Mar. 1855, Ruffin Papers, VHS.

35. T. Stanly Beckwith to Ruffin, 21 Aug. 1854; Ruffin to T. Stanly Beckwith, 25 Sept. 1854 (not sent); Ruffin to Elizabeth Sayre, 20 July 1860, Ruffin Papers, VHS.

36. Juliana Ruffin to Ruffin, five undated letters [1823]; Ruffin to Rebecca Cocke Ruffin Woodlief, 23 Mar. 1823; Juliana Coupland to Ruffin, 1, 19 Mar., 8 Sept. 1832; Ruffin to Juliana Coupland, 12 Jan. 1832, Ruffin Papers (Section 5), VHS.

37. Dandridge Spotswood, "Notes from the Records of Petersburg," in *Virginia Will Records* (Baltimore: Genealogical Publishing Co., 1982), 258.

38. Juliana Coupland to Ruffin, 14 Dec. 1833, Ruffin Papers, VHS.

39. For comparison, see Lebsock, *Free Women of Petersburg*, 54–86.

40. Edmund Ruffin, Indenture to J. C. and E. Ruffin, Jr., 2 Feb. 1857, Prince George County Deed Book 24, 330–31, Prince George Court House,

Va. The interpretation here differs in minor respects from Lebsock's account of the Ruffin estate in *Free Women of Petersburg*, 62. Ruffin's indenture clearly established two trustees, not one, and for Agnes's benefit it limited their powers. Both interpretations see the trust fund as a device to protect women from the legal, arbitrary power husbands could exercise over the property of wives.

41. Lebsock, *Free Women of Petersburg*, 23–24; Joan R. Gunderson and Gwen Victor Gampel, "Married Women's Legal Status in Eighteenth-Century New York and Virginia," *William and Mary Quarterly*, 3d ser., 39 (1982): 114–34; Rosengarten, *Tombee*, 30, 108–11. For similar provisions in Illinois see Faragher, *Sugar Creek*, 106–9.

42. In 1857 Ruffin said he had given Agnes $2,000 more than he had given Julian, and $3,000 more than to all the other children: Ruffin, *Diary*, 1:44 (10 Mar. 1857); Ruffin to T. Stanly Beckwith, 25 Sept. 1854 (not sent), Ruffin Papers, VHS.

43. In this case, power was seized by the family of Edmund Ruffin and his favored, responsible children. More simply, the collective family, composed of Ruffin with his children and their spouses, was assuming powers over the Beckwiths, who constituted just one member household in the collective family.

44. Julian C. Ruffin to Ruffin, 14 Mar. 1855, Ruffin Papers, VHS. Ten years later, in fulminating against the U.S. policy requiring Southerners to take an oath of allegiance, Ruffin did draw an analogy between the oath and "the solemn vows of the marriage service." He thought such vows were made too lightly, particularly when taken "to serve mercenary interests": Edmund Ruffin, Diary (manuscript), 4015 (13 May 1865), LC. He probably did not subscribe to Julian's view of marriage as an institution that could be severed only by death, an idea his Protestant soul must have regarded as an anachronism.

45. Margaret Stanly Beckwith believed later that Ruffin, together with Edmund, Jr., and Julian, had tried to persuade Agnes to separate from Beckwith and to remain at Woodbourne in 1857: Beckwith, "Personal Reminiscences," 1:23.

46. Edmund Ruffin, Jr., to Ruffin, 4 Mar. 1857, Ruffin Papers, VHS. Julian criticized Agnes for failure to anticipate the high cost of providing for a large family in Petersburg, "which every body else, except herself & husband, could so plainly foresee"; Julian C. Ruffin to Ruffin, Monday morning [1858] (Section 17), Ruffin Papers, VHS. Edmund, Jr., revealed contempt for Beckwith's medical practice, noting sardonically that his son was recovering from an illness "without using any thing else but Beckwith pills": Edmund Ruffin, Jr., to Ruffin, 17 Nov. 1858. Elizabeth told her father Beckwith was an "alien" and "stranger" who had "wasted your substance much": Elizabeth Sayre to Ruffin, 14 July 1860. Agnes had become

aware of their criticisms by 1863, when she demanded explanations from Ruffin and Julian: Agnes Ruffin Beckwith to Ruffin, 21 Jan. 1863, Ruffin Papers, VHS. Margaret Beckwith said that her father took one son with him when he returned to Petersburg (though she recalled the year as 1856): Beckwith, "Personal Reminiscences," 1:24.

47. Ruffin, *Diary*, 1:6, 22, 79, 89 ("Introduction to the attempt," 2 Jan., 31 May, 15 July 1857).

48. Ibid., 1:79, 158 (31 May 1857, 20 Feb. 1858).

49. Agnes Beckwith to Ruffin, 9 Jan. 1863, Ruffin Papers, VHS.

50. Ruffin to Agnes Ruffin, fragment of draft of letter, [13 Jan. 1863] (Section 25), Ruffin Papers, VHS.

51. Agnes Beckwith to Ruffin, 21 Jan. 1863; Ruffin to Agnes Beckwith, 26 Jan. 1863, Ruffin Papers, VHS.

52. U.S. Census, Population Schedules, Hanover County, Va., 1860, 403, NA (microfilm).

53. Ruffin, *Diary*, 1:42; 2:553 (1 Mar. 1857, 23 Jan. 1863).

54. The sister was Mary Grymes Sayre: "Sayre Family," *VMHB*, 3 (1896): 96; Gabrielle Maupin Bielenstein, "Genealogy for the Descendants of Hester Vanbibber Braxton (1827–1909) and Robert Williamson Tomlin (1813–1862)," typescript, 1984, entry for Carter Braxton II, VSL; *Index to Marriage Notices in the Southern Churchman,* 2 vols. (Richmond: Historical Records Survey of Virginia, 1942), 2:166; Steven A. Colvin, *On Deep Water* (Verona, Va.: McClure Printing Co., 1983), 23–29.

55. Ruffin, "Incidents," 1:214; *Richmond Enquirer*, 26 Apr., 3 Sept., 1850.

56. Julian C. Ruffin to Ruffin, 11 Sept. 1852, Ruffin Papers, VHS.

57. Julian C. Ruffin to Ruffin, 8 Oct. 1852, Ruffin Papers, VHS.

58. Concerning the traditional dimensions of this kind of conflict, see Michael Verdon, "The Stem Family: Toward a General Theory," *Journal of Interdisciplinary History*, 10 (1979): 87–105; and Natalie Zemon Davis, *The Return of Martin Guerre* (Cambridge: Harvard Univ. Press, 1983), 51–61.

59. Julian C. Ruffin to Ruffin, 8 Oct. 1852, Ruffin Papers, VHS.

60. When Elizabeth died in 1860, her trust fund, administered by Edmund, Jr., and Julian, reverted to Ruffin and then to the general family holdings: Ruffin, Will, 20 Oct. 1862, with codicil 18 May 1863, typescript copy in possession of Marion Ruffin Jones, Walkerton, Va. The official copy of this will in Hanover County appears to have been destroyed in the Civil War.

61. Ruffin, *Diary*, 1:6; 2:552–53 ("Introduction to the attempt," 23 Jan. 1863); Edmund Ruffin, "Memorandum of agreement & contract between Edmund Ruffin & Julian C. Ruffin," 1854, Ruffin Papers, VHS.

62. Elizabeth Sayre to Brother, 26 Sept. [1857], Ruffin Papers (Section 16), VHS.

63. William Sayre to Ruffin, 13 June 1858, Ruffin Papers, VHS; Ruffin, *Diary*, 2:553–54, 595 (23 Jan., 8 Mar. 1863).

64. Edmund Ruffin, Jr., to Ruffin, 10 Jan. 1856, Ruffin Papers, VHS.

65. Mildred Ruffin to Ruffin, 21 Apr. 1858, Ruffin Papers, VHS.

66. Ruffin, *Diary*, 1:343, 345 (22, 29 Sept. 1859).

67. Ibid., 1:346; 2:133 (1 Oct. 1859, 15 Sept. 1861). In fact, Mildred's property was placed in a trust fund administered by William Sayre, making him the trustee for Mildred should Burwell die; but Burwell became the effective owner of Mildred's portion and did in fact gain title to it when she died in 1862.

68. Ibid., 1:359 (21 Nov. 1859).

69. Ibid., 1:358, 359 (21, 22 Nov. 1859). This was a later account of the scene, which occurred 4 Oct. 1859.

70. Ruffin to Edmund Ruffin, Jr., 14 Jan 1860, Ruffin Papers, VHS; Ruffin, *Diary*, 1:378–79, 391; 2:554 (11 Dec. 1859, 12 Jan. 1860, 23 Jan. 1863). In 1861, however, Ruffin returned as a gift $2,500 in bonds that Sayre had signed as part of his payment for Elizabeth's share in Marlbourne: William Sayre to Ruffin, 12 Mar. 1861, Ruffin Papers, VHS. As the Civil War came near Richmond, the Ruffins needed Sayre, who remained at Marlbourne until the first Union occupation of the farm. Sayre kept his affiliation with the family through the end of the war.

71. Ruffin, *Diary*, 1:345 (30 Sept. 1859).

72. Ibid., 2:552 (23 Jan. 1863). The purchase was completed 9 Feb. 1863: see ibid., 2:573 (9 Feb. 1863).

73. Ibid., 2:552 (23 Jan. 1863).

74. For an interpretation of child rearing that emphasizes the value of honor in antebellum Southern culture, see Bertram Wyatt-Brown, *Southern Honor: Ethics and Behavior in the Old South* (New York: Oxford Univ. Press, 1982), 117–98. Ruffin did not subscribe to the traditional code described by Wyatt-Brown, who sees Ruffin as an exceptional Southerner (ibid., 178). Ruffin would have been horrified had he produced a grown son like Thomas B. Chaplin, whose journal recorded much idleness, play, and failure, but very little work: Rosengarten, *Tombee*, 327–481.

75. Edmund Ruffin, Jr., to Ruffin, 25 Feb. 1850, 30 June 1854; Julian C. Ruffin to Ruffin, 8 Oct. 1849, 27 Sept. 1850, 13 Dec. 1861, Ruffin Papers, VHS.

76. Charles L. Ruffin to Ruffin, 10 Jan. [1851], Ruffin Papers, VHS.

77. Ibid.

78. Charles wrote to Edmund, Jr., in 1852 that he was "at work without any pay," and Edmund feared he had no prospects: Edmund Ruffin, Jr., to Ruffin, 30 June 1852, Ruffin Papers, VHS.

79. Ruffin to Charles L. Ruffin, 19 Oct. 1857 (draft), Ruffin Papers, VHS.

80. Ruffin, *Diary*, 2:468 (20 Oct. 1862); Peebles, *Peebles Ante 1600–1962*, 80; U.S. Census, Agriculture Schedules, Prince George County, Va., 1860, 507, VSL (microfilm). The farm was worth $3,100 in 1860.

81. Ruffin to Charles L. Ruffin, 19 Oct. 1857, draft, Ruffin Papers, VHS. See also Ruffin's account of this episode in his *Diary*, 1:114–15 (18 Oct. 1857).

82. Elizabeth died from complications of this pregnancy.

83. Elizabeth Sayre to Ruffin, 14 July 1860, Ruffin Papers, VHS.

84. Charles, a twin of Ella and the last-born son, was thirteen when his mother died in 1846. He was eighteen years younger than Edmund, Jr., almost a full generation younger than his oldest brother.

85. Elizabeth Sayre to Ruffin, 14 July 1860, Ruffin Papers, VHS.

86. Ibid.

87. Ruffin to unnamed correspondent, 1 June 1857 (draft), Ruffin Papers, VHS. Ruffin did not reveal the identity of his correspondent, whom he attempted to convert to total abstinence from all alcoholic beverages. The timing suggests the man was a member of the North Carolina Ruffin family.

88. Ruffin to Elizabeth Sayre, 20 July 1860, Ruffin Papers, VHS.

89. Ibid.

90. Ibid.

91. Ibid.

92. Ibid.

93. Edmund Ruffin, Will, 1 Mar. 1856, with codicil 4 Sept. 1862, typescript copy in possession of Marion Ruffin Jones, Walkerton, Va.; Ruffin, *Diary*, 2:468 (20 Oct. 1862).

94. Ruffin died without discovering Charles's virtues or giving him approval. Ruffin supported his son's application for a commission in the Confederate army in 1861, but Charles lacked enthusiasm for the war and had to be urged toward the fighting, about which Ruffin demanded details. In 1862 Ruffin was mortified to discover that Charles was not, as thought, on sick leave in northern Virginia, but was "in Richmond (at Exchange Hotel,) & apparently in good health." All three Ruffin sons felt pressure during the war because of their father's role in secession, which added to the difficulties of having a famous, achieving father. Dr. David Ruffin of Statesboro, Ga., in unpublished manuscripts, has offered a sympathetic understanding particularly of Charles. On the war episodes, see Charles L. Ruffin to Ruffin, 29–30 June 1861; Ruffin to Jefferson Davis, 27 Aug. 1861; Ruffin to Capt. George B. Cuthbert, 12 May 1862, Ruffin Papers, VHS. See also Ruffin, *Diary*, 2:37–38, 135, 311 (29 May, 21 Sept., 23 Sept., 1861; 21 May 1862); Rebecca Wormeley Meade to John Meade, 4 June 1861, Ruffin and Meade Papers, SHC.

95. Ruffin, *Diary*, 2:468 (20 Oct. 1862).

96. Ibid., 2:573 (9 Feb. 1863).

97. Edmund, Jr., and Julian disapproved of Ruffin's decision to rent his own quarters in Richmond and repeatedly urged him to join their families: Julian C. Ruffin to Ruffin, 13 Dec. 1861; Edmund Ruffin, Jr., to Ruffin, 11 Feb., 15 Feb. 1862, Ruffin Papers, VHS.

Notes to Chapter Five

1. On the emergence of full-time careers in reform see Ronald G. Walters, *American Reformers, 1815–1860* (New York: Hill and Wang, 1978), 13–14. From this perspective, there were striking similarities between the careers of Edmund Ruffin and William Lloyd Garrison; had he been more of a perfectionist, Ruffin might be viewed as a Garrison of the South and secession. For a contrast, see John L. Thomas, "Romantic Reform in America, 1815–1865," *American Quarterly*, 17 (1965): 656–81.

2. Rebecca Ruffin to Julian Ruffin, 6 Jan. 1846, Ruffin and Meade Papers, SHC.

3. Ruffin, "Incidents," 2:187–88, 196, 215–18.

4. Ibid., 3:255.

5. Ruffin, "Farming Profits," 2–11. The essay was republished in the *Southern Planter*, 9 (1849): 226-37.

6. Ruffin, "Incidents," 2:190.

7. Ibid., 2:220.

8. Ibid., 3:255–56. Ruffin used almost identical terms to describe his 1839 sale of Coggin's Point farm to Edmund, Jr. "The first sale & entire transference of control of the farm, relieved me of what had become a grievous burden," he wrote in 1851. Clearly his mood had shifted against farming. See Ruffin, "Incidents," 2:141.

9. Ruffin, *Diary*, 1:5 ("Introduction to the attempt").

10. Edmund Ruffin, Will, March 1856, typescript copy in possession of Marion Ruffin Jones, Walkerton, Va. Ruffin destroyed the original manuscript of the 1856 will; this typescript is the only copy seen by the author.

11. Ruffin, *Diary* ("Introduction to the attempt"), 1:7.

12. Ibid., 1:7, 16.

13. Ibid., 1:16.

14. Ibid., 1:313, 335–36 (2 July, 27 Aug. 1859).

15. Ibid., 2:418 (17 Aug. 1862). This rate of purchase would have created a significant holding. Ruffin had been collecting books since 1813, creating over those fifty years a library that could have contained two thousand volumes; his son's collection probably approached the same size: Ruffin, Diary (manuscript), 36-1138 (22 Jan. 1857–15 Dec. 1860), LC.

16. Letter, 11 Aug. 1862, in Ruffin, *Diary*, 2:417, n. 32. Another letter, from a Michigan soldier killed at Second Manassas, also testified to

the scale of the holdings: "He left the largest library I ever saw"; ibid., 2:576, n. 28.

17. Ruffin, *Diary*, 1:62, 283, 415, 421, 554 (2 May 1857, 18 Feb. 1859, 25–27 April 1860, 22 May 1860, 20 Feb. 1861). In 1859 Sayre subscribed to four reviews and *Blackwood's Magazine*; Ruffin, *Diary*, 1:327 (3 Aug. 1859).

18. On the function of family libraries in Virginia in the late eighteenth century, see John R. Barden, "Reflections of a Singular Mind: The Library of Robert Carter of Nomony Hall," *VMHB*, 96 (1988): 85. Carter had three thousand volumes.

19. Ruffin, *Diary*, 1:62 (3 May 1857).

20. Ibid., 1:61–62 (1 May 1857). The book was published as *Agricultural, Geological, and Descriptive Sketches of Lower North Carolina, and the Similar Adjacent Lands* (Raleigh: Institution for the Deaf and Dumb, and the Blind, 1861).

21. In this he followed practices common among contemporary reformers and writers in the North, among them Harriet Beecher Stowe, Theodore Dwight Weld, Angelina Grimke, Sarah Grimke, Ralph Waldo Emerson, Henry David Thoreau, and Nathaniel Hawthorne. The home was a common place of intellectual activity throughout the first half of the nineteenth century.

22. Edmund Ruffin, "Memorandum of agreement & contract between Edmund Ruffin & Julian C. Ruffin," 1854, Ruffin Papers, VHS; Ruffin, *Diary*, 1:5–6 ("Introduction to the attempt").

23. Ruffin described as ideal his working conditions during a visit in 1861 at Judge Thomas Ruffin's house in North Carolina. There he was permitted to seclude himself in his own room to read and write for hours, not interfering with family routines; then he would emerge for conversation when convenient. See Ruffin, *Diary*, 2:123 (3 Sept. 1861).

24. On 7 July 1860, for example, Ruffin rose at 4:00 a.m. to start a journey to Richmond and Ruthven: Ruffin, *Diary*, 1:441 (7 July 1860).

25. Ibid., 1:61–62 (1, 3 May 1857).

26. Ibid., 1:62, 378 (2 May 1857, 11 Dec. 1859).

27. He criticized this flaw in his own writing: Ruffin, Diary (manuscript), 3988 (25 April 1865), LC.

28. Ruffin, *Diary*, 1:15 ("Introduction to the attempt").

29. Ibid., 1:232 (25, 26 Sept. 1858).

30. Ibid., 1:42–46 (2–21 Mar. 1857).

31. Ibid., 1:440 (1 July, 1860).

32. At Thomas Ruffin's house, he reported, "I am left, just as I would wish, to interfere with no one's business or pleasure, & to read, (for which there are plenty of books,) or write in my room, or to converse, without

requiring the notice of, or annoying any one." Ruffin, *Diary*, 2:123 (3 Sept. 1861).

33. Ibid., 1:441 (11 July 1860).

34. Ibid., 1:440–45 (1–31 July 1860).

35. Ruffin to James Henry Hammond, 17 May 1845, James Henry Hammond Papers, LC.

36. Edmund Ruffin, "Supplemental Report of the Agricultural Survey for 1843," *Southern Agriculturist*, 2d ser., 4 (1844): 122–27; Edmund Ruffin, "Desultory Observations on the Application and Action of Putrescent Manures," *Southern Planter*, 6 (1846): 135–42.

37. Ruffin, "Farming Profits," 2–11.

38. His writings under the series title "Essays on Various Subjects of Practical Farming" were as follows: "On Draining," *American Farmer*, 6 (1850): 5–8, 33–38, 90–95, 128–31, 177–82; "On Clover Culture, and the Use and Value of the Products," *American Farmer*, 6 (1851): 257–60, 291–93; "On Harvesting Corn-Fodder—Different Methods Compared," ibid., 422–26; "Management of Wheat Harvest," ibid., 453–60; "The Advantages of Ploughing Land in Wide Beds," *American Farmer*, 7 (1851): 20–22, 49–51; "The Excavation of Marl Pits, and Carrying Out and Applying of Marl," *American Farmer*, 7 (1851): 208–11, and 8 (1852): 239–42. He also published the following: "Petition of the Committee of the State Agricultural Club," *Governor's Message and Annual Reports*, doc. 61 (1850); "Petition to the General Assembly of Virginia," *Southern Planter*, 11 (1851): 65–73.

39. Ruffin, *Diary*, 1:15 ("Introduction to the attempt").

40. Ibid., 1:42, 46–48 (2–28 March 1857).

41. Edmund Ruffin, *Anticipations of the Future, to Serve as Lessons for the Present Time* (Richmond: J. W. Randolph, 1860; repr., Freeport, N.Y., Books for Libraries Press, 1972).

42. Ruffin, *Diary*, 1:407–8, 415, 416 (26, 29 Feb., 20 Apr., 1 May 1860).

43. Edmund Ruffin, "A Lecture on the Promotion of Agricultural Improvement," *American Farmer*, 6 (1851): 221–31.

44. Ruffin, "Incidents," 3:229, 234, 245–46; Ruffin, "Address to the Virginia State Agricultural Society," 8–16.

45. Ruffin, "Lecture on Agricultural Improvement," 225–29.

46. In one proposal Ruffin took a stand against modern developments. He attributed the success of Northern agricultural periodicals to their employment of traveling agents; instead of recommending that Southern publishers adopt the agency system, he urged his Easton audience to resist the appeals of Northern agents and to subscribe to the more expensive publications from the South; "Lecture on Agricultural Improvement," 230.

47. Edmund Ruffin, "Southern Agricultural Exhaustion," 375, 378, 383–87.

48. All through the *Farmers' Register* Ruffin inserted plans for Virginia that included draining swamps and small mill ponds (whose size he wanted to limit by state law); regulating public health, building canals, roads, railroads, and fences; and conducting geological and agricultural surveys. On railroads, for example, see [Edmund Ruffin], "What is the Best Route, Through Central Virginia, for a Railway to the Southwest," *Farmers' Register*, 4 (1836): 309–12, 369–74. His earliest statement on railroads appeared in 1832: Ruffin, *Essay on Calcareous Manures*, 147, note. In 1840, sobered by losses in his railroad investments, Ruffin wrote a comment critical of railway schemes: "Remarks on the Soils in General, and Particularly the Ridge Lands, of Eastern Virginia, *Farmers' Register*, 8 (1840): 168–71. He regained his enthusiasm, however, in "Notes of a Steam Journey," 243–54. For a partial bibliography of Ruffin's writing in this vein, see Swem, *Analysis of Ruffin's Farmers' Register*, 57, 59–63, 90–91.

49. Ruffin, *Diary*, 1:10, 12, 244, 352 ("Introduction to the attempt," 2 Nov. 1858, 2 Nov. 1859); Ruffin, "Incidents," 3:230; Virginia State Agricultural Society, *Journal of Transactions for the Years 1856–57* (n.p., n.d.), 17; Edmund Ruffin, "Report of the Agricultural Commissioner," *Southern Planter*, 15 (1855): 5–7.

50. Ruffin, "Incidents," 3:235; *Washington, D.C., National Intelligencer*, 19 Nov. 1853.

51. Ruffin, "Report of the Commissioner," 5–6. Richardson (1795-1876) canvassed the state as agent for the Society and was credited with increasing its membership to more than five thousand: Charles W. Turner, "William H. Richardson, Friend of the Farmer," *Virginia Cavalcade*, 20 (1970–71): 14–20.

52. Ruffin, *Diary*, 1:322 (22 July 1859).

53. "Virginia State Agricultural Society," *Southern Planter*, 14 (1854): 74–77; Ruffin, *Diary*, 1:134–35 (26 Nov. 1857).

54. Philander, "Enormous Losses Caused by the Fence Law of Virginia," *Farmers' Register*, 1 (1834): 634–35, editor's note; [Edmund Ruffin], "On the Petition for a Change of the Law of Enclosures," *Farmers' Register*, 2 (1834): 402–3; [Edmund Ruffin], "Remarks [on Fences]," *Farmers' Register*, 3 (1835): 49–50.

55. *The Code of Virginia*, 2d ed. (Richmond: Ritchie, Dunnavant & Co., 1860), 494–95; Ruffin, *Diary*, 1:136 (10 Dec. 1857).

56. Ruffin, *Diary*, 1:150, 398–99 (22 Jan. 1858, 6 Feb. 1860); Thomas G. Baylor, Appomattox Ring Fence Association, to Ruffin, 28 Jan. 1860, Ruffin Papers, VHS.

57. Ruffin, *Diary*, 1:388–89 (5 Jan. 1860).

58. Edmund Ruffin ["A Virginian," pseud.], "The Armed Truce," *Charleston Mercury*, 7 Nov. 1851.

59. *Charleston Mercury*, 19 Nov. 1852.

60. The federal government and the state governments of Virginia, North Carolina, and South Carolina were beginning to fund publications in which his research appeared, however.

61. Ruffin passed through Washington in 1827, escorting his sister Elizabeth on a seven-week tour of the Northern states; Elizabeth Ruffin Cocke, Diary, 6:158–69 (25 Sept. 1827), Cocke Papers, SHC. In 1828 Ruffin took his son to New Haven to enroll him in a private school, though they did not pass through Washington on the journey north; there is no record of how he returned to Virginia in 1828 or how Edmund, Jr., was retrieved in 1829. See Ruffin, "School-Boy Letters of Edmund Ruffin, Jr.," 287–329. Ruffin's 1857 visit certainly was his first in a long time, for he spoke of meeting "former acquaintances" and being introduced to other men for the first time. On his third visit he confessed he did not know the city well enough to choose a good lodging or boarding house: Ruffin, *Diary*, 1:33, 174 (14 Feb. 1857, 15 Apr. 1858).

62. Ruffin, *Diary*, 1:33–41, 145–50, 173–82, 255–58, 261–74, 376–83, 429–38 (13–23 Feb. 1857; 14–24 Jan., 14–27 April, 16–23 Dec. 1858; 2–24 Jan., 8–19 Dec. 1859, 13–24 June 1860).

63. Ruffin, "Incidents," 3:229, 245–46, 254; Ruffin, "The Armed Truce"; Ruffin, *Diary*, 1:64–73, 183–84, 425–26, 496–99, 511–16, 530–33, 559–63, 573–610 (9–19 May 1857, 5–7 May 1858, 1–3 June 1860, 16–20 Nov. 1860, 19–26 Dec. 1860, 12–15 Jan. 1861, 3–9 Mar., 1861, 29 Mar.–21 Apr. 1861). On his visit in 1857 Ruffin recalled mournfully that his daughter Jane (who married in 1854 and died in 1855) had accompanied him on his previous time at St. Philip's Church, probably a reference to his 1852 journey: Ruffin, *Diary*, 1:73 (17 May 1857). Ruffin combined these trips to Charleston with visits to Thomas Ruffin in North Carolina and extended stays in Columbia, South Carolina, another city of importance in his pursuit of the secession cause.

64. Ruffin, *Diary*, 2:149–50 (16, 21 Oct. 1861).

65. John Clive and Bernard Bailyn, "England's Cultural Provinces: Scotland and America," *William and Mary Quarterly*, 3d ser., 14 (1957): 200–13. On the vitality of Richmond before the Civil War, see David Goldfield, *Urban Growth in the Age of Sectionalism: Virginia, 1847–1861* (Baton Rouge: Louisiana State Univ. Press, 1977), 97–138, 197; for implicit comparisons with nineteenth-century Charleston, see David Moltke-Hansen, "The Expansion of Intellectual Life: A Prospectus," in Michael O'Brien and David Moltke-Hansen, eds., *Intellectual Life in Antebellum Charleston* (Knoxville: Univ. of Tennessee Press, 1986), 3–44; Jane H. Pease and William H.

Pease, "Intellectual Life in the 1830s: The Institutional Framework and the Charleston Style," in O'Brien and Moltke-Hansen, 233–54.

66. Ruffin, *Diary*, 1:115–16, 120 (23 Oct., 6 Nov. 1857).

67. For topics discussed at the executive committee meeting and the fair of 1857, see Ruffin, *Diary*, 1:116–19 (24–30 Oct. 1857).

68. Ruffin recognized this function of the Society: Ruffin, *Diary*, 1:39 (20 Feb. 1857). In 1853 the Society published four such essays by Ruffin: Virginia State Agricultural Society: *Journal of Transactions*, 1 (1853): 10–49, 182–87.

69. W. Eugene Ferslew, *First Annual Directory for the City of Richmond* (Richmond: George M. West, [1859]), 214.

70. Ruffin, *Diary*, 1:120 (6 Nov. 1857).

71. Ibid., 1:246, (9 Nov. 1858); 2:153, 488, 497 (24 Oct. 1861; 11, 24 Nov. 1862). See also Randolph's ten-page advertisement in Ruffin, *Calcareous Manures*, 5th ed., following p. 493.

72. The results of some of this research appeared in his study of three types of Virginia counties: Ruffin, "Communication to the Virginia State Agricultural Society," 258–70; see also Ruffin, *Diary*, 1:342, 393 (21 Sept. 1859; 16, 18 Jan. 1860).

73. Ruffin, *Diary*, 1:389 (6 Jan. 1860).

74. Ibid., 1:304 (27 May 1859).

75. Ibid., 1:33, 64, 174 (14 Feb., 10 May 1857; 16 April 1858).

76. Ibid., 1: 39, 147, 174 (20 Feb. 1857; 19 Jan., 16 Apr. 1858).

77. Ibid., 1:65–72, 184, 225, 425, 514 (12–16 May, 1857, 6 May 1858, 18 Aug. 1858, 1 June 1860, 23 Dec. 1860).

78. Ibid., 1:81 (11 June 1857).

79. Ibid., 1:61 (29 Apr. 1857).

80. Ibid., 1:90 (18 July 1857).

81. "Discussion, on Wheat and Its Culture," *Journal of the Transactions of the Virginia State Agricultural Society, for the Years 1856–57* (n.p., n.d.), 29–32; Ruffin, *Diary*, 1:11 ("Introduction to the attempt").

82. Ruffin, *Diary*, 1:81 (11 June 1857).

83. Ibid., 1:134 (24 Nov. 1857).

84. Ibid., 1:172 (3 Apr. 1858).

85. Ruffin, "Incidents," 2:111–12. All copies of this edition were sold. Ruffin made no income from its sale; he said in 1853 he had intended only to circulate his ideas, not to make money from the book.

86. Ruffin, "Incidents," 2:146–47, 157; Edmund Ruffin, "List of Subscribers," 769–76; see also above, chap. 2, nn. 70, 89.

87. Ruffin, *Diary*, 1:39, 62 (20 Feb., 5 May 1857).

88. Ibid., 1:174, 226 (17 Apr. 1858, 15 Jan. 1859). Ruffin said he gave away five hundred copies of the colonization pamphlet, and that members of Congress had bought 2,100 to distribute.

89. Ibid., 1:408–9 (1 Mar. 1860).

90. Ruffin, "Incidents," 3:247; Edmund Ruffin, "Southern Agricultural Exhaustion," pp. 373–89.

91. Ruffin, *Diary*, 1:326, 331 (30 July–1 Aug. 1859, 19 Aug. 1859).

92. Ibid., 2:232 (10 Feb. 1862). *Anticipations of the Future* was published anonymously.

93. Ruffin, *Diary*, 1:471, 473 (1, 15 Oct. 1860).

94. Ibid., 1:554 (21 Feb. 1861).

95. Ibid., 1:174, 180, 255–57, 447, 450, 453, (17, 24 April, 16, 20 Dec. 1858; 7, 26, 29 Aug. 1860). In 1860 Ruffin and five other guests at the springs (including Philip St. George Cocke) formed a "Publication Society," furnishing $100 each to publish "books & pamphlets the best calculated to sustain the rights of the southern states": *Diary*, 1:453 (29 Aug. 1860).

96. Ruffin; *Agricultural, Geological, and Descriptive Sketches of Lower North Carolina*; Ruffin, *Diary*, 1:427, 473–74 (8 June 1860, 17 Oct. 1860); Ruffin to Thomas Ruffin, 26 Feb. 1859, in Hamilton, *Papers of Thomas Ruffin*, 3:21–22.

97. Ruffin, *Diary*, 1:400 (9 Feb. 1860).

98. Ibid., 1:428–29 (12 June 1860).

99. Ibid., 1:579 (5 Apr. 1861); 2:108 (17 Aug. 1861).

100. Ibid., 1:279–80 (4, 8 Feb. 1859).

101. Ibid., 1:328 (3 Aug. 1859).

Notes to Chapter Six

1. Ruffin, *Diary*, 1:7, 16 ("Introduction to the attempt").

2. Edmund Ruffin ["A Virginian," pseud.], "What Will Be the Results of the Northern Abolition Agitation?" *Richmond Enquirer*, 22 Jan., 25 Jan., 2 Apr. 1850.

3. The single case of Ruffin fits closely the general argument concerning motives for secession advanced in Gavin Wright, *The Political Economy of the Cotton South: Households, Markets, and Wealth in the Nineteenth Century* (New York: W. W. Norton & Co., 1978), 144–57; compare Genovese, *Political Economy of Slavery*, 266–70.

4. Edmund, Jr., professed his faith at a local Episcopal church near Beechwood in December 1849: Julian C. Ruffin to Edmund Ruffin, 7 Dec. 1849, Ruffin Papers, VHS.

5. Ruffin, *Diary*, 1:187, 375, 485–97, 526, 558, 571 (11 May 1858, 6 Dec. 1859, 7–16 Nov. 1860; 7 Jan., 28 Feb., 22 Mar. 1861); 2:5, 9–10 (22, 25 Apr. 1861).

6. On Ruffin's association with a "network" of Southern intellectuals after 1840, see Faust, *A Sacred Circle,* 1–6.

7. U.S. Congress, *Biographical Directory of the American Congress, 1774–1961* (Washington, D.C.: Government Printing Office, 1961), 1387; Ruffin, *Diary,* 1:222–25 (14–17 Aug. 1858).

8. Ruffin, "Incidents," 3:228–29, Ruffin Papers, VHS; Ruffin, *Diary,* 2:11–12, n. It may have been through Boulware that Ruffin first encountered George Fitzhugh, who did not become a close Ruffin associate. Late in 1861 Ruffin encountered Fitzhugh three times in the lobby of the Exchange Hotel, talking about war news. See *Diary,* 2:152, 157, 164 (23, 29 Oct., 11 Nov. 1861).

9. Ruffin, *Diary,* 1:341–42 (19 Sept. 1859). Their common ancestors were Nathaniel Harrison (1742–82) and Mary Ruffin Harrison (1739–67), who lived in Amelia County; Stanard, "Harrison of James River," *VMHB,* 34 (1926):187.

10. For evidence of Hammond's influence on Ruffin as early as 1845, see Mitchell, *Edmund Ruffin,* 59–60, 68–69.

11. Ruffin, *Diary,* 1:64, 71, 290 (10, 16 May, 1857, 28 Feb.–3 Mar. 1859); see also ibid., 1:64, n. 30; John Bachman, *The Doctrine of the Unity of the Human Race Examined by the Principles of Science* (Charleston, S.C.: C. Canning, 1850).

12. Ruffin, *Diary,* 1:53, n.

13. Ibid., 1:149 (22 Jan. 1858). In April Ruffin emerged from a conversation with General William L. Cazneau of Texas with the difficulty clearly in mind: "Amalgamation with this black & mongrel race is out of the question": *Diary,* 1:178 (20 Apr. 1858).

14. Ibid., 1:146–48 (16, 19, 20 Jan. 1858).

15. Ibid., 1:35, 145, 180 (15 Feb. 1857; 14 Jan., 25 Apr. 1858). In another conversation with Fisher, General John Tyler intruded with a "harangue" and "speech," spoiling a three-hour talk: *Diary,* 1:267, (16 Jan. 1859).

16. Ibid., 1:181 (25 Apr. 1858).

17. Ibid., 1:72–73 (16-18 May 1857).

18. Ibid., 1:213, 325 (11 July 1858, 28 July 1859).

19. Ibid., 1:332 (22 Aug. 1859).

20. J. Thomas Scharf, *History of Delaware,* 2 vols. (Philadelphia: L. J. Richards, 1888), 2:964–66.

21. Ruffin, *Diary,* 1:340 (12–13 Sept. 1859).

22. Ibid., 1:78, 147–48 (26 May 1857, 20 Jan. 1858).

23. Ibid., 1:256 (18 Dec. 1858). The Ruffin family also maintained close relations with Bishop William Meade of Virginia, a member of the American Colonization Society: *Diary,* 1:120–21 (7 Nov. 1857); 120, n. 17.

24. Ibid., 1:290 (28 Feb.–3 Mar. 1859).

25. One acquaintance who disagreed with Ruffin but apparently said nothing was Dr. Richard Eppes, who lived a few miles upstream from Beechwood: Shearer Davis Bowman, "Conditional Unionism and Slavery in Virginia, 1860–1861: The Case of Dr. Richard Eppes," *VMHB*, 96 (1988): 40–42.

26. Ruffin, *Diary*, 1:375, 378 (6, 9 Dec. 1859); *New York Herald*, 5 Dec. 1859. The incident probably happened as the *Herald* reported it. Ruffin denied the story, but given his growing outspokenness and his absorption in the John Brown affair, it seems unlikely the account was wrong.

27. Ruffin, *Diary*, 1:484 (7 Nov. 1860).

28. The *African Repository*, however, did publish a critical review of Ruffin's pamphlet on colonization in 1859: Ruffin, *Diary*, 1:328 (6 Aug. 1859).

29. On Ruffin and the *Richmond Dispatch*, see Ruffin, *Diary*, 1:498–99 (18 Nov. 1860). On the *Richmond Enquirer*, see ibid., 1:17, 20, 157, 206, 225, 267–68, 409, 494, 499, 538, ("Introduction to the attempt"; 28 Dec. 1856; 16 Feb., 1 July, 18 Aug. 1858; 16 Jan. 1859; 6 Mar., 13, 18 Nov. 1860; 29 Jan. 1861). On the *Richmond Examiner*, see ibid., 1:225, 283, 301, 311, 360, 378, 379, 390 (18 Aug. 1858; 15 Feb., 4 May, 22 June, 24 Nov., 10, 14 Dec. 1859; 9 Jan. 1860). On the *Richmond Index*, see ibid., 1:390, 392, 404, 406 (9, 13 Jan., 21, 24 Feb. 1860). On the *Richmond Whig*, see ibid., 1:236, 240, 360 (7, 25 Oct. 1858; 24 Nov. 1859).

On the *Southern Literary Messenger*, see ibid., 1:251, 536, 579 (29 Nov. 1858; 19, 22 Jan., 5 Apr. 1861). On the *Southern Planter*, see ibid., 1:341, 346, 351, 355, 383, 536 (17 Sept., 1, 28 Oct., 12 Nov., 19 Dec. 1859; 22 Jan. 1861).

Apparently only *The South*, edited by Roger Pryor, directly criticized Ruffin's published schemes for secession, after having published his constitution for an "Association of United Southerners": Ruffin, *Diary*, 1:200, 220–21 (9 June, 11 Aug. 1858).

30. Ruffin, *Diary*, 1:197 (31 May 1858).

31. Ibid., 1: 475 (19 Oct. 1860). As late as February 1861 Judge Ruffin was under pressure from women in the family to resist secession. In that month he received a letter from Sarah B. Ruffin (sister of the pro-secessionist congressman from North Carolina, Thomas Ruffin) urging the Judge to stand with the Union and keep the young Ruffin men in line. Sarah Ruffin, who lived in Philadelphia, was particularly caustic in her criticism of Edmund Ruffin. "I regret to perceive, from the News-papers," she wrote, "that our distinguished cousin Edmund Ruffin, of Va, has set such an example for the younger Ruffin's; as, to exert his influence, in the opposite direction: he has made a fatal mistake." Sarah B. Ruffin to Thomas Ruffin, 18 Feb. 1861, in Hamilton, *Papers of Thomas Ruffin*, 3:128–29.

32. Ruffin, *Diary*, 1:559, 572 (1, 24 Mar. 1861).

33. On Charles Ruffin's lack of enthusiasm for the war, see *Diary*, 2:135,

310–11 (23 Sept. 1861, 21 May 1862); Julian Ruffin's mother-in-law reported that neighbors in Prince George opposed secession in January 1861, and that Charles was reluctant to join the Palmetto Guard as late as June of that year; Rebecca Wormeley Meade to John Meade, 4 June 1861, Ruffin and Meade Papers, SHC.

34. Mildred Sayre to Ruffin, 4 Feb. 1861, Ruffin Papers, VHS.

35. Mildred Sayre to Ruffin, 19 Feb. 1861, Ruffin Papers, VHS.

36. Mildred Sayre to Ruffin, 29 Apr. [1861], Ruffin Papers, VHS.

37. On the general skepticism among secessionists that a war would occur, see Wright, *Political Economy of the Cotton South*, 146–47.

38. Mildred Sayre to Ruffin, 8 May 1861, Ruffin Papers, VHS.

39. Mildred Sayre to Ruffin, 26 May 1861, Ruffin Papers, VHS.

40. Mildred Sayre to Ruffin, 7 Sept. 1861, Ruffin Papers, VHS.

41. Ruffin, *Diary*, 1:186–87 (11 May 1858).

42. Ibid., 1:222–23 (14 Aug. 1858).

43. Ibid., 1:495–96 (15 Nov. 1860).

44. Ibid., 1:526 (7 Jan. 1861).

45. Ibid., 2:5 (22 Apr. 1861).

46. Ibid., 2:9–10 (25 Apr. 1861).

47. Ibid., 2:568–71 (7 Feb. 1863).

48. [Edmund Ruffin], "Cassandra—Warnings," *Charleston Mercury*, 21 July 1859; reprinted in Ruffin, *Diary*, 1:627–32.

49. Edmund Ruffin, "Consequences of Abolition Agitation," *De Bow's Review*, 22 (1857): 590–91; ibid., 23 (1857): 271–72, 550. These essays appeared originally in the *Richmond Enquirer* in December 1856, and were reprinted in Ruffin, *Anticipations of the Future*, 343–416; see especially 368–81, 389–403. Ruffin's 1860 tract became a fantasy in which the Union abandoned the effort to suppress secession after one significant, small battle in western Virginia.

50. In emphasizing the evolution of Ruffin's thought, the interpretation here differs significantly from that in Mathew, *Ruffin and the Crisis of Slavery*, 48–49.

51. Ruffin, "First Views," 661.

52. Ruffin, "Incidents," 2:138.

53. W. J. Dupuy to Ruffin, 13 Jan. 1828; Ruffin to Juliana Coupland, 26 Nov. 1831; Juliana Coupland to Ruffin, 14 Jan. [1832], Ruffin Papers, VHS. Apparently Ruffin did succeed in this strategy, at least through 1833.

54. Warner, *Benjamin Harrison*, 44; abstract of Coupland's will in Dandridge Spotswood, "Notes from the Records of Petersburg," *Virginia Will Records* (Baltimore: Genealogical Publishing Co., 1982), 258.

55. Elizabeth Ruffin to Ruffin, n.d. (Monday night), Ruffin Papers (Section 5), VHS. Elizabeth had not married when she wrote this letter, some time between 1828 and 1832.

56. Ruffin, *Diary*, 1:238 (20 Oct. 1858).

57. Edmund Ruffin ["A Slaveholder," pseud.], "Estimates of the Expenses and Profits of Rearing Slaves [Written in 1832]," *Farmers' Register*, 2 (1834): 253–55. Ruffin may have intended to include this essay as an appendix to the first edition of *An Essay on Calcareous Manures*. It was composed about the time he prepared that manuscript for publication, and before he began publishing the *Farmers' Register*.

58. Ruffin, "Some effects of slavery on agricultural profits," Appendix C in Ruffin, *Calcareous Manures*, 162.

59. Ibid., 163.

60. Ibid., 162–64.

61. Jesse Burton Harrison ["A Virginian," pseud.], *Review of the Slave Question, Extracted from the American Quarterly Review* (Richmond: T. W. White, 1833); Thomas R. Dew, *Review of the Debate in the Virginia Legislature of 1831 and 1832* (Richmond: T. W. White, 1832). Harrison was responding directly to Dew on behalf of the Virginia Colonization Society. See Alison Goodyear Freehling, *Drift Toward Dissolution: The Virginia Slavery Debate of 1831–1832* (Baton Rouge: Louisiana State Univ. Press, 1982), 208–210.

62. Edmund Ruffin, "Agricultural Review: Slavery and Emancipation," *Farmers' Register*, 1 (1833): 36.

63. Ibid., 36–41.

64. Ibid., 36, 48.

65. For a treatment of this Malthusian notion as it developed in 1863, see George M. Frederickson, *The Black Image in the White Mind: The Debate on Afro-American Character and Destiny, 1817–1914* (1971; Wesleyan ed., Middletown, Conn.: Wesleyan University Press, 1987), 158–59.

66. Ruffin, "Agricultural Review," 48. In the development of his thinking on slavery Ruffin followed a course much like that of the South as a whole, as analyzed in William Sumner Jenkins, *Pro-slavery Thought in the Old South* (Chapel Hill: Univ. of North Carolina Press, 1935), 48–106.

67. [Edmund Ruffin], "Movements of the Abolition Societies; and Anticipated Results," *Farmers' Register*, 3 (1835): 287–89.

68. Edmund Ruffin, "Sketch of the Progress of Agriculture in Virginia, and the Causes of Its Decline, and Present Depression," *Farmers' Register*, 3 (1835): 748–49.

69. Edmund Ruffin, "The Effects of High Prices of Slaves; Considered in Reference to the Interests of Agriculture, of Individuals, and of the Commonwealth of Virginia," *De Bow's Review*, 26 (1859): 653–56.

70. Ruffin, "Farming Profits," 2, 4, 8. The whole group of slaves had increased in value by 9.4 percent in five years, far short of the 6 percent annual return Ruffin usually expected on investments. He appears to have been pleased with this increase, however, in part because he was surprised

that it took place. More important, he now regarded his slaves—along with marl—as crucial factors in producing farm profits at Marlbourne.

71. Ruffin, "Address to the Virginia State Agricultural Society," 9.

72. Ruffin, "Address to the Virginia State Agricultural Society," 10, 13; Edmund Ruffin, *The Political Economy of Slavery* (Washington, D.C.: Lemuel Towers [1858]), 5; Ruffin, "Prices," 651. The publication date of the *Political Economy* pamphlet is often cited as 1857, though Ruffin's diary indicates it was published in 1858: Ruffin, *Diary*, 1:174–80 (17, 21, 24 Apr. 1858).

73. Ruffin, "Address to the Virginia State Agricultural Society," 10.

74. Ruffin, *Political Economy*, 20.

75. Ruffin, "Prices," 652.

76. Ruffin attributed the influence to Fisher in several places, most immediately in "Address to the Virginia State Agricultural Society," 12.

77. Ruffin, "Address to the Virginia State Agricultural Society," 10.

78. Ibid., 10.

79. The definitions of racism and racist ideology used here are adopted from Frederickson, *Black Image in the White Mind*, 2.

80. Edmund Ruffin, "Equality of the Races—Haytien and British Experiments; the Dogma of the Natural Mental Equality of the Black and White Races Considered," *De Bow's Review*, 25 (1858): 27.

81. Ruffin had begun to gather evidence for this idea in 1836. See his editor's notes to James Madison [of Prince Edward County], "Condition of the Descendants of a Number of Emancipated Slaves, in Prince Edward County," *Farmers' Register*, 4 (1836): 4; Edmund Ruffin, "Some of the Effects of West Indian Emancipation, as Stated by the Friends of That Measure," *Farmers' Register*, 4 (1836): 49–52.

82. Ruffin, "Equality," 28–38.

83. Edmund Ruffin, "Liberia and the Colonization Society," *De Bow's Review*, 27 (1859): 343–44.

84. Ruffin, "Equality," 28, 33–34.

85. Ibid., 31.

86. Ruffin, *Political Economy*, 11.

87. Ruffin, *Diary*, 1:332–33 (22 Aug. 1859). Ruffin wrote an article about Mackintosh for the *Fredericksburg News*.

88. In this, he provides strong evidence for Frederickson's thesis in *Black Image in the White Mind*, p. 65. Indeed, Ruffin's case indicates racial arguments had greater significance than antibourgeois values in justifying slavery.

89. Ruffin, *Diary*, 1:73, 498 (17 May 1857, 18 Nov. 1860).

90. Ibid., 1:321 (19 July 1859).

91. Ruffin, *Anticipations*, p. 55–56.

92. Ruffin, "Equality," 28.

93. Ibid., p. 29; Ruffin, *Diary*, 1:577 (4 Apr. 1861).

94. Ruffin, *Political Economy*, 22.

95. Stanley Elkins has depicted abolitionist thought as given to abstraction in *Slavery: A Problem in American Institutional and Intellectual Life* (Chicago: Univ. of Chicago Press, 1959), 27–28, 144.

96. Ruffin, *Diary*, 1:308 (2 June 1859).

97. Ibid., 1:290 (3 Mar. 1859); for an account of Bachman's influence, see Frederickson, *Black Image in the White Mind*, 83, 86.

98. In his journal Ruffin occasionally praised the abilities of individual slaves, indicating that he did perceive differences among them and that he assumed they were capable of good work. This awareness that some of his slaves were excellent workers must have strengthened his assumption that the preservation of slavery was necessary. See Ruffin, Marlbourne Farm Journal, 364, 420–21, 422 (4 Apr. 1849; 20, 27 June 1850), VSL. For a treatment of slave labor and Ruffin that leads to different conclusions, see Genovese, *Political Economy of Slavery*, 43–51.

99. Ruffin, *Political Economy*, 22. In their correspondence Ruffin and his son Edmund occasionally mentioned illnesses of slaves: see, for example, Edmund Ruffin, Jr., to Ruffin, 13 Mar. 1847, Ruffin Papers, VHS. For Ruffin's concern about working slaves during the malaria season, see Ruffin, "Essay—On Harvesting Corn-Fodder," 422. For interpretations of possible ethnic and racial differences in immunity and susceptibility to specific diseases, see Rosengarten, *Tombee*, 181; Todd L. Savitt, *Medicine and Slavery* (Urbana: Univ. of Illinois Press, 1978), 17–47; Rutman and Rutman, "Of Agues and Fevers," 34–35; Peter H. Wood, *Black Majority: Negroes in Colonial South Carolina from 1670 through the Stono Rebellion* (New York: Alfred A. Knopf, 1974), 86–91.

100. The tracts on slavery and race contain some of Ruffin's most prolix, digressive prose. He was much better at writing expository prose than polemic. In the latter he assumed the proper method was to argue from an accepted general proposition to "each of its minor parts"; Edmund Ruffin, "Slavery and Free Labor Defined and Compared," *Southern Planter*, 20 (1860): 1, 5. His 1858 pamphlet, *The Political Economy of Slavery*, covered thirty-one pages, eleven of which consisted of material he had published previously.

101. [Edmund Ruffin], Editor's note to Madison, "Condition of the Descendants," 4; see also Randall M. Miller, "Introduction," in Randall M. Miller, ed., *"Dear Master": Letters of a Slave Family* (Ithaca: Cornell Univ. Press, 1978), 33–36.

102. Ruffin, *Diary*, 1:120–21 (7 Nov. 1857).

103. Ruffin, "Progress of Agriculture," 749.

104. Ruffin, *Political Economy*, 14.

105. Ruffin, *Diary*, 1:143 (9 Jan. 1858).

106. Ruffin, "Address to the Virginia State Agricultural Society," 12.

107. Ruffin, "Progress of Agriculture," 749; Ruffin, *Political Economy*, 8. Ruffin's reading of Fletcher's biography and some of Fletcher's writings

established in Ruffin's thinking a criticism of free labor and class relations under Northern capitalism that has been attributed to the influence of George Fitzhugh. If chronology is evidence, the influence ran from Fletcher to Ruffin to Fitzhugh. Ruffin did not take seriously Fletcher's ironic proposal to place serfs in bondage again, but he did adopt Fletcher's analysis of the dilemma confronting laborers competing in a free labor economy. Ruffin knew Fitzhugh slightly and thought him a "profound thinker, though a careless writer." He claimed credit for expressing first many of Fitzhugh's ideas, though he remained bewildered by Fitzhugh's opposition to "interest or capital." This "opposition to the accumulation of capital," he said, was "foolish." Ruffin was one Tidewater planter who regarded Fitzhugh's stance against capitalism a pose. Ruffin, *Diary*, 1:215–16, 240–41 (21 July 1858, 26 Oct. 1858). Even in 1859, at the height of his defensiveness on slavery, Ruffin expressed his fears in words appropriate to a capitalist farmer who wanted to preserve profit-yielding capital investments in slaves. He feared "agricultural capital" in Virginia could no longer "yield a profit," he said. "The capital of the farmer in Virginia is made up mainly of land and slaves." See Ruffin, "Prices," 647, 649.

108. By 1863 Ruffin certainly assumed this belief had been embedded in his thinking through early experiences with slaves. In that year he scoffed at orders by U.S. General Nathaniel P. Banks that freedmen in Louisiana be hired by the year. "Every man raised among negro slaves knows that the scheme, with any variations of particular features, is sure of utter failure, & probably before the first diminished crops will be partially secured." The hirelings, he predicted, merely would become indolent. Ruffin, *Diary*, 2:601 (16 Mar. 1863). For a succinct discussion of historiographic issues concerning the relationship between slavery and ideas of race, see Eugene D. Genovese, *The World the Slaveholders Made: Two Essays in Interpretation* (New York: Pantheon Books, 1969), 103–6.

109. Ruffin, *Essay on Calcareous Manures*, 145, 156, 194. It must be remembered that in daily farm records Ruffin did occasionally notice that some slaves were excellent workers: see Ruffin, Marlbourne Farm Journal, 420–21 (20 June 1850). These particular observations, however, were not powerful enough to shatter the general categorizations of human beings he employed in writings more distant in time from particular experiences.

110. U.S. Congress, *Census for 1820* (1821; repr., New York: Luther M. Cornwall Co., n.d.), 24; U.S. Census, Manuscript Returns, Prince George County, Va., 1820, 54, NA (microfilm). The 1820 census recorded 4,323 slaves, 588 free blacks, and a total population of 8,030 in the county.

111. Map of the Vicinity of Richmond, Va., and Part of the Peninsula, in Calvin D. Cowles, comp., *Atlas to Accompany the Official Records of the Union and Confederate Armies* (Washington, D.C.: Government Printing Office, 1891–95), plate XCII.

112. Ruffin, *Diary*, 1:86–87 (4 July 1857); Edmund Ruffin, Jr., to Ruffin, 9 May 1863, Ruffin Papers, VHS. Zack remained at Marlbourne through May 1864, but he left by Christmas that year: Ruffin, Diary (manuscript), 3925, (22 Mar. 1865), LC. Jem Sykes was not literate, and apparently none of Ruffin's other slaves could read or write. Ruffin, therefore, did not perceive variations in intellectual abilities that might have manifested themselves more strikingly in literate individuals. Even when he did observe differences in the abilities of field hands, his perception was dominated by a pre-existing concept of blacks as a group. Thus he did not proceed to draw conclusions about human variation and potentiality. On Sykes' inability to read, see Ruffin, "Incidents," 2:188.

113. Ruffin, *Political Economy*, 3.

Notes to Chapter Seven

1. Ruffin, Diary (manuscript), 4089, 4099–100 (16, 17, 18 June 1865), LC. The date of Ruffin's death has been a matter of confusion. Ruffin's last entry in the diary indicates the date was 18 June, but internal evidence indicates he was confused about this. Other sources, including a letter by Edmund, Jr., and all but one of the death notices published in Richmond, Washington, Baltimore, and New York newspapers indicate that the suicide occurred on Saturday, 17 June. For a recent discussion of the date see David F. Allmendinger, Jr., and William K. Scarborough, "The Days Ruffin Died," *VMHB*, 97 (1989): 75–96; see also Betty L. Mitchell, " 'Superfluous Lags the Veteran on the Stage': The Death of the Confederate Edmund Ruffin," *Virginia Cavalcade*, 32 (1983): 126-33; and Mitchell, *Edmund Ruffin*, 287, n. 63.

2. Edmund Ruffin, Jr., to his sons, 20 June 1865, in "Death of Edmund Ruffin," *Tyler's* 193–95. This is the published text of Edmund's letter to his sons at Beechwood. The original has not been found. It is the only first-hand account of the suicide apart from Ruffin's, and the only letter by a family member dealing with the death. All but one of the newspaper accounts drew on evidence supplied to the *Richmond Whig* and *Richmond Republic*, apparently by Edmund, Jr. All but one gave the date as 17 June. The exception was the *Richmond Daily Times*, 20 June 1865, which said that Ruffin died on Sunday; that would have been 18 June. See *Richmond Whig*, 20 June; *Richmond Republic*, 20 June; *New York Herald*, 21 June; *New York Times*, 22, 23 June; *New York Tribune*, 22, 23 June; *Baltimore American and Commercial Advertiser*, 22 June; *Washington, D.C., National Intelligencer*, 22 June; and *Washington, D.C., Evening Star*, 22 June, 1865.

3. *Richmond Whig*, 20 June 1865. The *New York Tribune* republished this account on 23 June 1865.

4. Ruffin, Diary (manuscript), 4098 (16, 17, 18 June 1865), LC.

5. The text of the final entry indicated that Ruffin considered the "Memoranda" a separate document. As he approached the final paragraph of the diary proper, he said he had only to "add some directions in writing," referring to instructions about burial. These instructions he must have intended to complete after 10:00 a.m., when he signed the final entry: Ruffin, Diary (manuscript), 4098 (16, 17, 18 June 1865), LC. A fragment of an earlier note in Ruffin's hand survives, expressing a request for burial in South Carolina and a concern for his future reputation in Virginia. At one time it was thought to be a draft of a suicide note, but it appears to be an instruction for burial drafted before May 1864; see Edmund Ruffin, "Draft of his suicide note," Ruffin Papers, UVA.

6. Ruffin, Diary (manuscript), 4100 (18 June 1865), LC.

7. Ibid.

8. "Death of Edmund Ruffin," 193; "mussle" in original. Edmund, Jr., meant to say that Ruffin used the stick to push, not pull, the trigger.

9. Ibid., 194.

10. Ruffin, Diary (manuscript), 5 Jan. 1865, 3752–56, LC.

11. *Richmond Whig*, 20 June 1865.

12. Ruffin, Diary (manuscript), 4098, 4100 (16, 17, 18 June 1865), LC.

13. Ibid., 4095 (16, 17, 18 June 1865).

14. "Death of Edmund Ruffin," 193, 194.

15. *Richmond Whig*, 20 June 1865; *New York Tribune*, 23 June 1865. If this letter did exist, it apparently has not survived.

16. *New York Times*, 23 June 1865.

17. *Richmond Republic*, 20 June 1865 (account reprinted in *Baltimore American and Commercial Advertiser*, 22 June 1865); *New York Tribune*, 22 June 1865.

18. This interpretation survived into the twentieth century, together with its implication that Ruffin's career in reform ended in the symbolic failure of an old order. See Craven, *Edmund Ruffin, Southerner*, 235–59.

19. Ruffin, *Diary*, 1:583–601 (9–15 Apr. 1861).

20. Ibid., 2:54, 58, 59, 62, 70–72, 78, 88–91, 94–95 (1–23 July 1861).

21. Provost marshal's pass issued to Ruffin, 28 Mar. 1862, Ruffin Papers, UVA; Ruffin, *Diary*, 2:266 (28 Mar. 1862).

22. Ruffin, *Diary*, 2:267–272 (29 Mar.–2 Apr. 1862).

23. Ibid., 2:391–98 (30–31 July, 1862); U.S. War Department, *The War of the Rebellion: A Compilation of the Official Records of the Union and Confederate Armies*, ser. 1, vol. 11, part 2 (Washington, D.C.: Government Printing Office, 1884), 940–46.

24. Immediately after the Battle of Seven Pines east of Richmond, Ruffin secured a horse on 1 June 1862 and rode to inspect the field of battle. There

his long white hair made him a recognizable figure. A young man from the Petersburg regiment introduced himself and told Ruffin that his grandson Julian Beckwith had been "killed instantanously {sic} by a musket ball received in front, in the forehead"; Ruffin, *Diary*, 2:330 (1 June 1862).

25. Ruffin's suicide has implications for many themes in Southern history, symbolic event that it was. It can be made to fit most of the classic theories of suicide. Two recent studies have been helpful in interpreting this event: Ronald W. Maris, *Pathways to Suicide: A Survey of Self-Destructive Behaviors* (Baltimore: Johns Hopkins Univ. Press, 1981), which develops the notion of the suicidal life "career"; and Nancy J. Osgood, *Suicide in the Elderly* (Rockville, Md.: Aspen Systems Corp., 1985), which surveys recent literature.

26. He undertook this course of study as early as 1862, when he began to study the writings of Adam Clarke: Ruffin, *Diary*, 2:487–88 (10 Nov. 1862).

27. Ruffin, Diary (manuscript), 4089–93 (16, 17, 18 June 1865), LC; see also Ruffin's Bible notes, "Negative Propositions from the Epistles, maintained," begun 10 Apr. 1865, inserted in the manuscript diary after p. 4020.

28. Ibid., 4093–94 (16, 17, 18 June 1865).

29. Edmund Ruffin, Jr., to Edmund Ruffin, 7 Dec. 1849, Ruffin Papers, VHS.

30. U.S. Census, Agriculture Schedules, Prince George County, Va., 1860, 491, VSL (microfilm). In 1851 it had 733 arable acres; Edmund Ruffin, Jr., Plantation Diary, 1851–1873, 2 (1 Jan. 1851), SHC.

31. Ruffin, *Diary*, 2:426 (22 Aug. 1862); U.S. Census, Slave Schedules, Prince George County, Va., 1860, 424, NA (microfilm); U.S. Census, Slave Schedules, Charles City County, Va., 1860, 156, NA (microfilm). Edmund, Jr., declared his real estate was worth $73,000 that year, his personal property (including slaves), $160,000; U.S. Census, Population Schedules, Prince George County, Va., 1860, 337b, NA (microfilm). He accounted for 59 percent of the wealth listed by family members in the 1860 census (excluding the small sum listed for Charles, who was no longer part of the family enterprise).

32. U.S. Census, Agriculture Schedules, Prince George, 1860, 505, VSL (microfilm); U.S. Census, Slave Schedules, Prince George, 1860, 79b, NA (microfilm).

33. On the smallness of the house see Ruffin, *Diary*, 2:352 (23 June 1862); Elizabeth Ruffin to Julian C. Ruffin, 14 June 1845, Ruffin and Meade Papers, SHC.

34. Ruffin, *Diary*, 1:505 (27 Nov. 1860); 2:418 (17 Aug. 1862).

35. Ibid., 1:558–610 (1 Mar., 21 Apr. 1861). For much of this period Ruffin was able to secure passes or free tickets on Southern railroads.

36. Ibid., 2:54–97 (1–24 July 1861).

37. Ibid., 2:463, 614 (13 Oct. 1862, 2 Apr. 1863).

38. Ruffin feared that her departure, known to Union officials, would lead to pillaging at Marlbourne: Ruffin, *Diary*, 2:334, 337 (11 June 1862).

39. Ibid., 2:259, 315–19, 350–53, 658 (22 Mar., 25–26 May, 11, 22–25 June 1862; 16 May 1863).

40. Ibid., 2:401–2, 416 (3, 17 Aug. 1862); U.S. War Department, *Official Records*, ser. 1, vol. 11, part 2, 946–50.

41. Ruffin, *Diary*, 2:352, 409 (23 June, 8 Aug. 1862).

42. Ibid., 2:634–44 (4 May–9 June 1863).

43. Ibid., 2:399–400, n. (1 Aug. 1862).

44. Ibid., 2:420 (17 Aug. 1862).

45. Ibid., 2:633–45, nn. (4–9 May 1863).

46. Ibid., 2:368 (4 June 1862).

47. Ibid., 2:472 (24 Oct. 1862).

48. Ibid., 2:427 (22 Aug. 1862).

49. Ibid., 2:416, 426 (17, 22 Aug. 1862).

50. Edmund Ruffin, Jr., to Thomas Ruffin, 9 June 1865, in Hamilton, *Papers of Thomas Ruffin*, 3:456.

51. Ruffin, *Diary*, 2:351 (22 June 1862).

52. Ibid., 2:511 (13 Dec. 1862).

53. Ibid., 2:435, 308, 351, 416, 444, 511, 622, 624–25 (30 Apr., 19 May, 23 June, 17 Aug., 14 Sept., 13 Dec. 1862; 11, 17 Apr. 1863).

54. Ibid., 2:418 (17 Aug. 1862).

55. Letter, 11 Aug. 1862, reprinted in Ruffin, *Diary*, 2:417, n.

56. Ruffin, *Diary*, 2:307, 317, 338, 350 (18, 26 May; 11, 22 June 1862).

57. William was the carriage driver for Edmund, Jr. "There could not be a better qualified guide for all that neighborhood, & for half the county," Ruffin observed; ibid., 2:409–10 (8 Aug. 1862). See also U.S. War Department, *Official Records*, ser. 1, vol. 11, part 2, 946–50.

58. Ruffin, *Diary*, 2:338 (11 June 1862).

59. By 21 Apr. 1864 Julian had lost only five male slaves at Ruthven, which means that as many as seventeen of his slaves may have remained there; Ruffin to Juliana Coupland Dorsey, 20 June 1864, Dorsey and Coupland Papers, CWM.

60. Ruffin, *Diary*, 2:353 (25 June 1862). More than thirty were sent to a holding farm.

61. Ibid., 2:346, 351, 353 (18, 23, 25 June 1862).

62. Ibid., 2:351, 353 (23, 25 June 1862).

63. Ibid., 2:371, 375, 471, 477, 500, 506, 507, 511, 514 (7, 12 July, 24, 29 Oct., 29 Nov., 8, 12, 19 Dec. 1862).

64. Ibid., 2:511 (12 Dec. 1862).

65. In his relationship with slaves Ruffin resembled closely the interaction described in Gutman, *Black Family*, 291–93, 309–26. His particular case fits far less well the paternalism described in Eugene D. Genovese, *Roll, Jordan, Roll: The World the Slaves Made* (New York: Pantheon Books, 1974), 3–7, 74, 89–93, 97; what Genovese and others have described about the shock of slaveholders at witnessing their former slaves choose freedom certainly does apply to Ruffin, however.

66. Ruffin, *Diary*, 1:25 (20 Jan. 1857). Ruffin's granddaughter did mention a servant, Daniel, who must have waited on table at Marlbourne: Beckwith, "Personal Reminiscences," 1:16. This would have been Daniel Scott: Edmund Ruffin, Marlbourne Farm Journal, 12 (1844).

67. In his farm journal Ruffin seldom referred by name to individual slaves. Rather, he would refer to them collectively as "marlers" and "haulers," or he would give simply the number of people performing different kinds of work. For examples see Ruffin, Marlbourne Farm Journal, pp. 17, 118, 119, 133, 400 (12, 22 Feb., 3 Mar., 10 May 1845; 23 Jan. 1850). Incomplete lists of slaves at Marlbourne appear in ibid., 12, 55, 82, 364, 420–21 (1844, 4 Apr. 1849, 20 June 1850). Ruffin's published diary, edited by William K. Scarborough, contains the names of only ten slaves between 1857 and 1863, indicating how infrequently these people entered Ruffin's daily mental life. These were as follows: Zack, head plowman at Marlbourne, 1:110 (30 Sept. 1857); Titus, 1:139 (25 Dec. 1857); Ritter 1:298 (15 Apr. 1859); Jem Sykes, 2:368 (4 July 1862); Pinkey, 2:421 (17 Aug. 1862); old Adam, 2:430 (26 Aug 1862); Old Jerry, 2:345 (17 June 1862); William, 2:409–10 (8 Aug. 1862); John, 2:514 (19 Dec. 1862); and Abby, 2:591 (28 Feb. 1863). See also Lebsock, *Free Women of Petersburg*, 140.

68. Ruffin, *Diary*, 2:309 (20 May 1862).

69. Ibid., 2:284, 358 (17 Apr., 30 June 1862).

70. Ibid., 1:556–57 (26 Feb. 1861).

71. Ibid., 2:36, 301 (26 May 1861, 11 May 1862).

72. This estimate is conservative. The gross income at Marlbourne alone totalled $8,000 in 1858. Ruffin estimated that the ruined wheat crops of Marlbourne, Beechwood, and Evelynton in 1862 would have been worth $30,000, and that the clover would have yielded a larger amount: Ruffin, *Diary*, 1:250 (20 Nov. 1858); 2:426–27 (22 Aug. 1862). In 1860 Ruffin and his two eldest sons owned real estate listed at a combined value of $149,200, and personal property worth $245,943 (including slaves); U.S. Census, Population Schedules, Prince George, 1860, 337b, 401b, NA (microfilm); U.S. Census, Population Schedules, Hanover County, Va., 1860, 403, NA (microfilm).

73. Ruffin placed the loss at "half of all they were worth in property": Ruffin, *Diary*, 2:338 (11 June 1862).

74. Ibid., 2:320 (26 May 1862).

75. Ibid., 2:552 (23 Jan. 1863). Edmund, Jr., and Julian tried to sell Marlbourne and its slaves for these amounts in 1862: 2:476 (29 Oct. 1862).

76. In February 1862 the Confederate government assessed the value of forty-eight slaves at Evelynton at $14,220, an average of nearly three hundred dollars each: Edmund Ruffin, Jr., Plantation Diary, 277 (15 Feb. 1862), SHC. This assessment did not reflect market value.

77. In fact, Ruffin released his sons from their bonds in 1863 on the understanding that they would continue to provide him with some income from his reserved capital as long as he lived. This decision marked the legal end of Ruffin's competency: Ruffin, *Diary*, 2:559 (27 Jan. 1863).

78. Ruffin, Diary (manuscript), 3385–86 (29 May 1864), LC.

79. Ruffin, *Diary*, 2:514 (17 Dec. 1862).

80. Ibid., 1:595 (9 Mar. 1863).

81. Ibid., 2:338–39, 574, 592 (11 June 1862; 11 Feb., 4 Mar. 1863).

82. Ruffin to Juliana Coupland Dorsey, 20 June 1864, Dorsey and Coupland Papers, CWM.

83. His sons were still paying income to Ruffin in January 1864, though the amount had fallen to about twelve hundred dollars a year (Confederate dollars); Ruffin to C. G. Memminger, 22 Jan. 1864, Ruffin Papers, UVA.

84. Ruffin, Diary (manuscript), 3969, 3997, (16 Apr., 2 May 1865), LC.

85. Ibid., 4094, (16, 17, 18 June 1865).

86. Scarborough, "Ruffin Family," xxiii–xxvi.

87. Beckwith, "Personal Reminiscences," 1:60a; 2:11, VHS.

88. Ruffin, Diary (manuscript): 3367, 3369 (23, 24 May 1864), LC.

89. Ruffin to Juliana Coupland, 20 June 1864, Dorsey and Coupland Papers, CWM.

90. Julian C. Ruffin to Ruffin, 20 Apr., 2 May 1861, Ruffin Papers, VHS.

91. Ruffin, *Diary*, 2:32–33, 37, 113, 135, 253–54, 262, 310–11 (22, 28 May, 27 Aug., 23 Sept. 1861; 11, 26 Mar., 21 May 1862); Ruffin to Jefferson Davis, 27 Aug. 1861; Edmund Ruffin, Jr., to Ruffin, 21 July 1863, Ruffin Papers, VHS; Rebecca W. Meade to John Meade, 4 June 1861; Charlotte M. Ruffin to Rebecca W. Meade, 17 July 1863, Ruffin and Meade Papers, SHC.

92. Ruffin gave two grim assessments of the family's financial situation in April 1865, including losses to Julian's estate: Ruffin, Diary (manuscript), 3948, 3968–69 (3, 16 Apr. 1865), LC.

93. Edmund Ruffin, Jr., to Thomas Ruffin, 9 June 1865, in Hamilton, *Papers of Thomas Ruffin*, 3:457. Edmund Ruffin said his son had two "rich" farms, but not "a dollar of current money": Ruffin, Diary (manuscript), 4002 (5 May 1865), LC.

94. Provost marshal's pass, 28 Mar. 1862, Ruffin Papers, UVA; Ruffin, *Diary*, 1:107, 226–27, 396–97 (21 Sept. 1857; 28 Aug. 1858; 24 Jan., 2 Feb. 1860).

95. Ruffin first mentioned the trembling in his hand and his red face in June 1857, when he expressed his new concern that people would think he was a drunkard: Ruffin, *Diary*, 1:80–81 (8 June 1857).

96. Ibid., 1:146, 376–77 (18 Jan. 1858, 8 Dec. 1859).

97. Ibid., 1:464 (13 Sept. 1860). On boarding a train in Petersburg in 1863, Ruffin was introduced to a Confederate general with whom he rode all the way to Richmond, but whose name he could not catch. After arrival he discovered the man was none other than Gen. Benjamin Huger, for whom he had developed deep contempt: Ruffin, *Diary*, 2:565–66 (5 Feb. 1863).

98. Ibid., 1:526 (7 Jan. 1861).

99. Ibid., 1:583–88 (9–12 Apr. 1861). The question of whether Ruffin fired the first shot has been a matter of debate. He clearly thought he had, as did most people in the nineteenth century: Ruffin, Diary (manuscript), 3948 (3 Apr. 1865), LC.

100. Ruffin, *Diary* 1:594 (13 Apr. 1861). Ruffin composed the entry for this date on 23 April 1861, by which time he had recovered none of his hearing.

101. Ibid., 2:78, 81, 82, 85–86 (23 July 1861).

102. Ibid., 2:326, 630 (31 May 1862, 30 Apr. 1863). After breakfast on 6 April 1865, while walking alone from Redmoor to William Harrison's house, Ruffin heard cannon fire to the south and west; during the day he heard the cannonading as it came from a more westerly direction, and more distant. Among the military actions that day as Lee retreated toward Appomattox, Ruffin undoubtedly was hearing the encounter at Sayler's Creek, in Amelia County twenty miles southwest of Redmoor: Ruffin, Diary (manuscript), 3956 (6 Apr. 1865), LC.

103. Ruffin, *Diary*, 2:199 (24 Dec. 1861).

104. Ibid., 2:608 (27 Mar. 1863). Ruffin here acknowledged that he could not hear anything during a reunion with Boulware and old friends in Richmond.

105. Ibid., 2:394 (31 July 1862).

106. Ibid., 2:354–55 (27 June 1862).

107. Ibid., 2:394–97 (31 July 1862).

108. Ruffin did wear eyeglasses. A family portrait taken about 1851 shows him holding a book, and resting his glasses atop his forehead: see Illustrations.

109. Ruffin, *Diary*, 2:673–74 (2 June 1863). Though Ruffin may have been ill with a simple intestinal disorder, both he and members of the family interpreted his symptoms as a permanent difficulty. He appears to have been suffering from this disorder in May 1864, when he complained of "slight

internal pain," which wakened him in the night. That same month in 1864 Ruffin drafted instructions for his burial, feeling so feeble that he anticipated he would "die soon & suddenly, & almost without any immediately previous warning": Ruffin, Diary (manuscript), 3655, 3363 (17, 21 May 1864), LC. (His entry for 21 May contains an error in pagination; Ruffin reached p. 3369 and then repeated numbers beginning at 3362.)

110. Anne Ruffin ("Nanny"), Edmund, Jr.'s daughter, died at age twenty-two. It was she who "fitted up" Ruffin's room in the cottage at Beechwood in 1860, and who became his traveling companion, accompanying him to Kentucky in the autumn of that year: Ruffin, *Diary*, 1:453–70, 505 (1–27 Sept., 27 Nov. 1860).

111. Ibid., 2:673–74 (2 June 1863).

112. By 1861 he also apparently had lost most of his teeth: ibid., 2:77 (20 July 1862).

113. Julian C. Ruffin to Charlotte M. Ruffin, 17 May 1863; Ruffin to Charlotte M. Ruffin, 18 May 1864, Ruffin and Meade Papers, SHC; Ruffin to Juliana Coupland Dorsey, 20 June 1864, Dorsey and Coupland Papers, CWM; Edmund Ruffin, Jr., to Jane M. Ruffin, 1, 8 May 1864, typescript copies of letters in possession of Marion Ruffin Jones, Walkerton, Va. Lottie urged him to try "remedies" a physician would think "advisable": Charlotte M. Ruffin to Ruffin, 14 June 1864, Ruffin Papers, VHS. Ruffin's letter to Lottie on 18 May 1864, in which he described the burning of Chula, Va., was written without comment on a blank form of the Farmers' Mutual Fire Insurance Company of Virginia.

114. Since Ruffin was right-handed, a stroke might not have impaired his handwriting. The infection in 1859 occurred in his left hand: Ruffin, *Diary*, 1:299 (23 Apr. 1859), 2:86 (23 July 1861).

115. Ibid., 2:252 (10 Mar. 1862). This gloom did not lift: ibid., 2:291, 614 (30 Apr. 1862, 2 Apr. 1863).

116. Edmund Ruffin, Jr., to Thomas Ruffin, 9 June 1865, in Hamilton, *Papers of Thomas Ruffin*, 3:456.

117. "Death of Edmund Ruffin," 193.

118. Ruffin, Diary (manuscript), 3947, 3950 (3, 4 Apr. 1865), LC. A year earlier he complained of sleeplessness through much of the night, but he indicated this was "contrary to my late habits": ibid., 3363 (21 May 1864).

119. Ibid., 3948, 3950, 3996 (3, 4 Apr., 2 May 1865). Ruffin probably feared the U.S. government would apply a literal interpretation of the provision against treason set forth in the Constitution, Art. III, Sec. 3. He might have been concerned particularly about the last sentence of that section, which says, "The Congress shall have Power to declare the Punishment of Treason, but no Attainder of Treason shall work Corruption of Blood, or Forfeiture, except during the Life of the Person attainted."

120. Ruffin, Diary (manuscript), 4053 (5 June 1865), LC.

121. Ibid., 4029 (20 May, 1865).

122. Ibid., 4002, 4057 (5 May, 5 June 1865).

123. Ibid., 4036–37 (25 May 1865).

124. Ruffin, *Diary*, 1:208 (3 July 1858). See also Ruffin's reflections on his own role in restoring the fertility of farms his children inherited: ibid., 1:87–88 (7 July 1857).

125. Edmund Ruffin, Prayers for deceased family members, manuscript copies in possession of Marion Ruffin Jones, Walkerton, Va.; Edmund Ruffin, "Remembrance of Jane," 31, Ruffin Papers, VHS.

126. Ruffin, Diary (manuscript), 3367–68 (23 May 1864), LC. Family members reported him "greatly grieved" by the death of Nanny in 1863, however: [John R. Coupland] to [Sue H. Coupland], 19 Aug. 1863, Dorsey and Coupland Papers, CWM.

127. Edmund Ruffin, Jr., to Jane M. Ruffin, 24 May 1864, typescript copy in possession of Marion Ruffin Jones, Walkerton, Va.

128. Ruffin, *Diary*, 1:366–70 (30 Nov.–2 Dec. 1859).

129. Ibid., 1:371 (2 Dec. 1859).

130. Ibid., 2:92–93 (23 July 1861).

131. Ibid., 2:472–73 (24 Oct. 1862).

132. Ibid., 1:262 (5 Jan. 1859).

133. Ibid., 1:346, 348 (4, 18 Oct. 1859).

134. Ibid., 2:20 (4 May 1861).

135. Ruffin to Charlotte M. Ruffin, 21 May 1863, Ruffin and Meade Papers, SHC. Ruffin's sister Juliana and her son John were aware that Ruffin was waiting for death in 1863, thanks to a letter he had written to other relatives: [John R. Coupland] to [Sue H. Coupland], 19 Aug. 1863, Dorsey and Coupland Papers, CWM.

136. Ruffin, *Diary*, 1:262 (5 Jan. 1859); 2:531 (5 Jan. 1863).

137. Ibid., 2:106, 139 (12 Aug., 20 Sept. 1861). In July 1862 he declared, "It is better to be dead than to be deaf": ibid., 2:378–79 (17 July 1862).

138. Ibid., 1:302 (8 May 1859).

139. Ibid., 2:501 (1 Dec. 1862).

140. Rebecca W. Meade to John Meade, 31 Dec. 1861, Ruffin and Meade Papers, SHC.

141. William H. Harrison to Ruffin, 10 Jan. 1862, Ruffin Papers, UVA.

142. Ruffin speculated that most Southerners would not rejoice in the assassination, which he referred to once as a "deserved fate." He expressed regret, too, that Seward would recover. He repeated stories about Lincoln's mother having cohabited with a black man, and he made clear his opinion that Lincoln was "low & vulgar." At the same time, Lincoln's policy toward the South was less harsh than Ruffin had anticipated, a fact he kept in mind

that spring. Ruffin, Diary (manuscript), 3969, 3972, 3975, 3980, 4033–34 (17–21 Apr., 23 May 1865), LC.

143. Ibid., 4034 (23 May 1865).

144. Ruffin was reading *The Testimony of the Rocks* (1857) by English geologist Hugh Miller, whose suicide he interpreted as the result of "the overthrow of his intellect" and "confirmed insanity": Ruffin, *Diary*, 1:317–18 (8 July 1859). He had not changed his view since 1840, when he offered the same explanation of suicide to Thomas Cocke.

145. *The Code of Virginia*, 2d ed. (Richmond: Ritchie, Dunnavant & Co., 1860), 812, 820–22.

146. Ruffin, *Diary*, 2:487 (10 Nov. 1862); Clarke's commentaries appeared in an edition of the Bible published in New York between 1811 and 1825.

147. Ruffin, Diary (manuscript), 4089–93 (16, 17, 18 June 1865), LC. His assessment of the Bible on the issue of suicide was accurate.

148. Edmund Ruffin, "Statement of the closing scenes of the life of Thomas Cocke," 25 Feb. 1840, 4–7, Ruffin Papers, VHS.

149. Ruffin, Diary (manuscript), 4099 (18 June 1865), LC. Ruffin had expressed these ideas a year earlier in the draft of a letter to Edmund, Jr., which he entitled "My Last Directions." The letter was dated 17 May 1864 and was entered in the diary. Here Ruffin gave instructions about the burial of his body. "In the shirt & drawers in which I may happen to die, let my body remain." He would have his body wrapped only in an old sheet. He wanted a plain coffin of pine or common planks. "When depositing my coffin in the earth, I forbid that there shall be used the customary screen, or partition, of boards, to separate the coffin from contact with the filling mass of earth; or that any other means shall be used to retard the earliest nearest approach & later joining of 'earth to earth,' which is inevitable, & cannot occur too soon." Even at this point, before he had decided upon suicide, he expressed his opposition to ostentatious funerals and forbade such a ceremony for himself. In a postscript he revealed that he had discussed these arrangements with his son, exactly as Thomas Cocke had done with him in 1840. Ruffin did not know that Julian had been killed the previous day: ibid., 3355–57 (17 May 1864). Ruffin did not request that his body be wrapped in a Confederate flag.

150. Ibid., 4099 (18 June 1865).

151. Allmendinger and Scarborough, "Days Ruffin Died," 75–96.

152. "Death of Edmund Ruffin," 194.

153. Ruffin, "Closing scenes," 8. The *Richmond Whig* gave details of the bloody scene (*Richmond Whig*, 20 June 1865); the *Richmond Republic* noted that the "upper portion of his head was entirely blown off" (*Richmond Republic*, 20 June 1865).

154. "Death of Edmund Ruffin," 194. Edmund, Jr., appears to have

had no draft team or vehicles for such a journey that spring. Harrison had lent his team and wagon to the Ruffins in April to move Lottie's possessions to Petersburg: Ruffin, Diary (manuscript), 3969 (17 Apr. 1865), LC. On at least one previous occasion Harrison had offered a horse to Edmund, Jr., to ride from Petersburg into Amelia County: Edmund Ruffin, Jr., to Ruffin, 24 May 1862, Ruffin Papers, VHS.

155. "Death of Edmund Ruffin," 194.

Selected Bibliography

Primary Sources

Manuscript Collections

Archives Division, Virginia State Library, Richmond:
   Edmund Ruffin, Ledger and Accounts, 1828–1830, 1855–1865.
   Edmund Ruffin, Marlbourne Farm Journal, 1844–1851.
College Archives, Swem Library, College of William and Mary, Williamsburg, Va.:
   Account of Receipts and Expenditures of William & Mary College, 1808, 1809, 1810, 1811.
   Bursar's Book, 1754–70.
Library of Congress, Washington, D.C.:
   Edmund Ruffin Diary (page references are to Ruffin's numbers).
Manuscripts Department, University of Virginia Library, Charlottesville:
   Gooch Family Papers.
   Mrs. Maria Parker Papers.
   Edmund Ruffin Papers.
Manuscripts and Rare Books Department, Swem Library, College of William and Mary, Williamsburg, Va.:
   Blow Family Papers.
   Dorsey and Coupland Papers.
Southern Historical Collection, University of North Carolina Library, Chapel Hill:
   Harrison Henry Cocke Papers (Elizabeth Ruffin Diary).
   John Perkins Papers.
   Edmund Ruffin Papers.
   Edmund Ruffin, Jr., Plantation Diary, 1851–1873.
   Ruffin and Meade Family Papers.
   Thomas Ruffin Papers.

University Archives, University of Virginia Library, Charlottesville:
  Matriculation Books, 1825–1880 (microfilm).
Virginia Historical Society, Richmond:
  Albemarle Parish Register, 1721–1787.
  Margaret Stanly Beckwith, "Personal Reminiscences, 1844–1865."
  Cocke Family (of Dinwiddie County) Papers.
  Dupuy family Bible records.
  Hugh Blair Grigsby Papers.
  Edmund Ruffin Papers.
  Skipwith Family Papers.

Public Records

Archives Division, Virginia State Library, Richmond:
  Hanover County, Va., Records:
    Land Tax Book, 1850 (microfilm).
  James City County, Va., Records:
    Land Tax Book, 1810 (microfilm).
    Personal Property Tax List, 1810 (microfilm).
  Mutual Assurance Society of Virginia Policies (microfilm).
  Prince George County, Va., Records:
    Land Tax Books, 1809, 1810, 1814 (microfilm).
    Personal Property Tax Lists, 1812, 1814, 1815 (microfilm).
  Surry County, Va., Records:
    Will Book 10a, 1768–79 (microfilm).
    Order Books, 1757–63, 1789–94, 1795–1800, 1804–07 (microfilm).
  U.S. Census, Agriculture Schedules, Hanover County, Va., 1850
    (microfilm).
  U.S. Census, Agriculture Schedules, Hanover County, Va., 1860
    (microfilm).
  U.S. Census, Agriculture Schedules, King William County, Va., 1850
    (microfilm).
  U.S. Census, Agriculture Schedules, Prince George County, Va., 1850
    (microfilm).
  U.S. Census, Agriculture Schedules, Prince George County, Va., 1860
    (microfilm).
Hanover County Court House, Hanover, Va.:
  Register of Deaths, 1853–1871.
National Archives, Washington, D.C.:
  U.S. Census, Population Schedules, Hanover County, Va., 1850
    (microfilm).

U.S. Census, Population Schedules, Hanover County, Va., 1860 (microfilm).

U.S. Census, Manuscript Schedules, Prince George County, Va., 1810 (microfilm).

U.S. Census, Manuscript Schedules, Prince George County, Va., 1820 (microfilm).

U.S. Census, Manuscript Schedules, Prince George County, Va., 1830 (microfilm).

U.S. Census, Manuscript Schedules, Prince George County, Va., 1840 (microfilm).

U.S. Census, Population Schedules, Prince George County, Va., 1850 (microfilm).

U.S. Census, Population Schedules, Prince George County, Va., 1860 (microfilm).

U.S. Census, Manuscript Schedules, Sussex County, Va., 1810 (microfilm).

U.S. Census, Slave Schedules, Charles City County, Va., 1850 (microfilm).

U.S. Census, Slave Schedules, Charles City County, Va., 1860 (microfilm).

U.S. Census, Slave Schedules, Dinwiddie County, Va., 1850 (microfilm).

U.S. Census, Slave Schedules, Dinwiddie County, Va., 1860 (microfilm).

U.S. Census, Slave Schedules, Hanover County, Va., 1850, (microfilm).

U.S. Census, Slave Schedules, Hanover County, Va., 1860, (microfilm).

U.S. Census, Slave Schedules, Prince George County, Va., 1850 (microfilm).

U.S. Census, Slave Schedules, Prince George County, Va., 1860 (microfilm).

Prince George County Court House, Prince George, Va.:

Deed Book, 1787–92.

Deed Book 24, 1855–58.

Surry County Court House, Surry, Va.:

Marriage Register, 1768–1853.

Register of Albemarle Parish, typescript copy, 1938.

Will Book 1, 1792–1804.

Newspapers

Baltimore American and Commercial Advertiser.
Charleston Mercury.
New York Herald.
New York Times.
New York Tribune.

Petersburg Intelligencer.
Richmond Daily Times.
Richmond Enquirer.
Richmond Visitor.
Richmond Whig.
Virginia Gazette (Williamsburg).
Washington, D.C., Evening Star.
Washington, D.C., National Intelligencer.

Published Documents

[Boulware, William]. "Edwin Ruffin, of Virginia, Agriculturist." *De Bow's Review*, 11 (1851): 431–36.
The Code of Virginia. 2d ed. Richmond: Ritchie, Dunnavant and Co., 1860.
Davy, Humphry. *Elements of Agricultural Chemistry.* Fredericksburg, Va.: William F. Gray, 1815.
"Death of Edmund Ruffin." *Tyler's Quarterly Historical and Genealogical Magazine*, 5 (1924): 193–95.
Dew, Thomas R. *Review of the Debate in the Virginia Legislature of 1831 and 1832.* Richmond: T. W. White, 1832.
"Discussion, on Wheat and Its Culture." *Journal of the Transactions of the Virginia State Agricultural Society, for the Years 1856–57* (n.p., n.d.), 29–32.
Ferslew, W. Eugene. *First Annual Directory for the City of Richmond.* Richmond: George M. West, [1859].
Fisher, Elwood. *Lecture on the North and the South.* Washington: John T. Towers, 1849.
Fontaine, William Spotswood. "A Statement of the Number of Acres of Land Which Had Been Marled in the County of King William, at the Time of Taking the Census in 1840." *Farmers' Register*, 10 (1842): 488.
Hamilton, J. G. de Roulhac, ed. *The Papers of Thomas Ruffin.* 4 vols. Raleigh, N.C.: Edwards and Broughton Printing Co., 1918–20. Reprint. New York: AMS Press, 1973 (page references are to reprint edition).
Harrison, Jesse Burton ["A Virginian," pseud.]. *Review of the Slave Question, Extracted from the American Quarterly Review.* Richmond: T. W. White, 1833.
Madison, James [of Prince Edward County]. "Condition of the Descendants of a Number of Emancipated Slaves, in Prince Edward County." *Farmers' Register*, 4 (1836): 3–4.
Malthus, Thomas Robert. *An Essay on the Principle of Population.* London: J. Johnson, 1798. Reprint. New York: St. Martin's Press, 1966 (page references are to reprint edition).

————. *An Essay on the Principle of Population.* 6th ed. 2 vols. London: J. Murray, 1826.

————. *A Summary View of the Principle of Population.* London: John Murray, 1830. Reprinted in D. V. Glass, ed., *Introduction to Malthus.* New York: John Wiley and Sons, Inc., 1953. (Page references are to Glass edition.)

Philander [pseud.]. "Enormous Losses Caused by the Fence Law of Virginia." *Farmers' Register*, 1 (1834): 634–35.

Review of *An Essay on Calcareous Manures*, by Edmund Ruffin. *American Journal of Science and Arts*, 30 (1836): 138–63.

Review of *An Essay on Calcareous Manures*, by Edmund Ruffin. "Calcareous Manures." *Cultivator*, 2 (1835): 66–68.

Ruffin, Edmund. "Address to the Virginia State Agricultural Society, on the Effects of Domestic Slavery on the Manners, Habits and Welfare of the Agricultural Population of the Southern States." Supplement to the *Southern Planter*, 13 (1853): 8–16. (This address appears after the February 1852 issue in the American Periodical Series microfilm.)

————. *Agricultural, Geological, and Descriptive Sketches of Lower North Carolina, and the Similar Adjacent Lands.* Raleigh: Institution for the Deaf and Dumb, and the Blind, 1861.

————. "Agricultural Review: Slavery and Emancipation." *Farmers' Register*, 1 (1833): 36–48.

————. "Answers to General Queries on Marling, in Regard to Green-Sand Marl Used on the Pamunkey River Lands." *Farmers' Register*, 9 (1841): 20–21.

————. "Answers to the General Queries on the Effects of Marl . . . in Regard to Some Farms in James City and Surry Counties." *Farmers' Register*, 9 (1841): 264–68.

————. *Anticipations of the Future, to Serve as Lessons for the Present Time.* Richmond: J. W. Randolph, 1860. Reprint. Freeport, N.Y.: Books for Libraries Press, 1972 (page references are to reprint edition).

————. ["A Virginian," pseud.]. "The Armed Truce." *Charleston Mercury*, 7 Nov. 1851.

[————]. "Cassandra—Warnings." *Charleston Mercury*, 21 July 1859. Reprinted in Ruffin, *Diary*, 2:627–32.

————. "Communication to the Virginia State Agricultural Society: Some of the Results of the Improvements of Land by Calcareous Manures." *Southern Planter*, 12 (1852): 258–70.

————. "Consequences of Abolition Agitation." *De Bow's Review*, 22 (1857): 583–93; 23 (1857): 266–72, 385–90, 546–52.

————. "Desultory Observations on the Police of Health in Virginia—as It Is, and as It Ought to Be." *Farmers' Register*, 5 (1837): 154–71.

————. *The Diary of Edmund Ruffin*, ed. William K. Scarborough. 2

vols. to date. Baton Rouge: Louisiana State University Press, 1972– (page references are to the Scarborough edition unless otherwise indicated).

————. "The Effects of High Prices of Slaves; Considered in Reference to the Interests of Agriculture, of Individuals, and of the Commonwealth of Virginia." *De Bow's Review*, 26 (1859): 647–57.

————. "Equality of the Races—Haytien and British Experiments; the Dogma of the Natural Mental Equality of the Black and White Races Considered." *De Bow's Review*, 25 (1858): 27–38.

————. *An Essay on Calcareous Manures*. Petersburg, Va.: J. W. Campbell, 1832. John Harvard Library edition edited by J. Carlyle Sitterson. Cambridge: Harvard University Press, 1961 (page references are to John Harvard Library edition unless otherwise indicated).

————. *An Essay on Calcareous Manures*. 5th ed. Richmond: J. W. Randolph, 1852.

————. "Essays on Various Subjects of Practical Farming: The Advantages of Ploughing Land in Wide Beds." *American Farmer*, 7 (1851): 20–22, 49–51.

————. "Essays on Various Subjects of Practical Farming: The Excavation of Marl Pits, and Carrying Out and Applying of Marl." *American Farmer*, 7 (1851): 208–11, and 8 (1852): 239–42.

————. "Essays on Various Subjects of Practical Farming: Management of Wheat Harvest." *American Farmer*, 6 (1851): 453–60.

————. "Essays on Various Subjects of Practical Farming: On Clover Culture, and the Use and Value of the Products." *American Farmer*, 6 (1851): 257–60, 291–93.

————. "Essays on Various Subjects of Practical Farming: On Draining." *American Farmer*, 6 (1850): 5–8, 33–38, 90–95, 128–31, 177–82.

————. "Essays on Various Subjects of Practical Farming: On Harvesting Corn-Fodder—Different Methods Compared." *American Farmer*, 6 (1851): 422–26.

————. "Estimate of the Increased Value of Property in King William County, Caused by Marling." *Farmers' Register*, 10 (1842): 489–90.

————. ["A Slaveholder," pseud.]. "Estimates of the Expenses and Profits of Rearing Slaves [Written in 1832]." *Farmers' Register*, 2 (1834): 253–55.

————. "Farming Profits in Eastern Virginia: The Value of Marl." *American Farmer*, 5 (1849): 2–11.

————. "First Views Which Led to Marling in Prince George County." *Farmers' Register*, 7 (1839): 659–67.

————. "The Former Poor and Exhausted Condition, and Earliest Subsequent Improvements, by Marling, of Coggin's Point Farm." *Farmers' Register*, 7 (1839): 112–16.

_____. "General Remarks on the Causes of, and Means of Preventing the Formation of Malaria, and the Autumnal Diseases Which Are the Effects of It, in Virginia." *Farmers' Register*, 5 (1837): 41–43.

_____. "Investigating the Effects of Marling." *Farmers' Register*, 8 (1840): 446–47.

_____. ["A Gleaner," pseud.]. "James City Soils, and Resources for their Improvement." *Farmers' Register*, 1 (1833): 108–9.

_____. " 'Jottings Down' in the Swamp." *Farmers' Register*, 7 (1839): 698–703.

_____. "A Lecture on the Promotion of Agricultural Improvement." *American Farmer*, 6 (1851): 221–31.

_____. "Liberia and the Colonization Society." *De Bow's Review*, 26 (1859): 415–29; 27 (1859): 55–73, 336–44, 392–402, 583–94.

_____. "List of Subscribers." *Farmers' Register*, 1 (1834): 769–76.

_____. "Memoranda of the General System of Cultivation and Improvement Practised by Fielding Lewis, Esq., of Wyanoke." *Farmers' Register*, 1 (1833): 17–24.

_____. "Minutes of Agricultural Facts and Observations, Collected and noted by the Agricultural Commissioner." *Southern Planter*, 14 (1854): 193–96, 257–59, 289–91, 321–32.

[_____]. "Movements of the Abolition Societies; and Anticipated Results." *Farmers' Register*, 3 (1835): 287–89.

_____. "Mr. Ruffin and the Marling System." *Charleston Mercury*, 5 Feb. 1844.

_____. "Notes of a Steam Journey." *Farmers' Register*, 8 (1840): 243–54.

_____. "Notes of a Three-Days Excursion into Goochland, Chesterfield, and Powhatan." No. IV, "Some Account of the Farming of Richard Sampson, Esq., of Goochland." *Farmers' Register*, 5 (1837): 364–73.

_____. "Observations on the Earliest Marled District of Prince George County." *Farmers' Register*, 8 (1840): 484–97.

_____. "On the Composition of Soils, and Their Improvement by Calcareous Manures." *American Farmer*, 3 (1821): 313–20.

[_____]. "On the Petition for a Change of the Law of Enclosures." *Farmers' Register*, 2 (1834): 402–3.

_____. "On the Soils, and Marling Improvements of King William County." *Farmers' Register*, 9 (1841): 21–28.

_____. "On the Sources of Malaria, or of Autumnal Diseases, in Virginia, and the Means of Remedy and Prevention." *Farmers' Register*, 6 (1838): 216–28.

_____. "Petition to the General Assembly of Virginia." *Southern Planter*, 11 (1851): 65–73.

_____. "Plan for Procuring and Publishing a General Report of the Practical Effects of Marling." *Farmers' Register*, 5 (1837): 509–11.

————. *The Political Economy of Slavery*. Washington: Lemuel Towers [1858].

————. "Queries in Regard to Prevalent Diseases Produced by Local Causes." *Farmers' Register*, 10 (1842): 68–69.

[————]. "Remarks [on Fences]." *Farmers' Register*, 3 (1835): 49–50.

————. "Remarks on the Soils and Agriculture of Gloucester County." *Farmers' Register*, 6 (1838): 178–91, 193–94.

————. "Remarks on the Soils and Marling of the Pamunkey River Lands." *Farmers' Register*, 8 (1840): 679–90.

[————]. "Remarks on the Soils in General, and Particularly the Ridge Lands, of Eastern Virginia." *Farmers' Register*, 8 (1840): 168–71.

————. "Report of the Agricultural Commissioner." *Southern Planter*, 15 (1855): 5–7.

————. *Report of the Commencement and Progress of the Agricultural Survey of South Carolina, for 1843*. Columbia, S.C.: A. H. Pemberton, 1843.

————. "Report to the State Board of Agriculture, on the Brandon Farms." *Farmers' Register*, 10 (1842): 274–82.

————. "Report to the State Board of Agriculture on the Most Important Recent Improvements of Agriculture in Lower Virginia—and the Most Important Defects Yet Remaining." *Farmers' Register*, 10 (1842): 257–66.

————. "The Results of Marling in the Country about Williamsburg." *Farmers' Register*, 8 (1840): 415–18.

————. ["A Gleaner," pseud.]. "Rough Notes upon Some of the Agricultural Improvements of Charlotte, and the Adjacent Counties." *Farmers' Register*, 4 (1836): 374–77.

————. "Ruffin's Agricultural Address." *Farmers' Cabinet*, 8 (1844): 270–72.

————. "Sketch of the Progress of Agriculture in Virginia, and the Causes of Its Decline, and Present Depression." *Farmers' Register*, 3 (1836): 748–60.

————. "Slavery and Free Labor Defined and Compared." *Southern Planter*, 19 (1859): 723–41; 20 (1860): 1–10.

————. "Some of the Effects of West Indian Emancipation, as Stated by the Friends of That Measure." *Farmers' Register*, 4 (1836): 49–52.

————. "Southern Agricultural Exhaustion, and Its Remedy." U.S. Congress. Senate. *Report of the Commissioner of Patents for the Year 1852: Part II, Agriculture*. 32d Cong., 2d sess., 1852, Executive Document 55. Washington, D.C.: Robert Armstrong, Printer, 1853. 373–89.

————. "Supplemental Report of the Agricultural Survey for 1843." *Southern Agriculturist*, 2d ser., 4 (1844): 122–27.

————. "Supplementary Chapter to 'An Essay on Calcareous Manures.' " *Farmers' Register*, 1 (1833): 76–79.

———. "The True and False Doctrines Respecting High Prices of Provisions." *Farmers' Register*, 4 (1837): 754–59.

———. ["A Gleaner," pseud.]. "View of Part of York, and the Back River Lands." *Farmers' Register*, 3 (1835): 414–16.

[———]. "What Is the Best Route, Through Central Virginia, for a Railway to the Southwest." *Farmers' Register*, 4 (1836): 309–12, 369–74.

———. ["A Virginian," pseud.]. "What Will Be the Results of the Northern Abolition Agitation?" *Richmond Enquirer*, 22 Jan., 25 Jan., 2 Apr. 1850.

———. "Writers of Anonymous Articles in the Farmer's Register." *Journal of Southern History*. 23 (1957): 90–102.

Ruffin, Mrs. Kirkland, ed. "School-Boy Letters of Edmund Ruffin, Jr., 1828–1829." *North Carolina Historical Review*, 10 (1933): 287–329.

Taylor, John. *Arator: Being a Series of Agricultural Essays, Practical and Political in Sixty-Four Numbers*. Petersburg, Va.: Whitworth and Yancey, 1818. Liberty Classics edition edited by M.E. Bradford. Indianapolis: Liberty Fund, Inc., 1977 (page references are to the Liberty Classics edition).

U.S. Congress. *Census for 1820*. Washington: Gales & Seaton, 1821. Reprint. New York: Luther M. Cornwall Co., n.d. (page references are to reprint edition).

U.S. Census Bureau. *Heads of Families at the First Census of the United States Taken in the Year 1790, Records of Enumerations: 1782 to 1785, Virginia*. Washington, D.C.: Government Printing Office, 1908.

Virginia State Agricultural Society. *Journal of Transactions*, 1: 1853. Richmond: P. D. Bernard, 1853.

Virginia State Agricultural Society. *Journal of Transactions for the Years 1856–57*. N.p., n.d.

"Virginia State Agricultural Society." *Southern Planter*, 14 (1854): 74–77.

Walker, George Henry. "Extracts from the Manuscript Notes of a Farmer: Letter IV." *Farmers' Register*, 3 (1836): 601–3.

Genealogical Sources

Bielenstien, Gabrielle Maupin. "Genealogy for the Descendants of Hester Vanbibber Braxton (1827–1909) and Robert Williamson Tomlin (1813–1862)." Typescript, 1984. Entry for Carter Braxton II. Archives Division, Virginia State Library, Richmond.

Boddie, John Bennett, comp. *Births, Deaths and Sponsors, 1717–1778, from the Albemarle Parish Register of Surry and Sussex Counties, Virginia*. Redwood City, Calif.: Pacific Coast Publishers, 1958.

———. *Southside Virginia Families*. 2 vols. Redwood City, Calif.: Pacific Coast Publishers, 1955–56.

————. *Virginia Historical Genealogies*. Redwood City, Calif.: Pacific Coast Publishers, 1954.

"The Cocke Family of Virginia." *Virginia Magazine of History and Biography*, 5 (1897–98): 71–91, 185–89.

Crozier, William Armstrong, ed. *Williamsburg Wills*. Baltimore: Southern Book Company, 1954.

Fothergill, Augusta B., and John Mark Naugle, comps., *Virginia Tax Payers, 1782–1787, Other Than Those Published by the United States Census Bureau*. Richmond, 1940. Reprint. Baltimore: Genealogical Publishing Co., 1986 (page references are to reprint edition).

Genealogies of Virginia Families: From the Virginia Magazine of History and Biography. 5 vols. Baltimore: Genealogical Publishing Co., 1981.

Hart, Lyndon H., III. *Surry County, Virginia, Wills, Estate Accounts and Inventories, 1730–1800*. Easley, S.C.: Southern Historical Press, 1983.

Index to Marriage Notices in the Southern Churchman. 2 vols. Richmond: Historical Records Survey of Virginia, 1942.

Knorr, Catherine Lindsay, comp. *Marriage Bonds and Ministers' Returns of Surry County, Virginia, 1768–1825*. Pine Bluff, Ark.: The Perdue Company Duplicating Service, 1960.

"Marlbourne." Hanover Historical Society, *Bulletin*, no. 7 (Nov. 1972): 1–3.

"Marriage and Death Notices from 'The Visitor.'" *Virginia Genealogical Society Quarterly*, 7 (1969): 56–66.

Meade, William. *Old Churches, Ministers and Families of Virginia*. 2 vols. Philadelphia: J. B. Lippincott Co., [1857].

Peebles, Anne B. *Peebles Ante 1600–1962*. [Washington, D.C.]: J. Hughlett Peebles, [1962].

Ruffin, David. Genealogical history of the Ruffin family (untitled), 1984. Unpublished manuscript in possession of David Ruffin, Statesboro, Ga.

Ruffin, E. Lorraine. "Descendants of Edmund Ruffin, the Great Agriculturist . . . ," *Tyler's Quarterly Historical and Genealogical Magazine*, 22 (1941): 242–56.

Ruffin, Edmund. "Ruffin Family Genealogy, Compiled May 1, 1856, at Beechwood, Prince George Co., Va." Manuscript, Virginia Historical Society, Richmond.

"Ruffin Family." *William and Mary Quarterly*, 1st ser., 18 (1910): 251–58.

"Sayre Family." *Virginia Magazine of History and Biography*, 3 (1896): 96.

Scarborough, William K. "The Ruffin Family: Children and Grandchildren of Edmund Ruffin," in Ruffin, *Diary*, ed. Scarborough, 2:xiii–xxvi.

Slaughter, Philip. *A History of Bristol Parish, Va., with Genealogies of Families Connected Therewith*. 2d ed. Richmond: J. W. Randolph, 1879.

Smith, Claiborne Thweatt, Jr. *Smith of Scotland Neck: Planters on the Roanoke.* Baltimore: Gateway Press, 1976.

Stanard, W. G. "Harrison of James River." *Virginia Magazine of History and Biography*, 34 (1926): 183–87; 39 (1931): 173–77. Also in *Genealogies of Virginia Families*, 1981, 687–844.

"Travis Family." *William and Mary Quarterly*, 1st ser., 18 (1910): 141–44.

Travis, Robert J. *The Travis (Travers) Family and Its Allies.* Savannah: Bowen Press of Decatur, Ga., 1954.

"Virginia Council Journals, 1726–1753." *Virginia Magazine of History and Biography*, 37 (1929): 323–26.

Virginia Genealogical Society. *Marriages and Deaths from Richmond, Virginia, Newspapers, 1780–1820.* Richmond: Virginia Genealogical Society, 1983.

Virginia Will Records. Baltimore: Genealogical Publishing Co., 1982.

Warner, Pauline Pearce. *Benjamin Harrison of Berkeley, Walter Cocke of Surry: Family Records I.* Tappahannock, Va., n.p., 1962.

Weisiger, Benjamin B., III, comp. *Prince George County, Virginia, Miscellany: 1711–1814.* Richmond, 1986.

Secondary Sources

Allmendinger, David F., Jr. "The Early Career of Edmund Ruffin, 1810–1840." *Virginia Magazine of History and Biography*, 93 (1985): 127–54.

Allmendinger, David F., Jr., and William K. Scarborough. "The Days Ruffin Died." *Virginia Magazine of History and Biography*, 97 (1989): 75–96.

Bowman, Shearer Davis. "Conditional Unionism and Slavery in Virginia, 1860–1861: The Case of Dr. Richard Eppes." *Virginia Magazine of History and Biography*, 96 (1988): 31–54.

Bruce, Kathleen. "Virginian Agricultural Decline to 1860: A Fallacy." *Agricultural History*, 6 (1932): 3–13.

Carr, Lois Green, and Lorena S. Walsh. "The Planter's Wife: The Experience of White Women in Seventeenth-Century Maryland." *William and Mary Quarterly*, 3d ser., 34 (1977): 542–71.

Censer, Jane Turner. *North Carolina Planters and Their Children, 1800–1860.* Baton Rouge: Louisiana State University Press, 1984.

Colvin, Steven A. *On Deep Water.* Verona, Va.: McClure Printing Company, 1983.

Craven, Avery. *Edmund Ruffin, Southerner: A Study in Secession.* New York: D. Appleton and Co., 1932. Reprint. Hamden, Conn.: Archon Books, 1964 (page references are to reprint edition).

——————. *Soil Exhaustion as a Factor in the Agricultural History of Virginia and Maryland, 1606–1860.* Urbana: University of Illinois, 1926.

Cutter, W. P. "A Pioneer in Agricultural Science," *Yearbook of the United States Department of Agriculture, 1895.* Washington, D.C.: Government Printing Office, 1896, 493–502.

Demaree, Albert Lowther. *The American Agricultural Press, 1819–1860.* New York: Columbia University Press, 1941.

Donald, David. "The Proslavery Argument Reconsidered." *Journal of Southern History*, 37 (1971): 3–18.

Earle, Carville V. "Environment, Disease, and Mortality in Early Virginia." In Tate and Ammerman, 1979, 96–125.

Faust, Drew Gilpin. *James Henry Hammond and the Old South: A Design for Mastery.* Baton Rouge: Louisiana State University Press, 1982.

——————. *A Sacred Circle: The Dilemma of the Intellectual in the Old South, 1840–1860.* Baltimore: Johns Hopkins University Press, 1977.

Frederickson, George M. *The Black Image in the White Mind: The Debate on Afro-American Character and Destiny, 1817–1914.* New York: Harper Row, 1971. Reprint. Wesleyan edition, Middletown, Conn.: Wesleyan University Press, 1987 (page references are to Wesleyan edition).

Freehling, Alison Goodyear. *Drift Toward Dissolution: The Virginia Slavery Debate of 1831–1832.* Baton Rouge: Louisiana State University Press, 1982.

Gates, Paul W. *The Farmer's Age: Agriculture, 1815–1860.* New York: Holt, Rinehart and Winston, 1960.

Genovese, Eugene D. *The Political Economy of Slavery: Studies in the Economy and Society of the Slave South.* New York: Pantheon Books, 1965.

——————. *Roll, Jordan, Roll: The World the Slaves Made.* New York: Pantheon Books, 1974.

——————. *The World the Slaveholders Made: Two Essays in Interpretation.* New York: Pantheon Books, 1969.

Goldfield, David. *Urban Growth in the Age of Sectionalism: Virginia, 1847–1861.* Baton Rouge: Louisiana State University Press, 1977.

Gray, Lewis C. *History of Agriculture in the Southern United States to 1860.* 2 vols. Washington, D.C.: Carnegie Institution of Washington, 1933.

Gutman, Herbert. *The Black Family in Slavery and Freedom, 1750–1925.* New York: Pantheon Books, 1976.

Hall, Peter Dobkin. *The Organization of American Culture, 1700–1900.* New York: New York University Press, 1982.

Hallam, H. E. *Rural England, 1066–1348.* Brighton, U.K.: Harvester Press. Atlantic Highlands, N.J.: Humanities Press, 1981.

Hallock, Judith Lee. "The Agricultural Apostle and His Bible: Edmund

Ruffin and the *Farmers' Register.*" *Southern Studies*, 23 (1984): 205–15.

Herndon, G. Melvin. "Agricultural Reform in Antebellum Virginia: William Galt, Jr., a Case Study." *Agricultural History*, 52 (1978): 394–406.

Isaac, Rhys. *The Transformation of Virginia: 1740–1790.* Chapel Hill: University of North Carolina Press, 1982.

Jenkins, William Sumner. *Pro-slavery Thought in the Old South* Chapel Hill: University of North Carolina Press, 1935.

Johnson, Michael P. "Planters and Patriarchy: Charleston, 1800–1860." *Journal of Southern History*, 46 (1980): 45–72.

Kenzer, Robert C. *Kinship and Neighborhood in a Southern Community: Orange County, North Carolina, 1849–1881.* Knoxville: University of Tennessee Press, 1987.

Lebsock, Suzanne. *The Free Women of Petersburg: Status and Culture in a Southern Town, 1784–1860.* New York: W. W. Norton and Co., 1984.

Lewis, Jan. *The Pursuit of Happiness: Family and Values in Jefferson's Virginia.* Cambridge, U.K.: Cambridge University Press, 1983.

Mathew, W. M. "Agricultural Adaptation and Race Control in the American South: The Failure of the Ruffin Reforms." *Slavery & Abolition: A Journal of Comparative Studies*, 7 (1986): 129–47.

———. *Edmund Ruffin and the Crisis of Slavery in the Old South: The Failure of Agricultural Reform.* Athens: University of Georgia Press, 1988.

———. "Edmund Ruffin and the Demise of the *Farmers' Register.*" *Virginia Magazine of History and Biography.* 94 (1986): 3–24.

———. "Planter Entrepreneurship and the Ruffin Reforms in the Old South, 1820–60." *Business History*, 27 (1985): 207–21.

McCoy, Drew. *The Elusive Republic: Political Economy in Jeffersonian America.* Chapel Hill: University of North Carolina Press, 1980.

———. "Jefferson and Madison on Malthus: Population Growth in Jeffersonian Political Economy." *Virginia Magazine of History and Biography*, 88 (1980): 259–76.

Mitchell, Betty L. *Edmund Ruffin: A Biography.* Bloomington: Indiana University Press, 1981.

———. " 'Superfluous Lags the Veteran on the Stage': The Death of Confederate Edmund Ruffin." *Virginia Cavalcade*, 32 (1983): 126–33.

Moltke-Hansen, David. "The Expansion of Intellectual Life: A Prospectus." In *Intellectual Life in Antebellum Charleston*, O'Brien and Moltke-Hansen, eds., 3–44.

Oakes, James. *The Ruling Race: A History of American Slaveholders.* New York: Alfred A. Knopf, 1982.

O'Brien, Michael, and David Moltke-Hansen, eds. *Intellectual Life in Antebellum Charleston.* Knoxville: University of Tennessee Press, 1986.

Pease, Jane H., and William H. Pease. "Intellectual Life in the 1830s: The Institutional Framework and the Charleston Style." In *Intellectual Life in Antebellum Charleston*, O'Brien and Moltke-Hansen, eds., 233–54.

Rosengarten, Theodore. *Tombee: Portrait of a Cotton Planter*. New York: William Morrow and Co., 1987.

Rutman, Anita H. "Still Planting the Seeds of Hope: The Recent Literature of the Early Chesapeake Region." *Virginia Magazine of History and Biography*, 95 (1987): 3–24.

Rutman, Darrett B., and Anita H. Rutman. " 'Now-Wives and Sons-in-Law': Parental Death in a Seventeenth-Century Virginia County." In *The Chesapeake in the Seventeenth Century*, Tate and Ammerman, eds., 153–82.

————. "Of Agues and Fevers: Malaria in the Early Chesapeake." *William and Mary Quarterly*, 3d ser., 33 (1976): 31–60.

Scarborough, William K. "Introduction." In Edmund Ruffin, *The Diary of Edmund Ruffin*. Vol. 1. Ed. William K. Scarborough. Baton Rouge: Louisiana State University Press, 1972, xv–xlv.

————. "Introduction." In Edmund Ruffin, *The Diary of Edmund Ruffin*. Vol. 2. Ed. William K. Scarborough. Baton Rouge: Louisiana State University Press, 1976, xiii–xxii.

Savitt, Todd L. *Medicine and Slavery: The Diseases and Health Care of Blacks in Antebellum Virginia*. Urbana: University of Illinois Press, 1978.

Scott, Anne Firor. *The Southern Lady: From Pedestal to Politics, 1830–1930*. Chicago: University of Chicago Press, 1970.

Sheridan, Richard C. "Mineral Fertilizers in Southern Agriculture." In James X. Corgan, ed., *The Geological Sciences in the Antebellum South*. University, Ala.: University of Alabama Press, 1982, 73–82.

Sitterson, J. Carlyle. "Edmund Ruffin, Agricultural Reformer and Southern Radical." Introduction to Ruffin, *Essay on Calcareous Manures*, vii–xxxiii.

Smith, Daniel Blake. *Inside the Great House: Planter Family Life in Eighteenth-Century Chesapeake Society*. Ithaca: Cornell University Press, 1980.

————. "Mortality and Family in the Colonial Chesapeake." *Journal of Interdisciplinary History*, 8 (1978): 403–27.

Smith, Kenneth L. "Edmund Ruffin and the Raid on Harper's Ferry." *Virginia Cavalcade*, 22 (1972): 29–37.

Stohrer, Freda F. "*Arator*: A Publishing History." *Virginia Magazine of History and Biography*, 88 (1980): 442–45.

Sutton, Robert P. "Nostalgia, Pessimism, and Malaise: The Doomed Aristocrat in Late-Jeffersonian Virginia." *Virginia Magazine of History and Biography*, 76 (1968): 41–55.

Swem, Earl G. *An Analysis of Ruffin's Farmers' Register, with a Bibliography of Edmund Ruffin*. Virginia State Library, *Bulletin*, 11. Richmond: Davis Bottom, 1919.

Tate, Thad W., and David L. Ammerman, eds. *The Chesapeake in the Seventeenth Century: Essays on Anglo-American Society & Politics*. New York: W. W. Norton and Co., 1979.

Taylor, William R. *Cavalier and Yankee: The Old South and American National Character*. New York: George Braziller, 1961.

Turner, Charles W. "Virginia Agricultural Reform, 1815–1860." *Agricultural History*, 26 (1952): 80–89.

Uhlenberg, Peter. "Death and the Family." *Journal of Family History*, 5 (1980): 313–20.

Walsh, Lorena S. "'Till Death Us Do Part': Marriage and Family in Seventeenth-Century Maryland." In *The Chesapeake in the Seventeenth Century*, Tate and Ammerman, eds., 1979, 126–52.

Walsh, Lorena S., and Russell R. Menard. "Death in the Chesapeake: Two Life Tables for Men in Early Colonial Maryland." *Maryland Historical Magazine*, 69 (1974): 211–27.

Wells, Robert V. *Uncle Sam's Family: Issues in and Perspectives on American Demographic History*. Albany: State University of New York Press, 1985.

Williams, Raymond. *Cobbett*. New York: Oxford University Press, 1983.

Wright, Gavin. *The Political Economy of the Cotton South: Households, Markets, and Wealth in the Nineteenth Century*. New York: W. W. Norton and Co., 1978.

Wyatt-Brown, Bertram. "The Ideal Typology and Ante-Bellum Southern History: A Testing of a New Approach." *Societas*, 5 (1975): 1–29.

———. "Proslavery and Antislavery Intellectuals: Class Concepts and Polemical Struggle." In *Antislavery Reconsidered: New Perspectives on the Abolitionists*, Lewis Perry and Michael Fellman, eds. Baton Rouge: Louisiana State University Press, 1979, 308–36.

———. *Southern Honor: Ethics and Behavior in the Old South*. New York: Oxford University Press, 1982.

Index